ANCIENT MODELS OF MIND

How does god think? How, ideally, does a human mind function? Must a gap remain between these two paradigms of rationality? Such questions exercised the greatest ancient philosophers, including those featured in this book: Socrates, Plato, Aristotle, the Stoics and Plotinus. This volume encompasses a series of studies by leading scholars, revisiting key moments of ancient philosophy and highlighting the theme of human and divine rationality in both moral and cognitive psychology. It is a tribute to Professor A. A. Long, and reflects multiple themes of his own work.

ANDREA NIGHTINGALE is Professor of Classics and Comparative Literature at Stanford University. She is the author of *Genres in Dialogue: Plato and the Construct of Philosophy* (1995), *Spectacles of Truth in Classical Greek Philosophy:* Theoria *in its Cultural Context* (2004), and *"Once out of Nature": Augustine on Time and the Body* (forthcoming). She has won a Guggenheim Fellowship, an ACLS Fellowship, and a fellowship at the Stanford Humanities Center. She has been a Stanford Fellow (2004–6) and is presently serving as a Harvard Senior Fellow of the Hellenic Center (2009–2013).

DAVID SEDLEY is Laurence Professor of Ancient Philosophy at the University of Cambridge, where he is also a Fellow of Christ's College. He is the author of *The Hellenistic Philosophers* (1987, with A. A. Long), *Lucretius and the Transformation of Greek Wisdom* (1998), *Plato's* Cratylus (2003), *The Midwife of Platonism: Text and Subtext in Plato's* Theaetetus (2004), and *Creationism and its Critics in Antiquity* (2007), based on his 2004 Sather Lectures. He edited *Oxford Studies in Ancient Philosophy* from 1998 to 2007. He is a Fellow of the British Academy, and a Foreign Honorary Member of the American Academy of Arts and Sciences.

ANCIENT MODELS OF MIND

Studies in Human and Divine Rationality

EDITED BY

ANDREA NIGHTINGALE

AND

DAVID SEDLEY

CAMBRIDGE
UNIVERSITY PRESS

CAMBRIDGE UNIVERSITY PRESS
Cambridge, New York, Melbourne, Madrid, Cape Town, Singapore,
São Paulo, Delhi, Dubai, Tokyo, Mexico City

Cambridge University Press
The Edinburgh Building, Cambridge CB2 8RU, UK

Published in the United States of America by Cambridge University Press, New York

www.cambridge.org
Information on this title: www.cambridge.org/9780521113557

First published 2010

Printed in the United Kingdom at the University Press, Cambridge

A catalogue record for this publication is available from the British Library

Library of Congress Cataloging in Publication data
Ancient models of mind : studies in human and divine rationality / edited by
Andrea Wilson Nightingale, David Sedley.
p.   cm.
Includes bibliographical references and index.
ISBN 978-0-521-11355-7 (hardback)
I. Philosophy of mind – History.   2. Philosophy, Ancient.   I. Nightingale, Andrea Wilson.
II. Sedley, D. N.   III. Title.
B187.M55A53   2010
128'.20938 – dc22   2010023578

ISBN 978-0-521-11355-7 Hardback

For Tony Long

Contents

Contributors

SARA AHBEL-RAPPE, Professor of Greek and Latin in the Department of Classical Studies, University of Michigan at Ann Arbor

RICHARD BETT, Professor of Philosophy and Classics, Johns Hopkins University

LUCA CASTAGNOLI, Lecturer in Ancient Philosophy, Department of Classics and Ancient History, Durham University

ALAN CODE, Board of Governors Professor of Philosophy, Rutgers University

JAMES KER, Assistant Professor of Classical Studies, University of Pennsylvania

KATHRYN A. MORGAN, Professor of Classics, University of California, Los Angeles

ANDREA NIGHTINGALE, Professor of Classics and Comparative Literature, Stanford University

GRETCHEN REYDAMS-SCHILS, Professor in the Program of Liberal Studies and Concurrent in the Department of Philosophy, University of Notre Dame

DAVID SEDLEY, Laurence Professor of Ancient Philosophy, University of Cambridge

ALLAN SILVERMAN, Professor of Philosophy, Ohio State University

STEPHEN WHITE, Professor of Classics and Philosophy, University of Texas at Austin

KENNETH WOLFE, Tutor at St John's College, Santa Fe

Introduction

Andrea Nightingale and David Sedley

This book started life at a conference which its two editors organized to honour Tony Long, better known to the world of scholarship as A. A. Long. It was held at his own university, the University of California, Berkeley, in September 2007, to mark his 70th birthday. "Models of Mind" was known to us as the working title of a long-term project of Long's own, and seemed to us to capture a theme that has, more than any other, been the hallmark of his truly seminal contribution to the study of ancient philosophy over four decades and more.

Tony Long was born in England in 1937. Since 1991 he has been Irving Stone Professor of Literature in the Department of Classics at Berkeley, where he is also an affiliated professor in the departments of Philosophy and Rhetoric. But his education and the first part of his professional career were set elsewhere. He took his BA and PhD degrees at University College London. There, among many leading scholars who taught and influenced him, special mention must be made here of David Furley, whose exceptional incisiveness and intellectual clarity in the study of ancient philosophy clearly passed from teacher to pupil. However, Long was not yet specializing in ancient philosophy, and his doctoral thesis (completed in 1964 under T. B. L. Webster) was in fact on Sophocles, later becoming the basis of his highly regarded 1968 book *Language and Thought in Sophocles: A Study of Abstract Nouns and Poetic Technique*.

It was during his tenure of his first three posts – the first at Otago, New Zealand, the second at the University of Nottingham, and the third back at his alma mater – that Long developed his interest in Stoicism. This started from a study of Plutarch's anti-Stoic works, and led on, in his early years as a lecturer at UCL, to his organization of a seminar on Stoicism at the Institute for Classical Studies. That period saw the emergence of some of his own classic papers on Stoic ethics, logic, and epistemology, and the publication of his 1971 edited anthology, *Problems in Stoicism*, covering all the major areas of Stoic thought, which nearly four decades after its publication continues to be regularly consulted and cited.

During the 1970s, the study of Stoicism enjoyed a remarkable renaissance. In this period, Stoicism was, almost for the first time, taken seriously as philosophy, on a par with the work of Plato and Aristotle. The rehabilitation of Stoic ethics that was a key part of this renaissance was due more than anything else to Tony Long's seminal studies, and to now classic studies by others that he put on the map by the timely publication of *Problems in Stoicism*. During his career he has published on a comprehensive range of ancient philosophers and topics, but a very substantial proportion of his total output has been on Stoic ethics, including approximately thirty articles, his scholarly edition (1992, with Guido Bastianini) of the Hierocles papyrus, and his brilliant 2002 book on Epictetus. It is no exaggeration to say that, cumulatively, these studies have transformed the scholarly landscape.

It was also during the seventies, 1974 to be exact, that Long published his celebrated book *Hellenistic Philosophy*. Frequently reprinted, it has also been translated into seven languages. Thirty-five years after its original publication, it remains a uniquely accessible, lucid, and inspiring introduction to its subject. It has been complemented since by the two-volume sourcebook *The Hellenistic Philosophers* (1987, co-authored with David Sedley). His other publications on Hellenistic philosophy are too numerous to describe here, but two in particular can be picked out, because they exemplify his special gift for shedding light on the period by focusing on its heritage from earlier traditions. "Heraclitus and Stoicism" (1975–76) and "Socrates in Hellenistic philosophy" (1988) remain, decades after their publication as journal articles, *the* classic studies of their respective topics.

After UCL, Long spent the years 1973–83 as distinguished holder of the Gladstone Professorship of Greek at the University of Liverpool, and as a key member of the Manchester–Liverpool ancient philosophy group, whose other regular participants included A. C. Lloyd, Henry Blumenthal, and George Kerferd. Long moved to Berkeley in 1983, and has remained there to the present.

It is impossible to do justice in a short space to the extraordinary range and depth of Tony Long's publications, which are listed in full at the end of this volume. In addition to his huge contribution to ancient philosophy, he has never abandoned his original interest in Greek literature, on which he has published a steady stream of articles over the years. Satisfyingly, his literary and philosophical skills came together in two classic articles on Homer, one on the Homeric value system (1970), the other on Stoic readings of Homer (1992).

Tony Long has received widespread recognition for his exceptional contribution to scholarship. Many honours could be listed, but we will restrict ourselves here to two tokens of his extraordinary standing among his peers: his election in 1992 as a Corresponding Fellow of the British Academy, and in 2009 as a member of the American Philosophical Society.

II

At the September 2007 conference in Tony Long's honour, there were ten speakers. Of these, nine were former students of Long's, all now holding posts in high-ranked universities and colleges. The tenth was Alan Code, who had been Long's close colleague at UC Berkeley for many years. The papers of these speakers have evolved into ten of the twelve chapters in the present volume. (The remaining two chapters have been contributed by us, the two editors, ourselves former graduate students of Long.) Ten others of those who attended the conference generously acted as commentators on the papers. These were Keimpe Algra, Ruby Blondell, Chris Bobonich, Myles Burnyeat, John Ferrari, Mary-Louise Gill, Jean-Baptiste Gourinat, Brad Inwood, Richard McKirahan, and Henry Mendell. We express our warm thanks to all of these; to the UC Berkeley Department of Classics and the Townsend Center, which generously funded the event; and finally, to Michael Sharp, Joanna Breeze, and Nigel Hope, and two anonymous referees for Cambridge University Press.

III

In this collection of studies, three familiar Greco-Roman standards of rationality are placed under joint-examination: (a) the divine intellect; (b) a perfected human being, whether this be Socrates or the idealized sage postulated by Stoicism; and (c) the inherent powers and structure of human reason.

The search for a model of intellectual understanding is an early and recurrent feature of Greek thought. It is visible, for example, in the early Greek thinkers (we here heed Tony Long's plea not to call them "Presocratics") Xenophanes, Heraclitus, and Parmenides. These authors all contrast the perfect knowledge possessed by the gods with the blinkered limitations of the human perspective, adding their own expressions of relative optimism or pessimism about our capacity to transcend the latter and aspire

to the former. In Plato the same motif becomes the ideal summed up as
"becoming as like god as is possible"; and he is followed in this by nearly
all subsequent philosophers until the end of antiquity, including thinkers
as diverse as Aristotle and Epicurus. There can be little doubt that not only
the earliest but also the most enduring model proclaimed for the human
intellect is god.

The chief competing paradigm is the human sage. Although the tradition of the revered sage is no doubt as old as civilization, its penetration
into philosophy is due above all to two figures, one of them elusive and
legendary, the other very much flesh and blood. The former is Pythagoras
(sixth century BCE), whose superior understanding was linked in particular
to his reported recollection of many past lives. The latter is Socrates, whose
name will be omnipresent in this book. Condemned to death by an Athenian jury in 399 BCE, Socrates became the first philosophical martyr, a fact
which bulks large among the reasons for his subsequent canonization as a
philosophical paradigm. Stoicism, which emerged a century after Socrates'
death, is in large measure an attempt to construct a formalized Socratic
philosophy; the figure of the sage, around whom much Stoic theorizing is
built, is recognizably modelled on Socrates.

Although he seems to have deliberately stayed at the margins of political activity, Socrates portrayed his own conduct in Athens as a divinely
ordained mission to make the citizens better people. There was therefore
little doubt that the paradigm of a human life that he bequeathed was
a deeply moral one. But the burning question of how others might set
about achieving the same understanding for themselves led Socrates' followers, and above all Plato, to look for the ultimate sources of his insights.
Once these were located in a higher reality (in Plato's case, the "Forms"),
it became legitimate to wonder whether perfect human happiness might
not lie in enjoying pure contemplative knowledge of that reality, rather
than in the same knowledge's application to the here-and-now. Whether
the chosen paradigm turned out to be god or a perfected human being like
Socrates, the question remained: in what aspects is this ideal model to be
emulated? Whether the imitation was seen as intellectual, moral, or both
in equal measure is a question that has to be addressed independently for
each thinker or school, from Plato to the Neoplatonists.

A third perspective, complementary to the first two, finds its model of
mind not in paradigmatic individuals but in the powers of reason as such.
Reason, whether found in god, in a Socrates-figure, or in you or me, is
essentially one and the same power, albeit developed to different degrees.
The philosopher's task is therefore to uncover the structure of reason itself,

in order to put it on a completely firm basis and to progress towards realizing its full capacity. This is what led both Aristotle and the Stoics to develop their own respective systems of logic and of scientific reasoning.

We have chosen to put the essays in chronological order, starting with Socrates and ending with Plotinus. In different ways, these contributions reflect at least one of the three issues listed above: (a) the divine intellect; (b) a perfected human being, whether this be Socrates or the idealized sage postulated by Stoicism; and (c) the inherent powers and structure of human reason. After listing and describing these essays, we will briefly discuss the ways in which they interact with one another. As we will suggest, each essay shows how at least one ancient philosopher explores and, in some cases, posits a particular "model of mind."

(1) Andrea Nightingale, in "Plato on *aporia* and self-knowledge," argues that Socrates' "disavowal of knowledge" in the early dialogues evinces a specific kind of self-knowledge. In Plato's mature work, the philosophical "self" – and thus "self-knowledge" – is achieved by the interaction of the individual person on earth and his or her incorporeal (and impersonal) "reason", which contemplates the Forms.

(2) Sara Ahbel-Rappe, in "Cross-examining happiness: reason and community in the Socratic dialogues of Plato," defends an unorthodox interpretation of Socrates' ethics, arguing against "egoistic eudaimonism." Socrates, she argues, places others on a par with himself as the intended beneficiaries of moral choice. This non-egocentric ethical philosophy is based in part on an interpretation of Socrates' "divine mission" in the *Apology* and other early dialogues.

(3) Kathryn A. Morgan's "Inspiration, recollection, and *mimēsis* in Plato's *Phaedrus*" addresses the status of madness and divine inspiration in Plato's cognitive hierarchy. She links "inspiration" to the Platonic ideal of imitating the divine. Plato, she argues, turned away from traditional religion and towards the realm of the "divine" Forms in his efforts to conceptualize the "*enthousiasmos*" of the philosopher.

(4) David Sedley, in "Plato's *Theaetetus* as an ethical dialogue," maintains that in Plato's own taxonomy this work counts as ethical because its topic, knowledge, is an intellectual virtue, most fully captured in the dialogue's Digression, where intellectual divinization emerges as the truest realization of "justice." This ultimate convergence between intellectual and moral virtue in Plato's ethical thinking is then further explored through the case of temperance, *sōphrosunē*, a virtue in which young Theaetetus is declared to have progressed at the end of the dialogue.

(5) Allan Silverman, in "Contemplating divine mind," focuses on the theme of godlikeness as Plato's and Aristotle's ethical ideal, comparing their respective conceptions of god (in Plato's case, the creator god of the *Timaeus*) and drawing the consequences for their respective views of an ideal human life. The chapter is notable for the sharp contrast it makes between Plato and Aristotle on this score – the ideal Platonic life does not, as often thought, involve a flight from the human world, but Aristotle's may do so. He bases this in particular on the key role of the Good in the Plato's conception of the highest learning.

(6) Alan Code, in "Aristotle and the history of skepticism," moves the spotlight onto distinctively human rationality. Aristotle, he argues, made a constructive use of skeptical puzzles in his efforts to find secure first principles for knowledge. Code highlights Aristotle's rejection of the requirement that knowledge must always be backed up with proof or demonstration; indeed, even puzzles that have not been fully solved do not present an obstacle to the search for principles.

(7) Stephen White's "Stoic selection: objects, actions, and agents" scrutinizes one aspect of the nature of moral thinking in Stoic ethics. Starting from what may seem a terminological technicality concerning the Stoic concept of moral "selection," he develops a novel analysis of the mode of deliberative reasoning that, at least in its ideal form, characterizes the Stoic sage.

(8) Richard Bett, in "Beauty and its relation to goodness in Stoicism," keeps the focus on the Stoic value system. He shows how two apparently distinct kinds of beauty, that of soul and that of body, are – when viewed from a cosmic perspective – inseparable in Stoic eyes, given that the paradigm of beauty is the supremely rational beauty of the world itself. Bett also shows that the two kinds of beauty coalesce at a lower level, in Stoic erotic theory.

(9) Luca Castagnoli, in "How dialectical was Stoic dialectic?," examines a style of rational thought regarded as distinctively human – although, as he points out, it was said that, *if* the gods used dialectic, it would be that of Chrysippus. His question is whether, as in the case of its direct forerunner – Socratic dialectic – any significant part is played in Stoic "dialectic" by interpersonal interrogation, as the literal meaning of the term implies. He defends a strongly positive answer, based on close examination of the Stoic self-refutation argument against the denial of proof.

(10) James Ker, in "Socrates speaks in Seneca, *De vita beata* 24–28," offers a detailed examination of how Seneca, as a Stoic, appropriates the name

and voice of Socrates to provide a moral paradigm fit for his own Roman context. Ker focuses in particular on *De vita beata*, arguing that Seneca uses Socrates to argue for various Stoic positions, including the Stoic doctrine of "preferred indifferents."

(11) Gretchen Reydams-Schils, in "Seneca's Platonism: the soul and its divine origin," charts Seneca's incorporation into his Stoicism of motifs drawn from Plato's dualism of divine and human realms. She pays particular attention to the Platonic antitheses between human and divine reason, the intelligible and sensible worlds, and body and soul, showing how Seneca, by exploiting the resources of Stoicism, is able to maintain a careful distance from contemporary Platonism.

(12) Finally, Kenneth Wolfe, in "The status of the individual in Plotinus", maintains the focus on this divine–human dualism by examining how Plotinian metaphysics divinizes the human rational self, linking it to the transcendent realm through a doctrine of individual forms. Plotinus, he claims, argued that there were forms for all human individuals; knowing the essence of a particular sensible human being, then, entails knowing his or her intelligible form.

Essays 1–5 and 11–12 deal with the interrelation between (a) the divine mind and (c) human reason. The remaining essays focus mainly on (c) human reason taken in its own right. But (b), the paradigmatic sage, identified with or inspired by the figure of Socrates, is a prominent linking theme, especially in chapters 1–4 and 7–10. Other recurrent motifs include the requirement of self-knowledge (chapters 1, 4, 12), and the constructive role of puzzlement in intellectual progress (chapters 1 and 6).

All who have contributed these chapters were eager to give a concrete expression to the special affection in which they hold Tony Long, as a scholar, as a teacher, and above all as an exceptional human being. He has done a huge amount for his pupils to make them what they now are, but has never expected that they should adopt his own intellectual style. All have benefited from the model that he has provided, as well as from his unfailing advice and support both during their graduate studies and afterwards. But he has always encouraged independence and diversity. It is to be hoped that this book will serve as a testament to his success.

CHAPTER I

Plato on aporia *and self-knowledge*

Andrea Nightingale

I am honored to dedicate this essay to my dear friend and mentor, Tony Long. This small offering stands in for my great admiration for this man. I thank Tony for his generosity, his brilliance, and his greatness of soul.

Consider the famous Delphic pronouncement, "know thyself." In archaic and classical Greece, self-knowledge or *sōphrosunē* involved an understanding of oneself in relation to others, both human and divine.[1] The man who "knows himself" understands human limits and does not attempt to overstep these boundaries. The *sōphrōn* knows his place in relation to the gods and understands his station in society.[2] Challenging traditional views, Plato offers new, philosophical "selves" who achieve different modes of self-knowledge. In the early dialogues, Plato portrays a philosopher who comes to know himself even as he seeks for truths that he cannot fully grasp.[3] And, in the middle dialogues, Plato introduces an incorporeal soul that contemplates the Forms and understands itself in relation to these beings. This transmigrating soul, however, is incarnated in a specific person in a given place and time: the incarnated soul shuttles back and forth from a personal life on earth to an impersonal "vision" of higher realities. This "double life" of the soul generates a new kind of self. In these texts, Plato transforms the Greek command to "know thyself." As Long

---

[1] For general studies of *sōphrosunē* in the context of classical Greek literature, see North 1966 and Rademaker 2005.

[2] As Annas 1985: 121 puts it: "in the ancient world the individual personality was not the relevant self to know. What is relevant is knowing myself in the sense of knowing my place in society, knowing who I am and where I stand in relation to others. The self-knowledge that is *sōphrosunē* has nothing to do with my subconscious and everything to do with . . . 'my station and duties.'"

[3] See Annas 2002 for a criticism of the early–middle–late division of the Platonic dialogues. I do not want to comment on the dating of the dialogues. For my purposes, what matters is that the "early" Socratic dialogues are ethical and the "middle" dialogues introduce incorporeal beings (the Forms and the soul), and set forth a metaphysical system that places the soul in relation to the Forms.

has taught us, the Greek philosophers offered radical reconceptualizations of the "self."[4] I want to explore the new "selves" that Plato dramatized and conceptualized in his explorations of self-knowledge.

SOCRATIC SELF-KNOWLEDGE

In Plato's early dialogues, Socrates famously claimed that he did not possess knowledge. In recent scholarship, many have argued that Socrates spoke truthfully (rather than ironically) in making this assertion. But, in some dialogues, Socrates advances ethical claims and propositions that he appears to "know."[5] In order to account for Socrates' avowals and disavowals of knowledge, scholars have argued that Socrates uses the word "know" in two different senses. Vlastos – whose argument has been especially influential – differentiates between "expert knowledge" and "elenctic knowledge." He identifies "expert knowledge" as deductive: truth is deduced from fundamental, self-evident principles and is both necessary and indubitable. As Vlastos claims, Socrates does not possess "expert knowledge" but rather "elenctic knowledge," which is attained when an argument or proposition has withstood repeated elenctic testing. Unlike "expert knowledge," "elenctic knowledge" is always subject to refutation in future discussions, and is thus provisional and open to doubt. Vlastos argues that Socrates possesses this non-expert, "elenctic knowledge," even as he persists in searching for something more certain.[6]

Many scholars have accepted the distinction that Vlastos draws between expert and non-expert knowledge, though they have raised questions about the nature of "expert" knowledge. Nehamas and Woodruff, for example, reject Vlastos' claim that "expert knowledge" is deductive. Rather, they identify "expert knowledge" as the "technical knowledge" exhibited by craftsmen.[7] "Technical knowledge" is based on principles and techniques that can be tested, explained, and taught. On this account, Socrates denies that he possesses "technical knowledge" of virtue. Nehamas and Woodruff, however, agree with Vlastos that the practice of the elenchus leads to the wisdom that Socrates *does* possess: an "elenctic knowledge" that is

---

[4] See Long 1992 and 2001 on the "self" in Greek philosophy.

[5] See Wolfsdorf 2004 for a detailed discussion of the six "sincere" Socratic "avowals of knowledge" in the early dialogues. As he claims, one cannot simply lift these "avowals" out of their literary context – each claim has its own hermeneutic and epistemological status.

[6] Vlastos 1994: 42–48.

[7] Nehamas 1999a: 73–80 and *passim*, 1999b: ch. 2, Woodruff 1992. See also Reeve 1989: 37–45 and Roochnik 1996: ch.4.

non-expert and non-technical.[8] It is this kind of knowledge that allows Socrates to advance certain propositions that he takes to be (provisionally) true. In the *Apology*, for example, he claims that "to do injustice and to disobey a superior, whether human or divine, is bad and shameful" (29b). And, as he says in the *Crito*, "one should never return an injustice or harm a human being, no matter what one suffers at their hands" (49c).

I agree with Nehamas and Woodruff's conception of "expert" and "non-expert" knowledge. I also accept that Socrates possesses non-expert, "elenctic knowledge" of some principles and propositions that he has repeatedly tested in debates. But, as I will suggest, Socrates possesses another kind of knowledge that cannot be identified as "elenctic." I identify this as "self-knowledge," which is achieved in part by way of the elenchus but is not itself the object of elenctic inquiry.

In order to explicate this third mode of knowledge, let us consider the distinction between (1) the judgment of another person's epistemic condition, and (2) self-reflexive awareness of one's own epistemic condition.

How do we judge another person's epistemic condition? In examining Socrates' case, for example, we scholars have asked whether he possesses knowledge of the virtues that he seeks. To make this judgment, we must first examine his claims that he does not possess knowledge. Does Socrates make this claim sincerely or ironically? If we decide to take him at his word, we must ask whether the knowledge that he disavows is deductive knowledge, "craft" knowledge, or some other form of knowledge. And we must also investigate Socrates' "non-expert knowledge" of certain ethical propositions, which he repeatedly affirms. If we agree that Socrates does have some kind of knowledge of these propositions, we must then identify this mode of knowledge: is it "elenctic knowledge," true belief, or some other form of knowledge? Scholars have rightly posed these questions, but have not addressed the fact that we are judging Socrates' epistemic state *as outsiders*.[9] As external judges, we determine whether Socrates' disclaimers of knowledge are sincere, and we decide on what sort of knowledge he possesses. As outsiders, we investigate Socrates' dialectical inquiries and

---

[8] Reeve 1989: 37–53; Woodruff 1992; Nehamas 1999a: 73–80; cf. Irwin 1977: 89 and 1995: ch. 2, esp. 27–29, who argues that the difference is not between two kinds of knowledge but rather between knowledge and true belief.

[9] Clearly, we are judging the epistemic status of fictional character. But, for all intents and purposes, we use the same "external" mode of judgment when we assess real people. A literary text does of course offer a (large or small) set of "clues" about a character; but we look for these same kinds of clues in our dealings with actual people.

thus form a judgment about his epistemic state.[10] In the same way, Socrates assesses the epistemic condition of others – from an external position, he judges that they do not possess knowledge, basing this judgment on their inability to defend their own views.

I turn now to the "self-reflexive awareness" of one's own epistemic condition. Socrates exemplifies this mode of self-awareness when he says that he is aware that he does not possess knowledge (e.g., *Apology* 21b). Here, Socrates investigates *his own* epistemic condition, which he discovers by way of argument and self-reflection. In particular, he judges his own inability to "give an account" of the nature of virtue; he admits to bafflement and frustration in his ongoing attempts to gain knowledge of virtue. He thus becomes aware that he has bumped up against his own epistemic limits – he is "self-reflexively aware" of his intellectual capacities and limitations. In his own view, Socrates believes that he does not possess "divine knowledge." Note that he can only achieve this self-understanding when he has extensively explored his own ideas, arguments, capacities, and actions. Of course his failure to achieve knowledge does not make Socrates stop inquiring, stop seeking to better himself; he carries on testing himself and finding new arguments in his search for truth. But, in spite of a lifetime of effort, he claims that he has not achieved true knowledge and is fully aware of this. In my view, this "self-reflexive awareness" is, itself, a kind of wisdom. For Socrates explicitly claims that he is "wiser" than others in this regard. As he puts it in the *Apology*, "just as I do not know, I do not think I know" (21b). Obviously, Socrates' lack of knowledge does not in itself make him wise or good (indeed Socrates identifies this as a defect). But his *awareness* of his epistemic limitations does constitute a kind of ethical wisdom, since it reveals his understanding of a truth about himself.

Socrates' self-proclaimed awareness of his own intellectual limitations evinces an understanding of his distance from truth and divinity. Socrates achieves this self-awareness, in part, by interacting with his fellow humans: he investigates his own ideas by debating with other people (and he invites them to correct his errors). And he also engages in practical activities that test his capacity to enact the virtues. Ultimately, however, he must look into himself and reach an honest assessment of his own capacities and limits. In doing this, he comes to see that he has not achieved knowledge and may never do so. His awareness that he does not possess knowledge taps into desire (it reveals a lack): he longs for a wisdom that he does

---

[10] We should also take under consideration the fact that Socrates does not bring his aporetic questions to positive and fixed conclusions in the early dialogues.

not yet possess. But this self-reflective awareness also reveals his capacities and limitations, his failures and successes. Socrates' claim in the *Apology* that he has "human" rather than "divine" knowledge indicates that he has discovered his own limits and boundaries. Given that Socrates makes this statement at the end of a lifetime of elenctic inquiry, we may be tempted to conclude that he has discovered not only his own limited capacities but the epistemic limitations of all human beings. But Socrates' claims about the ignorance of others – about the intellectual shortcomings of his interlocutors and fellow Athenians – are categorically different from the claims he makes about his own ignorance. For the knowledge he has of himself is based on data that he does not have direct access to in others – it is discovered by way of self-testing and self-inspection.

We should not, then, treat Socrates' disavowal of knowledge as a simple assertion about the presence or absence of knowledge – as a propositional claim about an epistemic state. It is, rather, the enactment of a form of ethical wisdom. What sort of ethical wisdom is this? Reeve claims that Socrates' disavowal of knowledge is commendably antihubristic and is certainly a part of "human" wisdom. But, as he argues, there must be some positive content to Socratic wisdom: "otherwise anyone who recognized that he lacked such knowledge would possess human wisdom and be as wise as Socrates, even if his recognition was the result of general skepticism or below-normal intelligence."[11] Reeve suggests, then, that the disavowal of knowledge does not, by itself, reflect ethical wisdom since unintelligent people who have not tested their own views can make this same claim. Reeve therefore argues that the wisdom that Socrates possesses must combine "negative" disavowals of knowledge with "positive" assertions of moral propositions based on non-expert knowledge. In my view, Socrates' disavowal of knowledge is the result of philosophical self-reflection. "Unintelligent people" cannot achieve Socratic self-knowledge simply by saying that they don't know something. Only a philosopher can correctly grasp his own epistemic limits. Indeed, Socrates claims that he is wiser than others precisely because he is aware of the fact that he does not have knowledge of the virtues. In reflecting on his own ignorance and epistemic capacities, Socrates exhibits self-knowledge – a knowledge that he can only find by testing and examining himself. This knowledge is "positive," but is completely distinct from propositional knowledge.[12]

---

[11] Reeve 1989: 35; see also Woodruff 1992: 99 and passim; Vlastos and Nehamas do not discuss this kind of knowledge.

[12] See Roochnik 1996: ch. 4, who sees Socratic knowledge as the knowledge of *ta erōtika*, which he identifies as a knowledge of the desiring human psyche. This knowledge is indeterminate and

Socrates' "self-referential awareness," then, must be distinguished from both technical (expert) and elenctic (non-expert) knowledge. This is "self-knowledge," which one cannot discover by making it the *object* of elenctic inquiry and philosophical argumentation. We can of course ask "what is self-knowledge?" and pursue this question in a philosophical inquiry, but this will tell us little or nothing about our own epistemic state and will not produce self-knowledge. To be sure, the practice of testing ideas and beliefs via elenctic discussions is a precondition for developing Socratic self-knowledge. But only when one combines this philosophical practice with introspection and self-testing (in discourse and praxis) can one achieve Socratic self-knowledge. Clearly, a correct understanding of one's present condition allows one to find ways to develop one's intellectual and ethical abilities. For Socrates, knowing oneself is a crucial element in ethical action. A self-ignorant person cannot make good choices and will inevitably engage in bad actions.

Let us look briefly at the *Charmides*, which offers an extensive investigation of self-knowledge. In the *Charmides*, the definition of self-knowledge "meets with terrible difficulties throughout the dialogue."[13] The dialogue ends in *aporia*, but its failure to apprehend self-knowledge is nonetheless instructive. The latter part of the dialogue focuses on Critias' claim that *sōphrosunē* is "self-knowledge" and Socrates' refutations of his arguments for this position. This discussion begins when Critias says that if Socrates denies that *sōphrosunē* is self-knowledge (τὸ γιγνώσκειν αὐτὸν ἑαυτόν) he himself will "give a demonstration of this" (τούτου σοι διδόναι λόγον, 165b). To Critias' confident – and conceited – claim, the self-knowing Socrates says: "I myself do not know" the truth of this matter (165b–c). Socrates proceeds to ask whether there is an *object* of self-knowledge that is distinct from the knowledge itself, just as the heavy and the light are the objects of the art of weighing and are distinct from the act of weighing (166a–b). Critias answers that *sōphrosunē* differs from other modes of knowledge in that it does not have something distinct from itself as an object, but is rather "a knowledge of other knowledges and of itself" (ἡ . . . τῶν τε ἄλλων ἐπιστημῶν ἐπιστήμη ἐστὶ καὶ αὐτὴ ἑαυτῆς, 166c, e).

Here, Critias makes an important move, shifting from the Delphic notion of *sōphrosunē* as "knowing oneself" to the quite different conception

---

thus resistant to technical modes of investigation. Roochnik comes close to my conception of self-knowledge, though he does not make the distinction between "self-referential" knowledge of oneself and "external" judgment of others.

[13] Roochnik 1996: 120

of self-knowledge as the "knowledge of knowledges."[14] Ignoring the fact that the object of self-knowledge must in some sense be the self (whatever that is), Critias advances the specious claim that self-knowledge is the "knowledge of knowledges." By identifying (reflexive) "self-knowledge" with the (non-reflexive) "knowledge of knowledges," Critias indicates that the person with *sōphrosunē* will have knowledge of his own knowledge *and that of other people* (167a). But the knowledge of the epistemic states of others is not self-knowledge. When we judge others, we may use some of the same criteria that we use in judging our own epistemic condition, but these are two very different kinds of judgment. First and foremost, we have access to ourselves that we do not have of others.[15] In addition, testing and acknowledging one's own epistemic and moral state – and thus gaining self-knowledge – allows one to make better choices and act more wisely. Correlatively, one's judgment of others (even if it is correct) does not help that person to become better or wiser.

By the end of the *Charmides*, Socrates says that their inquiry has produced "nothing good." Indeed, as he claims, he and Critias have made a number of claims that were not proven by argumentation. Socrates focuses in particular on Critias' discussion of the "knowledge of knowledges" (175a–c). As I have suggested, the trouble begins when Critias identifies "self-knowledge" with the "knowledge of knowledges." By ignoring the self-reflexive nature of self-knowledge, Critias paves the way for the numerous refutations that follow. During the discussion, Socrates does not correct this mistake or articulate the distinction between the (non self-reflexive) judgment of other people's epistemic states and the (self-reflexive) assessment of one's own epistemic state. Rather, he pushes Critias' claim to various absurd conclusions. But it is worth noting that, immediately after Critias first states that self-knowledge is the "knowledge of other knowledges and of itself," Socrates says that his own goal is to "*investigate myself* and what I am saying, since I fear that I might unwittingly think that I know something, when I don't" (166c–d, my italics). Socrates thus offers a pointed reminder that *sōphrosunē* is a self-reflective form of knowledge. Indeed, Socrates explicitly says that, in this philosophical discussion, he is investigating himself in an effort to avoid the conceit of knowledge.[16]

---

[14] This move is the central focus of many scholarly discussions of the dialogue. See, e.g., Tuckey 1951: 33–8 (and appendices I and III), Santas 1973: 119–20, Dyson 1974, Annas 1985: 133–36, McKim 1985, Coolidge 1993.

[15] In Plato, we see evidence for this in cases of deception: the liar or ironist can conceal his views from others.

[16] See also *Charmides* 160d–e, where Socrates tells Charmides to "look into yourself" in his search for the nature of *sōphrosunē*.

Socrates does not, then, exhibit a technical "knowledge of knowledges" but rather a self-knowledge that is a part of ethical wisdom. Critias, by contrast, refuses to confront his own ignorance:

When Critias heard these things and saw that I was in a state of *aporia*, he seemed to be seized by *aporia* himself because of my *aporia* – just as those people who see someone near them yawning are affected in the same way. But since he always aims for a good reputation, he was ashamed to admit in front of those present that he could not decide on the things I was asking him, and so he said something very indistinct, hiding his *aporia*. (169c–d)

Here, vanity and the desire for esteem prevent Critias from confronting his own ignorance. His inability to "know himself" is an ethical as well as epistemic failure.[17]

As the passage above indicates, Socrates clearly links *aporia* with the awareness of his own ignorance. In fact, one could define Socratic *aporia* as the combination of the lack of expert knowledge and the *self-knowing awareness of this lack*. Since self-knowledge is a form of ethical wisdom, Socratic *aporia* has an epistemic and an ethical component: epistemically speaking, Socrates does not possess knowledge; he does not know the truth about virtue, and is therefore (at least for the time being) "at a loss." But *aporia* is not ignorance pure and simple. For *aporia* includes the awareness that one is stuck or lost. A person who is not aware of being lost – not aware that he is mistaken or ignorant about something – is not in a state of *aporia*. He is simply lost or ignorant. To experience *aporia* is to enter into the awareness of *one's own* lack of knowledge – a self-awareness that Socrates exhibits and attempts to evoke in others. In fact, Socrates sometimes sounds as if his aim in dealing with his interlocutors is to lead them out of self-conceit into a state of *aporia* – and thus to the disavowal of knowledge – rather than to bring their elenctic discussions to firm conclusions.[18] As Socrates says in the *Apology*, "surely this is the most reprehensible form of ignorance, that of thinking one knows what one does not know" (29b). By showing the Athenians who think they are wise that they are not wise, he claims, he brings aid to his fellow citizens (30d–31b) and also serves the god Apollo (23b). He clearly believes that an individual who moves away from the conceit of knowledge to an awareness of ignorance will become a *better person*. The conceit of knowledge is an ethical, and not just an epistemic,

---

[17] See also *Philebus* 48c–49a, where Socrates claims that the opposite of self-knowledge (*gnōthi seauton*) is a form of ignorance that leads us to overestimate our wealth and personal appearance as well as our virtuousness.

[18] Of course there is much more to say about Socrates' mission, its motives, and aims. This goes beyond the scope of this essay.

failure; and thus the move from ignorance to *aporia* constitutes significant ethical improvement, even though the person who experiences *aporia* does not possess the knowledge of virtue. The person who experiences Socratic *aporia* has achieved a greater degree of self-knowledge and rid himself of vanity and self-delusion.[19]

Is the experience of *aporia* in regard to any field of inquiry good for a person, or only *aporia* concerning ethical questions and issues? For example, are we better people when we admit that we don't know the answer to a mathematical problem? Does this admission constitute a gain in self-knowledge and better our ethical condition? In Plato's early dialogues, Socrates focuses exclusively on ethical questions, which he calls "the most important of issues" (*Apology* 22d). It would seem, then, that falsely believing that one possesses knowledge about ethical issues would be more damaging to the soul than overestimating one's expertise in mathematics. If we wrongly think that we understand what is good and bad, this will affect our actions and thus our very lives. For example, in the *Apology*, Socrates addresses the traditional belief that death is evil: "to fear death is nothing other than to think oneself wise when one is not wise, for it is to think one knows what one does not know; in fact nobody knows if death is the greatest of goods to man, but they fear it as if they knew that it is the greatest of evils" (*Apology* 29a). This example shows the ethical ramifications of the false claim to know what is good and bad, for this *lack of self-awareness* leads one into a state of fear which can affect a wide range of one's choices and actions. Nonetheless, I think it can be argued that *any* false claim to knowledge – even concerning a value-neutral field such as carpentry or mathematics – marks an ethical failure.[20] For the presence of any kind of self-conceit reveals a person's vanity and self-deception. The very claim to know something that one has not fully explored and mastered is rooted in self-delusion.

APORIA AND CONTEMPLATION

Socrates' *aporia*, I have argued, is part and parcel of his self-knowledge – it is not just a cognitive condition but a mode of ethical wisdom. I turn now to the middle dialogues, where Plato advances the claim that the philosopher, in human life, can attain at least a partial apprehension of the Forms. Does the philosopher who contemplates the Forms achieve self-knowledge? Let

[19] See also *Theaetetus* 210b–c and *Sophist* 230b–c.
[20] Of course, in the middle and late dialogues, Plato does not consider mathematics an ethically neutral discipline.

us look first at Plato's treatment of *aporia*. In the *Meno*, Meno says that he had heard that Socrates is man who goes around in a state of *aporia* and makes others feel *aporia* as well (80a). After conversing with Socrates, he adds that he himself is now "full of *aporia*" and compares Socrates to a stingray that numbs its victims: "I am numb in both my soul and my tongue," Meno says, "and am not able to answer you. And yet I have given many speeches on virtue before many men on countless occasions, and I spoke very well, as I thought; but now I cannot say anything at all about virtue" (80a–b). Socrates responds that the analogy is apt if the stingray that numbs others is itself also numb. For, as he claims, he himself does not know what virtue is and "experiences more *aporia* than anyone" (80c–d). This treatment of *aporia* is in keeping with the *Charmides*: Socrates experiences *aporia* and thus sees his own lack of knowledge. In the *Meno*, Socrates also reduces his confident interlocutor to *aporia*: Meno admits that he is at a loss. This passage clearly links *aporia* to the disavowal of knowledge and the ethical "self-knowledge" that we saw in the early dialogues (and, correlatively, Meno's conceit of knowledge clearly signals a deficiency in this kind of ethical wisdom).

But the *Meno* differs from the early dialogues in that it offers a second, rather different conception of *aporia*. This is found later in the text, after Socrates has set forth the theory of recollection. In the midst of his dialogue with the slave-boy about a geometry problem – which demonstrates the process of recollection – Socrates says to Meno that the slave-boy did not know the answer to the problem when it was first posed. "At that point," Socrates says, "the boy thought that he knew, and answered confidently as if he did know, and he did not feel that he was in a state of *aporia*; but now he feels that he is in *aporia* and, in addition to not knowing, he does not think that he knows" (84a–b). Socrates goes on to say that the slave-boy is better off now that he is in a condition of *aporia*, since this will lead him "to discover (πρὸς τὸ ἐξευρεῖν) in what way the matter holds" (84b). In fact, the boy would not have "attempted to inquire or learn (ζητεῖν ἢ μανθάνειν) what he thought he knew . . . until he fell into *aporia*, realized that he did not know, and then felt a desire to know" (84c). Socrates adds that "out of this *aporia*" (ἐκ ταύτης τῆς ἀπορίας) the slave-boy will "discover" (ἀνευρήσει) the solution to the problem by responding to his questions (84c–d).

In this scene, Socrates knows the answer to the geometry problem and is not himself in a state of *aporia*: using his mathematical expertise, he can bring the slave-boy into *aporia*, which leads to the discovery of the correct answer. Socrates explicitly says that the slave-boy is better off when he moves from false confidence to *aporia*, but this is not because he has become humbler and more self-knowing. Rather, his *aporia* spurs him to "learn" and "discover" the truth. The slave-boy's *aporia* appears to be a cognitive awareness of ignorance that serves a purely instrumental purpose: it motivates him to search for the truth.[21] Socrates does not suggest here that *aporia* is an ethical state or a condition that generates self-knowledge. On the contrary, he identifies the *aporia* as the simple recognition of an epistemic error which serves to point the boy in the direction of knowledge. Indeed, once the slave-boy recognizes his error, he proceeds to "recollect" the solution to the problem and leave his *aporia* behind.

Many scholars have argued that, in the middle-period dialogues, Plato sets forth a new philosophical system. In contrast to the early, aporetic dialogues, Plato claims that the philosopher can, to some extent, attain the truth that evaded Socrates. The philosopher achieves this by engaging in dialectic and contemplating the Forms. To the extent that the philosopher's inquiries have led to truth, he has exited from perplexity. The *aporia* that is left behind, we may infer, is purely cognitive and has no ethical or existential valence. It is an epistemic perplexity that is merely instrumental: it awakens desire and leads to knowledge. It is not a form of self-knowledge or ethical wisdom.

In *Republic* 7, Socrates offers another account of *aporia* in his discussion of the education of the philosopher-kings. As he claims, "some of our sensory experiences do not provoke the mind toward inquiry, since the senses judge them adequately, whereas others invite the mind to inquire because the senses offer nothing that can be trusted" (523a–b). For example, sensory perception can convey to the soul that something is both hard and soft; in this case, "the soul experiences *aporia*" since it cannot understand how the same thing can be both hard and soft (524a). This also occurs in the perception of number, since the same thing can appear to be both one and many. "But if something opposite to it is always seen at the same time, so that it does not appear to be one more than the opposite of one [i.e. many], a person would need some way to judge the matter. The soul would be compelled to experience *aporia* and to investigate – arousing the thought within it – and to ask what the one is in itself" (524e–525a). As Socrates explains, this state of *aporia* leads to a philosophical inquiry that turns the soul towards the study of the Forms; ultimately, this leads the philosopher to the "vision of being" (525a). Here, the *aporia* is purely epistemic – it is an intellectual response to conflicting perceptions and ideas. According

---

[21]   As Matthews 1999: ch. 7 rightly observes.

to Plato, the philosopher can only settle this matter by moving from the sensible to the intelligible realm, from appearance to reality. The experience of *aporia*, then, redirects the rational part of the soul towards intelligible reality – it is a step along the soul's journey towards the Forms.

We find a similar explanation of "epistemic *aporia*" in Aristotle. At the opening of *Metaphysics* book 3, Aristotle offers an account of *aporia* that clearly alludes to Plato's Allegory of the Cave:

For those who wish to get rid of perplexity (εὐπορῆσαι), it is useful to go through all the puzzles (διαπορῆσαι) thoroughly. For the subsequent certainty (εὐπορία) is a release (λύσις) from the previous perplexities (τῶν . . . ἀπορουμένων), but it is not possible for people to loosen the bonds (λύειν . . . τὸν δεσμόν) when they are ignorant of them. But the *aporia* of the mind (ἡ τῆς διανοίας ἀπορία) reveals the presence of this condition in a given inquiry. For insofar as [the mind] is in *aporia*, it experiences (πέπονθε) something similar to men who have been put in bonds (τοῖς δεδεμένοις); for in both cases it is impossible to move forward. (3.1.995a)

Here, Aristotle says that the mind experiences itself as being fettered, stuck at some point in an investigation. He does not identify *aporia* with the bonds themselves; rather, it is the *awareness* of the bonds that produces *aporia* (which, we infer, stands in opposition to "*ignorance* of the bonds"). Clearly, people can have "mind-forged manacles" (as Blake put it) without being aware of this. As Aristotle claims, *aporia* reveals the presence of these fetters and points to a problem that needs to be solved. When the mind discovers the solution to the puzzles, it exits from *aporia* and is "released" from ignorance.

Clearly, this passage from Aristotle – with its talk of "bondage" (δεσμός) and "release" (λύσις) – echoes the language of the Allegory of the Cave. But Aristotle's example diverges from Plato's notion of *aporia* and contemplation. Let us recall Plato's portrayal of the philosophical journey in the Allegory of the Cave: "Picture men in a sort of subterranean, cavernous dwelling (οἰκήσει)," Socrates says, "having been, since childhood, in fetters (ἐν δεσμοῖς)." After describing the inside of the cave and its deluded denizens, Socrates goes on to discuss the soul's "release and healing from the bonds and from ignorance" (αὐτῶν λύσιν τε καὶ ἴασιν τῶν τε δεσμῶν καὶ τῆς ἀφροσύνης, 515c). He then describes what happens when a person in the cave "is released and compelled to stand up suddenly and turn his head around and to walk and look upwards towards the light" (515c). At first, this person experiences pain and is blinded by the light streaming into the cave from the higher world. Now comes *aporia*: "and if someone should compel him, by questioning, to say what each of the things at hand really is, don't you think that he would experience *aporia* and believe that the things he saw before were truer than the things that are now being revealed to him?" (515d). Here, it is *after* he is released from bonds that the person feels *aporia*. In Aristotle, by contrast, *aporia* reveals that the mind is in fetters, not yet released. Indeed, the soul that experiences *aporia* in Plato's narrative has entered a sort of existential and epistemic no-man's-land, since it no longer dwells at the back of the cave in chains but has not yet journeyed into the light. At this point, Socrates says, "if he were compelled to look at the light, he would feel pain in his eyes and, turning around, flee back (φεύγειν ἀποστρεφόμενον) to those things which he could see" (515e).

In Plato's Allegory, *aporia* occurs when the soul is exiled from its original "home" (οἴκησις, 514a, 516c) and "compelled" to journey to (as yet) unknown regions. The fact that the perplexed soul wishes to flee back to its original dwelling indicates that *aporia* resembles the experience of homelessness. The soul is "at a loss" existentially, since it has experienced deracination and disorientation. And its *aporia* also has an ethical dimension, since it is a necessary part of the soul's "release" and "healing" – its escape from the deluded and debased life within the cave. Socrates, in fact, compares the region inside the cave to the land of the dead (516d–e), and he even identifies the soul's later journey back into the cave as a "*katabasis*" (516e) – a standard term for a journey down to Hades. The philosopher's *aporia* when he escapes from chains, then, reflects his awareness that he is "lost," both epistemically and ethically. In Plato's mythic language, the soul is the protagonist in a narrative of captivity and release; it moves from deadly and harmful delusions to the vision of goodness.[22]

In this passage, Plato's philosopher experiences *aporia* that is at once ethical and epistemological. Whereas Aristotle speaks of the mind's "release" from the bonds of epistemic error, Plato identifies the soul's "release" as a "healing" from an unhealthy (and *unheimlich*) condition as it journeys towards its proper abode (516c). In contrast to Plato, Aristotle does not describe the condition of bondage as painful or morally debased. Indeed he offers a very simple explanation of the analogy: it illustrates the fact that, just as men in bonds cannot move forward, so also the fettered mind can't make progress. In short, Aristotle describes a purely cognitive and epistemic phenomenon: *aporia* is not an ethical condition and is not linked to self-knowledge.

As we have seen, at times Plato identifies *aporia* as a purely epistemic experience, while at others he indicates that it has ethical dimensions as

---

[22] Note the direct reference to Odysseus' journey to the underworld at 516d–e.

well. Obviously, the philosopher journeys to contemplate the Forms in order to escape from epistemic perplexity and come to know the truth. But, as Plato indicates in the Allegory of the Cave, the journey to the Forms (and back) has an ethical aspect that goes beyond mere rational contemplation.

CONTEMPLATION AND SELF-KNOWLEDGE

Why should we believe that self-knowledge has anything to do with the soul's "vision" of the Forms? Consider *Phaedrus* 229e–230a:

I have no leisure [for investigating mythical creatures]. And the reason, my friend, is this. I don't yet know myself (γνῶναι ἐμαυτόν), as the Delphic inscription puts it. Since I am ignorant of this, it seems ridiculous to investigate matters concerning others (ἀλλότρια). And I therefore ignore these things . . . and, as I was saying just now, I investigate not them but myself (σκοπῶ οὐ ταῦτα ἀλλὰ ἐμαυτόν), to discover whether I am a beast more complex and savage than the Typhon, or a gentler and simpler creature, sharing in my nature some divine and untyphonic lot.

Here, Socrates makes a statement that resembles some of his claims found in the early dialogues. But this passage contains some important differences. In particular, Socrates seeks to know himself by understanding his relation to beasts and to gods. Is he simple or complex, gentle or savage, divine or bestial? Socrates wants to "know himself" both ethically and ontologically.[23] Of course this passage clearly anticipates the image of the human soul as a charioteer with two horses in Socrates' second speech. As the charioteer analogy suggests, the human soul is complex (though one should note that the divine souls are also portrayed as having horses and chariots – they seem to be more complex than simple). But, more importantly, Socrates says that the soul becomes divine by virtue of its nearness to the Forms.[24] Here, Plato indicates that a philosophical soul can become (more) divine by seeing the Forms and achieving contemplative knowledge.

In the *Phaedrus*, Socrates links his search for self-knowledge to his understanding of the soul and its relation to the Forms. In order to achieve self-knowledge, Socrates must first comprehend that the soul is immortal and

---

[23] As Griswold 1986: 43 observes, "Socrates wishes to know himself in particular (and not just 'the soul' or 'human nature') in order that he may lead the life that is best. The centrality of leading one's life in the best possible way supplies a clue as to why self-knowledge must ultimately return to the level of an individual's knowledge of himself in particular."

[24] *Phaedrus* 249c: διὸ δὴ δικαίως μόνη πτεροῦται ἡ τοῦ φιλοσόφου διάνοια· πρὸς γὰρ ἐκείνοις ἀεί ἐστιν μνήμῃ κατὰ δύναμιν, πρὸς οἷσπερ θεὸς ὢν θεῖός ἐστιν.

not bounded by its life on earth. In the central speech in the *Phaedrus*, Plato places the soul in a cosmic context, tracing its history back to a preincarnate state. Plato thus tells a "story of the soul" that defines it in relation to the gods and Forms even as it acknowledges its (periodic) bodily incarnations. How, then, does Plato link the soul to a specific "self"? Note, first of all, that different souls have contemplated the Forms in different degrees in the pre-incarnate period of their lives. In addition, souls are differentiated according to their affinity to specific deities (248a, 252c–253c). Here, Plato moves from undifferentiated souls to soul-types. But how does this lead to a self? Plato does not address this question explicitly, but he does offer an indirect response.

In the *Phaedrus*, Plato locates the myth in the context of a dialogue between two quite specific characters, one of whom is energetically seeking self-knowledge. As in all his dialogues, Plato places the specificity of the characters in a dialogical relation to the general and abstract ideas being discussed.[25] The drama of the dialogue – with its characters, narratives, and events – corroborates but also complicates the issues set forth in the arguments. In this narrative, the characters' lives and personalities enrich and illuminate the intellectual arguments. Thus Socrates' highly idiosyncratic persona (and Phaedrus' more ordinary personality) affect our interpretation of the dialogue as a whole and the account of the soul in particular. And the same can be said about the other dialogues which discuss the soul (in mythic or analytic discourse). Socrates' personal search for wisdom and self-knowledge is placed in a fruitful interaction with his accounts of the contemplative activities of impersonal philosophical souls.

Let us look again at the myth in the *Phaedrus*, where Socrates describes a man and boy engaging in a philosophical love affair on earth. Socrates places these figures in a cosmic context that includes the preincarnate period of their lives. For example, when the philosophical lover gazes on the beautiful boy, he recollects the Form of Beauty, thus connecting up his present human self with his former theorizing soul. This indicates that the soul maintains some sort of continuity through time, and that its past experiences affect the present (just as the present affects the future). In connecting the present moment on earth with a former moment of non-incarnate theorizing, the lover begins to experience a transformation that alters his very identity. By "remembering" his preincarnate visions and getting a glimpse of this higher reality, he sees that his soul is not bounded, either temporally or spatially, by this particular earthly life. In

---

[25] See Blondell's excellent treatment of this issue in 2002: ch.1 and passim.

addition, he comes to see that his present actions affect his everlasting life in the future. Indeed, these actions will determine the "place" where he will dwell after death. By locating the soul of the lover in a cosmic "chronotope," Plato places the soul in relation to the incorporeal gods and the Forms while also showing its (present) incarnation in an earthly place.[26] The lover is both a social, earthly person and a player in the divine cosmos. As Socrates says later in the dialogue, the philosopher should strive to discover the truth and to perfect his discourse "not for the sake of speaking and acting in relation to men, but so that he can speak and act in all things, as far as possible, in a manner that pleases the gods" (273e–274a). And this is precisely what Socrates himself attempts to do – to use his reason to move up towards the gods and the Forms. He not only wants to "see" the Forms but to "know himself" in relation to these higher beings. He achieves self-knowledge in part by reflecting on his own epistemic and moral state. But he also gains this knowledge by theorizing the Forms and thus finding himself in "a region of unlikeness" (to borrow a phrase from the *Statesman*). As Socrates makes clear, human and divine souls move and bring about change, whereas the Forms are unitary and changeless.

Plato, then, offers a notion of the self that differs radically from traditional Greek views. He does of course acknowledge that social and cultural forces contribute to the construction of the self, but he also claims that metaphysical and divine forces play a key role in self-formation. In order to attain self-knowledge, in sum, Socrates must not only examine his own arguments and actions (as in the early dialogues) but also understand the nature of the soul and its cosmic peregrinations and transformations. To grasp the nature of the soul, Socrates must apprehend its erotic desire for the Forms (and feel this desire in his own soul) and also contemplate the Forms themselves. Thus the theoretical contemplation of metaphysical reality – even if only partial – not only confers objective knowledge but also assists in the attainment of self-knowledge. Note, finally, that the dialogue does not define Socrates or the philosophical lover solely in terms of his incorporeal soul who "recollects" or "sees" a Form:[27] each of these characters shifts back and forth between this world and the next in the effort to comprehend the truth about the corporeal and incorporeal realms and his own relation to both.

---

[26] On the notion of the "chronotope" in Plato's dialogues, see Nightingale 2002.

[27] See Long 1992 for an excellent discussion of the "objective self." In Plato, the theorizing soul is akin to the "objective self"; but Plato offers a richer sense of the self by showing the interaction of the earthly person and the impersonal soul (see also Blondell 2002: ch. 1).

Plato makes a similar move in the Allegory of the Cave. In this myth, as we have seen, the philosopher "journeys" out of the darkness of the cave into the bright region of reality. He thus exits from the constraints of society and culture and enters into the presence of true being. Although Plato's use of the narrative mode has the effect of turning the rational part of the soul into a full-blown person – thus creating the famous "homunculus" problem – we must remember that it is reason alone (with its own erotic drive) that ascends to the Forms. But it is the philosopher living on earth who chooses to turn away from the human and terrestrial world and use his reason to contemplate the Forms. Plato suggests that the philosopher's soul can "remember" his former abode even as he gazes on the Forms:

When he recalls (ἀναμιμνησκόμενον) his first habitation and the "wisdom" there and the fellow-inmates that he formerly (τότε) lived with, wouldn't he consider himself happy in his transformation (τῆς μεταβολῆς), and pity those others? (516c)

At this moment, although his mind is contemplating the Forms, the philosopher is aware of the transformation he has gone through. He rejoices in his nearness to the Forms and distance from earth and its values. In addition, he remembers his former life: although the *Republic* does not make use of the doctrine of recollection, the Allegory portrays a sort of reverse-recollection in which the philosopher remembers the world and its shadowy multiplicity even as he engages in contemplation.[28] Either way, the philosopher uses his memory to connect his contemplating soul to his earthly person. As in the *Phaedrus*, it is this interplay between the earthly person and the contemplating soul that contributes to the formation of the philosophical "self."

Plato does not offer a definition of the self, nor does he explain the psychic or epistemological mechanics of self-knowledge. But we can, I think, make some general claims about Plato's notion of the self-knowledge that is achieved through contemplation. First of all, when contemplating, the rational part of the soul focuses on the Forms. The contemplating soul is not private or personal: it has detached itself from the bodily and social aspects of its earthly life. To some extent, the contemplating soul resembles Nagel's "objective self," except that Plato's contemplator looks solely at the Forms and not at physical objects.[29]

---

[28] Plato does not identify which faculty of soul is doing the remembering in this case. For my purposes, what matters is the general affirmation that the philosophical soul goes back and forth between this world and the next.

[29] Nagel 1986. Long 1992 rightly claims that Heraclitus' notion of the self anticipates Nagel's "objective self."

As I have suggested, the philosopher attains self-knowledge by moving back and forth between his particular life on earth and his contemplation of incorporeal realities – by understanding himself in both a corporeal and incorporeal context. Indeed, the activity of contemplation does have a self-referential aspect. While contemplating the Forms, the philosophical souls escape from perplexity and discover true Being: in the process, their self-understanding undergoes a radical change. In portraying the soul's "vision" of reality, Plato stages an ontological encounter between the human soul and the essences of the Forms.[30] Insofar as the soul "encounters" the Forms, it confronts and apprehends their unique ontology, their divine essences. In addition to gaining knowledge of these objects, the contemplating soul comes to understand its kinship to and difference from the divine essence of the Forms. This is not just a cognitive grasp of the qualities of similarity and difference. The soul self-referentially grasps its kinship with and difference from the Forms.[31] By seeing the Forms as both kindred and strange, the theorizing soul not only apprehends these beings but also comprehends its own ontological and existential status. The soul, then, does not investigate itself as an object but "knows itself" in relation to the Forms.

This kind of self-knowledge, like that of Plato's early Socrates, has an ethical dimension. But the self-knowledge of Plato's contemplative philosopher differs from Socrates, whose "self-referential awareness" leads him to see that he lacks knowledge. Plato's philosopher does possess at least some "divine" knowledge (though he may, when seeing one Form, be aware that he does not know other Forms, especially the Form of the Good). Indeed, it is precisely because the contemplative philosopher *has* achieved knowledge of some aspect of reality that he can understand his own nature in relation to these Beings. When a philosopher apprehends the Forms, he comes to understand the boundaries of his soul – his very nature as a soul – even as he contemplates the divine essence of the Forms. This understanding, I would suggest, is ethical and ontological but not identical to or coextensive with the objective knowledge of the Forms. In other words, when epistemic knowledge is achieved (even if only partially), the soul also comes to know itself in its ontological relation to a divine Other – it journeys to the boundary of ensouled being and sees something that is beyond. To the extent that it experiences its own boundaries and grasps its own

---

[30] See, e.g., *Symposium* 210e, *Republic* 490a–b, 500b–c, 515c–516e, *Phaedrus* 247a–c, 249c, 249e–250c, 254b.

[31] Note that, if the Forms were simply alien presences, the soul would not recognize them; but if they were utterly familiar, the soul would not be astonished.

ontological essence even as it gazes at the essence of the Forms, the contemplating soul attains a self-reflexive understanding. To this extent, the contemplative philosopher gains a sort of "soul-knowledge." Ultimately, however, he attains self-knowledge by moving back and forth between his contemplating soul and his earthly person: it is the interplay between these two that generates self-knowledge in the Platonic philosopher.

CHAPTER 2

Cross-examining happiness
Reason and community in Plato's Socratic dialogues
Sara Ahbel-Rappe

This essay is dedicated to A. A. Long. Tony has fostered a community of reason among his students, of whom I am privileged to be one.

INTRODUCTION: CONTESTING SOCRATIC EGOISM

There is a widespread understanding among historians of philosophy that ancient Greek ethics is largely or even entirely eudaimonist in structure. And yet, there are some deeply counter-intuitive consequences of a eudaimonist ethics. Ordinarily, we think that it is possible for us to benefit others for their own sake, a possibility that does not depend upon its being a condition of our own happiness. Egoism, the position attributed to Socrates by, e.g., Terence Irwin and Gregory Vlastos, claims that such independently arising, other-directed concern is irrational. Indeed, it seems that a growing consensus among scholars of Socratic ethics attributes to Socrates the thesis of eudaimonism, the view that an agent exclusively pursues her own well-being, as well as that of psychological egoism (i.e., that an agent acts in her own self-interest). According to the latter thesis, it is impossible for agents to be motivated to do anything other than what is in their own interest.[1]

Can it really be that Socrates is to be credited with the discovery of egoistic eudaimonism? Well aware that this association looms strongly in the mind of most informed readers, in what follows I attempt to show that there is a great deal of assumption and not much by way of strong evidence to support the attribution. In part I of this essay, I study the prudential principle, the thesis that everyone wishes to be happy, as it is deployed in the elenctic dialogues. Here I suggest that its deployment can be seen as strategic on the part of Socrates; we need not infer that Socrates' use of this thesis in elenctic contexts entails that he subscribes to the doctrine of

[1] Other examples of scholars who attribute to Socrates a doctrine of egoistic eudaimonism, the thesis that an agent must act in her own self-interest, are Reshotko 1996 and Penner and Rowe 2005. Their interpretations will be explored more fully below. A notable exception is Weiss 2006.

egoism. In part II, I turn to consider the issue of motivation as it applies to Socrates' own actions. Here I argue that egoistic eudaimonism, the agent's pursuit of her own wellbeing as the reason for action, does not adequately explain the accounts that the Platonic Socrates offers about his own motivations for his philosophical activity.[2] I test the prudential principle insofar as it applies to the paradigmatic case of Socrates himself. If the Socratic dialogues overwhelmingly offer a portrait of Socrates that is compellingly inconsistent with the doctrinal formulation of egoism, then perhaps we ought to reconsider the extent to which egoistic eudaimonism can truly be the platform of Socratic ethics.

Both Irwin 1995 and Vlastos 1991 construe Socratic ethics along the lines of egoism insofar as each interprets Socrates as analyzing human motivation in terms of an entirely self-regarding form of agency. For Irwin Socratic egoism amounts either to the claim that an agent simply cannot pursue anything other than his own happiness, or that to pursue any other aim would be irrational.[3] Vlastos apparently opts for a position that might be described as rational egoism when he writes that "the linchpin of Socratic ethics consists in the principle that I have most reason to do whatever promotes my own happiness."[4] More recent interpretations, including those of Reshotko 2006 and Penner and Rowe 2005, explicitly make Socrates into an egoist. So for example Reshotko assumes "that Socrates thinks that harm and benefit are always and only harm or benefit to the self."[5] Likewise, for Penner and Rowe, Socratic "desire for the good" is identified as:

DES. The desire for *whatever action* may be the best means currently available to me, in the circumstances I am in, to the end of maximizing the amount of happiness (or of ultimate good) that I will achieve over a complete life,

together with

BEL. the belief that this action here and now realizes the best means in question and thus instantiates the general characterization given in (DES).[6]

---

[2] I would add, although I will not make the argument in detail here, that there is no other tenet with which Socrates is today credited that so glaringly illustrates the difference between the doctrinal and what we might call the exemplary Socrates than the egoistic eudaimonism that Vlastos averred was the linchpin of Socratic ethics. The narratives that Xenophon, Aeschines, and above all Plato create surrounding the life and death of Socrates feature a Socrates who is supremely selfless, sacrificing his material possessions and his very life for the sake of continuing his god-given mission, that of awakening his fellow citizens from their nightmarish pursuit of wealth and power at the expense of virtue.

[3] Irwin 1995: 53. It does not matter to my argument here whether Socrates is understood to be someone who holds that actions other than self-regarding actions are irrational, or impossible.

[4] Vlastos 1991: 203.   [5] Reshotko 2005: 58.   [6] Penner and Rowe 2005: 218.

Penner and Rowe and Reshotko think that Socrates endorses a position that we can call *benign* egoism, the thesis that "denies that the good of one person can conflict with that of another."[7] As Kraut writes, the benign egoist "insists that no one will be worse off if we maximize our own good and assign priority to self-interested reasons," just because in some ways the welfare of others will be a part of one's own interest or own happiness. Likewise Penner and Rowe (2005: 215) tell us that Socrates teaches that one must "understand the place of the happiness of those around one in one's own happiness." Reshotko (2006: 65) reassures the reader that "Socrates would maintain that every time we think we can benefit by harming someone else, we are wrong. Either the act is, in the long run, harmful to us as well, or it is not the case that the act is, in the long run, harmful to someone else." For them, Socrates comes off as likable in the extreme: he enlarges the scope of what counts as self-interest so that it inevitably, invariably, and necessarily includes the interests of others. Yet if Socratic egoism is framed in this attractive way as both encompassing the other-regarding virtues and construing wellbeing so broadly that the interests of those around one should always be taken into account, what objections could one mount against it?

As Kraut says, the deciding factor in determining whether or not a philosopher is an egoist is not necessarily that she recommends maximizing her own good. Rather, she must also assign this principle "a basic and not merely instrumental role" in her moral philosophy; self-regarding reasons are either the best or the only kind of reason there is (Kraut 1989: 82). It is not that the Socrates we find in these modern portraits is selfish. Rather, I would argue that if Socrates is interpreted in this way, he is not an egoist at all precisely because he does not think that the reasons for actions can best be captured in terms of whether or not they are primarily self-beneficial. Sometimes, Plato represents Socrates as acting because he wishes to promote the wellbeing of others, irrespective of whether or not this activity will benefit himself. At other times Plato represents Socrates as acting because of the demands of justice, for the sake of the truth or for the sake of the good. Yet, I argue, nowhere does Plato represent Socrates as acting for his own sake primarily or in a self-interested way.

PART I: EVERYONE WISHES TO BE HAPPY

The thesis of Socratic egoism arises as a response to the prominence of what I will call the prudential principle, that is, the thesis that Socrates

---

[7] Kraut 1989: 81.

invokes in a number of arguments, to the effect that everyone desires the good or wishes to be happy. In the examples cited below Socrates begins the elenctic progression from the undisputed premise that everyone desires the good. In the *Gorgias*, he uses the premise to undermine Polus' point that the tyrants have the greatest power in the city; in the *Meno* he uses the paradox to refute Meno's definition of virtue – everyone wants good things, so wanting good things cannot be a distinguishing feature of the virtuous person. On the surface the prudential principle appears to reflect the structure of strategic, or self-interested action: "Who in the world does not wish to do well?" "Not a single one," said Clinias. As it is expressed in the *Protagoras*, the principle apparently guarantees that, first and foremost, we would choose our own good: that all things being equal, we would never sacrifice our benefits and accept a diminished good in place of a greater one.[8] Here are some of the texts that offer evidence for what I have called the prudential principle:

(1) *Gorgias* 468c2–6, Socrates speaking: "Therefore we do not want simply to slaughter or banish people from cities or appropriate their wealth; rather, if they prove beneficial, then we do want to commit these acts, whereas if they prove harmful, we do not want to commit them. For as you say, we want things that are good; we do not want what is neither good nor bad, nor do we want what is bad."

(2) *Gorgias* 468d1–6:

> Socrates: "If we make these agreements, then when someone, whether a despot or a politician, kills a man or banishes him from his city or appropriates his wealth, imagining it to be more advantageous for him, whereas in fact, it turns out to be more harmful for him, still this person is doing what seems best to him, is he not?"
>
> Polus: "Yes."
>
> Socrates: "Therefore is he also doing what he wants, since these acts are in fact harmful?"

(3) *Protagoras*, 358c6–d4, Socrates speaking: "Therefore, is it not the case," I said, "that no one advances toward bad things voluntarily, or toward what he imagines as bad? To go after what one believes to be bad, instead of the good, is not, it seems, in human nature and when one is compelled to choose between two evils, no one will choose the greater when he might choose the less."

---

[8] On interpretations of the particular problems that the *Protagoras* raises for a consistent theory of Socratic eudaimonism, see Rudebusch 1999.

(4) *Meno*: 77d7–78a8, Socrates speaking:

"Isn't it clear that these people, that is, those who don't recognize evils for what they are, don't desire evil but what they thought was good, whereas in actuality it was evil? Hence, those who do not recognize evil yet imagine it to be good clearly desire the good?"

Meno: "Yes, they at least probably do desire the good."

Socrates: "Now as for those whom you describe as desiring evils in the belief that they do harm to their possessor, surely they know that they will be harmed by evils?"

Meno: "They must."

Socrates: "And don't they believe that whoever is harmed, to the extent that he is harmed, is miserable?"

Meno: "They must believe this as well."

Socrates: "And that the miserable are unhappy?"

Meno: "I certainly think so."

Socrates: "Well, is there anyone who wants to be wretched and unhappy?"

Meno: "Not in my view, Socrates."

Socrates: "Therefore, no one wants what is bad, since no one wants to be in this condition. Since what is it to be wretched other than desiring bad things and obtaining them?"

(5) *Euthydemus* 278e3–279a1, Socrates speaking:

"Do we human beings all wish to do well? Or perhaps this question is one of those that I just now feared was ridiculous? For it is foolish, no doubt, even to ask such things. What human being does not want to do well?"

"Not a single one," said Clinias.

A glance at the above texts reveals several things. First, Socrates never argues for the truth of the premise that all people wish to be happy; indeed, he fears it may be foolish even to question it. Second, the interlocutor always agrees to the principle without argument. Because the interlocutors always agree to the prudential principle, since it is seemingly indefeasible, Socrates crucially deploys it in a number of elenctic refutations, as the texts above show. Here, I will emphasize the work that this principle is commonly thought to do in these texts, which are, as we have seen, frequently interpreted as underwriting a motivational structure that is rooted in egoism; the texts are thought to imply that "in all our rational actions we pursue our own happiness."

Apparently, what the reader finds over and over in these passages is a point about the structure of motivations: people are motivated to act with a view to enhancing their own wellbeing. Yet it is important not to isolate these exchanges from their dialectical contexts. One consideration involves the extent to which Socrates may or may not be seen as a doctrinal thinker, i.e., someone with a positive psychological or ethical doctrine that he advances or even teaches. At first glance, it might seem that this interpretation of the text follows rather straightforwardly from the frequency with which Socrates elicits agreement with the premise that "no one wants to be unhappy." Yet in the texts above, Socrates is asking about the beliefs of his interlocutors; he is asking a series of questions and not, let us note, making a series of didactic statements. Moreover, Socrates is talking to interlocutors who already possess various dispositions or intellectual commitments that can sometimes be linked to radical teachings about human nature advanced by Sophists.[9]

At *Protagoras* 356c8, the words "human nature" might remind the reader of the Sophistic teachings referenced, for example, in Thucydides or, indeed, in Callicles' remarks at *Gorgias* at 483 c8-d1: "I believe that nature herself demonstrates that it is just for the superior to win out over the inferior."[10] One of the features of the Socratic dialogues that lends them such a high degree of verisimilitude is the vivid way that Socrates is shown as combating Sophists and Sophistic theses in their own terms. In the *Gorgias* Socrates employs language that might be thought to have a Sophistic provenance, i.e., discourses that focus on the principle of wronging no one and the interdict against wronging in return. Compare Antiphon fragment 44c, which discusses the mutual incompatibility of the principle of non-harm and of conventional justice:

Bearing true witness for one another is regarded as just and no less useful for human pursuits. Now, whoever does this will not be just, if it is just to wrong no one and not be wronged oneself. For one who bears witness, even if his testimony is true, must nevertheless somehow wrong another . . . and be wronged himself inasmuch as the one testified against is convicted because of the testimony given by him, and loses either his money or his life because of this man to whom he does no wrong. Now in this he wrongs the one testified against, in that he harms one who is not wronging him; and he is himself wronged by the one testified against, in that he is hated by him for bearing true witness.[11]

---

[9] See Weiss 2006, passim, for an interpretation of passages in which it is the Sophists, not Socrates, who offer doctrinal pictures of human nature: Socrates uses their theses against them without thereby committing himself to any psychological theories, other than those entailed by common sense.

[10] An abbreviated way of referring to Sophistic teachings about human nature might be found in the reference to 'all human beings' at *Euthydemus* 278e6.

[11] Antiphon fragment 44c, *On Truth*, Pendrick 2002: 186–87.

Now Socrates famously argues that it is "worse to commit wrong than to be wronged," and that one who "receives his due" for the wrongdoing he commits is less miserable than one who acts unjustly with impunity (*Gorgias* 472e4). It is possible that Plato even has something like Antiphon's argument against injustice in mind in this dispute between Socrates and Polus. Thus, fifth-century sophisms and strategies fill the dialectical arguments of the Socratic dialogues with brilliant sparring. Nevertheless, this dialectical context does not prove the thesis of egoism to be Socratic, but rather shows us that caution should be exercised when we dogmatically attribute eudaimonism to Socrates as anything other than an antidote to the more savage variety of what could be called "amoral" egoism at work in the theses of the Sophists he combats.

Are there places in the dialogues where, on the contrary, Socrates espouses his own views about ethics, i.e., where he explicitly claims ownership, one might say, of a given position? At *Crito* 49a4–5, Socrates asks Crito the following question: "Do we say that one must never willingly do wrong or are there some ways in which one should do wrong and others in which one should not?"

Notice that in this articulation of the principle of non-harm, Socrates uses the word, "we say" (φαμέν). Unlike the passages cited above, Socrates here is talking about his *own* commitments, commitments that he shares with Crito. Socrates stipulates that one must never harm irrespective of the surrounding circumstances. Now of course, what is here represented as a Socratic commitment, that it is always wrong to harm another, may be an ethical principle that is independent of the prudential principle; or, alternatively, it may be derived from the prudential principle. But so far, we have noticed one crucial difference between what Socrates says here in the *Crito* and what we saw in the passages above: even in cases where Socrates talks about all human beings and stipulates that he himself is a member of this category, he is nevertheless inquiring about the interlocutor's beliefs.

Of course, most readers of the Socratic dialogues, in treating the principle of non-harm or, in another formulation, the Socratic paradox that it is better to receive than to commit injustice, argue that this stipulation appeals to eudaimonistic considerations that are in some sense prior to the principle of not committing injustice. For them, Socrates argues that it is because injustice turns out to be harmful to the person who commits it that one will be better off not committing injustice.

We turn now to consider this question: which has priority in the Socratic ethics of non-harm? Does Socrates advance this thesis on the basis of a prior egoism, and then demonstrate the irrationality of harming others due to the harm it brings to the agent, the one who commits injustice? Or is the interdict against injustice an independent moral principle? There are two passages in the Socratic dialogues where this question is most easily explored. They are:

Crito 49a4–5, quoted above, and *Gorgias* 475e4–6: "neither I nor you nor any man whatever would rather do than suffer wrong, for to do it is worse."

Crito 49a4–5 appears to offer us an ethical principle, the interdict against doing injustice, formulated in a way that is independent of eudaimonist reasoning. Yet in the *Crito*, Socrates operates at two levels simultaneously: the principle of non-harm is an agreement that he and Crito endorse and have endorsed over a lifetime of conversations about the importance of justice. On the other hand, Socrates also appears to offer eudaimonist grounds for this principle in the context of convincing Crito to apply the principle in their particular circumstances. The circumstances surrounding the argument are as follows. Socrates is in jail awaiting execution on capital charges of corrupting the youth of Athens and of atheism. The trial has perhaps gone horribly awry (it is possible that no one truly expected that Socrates would end up convicted and sentenced to death rather than exile or some lesser penalty).[12] Socrates' old friend Crito has made it clear to Socrates that it would be possible for Socrates' friends to offer a bribe to the prison official and for Socrates to escape his capital sentence. The conversation revolves around the justice or injustice of this action. Without going into the details of how, in refusing to honor the city's laws and await his punishment, Socrates would be committing an injustice and possibly harming others, it is enough to recall that at 49b3–6 he makes clear that the principle that one ought never to commit injustice is unrelated to any consequences for the agent:

Whether we must endure still more grievous sufferings than these, or lighter ones, is not wrongdoing inevitably an evil and a disgrace to the wrongdoer? Do we say this or not?

In our text, Socrates emphasizes that this agreement not to do harm will be the starting point of deliberation (ἀρχώμεθα ἐντεῦθεν βουλευόμενοι, 49d6). He is going to argue from this premise (ἐντεῦθεν), and determine which actions (escaping or remaining in prison) might be consistent with this underlying assumption. One other point should not escape our notice: in this passage, Socrates explicitly contrasts his *own* ethical commitments

---

[12] Cf. Nails 2006.

with those of the many. He says, "I am aware that this is and will be the view of a few" (49d2). Nevertheless, those who wish to emphasize the priority of eudaimonist considerations operating in the sphere of the Socratic injunction not to harm often cite *Crito* 47e6–7: "will our life be worth having, if that part of us is ruined which is harmed by injustice and improved by justice?" Here the argument is that the one who commits injustice harms his soul so that his life, under the circumstances of committing injustice, is not worth living. Hence he, the agent of the justice or injustice, is better off refraining from injustice.

Much could be said by way of response to this egoistic reading of the *Crito*. For example, the argument at 47a1 in particular turns on questions of philosophical authority – in this case, the question of whom one should lend one's obedience in matters of moral deliberation: "Has it been rightly stated that one should not honor all the opinions of human beings?" Crito is worried about what people will say about him if he allows Socrates to die in prison: "I am afraid people will think that this whole affair of yours has been conducted with a sort of cowardice on our part" (45e1). Perhaps they will assume he was too parsimonious to offer a cash incentive to the warden. Since Crito is particularly vulnerable to questions of reputation and allegiance, Socrates frames his argument to appeal to this kind of personality. Thus it is not a matter of supporting the principle of non-harm through an appeal to prior eudaimonist considerations, but rather a method of strengthening Crito's adherence to this prior principle. And here Socrates might well use eudaimonist considerations, given his assumption that all people, Crito included, wish to be happy. That is, Socrates can silence Crito's objections with an appeal to his fundamental egoism without himself embracing that egoism. Still, the text leaves us with a general question that hangs on such issues of interpretation. For Socrates, will appeal to eudaimonistic considerations trump his invocation of the principle of non-harm? Do the principles stand and fall together, at the very least?

Another passage relevant to this discussion is *Gorgias* 475e4–6, where Socrates is, as we saw above, discussing the interdict against committing injustice in slightly different language. Here Socrates says that it is worse to do than to receive injustice (κάκιον γὰρ τυγχάνει ὄν). The language of the passage is notoriously underdetermined in precisely this respect: Socrates leaves it unclear whether committing injustice is worse for the agent, worse for his or her victim, or simply worse in some non-consequential, ethical sense that has to do with the idea of moral badness or wrongness. Now the literature on this passage is vast and many scholars have concluded that the agreement Socrates secures with Polus turns on an equivocation in the argument.[13] Polus admits that doing injustice is more shameful than being the recipient of injustice, but wants to maintain that it can nevertheless actually be good, for example, to kill with impunity (469c). The argument exploits various shades of value that attend to the Greek words for "shameful" (*aischron*, which also has the connotation of "aesthetically displeasing"), "beautiful" (*kalon*, which also has the sense of "noble, respectable"), and the more generic "good" (*agathon*, which veers toward moral value but can denote utility as well) – words that are used in the evaluation of just and unjust actions.

Despite the prolific discussion of the question whether Socrates exploits ambiguity in the dialectic, in the end Socrates' point seems clear enough. He returns to the familiar topos of the intrinsic badness of injustice in the soul, on the analogy of poor health of the body: to commit injustice is to worsen the condition of the soul.[14] Thus it would seem that our debate has been decided and that Socrates' strategy against Polus ultimately involves the eudaimonist weighing of the consequences of injustice. In that case, Polus is self-deceived in thinking that people are securing their own good when they commit injustices. But the matter does not end here: the context of the argument with Polus still has to be considered. We should not lose sight of the fact that Socrates is arguing against Polus, a well-established protégé of the Sophist Gorgias. Socrates' interlocutor is someone who has been convinced that selfish egoism, the pursuit of desire for its own sake, and the fulfillment of one's own desires, all contribute to a satisfactory life. When Socrates argues with this person, he starts from the interlocutor's position of extreme egoism and is committed to steering him away from the narrow pursuit of self-interest. At this juncture, Socrates offers an argument that relies on an appeal to eudaimonist considerations. In that case, Polus ought to care more for his soul than for any advancement that he thinks will accrue to him through the practices of injustice. At any rate, we should notice that Socrates claims ownership of the view that it is worse to commit injustice than to receive it: "I and you and everyone else" (474b4).

[13] Cf. Weiss 2006: 85–93. Weiss locates the fallacy by means of which Socrates gains Polus' agreement in a sleight of hand by which Socrates easily substitutes morally loaded words for the morally neutral words that Polus employs in his axiology. Other commentators include Irwin 1995: 99–101, Vlastos 1991: 139–44. Vlastos argues that Socrates exploits an ambiguity in the argument by pretending to show that doing wrong is more painful for the wrongdoer, whereas in reality he has left the recipient of pain, the victim or the agent of harm, unspecified in the argument at 475c2–c8.

[14] *Gorgias* 477b5–8: "Do you consider there is an evil condition of the soul? And do you call this injustice and ignorance and cowardice and the like?"

PART II: THE GOOD OF OTHERS

So far we have studied the prudential principle in terms of its dialectical contexts. Nevertheless, we have not yet asked about its overall implications for the thesis of egoism. From the assumption that each of us desires to be happy, are we entitled to infer that each should pursue her own happiness, first and foremost? Again, the reader who is familiar with the literature on Socrates will no doubt think that the answer to this question is yes. Interpreters often assume that the prudential principle supports egoism. With regard to *Gorgias* 468b2 and to the Socratic dialogues in general, Vlastos writes as follows:

Here desire for happiness is strictly self-referential: it is the agent's desire for his own happiness and that of no one else. This is so deep-seated an assumption that it is simply taken for granted: no argument is ever given for it in the Platonic corpus. (Vlastos 1991: 203, n. 14)

When Reshotko writes (2006: 58) that "in addressing the assumption that Socrates thinks that harm and benefit are always and only harm or benefit to the self," the reader might wonder just who is making this "assumption." Does Plato assume this? Does the scholar herself make this assumption? A prior question will be, what justifies the inference from the prudential principle to the purported doctrine of Socratic egoism? In what follows, I will continue the thread developed in part i, where I tried to differentiate between statements endorsed by Socrates as his own ethical views and those he elicits from others. Here I want to show that when Socrates talks about his own motivations, he often refers to non-egoistic motivations. I want to offer these texts as reasons to reject Socratic egoism.

At the very least, the evidence of Plato's *Apology* shows that it is counter-intuitive to interpret the ethical exhortations of Socrates as motivated by his pursuit of his own happiness. In fact, one of the least studied aspects of Plato's Socrates is the concern that he shows for the welfare of all the members of his community. The *Apology* contains a number of statements that appear to be primarily other-regarding. For example, the Athenians require that Socrates suggest a counterproposal in exchange for his capital sentence, whereupon Socrates insists that what he ought to have from the state is a reward, since he has spent his life "conferring upon each citizen individually what [he] regard[s] as the greatest benefit" (36c3–4).

What motivates this Socratic activity? Does Socrates pursue the wellbeing of his community and bestow upon it "the greatest benefit" in pursuit of his own happiness? In practicing what he calls a service to the god, does

Socrates operate within the constraints of psychological egoism, according to which it is impossible for him to seek anything other than what is in his interest? In order to answer this question, we need to take into account several kinds of evidence. In the first place, we can notice what kinds of reasons Socrates invokes as an explanation for his activity; if there are multiple reasons, then we can try to sort out which have priority. Second, we can ask if Socrates appeals to the principle of eudaimonism to explain his philosophical activity.

As Plato has him say at 20e6–23c1, Socrates undertakes his lifetime of elenctic examination as a form of "*latreia*," i.e, as a service to Apollo (23c1). In this same passage, Socrates tells us that, as a result of his service, he is unable to undertake any action on his own behalf (οὔτε τι τῶν τῆς πόλεως πρᾶξαί μοι σχολὴ γέγονεν ἄξιον λόγου οὔτε τῶν οἰκείων, 23b8–9). Yet why did Socrates initially enter into this service? As Plato tells the story, Socrates is puzzled about the meaning of an oracle. He recognizes that Apollo cannot be lying when he claims that "no one" is wiser than Socrates; he uses the phrase, "it is not lawful." The Greek phrase here (οὐ γὰρ θέμις, 21b6) refers to matters of religious propriety. The suggestion is that Socrates embarks on his activity to fulfill a duty in recognition of an obligation for which there is divine sanction. Later in the speech, Socrates seems to recognize the service he renders to Apollo as a kind of order, station, or post: "Wherever one takes up his post in the belief that it is best or is assigned a post by a superior" (οὗ ἄν τις ἑαυτὸν τάξῃ ἡγησάμενος βέλτιστον εἶναι ἢ ὑπ' ἄρχοντος ταχθῇ, 28d6–8). In this later passage, Socrates gives two possible motivations for his continued practice of philosophy. Either he judges it best or else he is obeying the orders of a superior. This passage nowhere takes into account the benefit that would accrue to Socrates personally. He believes it to be best, but this best does not have to have self-reflexive properties. It may or it may not. To judge that by "best" Socrates means here "what is best for himself," is to prejudge the issue of Socratic egoism; only if we import an egoistic reading into the text do we have reason to regard this account as supporting the thesis of Socratic egoism.

One other passage is relevant to this discussion of Socrates' motivations in the *Apology*. At 25d9–e9, in the course of his cross-examination of Meletus, Socrates recognizes the eudaimonistic appeal that benefiting one's neighbors offers to the agent who bestows such benefit:

Are you so much wiser at your age than I am at mine that you understand that wicked people always do harm to their closest neighbors while good people do them good, but I have reached such a pitch of ignorance that I do not realize this, namely that if I make one of my associates wicked I run the risk of being harmed by him so that I do such a great evil deliberately, as you say? (*Apology* 25d9–e9; Grube translation)

Proponents of Socratic egoism cite this text in support of their position that Socrates is motivated to pursue his own happiness. We have at least a case of over-determination, where Plato offers us an account of Socrates that appeals to several considerations: the *latreia* that Socrates undertakes; the fact that Socrates considers his philosophical activity best; and Socrates' awareness of the eudaimonistic structure of human motivation generally. To harm others increases the probability that one will in turn be harmed by them; Socrates is arguing from probability at this point. His suggestion is that it is unlikely that he would harm fellow citizens. He can't seriously be admitting that he refrains from harming his fellow citizens because he would be likely to be harmed by them in turn, since Socrates believes that he has led a good life, and that a lesser person cannot harm a good man: "Neither Meletus nor Anytus can harm me – it would not be possible – since I don't think it is permitted for a better man to be harmed by a lesser one" (29c7–d1). Socrates does not seriously entertain the possibility that his fellow citizens might harm him.

To conclude this investigation of Socratic motivation in the *Apology*, we turn to *Apology* 33a1. Here Socrates announces the first and foremost consideration for him in deliberation concerning any action: a man who is good for anything ought not to calculate the chance of living or dying; he ought only to consider whether in doing anything he is doing right or wrong, acting the part of a good or a bad man. Plato introduces his character as explaining the path of deliberation that must be taken by a virtuous person: is the action just or not?[15] Here, Socrates offers reasons for action that are independent of eudaimonist considerations. It may or may not turn out to be the case that in performing such actions the agent will thereby be depriving herself of a good, such as life itself, or, alternatively, enhancing her life by acquiring the virtue of justice; nevertheless, these eudaimonist considerations do not orient the argument.

We also need to take into account the Socratic exhortation to care for the soul (*Apology* 29e2, τῆς ψυχῆς ὅπως ὡς βελτίστη ἔσται οὐκ ἐπιμελῇ; 30b1–2, ἐπιμελεῖσθαι μήτε χρημάτων πρότερον μηδὲ οὕτω σφόδρα ὡς τῆς ψυχῆς ὅπως ὡς ἀρίστη ἔσται). For Socrates, caring for the soul will mean discovering knowledge of the good. Yet knowledge of the good entails virtue, and if one is virtuous then one is good and therefore does good,

---

[15] Cf. Weiss 2006: 6–7; cf. also *Ap.* 32a6; *Crito* 48d1; *Gorg.* 522b9–c1, listed there by Weiss.

both for oneself and for others. Therefore, this exhortation to care for the soul raises the question of why one should care for the soul: should I do so because it is my soul, or because it is soul? In the *Apology*, Socrates makes the case that he cares for the souls of his fellow citizens on two grounds: first, his work is a service to the divine. Second, he feels affection for his fellow citizens (ἀσπάζομαι, 29d3) and acts toward them in the capacity of a father or older brother (31b4). Of course, we cannot tell from the outside whether or not a person is a eudaimonist; rather, if we listen to what they say about why they performed certain actions, we can get a sense of how viable the ascription of eudaimonism is to them. As I said at the outset, Socrates claims that he continues in the philosophical life because of his service to the god, because he sees his activity as making others more virtuous and therefore happy, because he cares for his fellow citizens, and because he strongly desires to discover the truth for its own sake. But it would be odd if his philosophy itself recommended the truth of egoistic eudaimonism.

Someone might argue that the *Apology* is not the text to turn to when trying to take stock of the question of Socratic egoism. After all, here if anywhere, Plato would be trying to polish the image of Socrates; why would he insist on Socrates' commitment to egoism in a text where he is defending his way of life to a crowd largely ignorant of philosophy, one that might assume an equation between Socratic egoism and Sophistic amoralism? This question seems fair enough, and certainly there ought to be passages outside of the *Apology* that address the question of Socratic motivation.

PART III: An alternative to the language of egoism in the Socratic dialogues

Above I hinted that some of the language that Socrates uses in framing the prudential principle echoes Sophistic theses about human nature; several of his interlocutors are practicing Sophists and it makes sense that he speaks to these people in terms of their own ideologies. Casting our gazes backwards into the fourth, fifth, and earlier centuries and following the line of Plato's vision we see that he made use of competing discourses in order to articulate ethical issues and rivalries rampant in his own world. For Plato also associates Socratic ethics with another kind of language, one that draws on a different set of metaphors that are borrowed from a rival (i.e. not a Sophistic) camp, one might say, among the various fifth-century intellectual movements. Plato consciously casts Socrates in an older tradition, associating him with the Pythagorean ethical discourse that utilizes the vocabulary of equality, friendship, and association among peers. Plato represents Socrates as sharing his ends with others, granting them equal access to the logos, using calculation, a mathematical metaphor, to dispel the grasp of greed, of *pleonexia*. In fact, Plato draws a contrast among fourth-century theorists, pitting Pythagorean ethical speculation against Sophistic constructs, including the conception of human nature as determined by the forces of brute, individual appetite. This contrast is most evident in the *Gorgias*, where Socrates opposes Callicles' vulgar, appetitive individualism with the metaphor of cosmic friendship and reciprocity. In the final section to this essay, I wish to draw attention to Socratic philosophy as a species of rational activity jointly undertaken for the mutual development of wisdom. I hope that these remarks will provide a rationale for criticizing the egoistic interpretation of Socratic philosophical activity.

One passage where the two systems, Sophistic self-aggrandizement and Pythagorean reciprocity, come into radical juxtaposition is *Gorgias* 508a5–8, where Socrates addresses Callicles. Here, introducing a number of mathematical images into the discussion, he claims: "It has no doubt escaped your notice that geometrical equality has the greatest force among gods and among men, whereas you think it is necessary to practice *pleonexia*, for you are neglectful of geometry." The language that Plato inserts into Socrates' repudiation of Calliclean hedonism and egoism has undeniable affinities with contemporaneous Pythagorean ethical vocabulary that emphasizes the importance of harmony and equality to justice. For example, fragment 3 of Archytas contains these signature Pythagorean terms:

Once *calculation* (*logismos*) was discovered, it stopped discord and increased *concord*. For people do not want more than their share, and *equality* exists, once this has come into being. For by means of calculation we will seek reconciliation in our dealings with others. Through this, then, the poor receive from the powerful, and the wealthy give to the needy, both in the confidence that they will have what is *fair* on account of this.

The words that Plato uses in the *Gorgias* passages, equality versus *pleonexia*, correspond closely to the ethical and political language of fourth-century BCE Pythagorean writing.[16] Of course, this language developed contemporaneously with Platonic formulations, and it is arguable that the contrast between justice and *pleonexia* is a part of common moral discourse in the fourth century. Yet this caution, not to be neglectful of geometry (*Gorgias*

---

[16] On the language of calculation versus *pleonexia* see Huffman on Archytas fragment 9 in Huffman 2005 *ad loc* from Aristoxenus' *Life of Archytas*.

508a8), also resonates with another Pythagorean allusion in the *Gorgias*, where at 507e3–4 Socrates admonishes Callicles that the life of *akolasia* is a life that makes friendship with another person impossible, and also precludes friendship with god. For Socrates the friendless life is an inherently evil life. The disorderly soul can enjoy no society with another (507a, d–e). Orderliness, *hosiotēs*, justice and temperance hold together the entire cosmos, including not only people, but also gods and indeed the heavens.

Partnership and friendship, orderliness, self-control, and justice hold together heaven and earth, and gods and men, and that is why they call this universe a world order, my friend, and not an undisciplined world order. (507e6–508a2)[17]

This valorization of friendship is independent of egoism, to the extent that it is an argument against egoism. Hence we see Socrates borrowing from the Pythagoreans as a reply to Sophistic theses.

In the *Charmides*, Socrates refers to the sharing of truth as the common good for all human beings:

So too now I say that this is what I am doing, investigating the argument especially on my own behalf, but perhaps as well on behalf of my other companions; or do you not think that it is a *common good* among virtually all human beings (κοινὸν οἴει ἀγαθὸν εἶναι σχεδόν τι πᾶσιν ἀνθρώποις), for each thing to be completely evident, as to what it is in reality? (*Charmides* 166d2–6)

And again in the *Gorgias* Socrates defends the elenchus on the grounds that knowing the truth is a common good for all human beings.

I think that it would be best for us to be eager for victory with regard to knowing the truth and falsity of each subject of argument, for it is a *common good for all* that it be manifest (κοινὸν γὰρ ἀγαθὸν ἅπασι φανερὸν γενέσθαι αὐτό). (505e4–6)

In these Socratic dialogues, Plato attributes a kind of universal generosity to Socrates, who pursues the truth on behalf of all human beings. To summarize, then, the Pythagorean cosmic language of friendship, reciprocity, and justice among gods and men, the equal and proportionate distribution of logos itself as a share of a divine good – all of this is present in the Socratic dialogues. The contrast between Sophistic and Pythagorean ethical vocabularies reveals that it is mistaken to identify egoism as the core of Socratic ethics. Insofar as there is an ethical dimension to the practice of the elenchus, and there undoubtedly is, Plato consistently associates

---

[17] On the importance of friendship and even cosmic friendship to Socrates see Woolf 2000: 14: "it is good for one to have, or to be, a well-structured soul as part of a community of well-structured souls. Socrates' emphasis on friendship (and his antipathy to friendlessness) has made it clear that this second principle is part of his full conception of the good life."

it with reasons for action that are fundamentally not self-regarding. The elenchus is dedicated to and is performed on behalf of all, on behalf of Socrates and anyone who participates in it. Socrates says in the *Charmides* that his reasons for acting are for the common good of all: "investigating the argument on my own behalf, certainly, but perhaps as well on behalf of my other companions" (166d2).

That friends share a common good is a claim adopted in the *Republic* (449c5) designed to fuse competing interests among the guardians via a psychic state, in which the terms "me" and "mine" are radically altered denotatively; the outcome is a community, a *koinonia*, in which each has the same end, the good of all. Not coincidentally, Plato defines the function of reason as "the good of the whole."

"Then in our city the language of harmony and concord will be more often heard than in any other. As I was describing before, when anyone is well or ill, the universal word will be 'with me it is well' or 'it is ill.'" "Most true." "And agreeably to this mode of thinking and speaking, were we not saying that they will have their pleasures and pains in common?" "Yes, and so they will." "And they will have a common interest in the same thing which they will alike call 'my own,' and having this common interest they will have a common feeling of pleasure and pain?" (463e3–464a4)

For a moment, let us take this text quite literally: in the ideal city, the philosophers will "have a common interest in the same thing" (464a4) or share the same ends. This phrase is crucial; it picks out a condition of mind that we may call, among other things, reciprocity, equality, and friendship.[18] As in the *Republic*, practitioners of the Socratic elenchus engage in pursuit of a common good.

This acting in concert in the name of true friendship can easily be overlooked; we can overemphasize the place of individual action, individual choice, and individual happiness. But rarely does Socrates act alone: in the Socratic dialogues, he is almost never alone. That Socrates leaves the porch in order to converse in the gymnasium, that he not only practices the justice of restraint from wrong action or illegal action, but actively befriends the souls of his fellow citizens, points to a teaching that, at root, is not adequately captured by egoistic eudaimonism. It involves considerations of duties to god, to one's fellow citizens, and to justice; it involves care for others at a cost to oneself; it involves active love, good will, and the

---

[18] Of course, the reader is free to object that I am arguing very loosely, insofar as I cite the *Republic* in invoking the moral psychology of the citizens of Callipolis to discuss the question of friendship in Socrates. Nevertheless, Plato's description of Socratic elenchus in terms of the pursuit of a common good does anticipate the *Republic*'s community of ends.

promotion of others' well being for their own sakes. And, above all, it involves considerations for truth for its own sake. Thus Socratic ethics is not an ancient version of egoistic eudaimonism, but an ethics of wisdom.[19]

---

[19] All translations of Plato are my own unless otherwise specified. Many thanks to David Sedley and Andrea Nightingale: they have gone beyond the call of duty as editors of this volume in so many ways. Tony Long's work on Socratic and Hellenistic ethics has been the chief inspiration for this essay. Thanks also to the 2004 Arizona Colloquium in Ancient Philosophy, to which a version of this essay was first presented. All errors of fact or judgment are, of course, solely my responsibility.

CHAPTER 3

Inspiration, recollection, and mimēsis in Plato's Phaedrus

Kathryn A. Morgan

For Tony Long:

πολὺ δ᾽ οἶμαι καλλίων σπουδὴ... ὅταν τις... λαβὼν ψυχὴν προσήκουσαν, φυτεύῃ τε καὶ σπείρῃ μετ᾽ ἐπιστήμης λόγους, οἳ ἑαυτοῖς τῷ τε φυτεύσαντι βοηθεῖν ἱκανοὶ καὶ οὐχὶ ἄκαρποι ἀλλὰ ἔχοντες σπέρμα, ὅθεν ἄλλοι ἐν ἄλλοις ἤθεσι φυόμενοι τοῦτ᾽ ἀεὶ ἀθάνατον παρέχειν ἱκανοί...

Plato, *Phaedrus* 276e–277a

Plato's *Phaedrus* obtrusively foregrounds issues of the rhetoric and reality of madness, inspiration, and *mimēsis*. In this most "poetic" of dialogues these issues are embodied by an (ironically?) inspired Socrates, and commentators have long been at a loss to nail down the precise ratio of play to seriousness in his myth of the charioteer.[1] This essay examines how the rhetoric of Socrates' famous palinode both raises and defuses problems that have perplexed commentators concerning the status of the poetic, prophetic, and initiatory lives in the scheme of the myth: why are such lives ranked low in one place, yet lauded at the beginning of the speech as the purveyors of the greatest blessings? The palinode, however, provides suggestive indications as to the possibility of a new model of inspiration. Not the least achievement of the speech is to use a conventional framework to present a radical rethinking of the impingement of the divine upon human consciousness. The rhetoric of the speech reflects a changing conception of reality, as a philosophical model of inspiration displaces Plato's (tendentious) presentation of the contemporary cultural realities of divine madness and influence. I hope this will prove a congenial contribution to a volume honoring my friend and teacher Tony Long, whose kindness and confidence have always been an inspiration, and with whom I first read the *Phaedrus* and began to develop many of the ideas presented here.[2] Socrates' palinode is concerned

---

[1] Verdenius 1962: 138, 149; Rowe 1986: 169; Janaway 1995: 162–66; Morgan 2000: 174–75, 226–27, 234.
[2] So also Morgan 2000: 210–41.

precisely with creating the outlines of a "model of mind," one of Tony's enduring interests; the activity of the philosophical lovers there is a process of psychic modelling.

The opening of the palinode is a rich, if problematic, mine for students of Plato's attitude to poetry and inspiration. Socrates wants to distance himself from his first formal speech in the dialogue, and from the speech of the orator Lysias that preceded it, speeches in which the speakers aimed to demonstrate that a young man would do better to yield to the sexual attentions of someone who was not passionately in love with him rather than to those of a lover. The lover is, Socrates maintained in his first speech, sick: jealous, greedy, irrational – the last person one would want to spend time with. Yet, following up an intuition given to him by his divine sign, Socrates feels the need to recant his slander of love. As the palinode begins, Socrates throws down the gauntlet by stating that his former argument only holds if madness is a simple evil, whereas, on the contrary, the greatest goods come about for humans through madness, as long as it is given by divine gift (θείᾳ . . . δόσει 244a). He then gives three examples of such goods. First, prophetic madness (μαντικῆ . . . ἐνθέῳ 244b), such as experienced by the priestesses at Delphi and Dodona. Second, telestic madness, which occurs within certain families, leads to prayers and service to the gods and comes upon means of purification and mysteries (244d–245a). The third kind comes from the Muses:

τρίτη δὲ ἀπὸ Μουσῶν κατοκωχή τε καὶ μανία, λαβοῦσα ἁπαλὴν καὶ ἄβα-
τον ψυχήν, ἐγείρουσα καὶ ἐκβακχεύουσα κατά τε ᾠδὰς καὶ κατὰ τὴν ἄλλην
ποίησιν, μυρία τῶν παλαιῶν ἔργα κοσμοῦσα τοὺς ἐπιγιγνομένους παιδεύει.

. . . possession and madness from the Muses, seizing a tender and untrodden soul, rousing it and setting it to Bacchic frenzy in the area of songs and other poetry, adorning the countless deeds of the ancients, educates future generations. (245a)

Just so, he argues, the madness of love is sent by the gods for the benefit of the lover and the beloved. And he will prove it.

In order to do so, he says, one must understand the truth about divine and human souls. The beginning of this proof is the famous immortality argument, after which he proceeds to liken the form of the soul to a charioteer and team of horses (245c–246b). Human souls have one black horse (problematic and seeming to represent the passions) and one white (obedient and seeming to represent shame). Divine souls have two white horses. Each of the twelve Olympian gods (with the exception of Hestia) leads a company of other gods and *daimones*, as well as human souls that have devoted themselves to the god. When the souls need to feed, they ascend up the vault of heaven; the well-balanced divine teams move easily, the human teams with difficulty. The divine teams stand upon the back of heaven and achieve uninterrupted contemplation of the Forms, whereas mortal teams see them with difficulty or not at all. Failure results in the loss of the wings of the soul and in incarnation (246d–248d). Depending on how much of the place beyond the heavens a soul has seen, it can be incarnated into a variety of different lives:

[the rule is to plant] the soul that has seen the most [in the place beyond the heavens] into that which will engender a man who will be a lover of wisdom or a lover of beauty or a musical and erotic man (φιλοσόφου ἢ φιλοκάλου ἢ μουσικοῦ τινος καὶ ἐρωτικοῦ) . . . fifthly into the generation that will have the life of a *mantis* or a life of mystery initiation (μαντικὸν βίον ἤ τινα τελεστικόν); in sixth place will fit a poetic life or some other life concerned with *mimēsis* (ποιητικὸς ἢ τῶν περὶ μίμησίν τις) . . . each soul does not arrive at the same place whence it came in less than ten thousand years . . . except the life of one who has philosophized without deceit or who has loved boys philosophically . . . . (248d–249a)

The top-rank life thus belongs to the lover of wisdom or beauty, devoted to the Muses and to love. The telestic or mantic lives come in fifth place, while the poetic or mimetic come sixth. The bottom belongs to the tyrant. Once in the body, human souls struggle to recollect their otherwordly vision and regrow their wings so that they may eventually escape incarnation. They are helped by the sight of beautiful bodies here on earth and may use the experience of love to help them gain a more speedy return to the divine realm. One aspect of a philosophical love affair is that the lover strives to make his beloved as like their mutual patron god as possible, searching in himself and using his memory to grasp the god. This is, then, no jealous or mean relationship, but one that brings happiness to both.

This brutally short and simplified summary of a very rich myth is enough, I hope, to bring out some of the issues that have vexed interpreters. Why does the speech begin by privileging the prophetic, telestic, and poetic states as those that bring the greatest happiness to mortals, but then relegate them to fifth and sixth place in the hierarchy of lives? Is love a kind of divine madness in the same sense as the first three types of madness?

INSPIRATION AND POSSESSION

In order to answer these related questions, we must first arrive at an adequate understanding of the way Plato is playing with contemporary notions of inspiration and possession. We start with the picture of the poet (and by extension, the rhapsode) in the *Ion*. There Socrates suggests that poets are moved by a "divine force" (θεία... δύναμις, 533d) and that the Muse makes them "divinely possessed" (ἔνθεοι ὄντες καὶ κατεχόμενοι, 533e). Such poets are out of their minds and act like Bacchants (534a). The point is made with considerable emphasis at 534b–d:

οὐ πρότερον οἷός τε ποιεῖν πρὶν ἂν ἔνθεός τε γένηται καὶ ἔκφρων καὶ ὁ νοῦς μηκέτι ἐν αὐτῷ ἐνῇ·... οὐ γὰρ τέχνῃ ταῦτα λέγουσιν ἀλλὰ θείᾳ δυνάμει,... διὰ ταῦτα δὲ ὁ θεὸς ἐξαιρούμενος τούτων τὸν νοῦν τούτοις χρῆται ὑπηρέταις καὶ τοῖς χρησμῳδοῖς καὶ τοῖς μάντεσι τοῖς θείοις, ἵνα ἡμεῖς οἱ ἀκούοντες εἰδῶμεν ὅτι οὐχ οὗτοί εἰσιν οἱ ταῦτα λέγοντες οὕτω πολλοῦ ἄξια, οἷς νοῦς μὴ πάρεστιν, ἀλλ' ὁ θεὸς αὐτός ἐστιν ὁ λέγων, διὰ τούτων δὲ φθέγγεται πρὸς ἡμᾶς.

he is not able to compose until he becomes divinely inspired and out of his senses and his mind is no longer in him... for they do not speak these things by skill but by divine power... this is why the god takes away their mind and uses them as his servants and singers of oracles and divine seers, so that we who hear may know that those who say these beautiful and worthwhile things are not those who are out of their minds, but the god himself is the one speaking and speaks to us through them.[3]

We note here the collocation of Bacchic inspiration, prophecy, and poetry that will be reflected in the first three types of madness listed in the *Phaedrus*: prophecy, telestic madness, and poetry.[4] In the *Ion* the aim is to disqualify poets and rhapsodes from any intellectual pretensions: they are passive vessels of the god.[5] It is disconcerting, therefore, to find what is fundamentally the same strategy used to praise poetic madness in the *Phaedrus*. Of course, the angle is slightly different; the focus is not, for the moment, on skilled deployment of divine knowledge but on divine benefaction. But a more fundamental question is how accurate a picture this paints of classical Greek beliefs about the sources of poetry. The work of Tigerstedt and Murray has gone a long way towards clarifying Plato's

---

[3] By quoting only *Ion* 533d–e and not the above passage as diagnostic of Plato's understanding of ἔνθεος, Leinieks 1996: 97 misrepresents Plato's views on the matter as implying that "being ἔνθεος does not mean that one has a god within him." He states that there is "no reason to doubt that the concept was the same in the fifth century as in Plato." As will become clear, I align myself with Tigerstedt 1970 and Murray 1981 in believing that Plato is talking about possession, and that his presentation of the experience is substantially different from that of earlier periods.

[4] Dionysiac possession was not the only kind of telestic madness (Linforth 1946: 171–72), but when Socrates summarizes the beginning of the speech later in the dialogue, he sets telestic madness under the patronage of Dionysus (256b).

[5] Murray 1992: 28–32. In the *Meno* (99c–100c), Socrates uses a similar tactic to characterize the knowledge (or lack of it) in politicians, who, when they are successful, are so by a "divine dispensation" (θείᾳ μοίρᾳ) and in this respect are like prophets.

moves here. Whereas older scholars tended to take Plato at his word and make this notion of poetic inspiration as ecstatic possession characteristic of the thought world of Archaic and Classical Greece, it now seems likely that Plato invented it, possibly under the influence of Democritus. He was aided in this endeavor by the association of prophecy with some form of divine possession.[6]

Plato's strategy in the case of inspiration is a part of a more general move to examine the consequences of common cultural beliefs. In this case, we may formulate the issue as a consideration of the meaning of the word ἔνθεος ("inspired, possessed"). What would it mean for a god to be "in" a human being? The concept evoked was generally one of divine empowerment. Although Leinieks has argued that it is "naive etymologizing" to imagine that the Greeks thought the god was actually "in" a person,[7] this seems too extreme a formulation. It is likely enough that most Athenians of the fifth century would not have worried about precise nuance and would have been content to think that the god inhabited the inspired person in a broad sense. Many societies interpret an altered state of consciousness in terms of spirit possession, where an alien spirit influences the possessed, although there are various ways of interpreting the nature of that influence.[8] As Murray has shown so well, early Greek literature draws no dichotomy between divine empowerment and individual skill.[9] Even in the case of prophecy, skill and inspiration coexist, so that in Aeschylus, Zeus can make Apollo's mind "inspired with skill" (τέχνης... ἔνθεον) before installing him at Delphi (*Eum.* 17), and Cassandra in the *Agamemnon* (1209) is seized by "inspired arts" (τέχναισιν ἐνθέοις).[10] In the *Ion*, then (and subsequently in the *Phaedrus*), Plato is engaging in precisely the kind of etymologizing deemed by Leinieks to be naïve: the god is in the poet and the poet is not responsible. But Plato is

---

[6] Tigerstedt 1970; Murray 1981: 87–88, 99; 1992: 32–34, 37–39. Cf. Verdenius 1962: 134–35.

[7] Leinieks 1996: 95.

[8] Maurizio 1995: 74 (for Maurizio [76] there is no question that in Plato ἔνθεος implies that a god is in the body). For a discussion of the vocabulary of ancient Greek possession and its implications, see Graf 2009.

[9] Murray 1992: 33–34.

[10] Plato's collocation of divine inspiration with Bacchic frenzy is an inheritance from the usage of the Attic tragedians (Aesch. *Sept.* 497–8; Soph. *Ant.* 963–4; Eur. *El.* 1032, *Tro.* 366–7) – not a pedigree that will have endeared the connection to him, and a good reason to take any praise of prophetic and Bacchic inspiration with a grain of salt. Aeschylus seems to have been interested in the mechanics of being ἔνθεος. His tragedy *Semele*, we are told (Schol. Apollon. Rhod *Argon.* I 636a), brought Semele on stage pregnant and inspired. Even those who touched her belly were also inspired (... ἐνθεαζομένην, ὁμοίως δὲ καὶ τὰς ἐφαπτομένας τῆς γαστρὸς αὐτῆς ἐνθεαζομένας). This must reflect a kind of physical pun: Semele is inspired because, quite literally, she has a god inside her.

never naïve. By following the logic of the word through to its conclusion, he can expose the ignorance he thinks underlies his culture's careless constructions of mortal and divine interaction. In the *Phaedrus* Socrates tells us that mortal notions of the makeup of the gods are not based on any reasoned argument. We simply haven't thought the matter through (247c). And having decided that our approach to the problem of inspiration is woolly-minded, Plato elaborates and emphasizes his point by developing an abstract vocabulary of inspiration. The noun *enthousiasmos* (ἐνθουσιασ-μός) appears first in Plato and Democritus (DK 68B18), while the adjective *enthousiastikos* (ἐνθουσιαστικός), the noun *enthousiasis* (ἐνθουσίασις), and verb *enthousiazō* (ἐνθουσιάζω) are first preserved in Plato.[11] This development of a technical vocabulary of course reflects a general interest in the technical analysis and criticism of poets starting in the second half of the fifth century, but also reveals how hard Plato wanted to explore and press the concept. Instead of illuminating a problematic issue (the madness of love) by something better known and generally agreed upon, Plato has Socrates connect it with an exaggerated interpretation of the cultural practice of poetry, prophecy, and initiatory purification, an interpretation that foregrounds direct divine intervention in the mortal world.

MADNESS AND INSPIRATION IN THE *PHAEDRUS*

As many commentators have recognized, the issue of inspiration is prominent in the first part of the dialogue.[12] Responsibility for Socrates' first speech praising the non-lover is assigned (in Rowe's listing) to the Muses, the place, Lysias, the Nymphs and Pan, and to Phaedrus.[13] Opinions differ as to how seriously we should take these claims, but it seems clear, as Nightingale has shown, that the play of alien voices within the soul should be contrasted with the authentic voice that the philosopher must develop for himself.[14] The palinode is instigated by Socrates' *daimonion*, attributed to Stesichorus, and later credited to the gods of the place and the cicadas (262d). Both speeches are presented as inspired, although only the second is

---

[11] Tragedy uses the verb ἐνθουσιάω.

[12] Flashar 1958: 125; Hackforth 1952: 36, 47; Rowe 1986: 153; Nightingale 1995: 159 with n. 56; Nicholson 1999: 125, 135–36; Morgan 2000: 214, 237–39; Scully 2003: 94–5. Socrates describes his enthusiasm for speeches as a kind of Corybantic possession at 228b and as Bacchic at 234d. At 235c–d he is filled up like a jug with material from the lyric poets and prose writers. Cf. 238c–d, where Socrates has suffered a "divine experience" connected with the "divine" nature of the place; it is possible that he will become "seized by the nymphs." Note that *nympholepsy* is held out as a threat, one that is marked as fulfilled at 241e.

[13] Rowe 1986: 163.   [14] Nightingale 1995: 159.

a genuine expression of Socrates' philosophical intuition. From the beginning of the palinode, then, as soon as the issue of poetic mania is raised, the reader is implicitly asked to meditate on the relationship between poetic creation and Socrates' own production.[15] Poetic inspiration is the third type of madness listed in the palinode, preceded by prophetic and telestic madness. Socrates displays aspects of these madnesses as well: he is a low-level seer at 242c, and, like a ritual practitioner, he knows an "ancient purification" (243a) for those who have sinned in the area of mythology. Rowe has argued that all three types of madness presented at the beginning of the palinode are contrasted by Socrates and subsumed in him, and I think this is correct.[16] What is particularly significant for present purposes is the effect that this realization has on interpreting the opening of the palinode. It makes us question immediately how authoritative these categories are, and in particular, what their relationship will be with philosophy.

The first three forms of madness in the speech are an interesting group. It seems clear from Socrates' statement at 245b, "I can narrate so many and still more fine deeds of madness that come from the gods," that they are supposed to be seen as examples, but they are in fact carefully chosen for their interconnections and to bring to mind conventional notions of divine influence. They also, however, allow space for Platonic re-presentation of these notions and of divine possession. There is indeed an ancient cultural connection between poetry and prophecy.[17] In the case of telestic madness it seems that the occasional tragic connection between prophecy and (metaphorical) Bacchic revelry has carried through into Socrates' presentation, although it is difficult to specify precisely how telestic madness operates.[18] In terms of the aims of the dialogue, the three madnesses evoke the idea of possession, which Socrates will later redescribe and reinterpret. In prophetic madness, the connection with the gods comes because the activity of prophecy has a god in it (ἐνθέῳ, 244b). Poetic madness is a kind of possession (κατοκωχή) and comes from the Muses (245a). Telestic madness causes people to take refuge in rituals and service to the gods, which lead in turn to purifications and mysteries. The sufferer is again said to be "possessed" (κατασχομένῳ, 244e). Here madness is listed as both

---

[15] Even when listening to Lysias' speech in Phaedrus' mouth, Socrates, possessed by Phaedrus' appreciation of the speech, joined in his Bacchic revelry (234d). Cf. Griswold 1986: 77.

[16] Rowe 1986: 170.   [17] Murray 1992: 33.

[18] See above, n. 10. For telestic madness Linforth 1946 is fundamental. Note too the convergence of the different forms, where telestic madness acts as an interpreter (προφητεύσασα, 244d), an image taken from the realm of prophecy. Poetic madness comes upon a soul that is "untrodden" and makes it into a bacchant with respect to poetry. The image here has elements of Bacchic and thus telestic imagery.

illness and cure: the madness is a divine gift when it is "correct" because it encourages people to put themselves into a right relationship with the gods.[19] We shall see that this is an important aspect of the philosophical love affair.

These three manifestations of madness are thus chosen both for their immediate Socratic resonance with the earlier pages of the dialogue and because they have a certain amount of intuitive plausibility in the Platonic universe. Possession was associated with (Dionysiac) purification and prophecy; poetry with prophecy and the kind of divine influence that Plato had tendentiously associated with possession and Bacchic ecstasy.[20] In terms of the purposes of the speech these examples establish successfully that certain traditional manifestations of "madness" may be connected with the divine realm and are beneficial. In each case a mortal is held or possessed by a god and we are encouraged to think that a god is in him or her.

Does erotic passion belong to this category? It would have been no stretch for an ancient audience to associate maddened passion and the lover who has lost control of himself with the kind of eros criticized in Socrates' *first* speech. Various well-known passages from lyric poetry, Sappho, Anacreon, and others, describe the force of Eros that overwhelms his victims.[21] It is also the paradigm that lies behind the rape of Oreithyia alluded to at the beginning of the dialogue: an Athenian princess swept away by a wind god overwhelmed by desire.[22] But this is, of course, the model that Socrates wants to refute. The purpose of the palinode is to show that the power of Eros results in good. The issue is, as Socrates sees, a theological one: "don't you consider Eros to be the son of Aphrodite and a god? ... If Eros is – as he is – a god or something divine, he could be nothing bad" (242d9–e4). Eros as active in traditional myth, as well as the passion he invokes, must then be reformulated in order to fulfill its function in the palinode. This project involves rethinking traditional notions of the cosmos and the nature of the divine. Thus Socrates will soon deny that the gods have physical bodies and, as we shall see, they will be toppled from their prior position as the summit of the universe. We note the significant slide in 242d–e from the description of Eros as "son of Aphrodite" to "god" to "something divine" (θεὸς ἤ τι θεῖον). Erotic madness as it is presented in the palinode will not be "possession" in the same sense that prophetic,

---

[19] Hackforth 1952: 59–60, although for Linforth 1946 madness is the cure only.
[20] Cf. Verdenius 1962: 134–37.
[21] Good lists of references are to be found (contents mostly overlapping) at Nehamas and Woodruff 1995: 88–92; Scully 2003: 100–05. Cf. Fortenbaugh 1966 for further discussion.
[22] Cf. Nightingale 1995: 159.

telestic, and poetic madness are, where a god invades the personality of a mortal and may even speak though his or her mouth. The possession model of the opening, used to characterize the first three types of madness, is incompatible with the later metaphysics that underlies the presentation of beneficial erotic madness. This later metaphysics in fact sweeps away the conceptual structure that underlies the presentation of divine madness at the beginning of the speech. It is the genius of the palinode that its rhetorical articulation initially obscures this incompatibility. By the time we notice it we have been presented with a different structure with which we may associate inspiration. Let us examine in more detail how this transformation occurs.

SUPERSEDING THE OPENING OF THE PALINODE

The very structure of the palinode dissociates the madness of eros from other madnesses and discourages us (at first) from examining too closely the connections between them. As Verdenius has pointed out, the different kinds of madness and their respective goods do not exist at the same level. Socrates does not, after describing the first three kinds of madness, immediately describe the fourth, but merely states that he could say more and that the existence of divine madness entails that the argument of love as madness does not necessarily mean that one should prefer a sober "friend" to a passionate one.[23] Erotic madness is not described at all. Socrates merely gives a promissory note: he will prove that it is granted by the gods in order to produce good fortune. The actual examination of erotic *mania* is separated from the opening survey of madness by just over four Stephanus pages because, we are told, we must first understand the truth about the soul. We are, therefore, first presented with the immortality proof, then with the image of the soul as charioteer and team and its associated cosmological sketch. The first mention of eros comes when we learn that the soul that has seen the most in the place beyond the heavens will be incarnated into a man who is "erotic" (ἐρωτικοῦ), linked here with the lover of wisdom (listed first), the lover of beauty, and the "musical" man – one associated with the Muses (248d). Then we are told that only someone who has pursued philosophy without guile or loved a boy in conjunction

---

[23] Verdenius 1962: 132, however, slightly misconstrues the argument at 245b–c. He claims that Socrates jumps immediately from establishing the category of divine madness to the conclusion that one need not be afraid to give in to a passionate lover (a conclusion that does not follow). In fact, Socrates claims only that the fact of madness is not *decisive*.

with philosophy can short-circuit the cycle of incarnation (249a). Only at
249b–d does madness enter the picture. Here we learn that

A man must understand what is spoken according to form, going from many perceptions to one thing gathered together by reason. This is recollection (*anamnēsis*)
of those things that our soul once saw when it travelled with god and looked
down on all the things that we now say exist, and looked up to what really exists.
Therefore only the mind of the philosopher grows wings; for it is always in proximity, through memory and to the extent of its power, to those things in proximity
to which a god is divine (πρὸς γὰρ ἐκείνοις ἀεί ἐστιν μνήμη κατὰ δύναμιν,
πρὸς οἷσπερ θεὸς ὢν θεῖός ἐστιν). A man using such reminders correctly [that
is sensations that remind us of the Forms], continually being initiated into the
perfect mysteries, alone becomes truly perfect. Standing apart from human cares
and being near to the divine, he is admonished by the many as being out of his
senses (παρακινῶν); they don't notice that he is divinely occupied (ἐνθουσιάζων).
(249b–d).

So far, then, the stress of the myth has been on the philosopher, whose
erotic aspects have been mentioned only in passing. It is the philosopher
who is thought to be out of his senses, whereas he is really ἐνθουσιάζων,
under divine influence. But how should we translate ἐνθουσιάζων here?
Most translators say that the philosopher is possessed, and this is certainly
how one would translate the word at the beginning of the palinode, or
in the *Ion*. But in what sense is he possessed? Surely not in the sense that
the prophetess has a god in her or the poet is taken over and possessed (in
Socrates'/Plato's portrayal). What we have heard about the gods and the
daimones since Socrates started his explanation of the nature of the soul
gives no indication that they enter into a mortal or possess him. This is
why I have chosen to render the phrase "divinely occupied,"[24] in order to
signal that a different process is at work. Rather than being invaded by
an outside force, the mind of the philosopher leaves the mortal world.[25]
The process of recollection allows him to use his memory to come as close
as he can to the Forms that inhabit the place beyond the heavens. It is
this phenomenon that makes him appear to the many as if he is out of
his senses and in erratic motion (παρακινῶν).[26] It is this that makes him
"possessed": mnemonic closeness to the Forms, not anything sent from
the gods. To recollect, therefore, is to be ἔνθεος, and this does not mean
that the divine thing you have in you is a god. The gods here are almost

---

[24] Suggested to me by David Blank.   [25] Griswold 1986: 75.
[26] The stress on motion is programmatic, given that the essence of the soul and the source of its
immortality in the *Phaedrus* is self-motion. Thus the lover is set in motion at 245b, and although
the many think this motion is out of control at 249d, they are wrong. This is the motion that is the
essence of psychic life.

incidental to the process of recollection and enthusiasm.[27] Indeed the gods themselves are divine – the θεοί are θεῖοι – because they can be close to the Forms and their psychic charioteers nourish themselves by gazing on them (247e).[28] Their divinity is, as it were, derivative.[29] The concept of divine possession, having something *theion* in you, has been reconfigured by the metaphysics of the myth before we ever get to the subject of erotic madness.[30] Being inspired is a question of being next to the divine (πρὸς τῷ θείῳ), by means of your memory. Rather than having a god in you, you are in the divine (to the extent that you can be).

Only now do we return to the fourth kind of *mania*. Socrates signals that this is the climax to which the entire speech has led (249d); he identifies this divine occupation of the philosopher with the transports of the lover:

When someone sees beauty here and recollects (ἀναμιμνῃσκόμενος) true beauty, he becomes winged, and as he becomes winged he desires to fly up, but cannot. He looks up like a bird, neglects what is below, and incurs the charge of being mad (αἰτίαν ἔχει ὡς μανικῶς διακείμενος). This, then, is the best of all the types of enthusiasm (πασῶν τῶν ἐνθουσιάσεων ἀρίστη) both for the one who has it and the one who shares it, and comes from the best source. He who shares in this madness and loves the beautiful is called a lover. (249d–e).

Eros is defined as the madness of someone who sees beauty here in this world, is reminded of the Form of Beauty, tries to fly up to it, and neglects what is here on earth. This is the best kind of enthusiasm/inspiration (*enthousiasis*) and this is what happens to the lover. A soul that has sufficient memory is driven out of itself (ἐκπλήττονται καὶ οὐκέτ' <ἐν> αὐτῶν γίγνονται, 250a) when it sees an earthly likeness of a Form, but doesn't understand what is happening to it. Plato may have coined the noun *enthousiasis* for this occasion. It occurs here for the first time in extant Greek literature and the novelty of vocabulary is one more indication that Plato is making Socrates formulate an interpretation of inspiration that gives new content to prior cultural forms, centering here on the ambiguities of divine presence in the self. When the lover is no longer "in" himself he is

---

[27] Contrast *Ion* 534e, where poems are divine (θεῖα) because they come from the gods (θεῶν), and the poets are the interpreters of whichever god they are possessed by.

[28] The nectar and ambrosia which, in the broader mythological tradition, confer immortality and are the food of the gods, are here given only to the horses. The idea of the food of the gods that in some sense makes gods what they are is retained and transferred to the Forms.

[29] De Vries 1969: 146–7; van Camp and Canart 1956: 112–15 ("auquels . . . un dieu doit sa divinité" [113]; "les dieux tout comme les hommes se nourrissent du Divin" [114]; Nicholson 1999: 180. Contra Hackforth 1952: 86 n. 3.

[30] Cf. Ferrari 1987: 118: the myth "radically revises the moral psychology of love . . . the philosophical way of life is a new way, which does not simply establish itself alongside the more ancient paths of inspiration, but . . . partly usurps their function."

striving for the world "above." He is not possessed by the god Eros; rather Eros is "something divine" because it is the force that moves the lover out of himself and spiritually upwards. Enthusiasm/inspiration is thus a reaction to likenesses that carries one to the divine realm. Inspiration is recollection.[31]

Socrates' return to the madness of love fulfils his earlier promise to show how it is "given by the gods in order to produce good fortune," but in a different sense than we had been led to expect. I hope to have shown that love is not given by the gods but is a reaction to a type of divinity that is metaphysically superior to the gods. The relationship of possession/inspiration has been depersonalized and systematized. Socrates himself has been inspired: not by the nymphs or the spirit of the place, but by his own yearning for the place beyond the heavens (250c). The clipped prose of the immortality proof, the narrative of the disembodied soul, the mystic description of the world of the Forms – all enter the rhetorical world of the palinode as an otherworldly intrusion. They model at the level of literary form the content that they describe. Just as the soul of the lover is swept away from everyday concerns, so a speech that aimed to examine the benefits of yielding to a lover is transformed by the need to place love in its correct relationship to the soul. The ringing declaration that "all soul is immortal" (245c) changes the conceptual as well as the rhetorical framework of the speech.[32]

MIMĒSIS AND THE GODS

If inspiration and being occupied by/with the divine are no longer caused by the intervention of individual deities, and the underpinnings of the first three types of divine madness at the opening of the speech cannot stand, we may well ask what role the gods are supposed to play in this new universe. We have seen them as leaders of the divine troops, models of perfect access to the place beyond the heavens. This intermediary modeling activity will continue in the later part of the speech, as we shall see, but the gods have not yet been implicated in the process of *enthousiasmos*. The connection is made at 251a:

---

[31] Carter 1967: 116; Morgan 2000: 218–23. Carter's approach to inspiration is similar to mine, but operates at a more general level. He notes in passing the issues involved in saying that the philosopher is "possessed" by Eros the god, but skirts the theoretical problem by asserting that the philosopher is "possessed by love, inspired by love" to search for knowledge.

[32] Compare *Rep*. 608d, as Socrates says to Glaucon, "Have you never perceived that our soul is immortal and never perishes?" to which Glaucon replies in amazement, "By Zeus, I haven't!" The discussion that then follows is capped by the Myth of Er.

He who has been recently initiated, the one who then saw much, when he sees a godlike face or bodily form that imitates beauty well (θεοειδὲς πρόσωπον ἴδη κάλλος εὖ μεμιμημένον) . . . looking upon him [the beloved] he reverences him as a god, and if he did not fear the reputation of excessive madness, he would sacrifice to his *paidika* as to a statue and god (ὡς θεὸν σέβεται, καὶ εἰ μὴ ἐδεδίει τὴν τῆς σφόδρα μανίας δόξαν, θύοι ἂν ὡς ἀγάλματι καὶ θεῷ τοῖς παιδικοῖς).

The lover suffers the symptoms of love when he sees "a godlike face." The participial clause here is informative: a godlike face is one that is a good representation of the Form of Beauty. The gods are paradigmatic in more ways than one.[33] They model the ascent to the place beyond the heavens and represent the Forms to us: the face of the beloved is like that of a god and like the Form. Moreover, the lover reveres the beloved "as a god," and if he were not afraid for his reputation, he would sacrifice to the *paidika* as to a statue of a god. This is a very rich formulation, as the image of the *agalma*, itself an image, introduces another layer of mediation between the world of the gods and the world the Forms on the one hand, and the sensible world on the other. When we sacrifice in front of an image of a god, we honor the statue for what it represents: the god. The first implication of this language, then, is that, even if he does not realize it, the lover reverences the beloved for that of which he is an image: beauty. It is worth noting also, that when the charioteer is dragged by the black horse towards the *paidika*, he falls back: "the memory of the charioteer when he sees the *paidika* is carried back to the nature of Beauty, and he sees it again, together with moderation, standing on its pure base" (βάθρῳ, 254b). *Bathron* can be a foundation, but also a statue base, and it is arguable that the Forms here are conceived in terms of a perfect cult statue.[34] In this instance, however, the statue would be paradoxically no image, but the reality, and as such worthy of religious awe and reverence. Yet gods cannot be removed from the equation. We honor the beloved as though he is a god, and we honor the reflection of the Form in him. We have also, however, seen that the gods are an important link between the Forms and humanity. Theirs is the perfected life of reason whose greatest achievement is successful contemplation of the Forms. They model successful ascent and themselves represent more perfectly than we do the qualities of the Forms. Nor is this the only way they are implicated in the process of inspiration. The next part of the palinode reveals that we live the recollective and philosophical life as a process of imitating the gods.

---

[33] The discussion here is a development of Morgan 2000: 223–35.
[34] I thank my student Renée Calkins for pointing out the significance of *bathron* here.

In her 1992 treatment of poetic inspiration, Murray asked how *mimēsis* and inspiration were connected, pointing out that in the *Ion* and the *Phaedrus*, Plato seems to be working with a model of poetry centered on inspiration, while in the *Republic*, he focuses on *mimēsis*.[35] As we have seen, poets in the *Phaedrus* are indeed shown as inspired, and yet we have also found good reason to suppose that when we are presented with the charioteer myth we should jettison this paradigm. This is reflected in the low ranking of the poetic life in the hierarchy of lives. How might our revised vision of inspiration help to construct a new version of *poiēsis*? Here I wish to carry further the insights of Murray (in her later work on Plato's Muses) and Rowe that Socrates and the philosopher are the real *mousikoi* and that the art of the Muse (*mousikē*) is best embodied in philosophy.[36] Inspiration and *mimēsis* combine in the lives of the philosophical lovers.

Let us consider first the imitation of the gods. As long as he is living his first incarnated life, each lover lives honoring and imitating as far as he can (ἐκεῖνον τιμῶν τε καὶ μιμούμενος εἰς τὸ δυνατὸν ζῇ, 252d) the god of whose *choros* he was a member, and this divine chorus leader also influences one's choice of beloved: a choreut of Zeus will choose a Zeus-like beloved, and "as if that very person were his god, he fashions him like an *agalma* and adorns him" (καὶ ὡς θεὸν αὐτὸν ἐκεῖνον ὄντα ἑαυτῷ οἷον ἄγαλμα τεκταίνεταί τε καὶ κατακοσμεῖ, 252d).[37] One chooses one's love on the basis of resemblance to a god and then works to strengthen the resemblance. This process of construction means that lovers must find out the details of their model wherever they can; they look within themselves and find a way "because they are forced to look intently towards the god, and grasping him in their memory, being inspired, they take from him their character and their habits, and to the extent that it is possible for a man they have a share of god" (διὰ τὸ συντόνως ἠναγκάσθαι πρὸς τὸν θεὸν βλέπειν, καὶ ἐφαπτόμενοι αὐτοῦ τῇ μνήμῃ ἐνθουσιῶντες ἐξ ἐκείνου λαμβάνουσι τὰ ἔθη καὶ τὰ ἐπιτηδεύματα, καθ᾽ ὅσον δυνατὸν θεοῦ ἀνθρώπῳ μετασχεῖν, 253a). In turn, they make their beloved as similar as possible to their own god:

καὶ ὅταν κτήσωνται, μιμούμενοι αὐτοί τε καὶ τὰ παιδικὰ πείθοντες καὶ ῥυθμί-
ζοντες εἰς τὸ ἐκείνου ἐπιτήδευμα καὶ ἰδέαν ἄγουσιν, ὅση ἑκάστῳ δύναμις,
οὐ φθόνῳ οὐδ᾽ ἀνελευθέρῳ δυσμενείᾳ χρώμενοι πρὸς τὰ παιδικά, ἀλλ᾽ εἰς
ὁμοιότητα αὐτοῖς καὶ τῷ θεῷ ὃν ἂν τιμῶσι πᾶσαν πάντως ὅτι μάλιστα
πειρώμενοι ἄγειν οὕτω ποιοῦσι.

---

[35] Murray 1992: 45.   [36] Rowe 1986: 181; Murray 2002. Cf. Morgan 2000: 235–37.
[37] See Belfiore 2006: 187, 204–07, for a good account of the importance of dance imagery here.

When they get hold of them they imitate their god themselves and persuade their beloved and assimilate his rhythm to the form and character of that god, as much as each one can, not employing jealousy or ill will unworthy of a free man, but trying to bring whomever they honor as much as they can into a thorough likeness to themselves and their god . . . (253b–c).

The account of the divine chorus leader has strong affinities with the picture of inspiration/enthusiasm at 249b–d. There the philosopher is close, through memory and as far as possible, to the things nearness whereunto make a god divine. As a result he is inspired, ἔνθεος. At 253a the lover looks intently towards his god and grasps him with his memory. Thus as far as is possible, he has a share in god and is inspired (ἐνθουσιῶντες). In both instances, being "inspired" is glossed as quasi-contact through memory with a pre-incarnation experience, although the gods are directly involved in the process of recollection only in the second passage.[38] It is also in the account of the patron gods that imitation/representation becomes an issue. *Mimēsis* here connotes emulation, acting like someone, rather than mimicking the appearance of someone or something (its derogatory meaning in *Republic* 10).[39] Once we free ourselves from thinking of *mimēsis* as mimicry and inspiration as literal possession, *mimēsis* can be seen as compatible with a re-imagined inspiration.[40] As we have seen, the gods model the ascent to the Forms and help communicate the divinity of the Forms to us. If the Forms source divinity for the gods and for us, divinity then seems to trickle down partly through direct recollection of the Forms, partly through conscious striving to imitate a model of successful access to the Forms. The injection of a different metaphysics, with a different relationship of the human mind to the divine, changes the playing field. We move from a traditional religious/mythological mode of inspiration to a philosophical one. In the former, as I have argued, inspiration is a mode of possession and incursion, whereas the latter is more complex.[41] Most significantly, philosophical inspiration is married to reason. Whereas the possessed poet or prophet is a passive instrument of the god, the philosopher must use

[38] Verdenius 1962: 143–4 draws a distinction between the two operations of memory here, privileging philosophical *anamnēsis* of the Forms and characterizing memory of one's patron god as based only on personal feelings. The two types of inspiration/*enthousiasmos* here are not identical, but there is no reason to believe that striving to imitate one's divinity must be seen as non-reflective and prephilosophical.

[39] For the distinction as it is played out in the *Republic*, see Nehamas 1999c [1982]: 258–9; Janaway 1995: 95.

[40] Cf. Murray 1992: 40–1, on the analogy between *Republic* 393c (where Homer assimilates himself to the speaker) and *Ion* 535b, where the term *mimēsis* is not used, but instead we are exploring inspiration.

[41] Rowe 1986: 170, Griswold 1986: 53, 75. Cf. the remarks of Nightingale 1995: 159.

his contact with the divine to help construct a deeper self-awareness and engage in systematic reflection.[42]

The question arises as to why, if Plato's reader is meant to realize that previous categories of inspiration have been superseded in the palinode, Plato does not simply have Socrates dismiss them as inaccurate. One might also wonder why Socrates' final invocation of Eros in the palinode (257a–b) is framed in entirely conventional terms. No complete answer can be given, but one might begin by stressing Socrates' lack of accurate knowledge about the metaphysical world and his notorious intellectual humility. When he compares the first three kinds of madness to the philosophical madness of love he is to some extent like the speaker later in the dialogue (260b–c), who talks about a donkey as if it is a horse because he doesn't know what a horse is really like. The ignorance is humorous, but it is at least well-intentioned. On the basis of two things in which he believes, the immortality of the soul and the existence of Forms, he creates a picture of erotic madness and connects it with familiar concepts of inspiration and possession. He is exercising his philosophical intuition.[43] But he cannot get bogged down in a minute discussion of which elements of conventional religious and mythological belief might or might not be accurate. This would be to do precisely what he rejects at the beginning of the dialogue: worry about where Boreas snatched Oreithyia or whether she was, in fact, snatched at all; or fret about composite mythological horsey beasts like the centaurs and Pegasus (or his own winged chariot team in the palinode?) (229c–230a). Socrates has more important goals than this, starting with his knowledge of himself, knowledge for which myth is one kind of heuristic device.

Thus the prayers, the gods, the religious oaths, and Socrates' ostentatious piety in the dialogue all contribute to a strong religious atmosphere, but do not compel commitment to conventional religious beliefs.[44] As Wilamowitz once commented, *Phaedr.* 246c–d ("because we have not seen and do not sufficiently understand, we invent god as an immortal creature that has a soul and a body united together for all time") shows that Plato was uncomfortable with the gods of mythology. He deployed them because of the place they held in traditional piety and was reluctant to a lay a hand on the customary forms of worship.[45] Wilamowitz attributes this to a

---

[42] On the move from intuitive and unconscious to rational and deliberate recollection, see Morgan 2000: 220–21. On the primacy of reason in philosophical inspiration, see Verdenius 1962: 148–49.

[43] Morgan 2000: 211.

[44] On the richness of references to gods and the divine in the *Phaedrus*, see Nicholson 1999: 135–36. Verdenius 1962: 147 finds the piety of the *Phaedrus* exaggerated, and connects it with developing Platonic pessimism about human capacity to attain knowledge unaided.

[45] Wilamowitz-Moellendorf 1959: 365, cited also at Nicholson 1999: 137.

readiness to find truth in ancient traditions, but if my analysis is correct, this cannot be the whole story. The imagined "truth" of inspiration, as we have seen, was far from the quasi-Bacchic possession of the tragic Cassandra and the rhapsode of the *Ion*. We are dealing with a two-level reading of the dialogue that uses conventional beliefs as a springboard for new thoughts. The vocabulary of inspiration is retained but developed and given different content. In a kind of bootstrapping manoeuvre, we need to use and then reject the theology that stands behind the first three kinds of madness, without stopping to deal in detail with theological questions beyond the scope of the present inquiry. The rhetorical strategy whereby the first three kinds of madness were separated from their philosophical and erotic counterpart by an intrusive metaphysics is also a sign of conversion.[46]

CONCLUSION: MEMORY, POETRY, AND MADNESS

The life of philosophical lovers encompasses at a higher level aspects of divine madness surveyed at the opening of the palinode. Prophetic madness, potentially, because the philosopher will look to the future of his soul and know what awaits it. Telestic madness because the philosopher alone becomes the perfected initiate, always being initiated into the perfect bliss of the Mysteries that are the Forms (249c) – an initiation that, like the results of telestic madness, will release the subject from present evils and render him safe in the future. The life of philosophical lovers encompasses poetic madness because philosophical eros is most likely to happen to a soul that has seen the Forms recently and is uncorrupted, just as poetic madness comes from the Muses upon a soul that is soft and untrodden upon (245a). The lovers, if all goes as it should, engage in a life of *mimēsis* and produce living *logoi* (to which we shall return). Most importantly, however, the philosophical lover, like the poet, has a particular relationship

---

[46] It is, therefore, an oversimplification to conclude that "Divine inspiration has become chameleon-like" because it is compatible both with a life of little value, and with a life of reason (Price 1989: 65). On this reading we are dealing with several different types of divine inspiration that coexist, while I maintain that although they coexist in the rhetoric of the dialogue, they do not at the level of its theology. Nor can I agree with Ferrari that the difference between the different types of inspiration can be glossed as a matter of historical perspective (Ferrari 1987: 118). To say that inspired love requires a different approach than the other three kinds of madness, partly because it has no historical pedigree, seems to me to invert matters: an historical pedigree is, rather, fashioned to create comfort with a different approach. My approach to inspiration in this dialogue comes closest to the notion of Platonic "transposition" discussed by Diès (1927: 268 and *passim*; cf. Flashar 1958: 125–26). He identifies as a fundamental Platonic rhetorical strategy the practice of bringing up a discourse of popular culture and then reworking it into an image of philosophy and the philosophical life.

with Memory. Mnemosyne in myth is the mother of the Muses – the very Muses who, as Murray has remarked, will be reconfigured as the patrons of philosophy in the myth of the cicadas that follows the palinode.[47] This traditional relationship reflects the importance of memory for a bard in the oral poetic tradition. Yet memory is also the power that in the metaphysics of the palinode brings us closer to the divine. Through memory the philosopher approaches the Forms and becomes inspired: he approaches the divine and becomes ἔνθεος. Through memory the lover grasps his god, gets a share of him or her, and becomes, again, inspired. The human ability to bring together many sensations into a whole gathered together by reason is the *anamnēsis*, recollection, of the things the soul saw in the place beyond the heavens. Memory is the power that drives a thoughtful human life, and is the engine of becoming inspired.

Just as in traditional poetic inspiration the bard's memory enables him to represent the past and engage in *mimēsis*, so too, the philosophical lover creates a way of life that is a work of art. He is, as Ferrari puts it, "the 'compleat' artist."[48] We have seen how the lover chooses a beloved who imitates beauty well, and then works to make him into the best possible representation of their god. He treats the beloved as a cult statue and strives to perfect it (note that Plato uses craft vocabulary here: τεκταίνεται, 252d). The philosophical life assimilates both lover and beloved into representations of their god. The vocabulary of imitation and likeness is obtrusive. Things on earth, like the beloved, that remind us of the Forms are *homoiōmata*, likenesses (250a6, b3), and imitate the Form. The lover lives imitating his god and bringing the beloved into a state of similarity to himself and the god.[49] No wonder that traditional poets and their traditional *mimēsis* rank so low in the dialogue's hierarchy of lives: why make dead motionless copies when you can make living and moving re-presentations? This thought returns us to criticisms of the poet in the *Ion* and *Republic*: that if they knew what they were writing about, they would create a real general (for instance), rather than his semblance.[50] It also feeds directly into the critique of written texts that will end the discussion of rhetoric at the close of the dialogue where writing things down in the belief that this makes them stable is castigated as foolish and illegitimate, compared with the living speech of the one who

---

[47] Murray 2002: 43–46.   [48] Ferrari 1987: 119.   [49] 253b8, cf. 253b1. Cf. Price 1989: 101.

[50] *Ion* 541b–e, *Rep* 599c–600a. The opening of the *Phaedrus* presents a chain of inspiration similar to that envisioned by the *Ion*. When Phaedrus delivers Lysias' speech, he is so overwhelmed by what he regards as its excellences that Socrates, his audience, speaks of joining in his Bacchic frenzy (234d). So too in the *Ion*, the rhapsode (Phaedrus in the *Phaedrus*) passes on the inspiration of the author (Lysias in the *Phaedrus*) to his audience.

knows (275d–277a). This speech can reproduce itself in another person and is "ensouled" (ἔμψυχον).[51] In the world of the myth, this would translate to the beloved, who is, quite exactly, the poetic creation of the lover, created in emulation of the gods and in honor of the Forms.

The palinode, then, presents us with a picture of eros as a master madness that subsumes the important aspects of the first three kinds of madness. It uses them as a means of persuasion (arguing that eros is similar to them) before creating a new world. It reconfigures inspiration as recollection, where the soul is impinged upon by the divine, but where the divine is sourced not in the gods of religion and mythology but in the divinity of the Forms, and where the gods are themselves dependent for their divinity on these same Forms. It reconfigures proper poetry as philosophy, an "art" of imitation, representation, assimilation to the divine models that exist in and above heaven, a *poiēsis* where instead of producing lifeless statues and dead discourse, we create ourselves and our beloveds as images of the divine, speaking, living *logoi.*[52]

---

[51] Dialectical exchange and analysis between the lover and beloved will help them move towards an advanced form of recollection that is the conscious product of reason (Morgan 2000: 219–22).

[52] Thanks are due to David Blank, Sarah Johnston, Andrea Nightingale, and Alex Purves for helpful discussions and comments on this essay.

CHAPTER 4

Plato's Theaetetus *as an ethical dialogue*

David Sedley

It is a privilege to be able to dedicate this essay to my teacher, mentor, colleague, co-author and friend Tony Long, with pleasant memories of many past conversations about the *Theaetetus*.

The *Theaetetus* is by common consent one of the classic texts in the history of epistemology. But would Plato himself understand and endorse this description? If "epistemology" were defined simply as "the study of *epistēmē*," it would be easy to answer affirmatively, *epistēmē* being after all the official topic of the dialogue. But does Plato recognize any area of philosophy that would correspond to what *we* call epistemology?

For the later Platonist tradition, "logic" had come to constitute one of the three parts of philosophy, alongside ethics and physics; and cognition of truth (often under the rubric "the criterion of truth") was in its turn recognized as a primary focus of "logic". Hence Platonist schematizations had no trouble in classing the *Theaetetus* as a "logical" dialogue if they so wished. The epitome of Plato preserved by Stobaeus (*Ecl.* 2.49.8–25) is able to say that the goal of "becoming like god" is set out by Plato in the *Timaeus* from the point of view of physics (φυσικῶς), in the *Republic* from the point of view of ethics (ἠθικῶς), and in the *Theaetetus* from the point of view of logic (λογικῶς). This classification of the *Theaetetus* as "logical" was not mandatory, however, and in fact in Thrasyllus' second Platonic tetralogy the dialogue was, although placed in a logical group, itself classed as "peirastic," in recognition of its primary focus on testing and exposing false views of knowledge rather than laying down the truth about it. Nevertheless, the idea of classifying the *Theaetetus* as an epistemological dialogue can, without excessive anachronism, be said to have made sense in a post-Platonic context.

How about Plato himself? How far does he go towards that eventual tripartition of philosophy into physics, ethics, and logic? Two passages offer a glimpse of the answer. At *Timaeus* 29b3–d3 he distinguishes just two kinds of discourse (λόγος): inherently unstable discourse about the sensible world, in other words physics; and inherently stable discourse about being. The latter kind of discourse acquires its stability from the fact that its proper objects are Forms, entities not subject to change. We are not required to limit this latter kind of discourse to the study of ontology as such, and it must in fact include the kind of work to which Platonic dialectic had been devoted in many previous dialogues, largely of ethical content, on the ground that the objects of ethical inquiry and definition are stable concepts, or, more specifically, Forms. As we encounter it in the dialogues, this kind of discourse admittedly does not take exclusively Forms as its subject matter, and includes plenty of empirically focused discussion, but at least ideally Plato viewed it as focused on Forms alone (*Rep.* 6.511b2–c2).

In the *Timaeus*, then, we are confronted with a *bipartition* of philosophy into (a) physics and (b) the study of stable being, the latter including ethics.

The second text, one which enables us to put some flesh on these bare bones, is the *Cratylus*. There the long series of etymologies set out in the central part of the dialogue takes as its subject matter a comprehensive set of philosophical terms, following an order which is anything but casual. It appears to offer us, in fact, a synopsis of Plato's own division of philosophy at the time of writing, and there is much waiting for us to learn if we start paying proper attention to it.[1] After working systematically through physics, the etymological excursus announces a switch to ethics, "the names . . . concerning virtue, such as wisdom and understanding and justice, and all the others of that kind" (411a3–4), which Socrates condemns *en bloc* (411b3–c5) as having been coined to convey the false impression that values are inherently unstable: for instance, he will shortly be decoding *phronēsis*, "wisdom", as *phoras noēsis*, "thinking of motion". The ensuing ethical survey then occupies in effect the entire remainder of the etymological excursus. Hence Plato's bipartition of philosophy proves to be into (a) physics and (b) ethics. How such a bipartition can be thought to exhaust the subject matter of philosophy will become clear in a moment.

The sequence within the ethical section is as follows:
(1) the virtues, in the presumably descending order
    (a) intellectual virtues (411d4–412b8);[2]

---

[1] I am here drawing on my findings in Sedley 2003: 156–58.

[2] A little anomalously, ἀγαθόν is considered in between (a) and (b), at 412b8–c6. The reason, I assume, is that it is here functioning in its role as the adjective whose abstract noun is ἀρετή, and hence as a proper lead-in to the moral virtues.

    (b) moral virtues (412c7–414a7);

    (c) technical virtues (414b7–415a7).

(2) The generic terms for moral evaluation (415a7–419b7).

(3) Terms from moral psychology (419b7–420e5).

(4) The more strictly logical terms "name," "truth," "falsity," "being," and "not-being," familiarly analysed in the *Sophist* (421a1–c2).

What was later to be separated off as "logic" is here unmistakably a part of ethics. That (4) is still part of the ethical section, and not a new beginning, is confirmed by the way in which it seamlessly continues to fill out Socrates' condemnation of ethical language as vitiated by a mistaken belief in instability.

The opening focus on knowledge terms and the closing focus on truth, by framing the whole account, confirm that intellectual understanding is integral to ethics. Coming from someone who had seriously contemplated the reduction of all virtue to knowledge, and who never retreated far from considering wisdom the best possible state of the soul, whether in our present life or at any rate after it, this classification should be anything but surprising.

Admittedly this bipartition, when compared with the later standard tripartition of philosophy into physics, ethics, and logic, appears unenlightening. If even a dialogue like the *Sophist* is, thanks to its concern with being and not-being, part of ethics, it may turn out that *all* Plato's dialogues, with the solitary exception of the *Timaeus*,[3] are likewise ethical, or alternatively that some, perhaps even including the *Cratylus* itself, fit nowhere in the scheme. It was only in later generations, when "logic" became a distinct third part of philosophy, that dialogues like *Cratylus*, *Parmenides*, and *Sophist* could be classified as logical, and partitioning philosophy gained real value as a didactic or hermeneutic tool. Nevertheless, the primitive bipartition is, however latently, a genuine part of Plato's own outlook, and understanding the consequently wide reach of Platonic ethics will prove to be an important part of the background to the *Theaetetus*.

Let us, with this goal in mind, turn to the sequence of intellectual virtues with which the *Cratylus*' ethical list opens. These are wisdom (*phronēsis*), judgement (*gnōmē*), intellection (*noēsis*), temperance (*sōphrosunē*), knowledge (*epistēmē*), understanding (*sunesis*), and wisdom again (this time *sophia*). The fact that they are followed almost immediately by a second

---

[3] Of course even the *Timaeus* has a large ethical content, but it was always treated as Plato's work on physics, and the *Cratylus* confirms this by treating its cosmological themes separately, before the ethics. See further Sedley 2003: 156–58.

group, consisting of justice (*dikaiosunē*) and courage (*andreia*), confirms that this first list is specifically a list of intellectual virtues. The one apparent anomaly is *sōphrosunē*, which we may well be inclined to think of as a moral rather than an intellectual virtue. I shall return to its anomalous status at the end of the essay, where it should become clear just why it does in fact belong properly among the intellectual virtues. All the other words in the first group are ones which emphasize intellectual understanding rather than moral disposition. They include not only the two terms conventionally translated "wisdom," namely *phronēsis* and *sophia*, but also *epistēmē*, the definiendum of the *Theaetetus*.

We thus have a prima facie expectation that Plato himself would view the *Theaetetus* as an ethical dialogue.[4] The second reason for that same expectation is the following. In the classic dialogues of definition, four of the five cardinal virtues had been tackled: piety in the *Euthyphro*, courage in the *Laches*, moderation in the *Charmides*, and justice in the *Republic*. The missing fifth cardinal virtue is wisdom. Why did Plato never complete the set by writing a dialogue on that? Or perhaps he did. It seems to me highly plausible that in the opening moves of the *Theaetetus* Plato is reassuring us that this dialogue is to be, at last, the missing treatment of exactly that virtue.

Socrates turns his conversation with the young mathematics student Theaetetus to the subject of learning (145d7–e7):

SOCR. ... Tell me, is to learn to become wiser about what one learns?
THT. Of course.
SOCR. And it is wisdom (*sophia*) that makes the wise wise?
THT. Yes.
SOCR. And I take it that this is nothing different from knowledge?
THT. What is?
SOCR. Wisdom. Or isn't it true that what people are knowledgeable about they are also wise about?
THT. What are you getting at?
SOCR. Knowledge and wisdom turn out to be the same thing?
THT. Yes.

This exchange shifts the topic of the dialogue to knowledge, where thereafter it stays. But why did Socrates choose to take so circuitous a route? He could simply have pointed out, exploiting a standard equivalence, that

---

4 In defending this thesis, I shall not be systematically cataloguing the ethical themes and implications present in the dialogue (cf. *Timaeus*, previous note). But for an account of the *Theaetetus* as ethical which does focus on its ethical themes, especially in the Digression, see van Ackeren 2003: 226–58.

to learn is to acquire knowledge. Instead he added an extra link to the inferential chain, by pointing out the identity of "wisdom" with "knowledge". This additional link in the chain is neatly explained by reference to an authorial strategy for reminding the reader that, in seeking to define knowledge, the *Theaetetus* will *ipso facto* be examining the virtue of wisdom. The interchangeability of "knowledge" and "wisdom," exploited here, has a good Socratic pedigree in the Platonic corpus: wisdom (normally *sophia* or *phronēsis*) is referred to as *epistēmē* in lists of the virtues at both *Protagoras* 330b4 and *Phaedrus* 247d7.

One might reasonably ask why, if the virtue of wisdom will be under examination in the dialogue, the kind of learning which gives Socrates his initial cue for mentioning wisdom should be mathematical learning such as that in which the young Theaetetus engages under Theodorus' instruction.

Here, as often in this dialogue, it is helpful to leave a gap between the author Plato and the speaker Socrates. That moral understanding must grow from the study of mathematics would be unlikely to occur to the barren midwife of others' ideas who is portrayed in the *Theaetetus*. For he represents, at least on the interpretation I have argued elsewhere,[5] a reversion to the inquisitive but self-confessedly ignorant Socrates portrayed in the early dialogues, presented here with hindsight not as a Platonist *avant la lettre*, but as Platonism's midwife, the open-minded inquirer whose interrogations unwittingly brought Plato's philosophy into the world.

If we assume this broad framework of interpretation, we must ask what in the present case are the Platonic developments to which Socrates' inquiries point forward. In the *Republic* the profound continuity between mathematical and moral education is the pivot on which the entire educational programme turns. There the trainee rulers are expected to spend ten years studying mathematics before they are ready to turn to dialectic, which itself in turn will culminate in the study of the Good. Only after that will they have the moral knowledge required of rulers. This doctrine is Plato's own, not traceable back to the Socrates of his early dialogues. In the *Theaetetus*, his recreated aporetic Socrates shows no inkling of any such link between mathematics and ethics, but Plato's authorial strategy keeps it in view for us. The young Theaetetus has already solved a problem in arithmetic by correlating two classes of number to two classes of geometrical figure, and has gone on to perform a similar operation for cubic numbers; in other words he has progressed from arithmetic, through plane geometry to solid

---

[5] Sedley 2004.

geometry, the first three stages of mathematical education in the *Republic*. In the future he wants Theodorus to teach him astronomy and harmonics (145d1–3), the remaining two bridge disciplines in the *Republic*. In the course of the dialogue itself he is going to be initiated into dialectic. And as we know from the proem, which recounts his death, he will go on to become a true *kalos kagathos* who conducts himself with exemplary heroism in time of war (142b6–8). The authorial subtext thus reveals that the teenager Theaetetus, already far advanced on the *Republic*'s educational programme, is on his way to moral virtue.

Having thus bridged the apparent gulf between mathematical and moral knowledge, we can largely dispel the worry that knowledge is considered in the *Theaetetus* from too narrowly epistemological a point of view to contribute to an ethical inquiry. That even non-moral knowledge is more morally relevant than one might at first have expected is itself a deeply Platonic subtext.

At the same time, the *Theaetetus* narrows the gap between intellectual and moral understanding in the reverse direction as well: moral knowledge is ultimately less distinctively moral than one might think. The place where such a narrowing becomes clearest is in the Digression which stands at the dialogue's exact centre (172a1–177c2). This excursus is occasioned by the observation (172b7–8) that even those who do not embrace wholesale Protagorean relativism sometimes adhere to *moral* relativism. Socrates' ensuing answer to moral relativism is a portrayal of the true philosopher as altogether detaching himself from the civic conditions that make moral standards appear inextricably context-dependent, and instead focusing on god as the absolute moral paradigm. Adherence to this divine standard turns out to transform moral understanding in an initially surprising way: although by emulating it the philosopher becomes "just", his is a derelativized justice which takes him far away from concern with justice as practised in familiar civic situations, and far even from care for the welfare of his fellow men. He is so focused on questions about universals, such as "What is a human being?", that he is barely aware whether his neighbour *is* a human being or not (174b1–6); and, by implication, he is so focused on inquiry into "justice and injustice themselves" that he has left behind such questions as "What injustice I am doing you, or you me?" (175b8–c2). True justice lies not in sorting out relative rights and wrongs in the law courts and other civic institutions, but in acquiring a radically non-perspectival, and in that sense godlike, level of understanding.

I am aware of the controversy surrounding this interpretation. I cannot return to its defence here, beyond remarking that it remains in my view the only natural and unforced reading of the passage. Those interpreters who have refused to accept it have also typically been unwilling to accept at face value the apparent meaning of other passages in Plato and Aristotle which similarly present the highest intellectual achievement as raising the philosopher above interpersonal morality. These include the ascent passage in the *Symposium*, which makes the ultimate achievement of love one that leaves behind personal affection for individuals, in favour of a direct union with the Beautiful itself; the concession in *Republic* VII that true philosophers will find a life of detached contemplation more fulfilling and desirable than one of discharging their civic duties, with the result that they will have to be "compelled" to play their part in government;[6] the declaration near the end of the *Timaeus* (89e3–90d7) that the highest form of human happiness lies not in harmony of the soul (*Republic* IV's analysis of moral virtue), but in the divinization of its immortal rational component alone; and Aristotle, *Nicomachean Ethics* X 6–8, where on the most natural and straightforward reading the contemplative life, in which the exercise of moral virtues plays no more than an incidental part, is the highest form of human happiness, outclassing any possible life centred on civic engagement. The pattern is in my view too emphatic and recurrent to be plausibly explained away each time. It is better to accept that, in the opinion of both Plato and Aristotle, the superiority of the intellectual to the moral virtues makes an intellectual or contemplative life superior to a moral life.

However, this precise way of putting it, in terms of contemplative versus moral, is Aristotelian. Plato's own view, as evidenced in the *Theaetetus*, is that the intellectual life which withdraws from civic engagement is itself the life of true "justice" (176a9–b2: "to become as like god as is possible . . . is to become just and holy, together with wisdom"). In other words, at the highest level of human attainment moral values are not abandoned, but instead are realigned as ultimately intellectual ones, characterized by an absoluteness which raises them higher than any interpersonal focus could take them. In the *Phaedo* the soul's escape into the realm of pure intellectual self-fulfilment had been seen as fully realizable only after death; but the *Theaetetus*, a dialogue which in true Socratic spirit de-emphasizes (although it does not exclude) the soul's expectations of post mortem survival, correspondingly locates that same escape ("to escape from here to there as quickly as possible", 176a9) within the confines of an incarnate human life. Even as a human being physically located in a city you can

---

[6] For the view that I am contesting here, cf. esp. Silverman (this volume).

become a godlike pure contemplator. The historical Socrates' political minimalism is, it seems, being interpreted with hindsight as hinting at this idealized realignment of virtue, away from the civic and towards the intellectual.

Here then is a second reason why we should hesitate to class the knowledge investigated in the *Theaetetus* as non-moral. At the highest level, moral understanding and pure intellectual understanding are not ultimately separable, because the former culminates in the latter. For Plato both the starting point and the highest achievement of moral living are essentially intellectual in character. This relative ranking of the moral and the intellectual, so hard for us to treat with sympathy but so central to ancient philosophical thought, is explicit in the *Theaetetus* digression, and does much to explain why, throughout the dialogue's definitional discussions, the moral implications of wisdom are not privileged over others.

At the end of the dialogue, Theaetetus has turned out after all not to be intellectually pregnant. Nevertheless, Socrates' midwifery has benefited him:

Suppose that in the future you try to become pregnant with other ideas, Theaetetus. If you succeed, you will be filled with better ideas thanks to today's investigation; and if you are empty, you will be less burdensome to those you associate with ἧττον ... βαρὺς τοῖς συνοῦσι), and nicer (ἡμερώτερος), thanks to your having the modesty not to think that you know things that you don't know (σωφρόνως οὐκ οἰόμενος εἰδέναι ἃ μὴ οἶσθα). (210b11–c4)

By being disabused of his pretensions to knowledge, Theaetetus has acquired a degree of *sōphrosunē*. What is this virtue, which puts in its first appearance only on the final page of the dialogue?

In Plato's well-known definition of it in *Republic* IV, *sōphrosunē* is self-control, taking the specific form of harmonious agreement among the three soul parts that reason should give the orders, and the other two obey them. But the term also has, prior to that, a Socratic history. In the *Charmides*, the dialogue which Plato devoted to its definition, it has often been noticed that the "self-control" conception of *sōphrosunē* is resoundingly absent. Instead, the definitions canvassed are, no doubt, as usual in order of increasing merit, (1) being laid-back (159b–160d), (2) modesty (αἰδώς, 160e–161b), (3) minding one's own business (161b–163c), (4) doing good (163d–e), (5) self-knowledge (164a–165b), and (6) knowing what one knows and what one does not know, i.e. knowledge of knowledge and ignorance (165b–175d). (Most interpreters find a seventh definition, "knowledge of good and bad," at 174d, but I do not believe it is intended as a definition.)

It should be clear that the reference to *sōphrosunē* at the end of the *Theaetetus* uses it in a sense far closer to these definitions from the *Charmides* than to the "self-control" aspect picked out in the *Republic*. If Theaetetus is disabused of the impression that he possesses knowledge, Socrates has said, he will be less burdensome company, thanks to his modesty in not thinking that he knows what he does not know. This echoes the picture presented by Charmides' three definitions (1–3), which jointly emphasize that possessors of *sōphrosunē* are not pushy towards others, and mind their own business. But it also, more specifically, takes up the implications of Critias' two main definitions (i.e. 5–6; definition 4, "doing good", is offered in passing and not seriously discussed). According to these, *sōphrosunē* is not merely self-knowledge, but more specifically self-knowledge with regard to one's state of knowledge or ignorance. This particular brand of intellectualism has often been recognized as being of Socratic inspiration. Socrates responds to Critias as follows:

> So the *sōphrōn* is the only person who will know himself and be able to determine what he does know and what he does not. And likewise with regard to others, he will be able to examine what someone knows and thinks he knows, in the case where that person knows, and on the other hand what someone thinks he knows but doesn't know. No one else will have this ability. And that's what being *sōphrōn*, *sōphrosunē*, and self-knowledge are, namely knowing what one knows and what one does not. (*Charmides* 167a1–7)

Socrates proceeds to attack this conception, on the ground that knowledge could not have knowledge and lack of knowledge as its object. His hostile reaction has caused some puzzlement, because Socrates' distinctive hallmark is widely seen as being, precisely, his avowed knowledge of his own (and others') ignorance. This is, indeed, seen as being his favoured interpretation, in the *Apology*, of what his own "wisdom," attributed to him by the oracle, in fact consists in (*Apol.* 23b). However, nowhere in Plato, Xenophon, Aristotle or any pre-Hellenistic source is Socrates ever represented as claiming to have knowledge of his own ignorance. At most he is prepared to say that he "knows that in reality he is worthless with regard to wisdom" (23b3–4, ἔγνωκεν ὅτι οὐδενὸς ἄξιός ἐστι τῇ ἀληθείᾳ πρὸς σοφίαν); that "For my own part, neither in a large way nor in a small one am I aware of being wise" (21b4–5, ἐγὼ γὰρ δὴ οὔτε μέγα οὔτε σμικρὸν σύνοιδα ἐμαυτῷ σοφὸς ὤν); and that "Just as I do not know, so too I do not even think I know" (21d5–6, ὥσπερ οὖν οὐκ οἶδα, οὐδὲ οἴομαι). All these formulations stop well short of the second-order knowledge claim, "I know that I know nothing," attributed to Socrates in the later tradition.[7] Hence I see no reason to take less than seriously the implications of his argument in the *Charmides*: any cognitive state must have a suitably correlated object or content distinct from itself, and cannot be merely self-reflexive. The joint message of the *Apology* and *Charmides* is that modest acceptance of one's own ignorance is an inherently desirable form of self-awareness, but that it cannot, on pain of incoherence, be interpreted as a self-reflexive branch of knowledge.

However, the philosophical motives of the limitation imposed in the *Charmides* are anything but clear. What would Socrates have lost, or risked, by allowing that one might in principle have knowledge of one's own knowledge or ignorance?[8] Plato's own longer-term motivation is likely to have lain in his growing conviction that knowledge, properly analysed as in the *Republic* and *Timaeus*, must have objective and unchangeable "being" as its object,[9] and that the subject's own psychological states are simply not suitable candidates for this.[10] If so, there is a natural appropriateness in the *Theaetetus*' closing reminder of the point, especially if one assumes, as I do, that the dialogue's failure to define knowledge is meant to open up a space which the *Republic*'s epistemology alone can fill.

What, at any rate, the close of the *Theaetetus* makes clear is the following. Young Theaetetus has been proved not to know what knowledge is. His own epistemic state, whether one of knowledge or of ignorance, is therefore something he cannot possibly be said to know, given only that you could not know that you are or are not in such and such a condition if you do not even know what that condition is. Despite this, he has grown in virtue: he is now less likely than before to think that he knows things which in fact he does not know, and it is in fact in that enhanced lack of pretension that

---

[7] Since I wrote the above, Gail Fine has published a full study of the topic (Fine 2008), arriving at a broadly similar conclusion. At *Alc.* 117b–118a (not discussed by Fine) Socrates does recommend – albeit without explicitly avowing it for himself – actual knowledge of one's own lack of knowledge. This is as far as I know unique in the Socratic dialogues, and might be added to the reasons for doubting the authenticity of *Alcibiades*.

[8] That knowledge about knowledge (albeit not about one's own knowledge) is possible is conceded at *Meno* 98b2–5, but that is the kind of cognition that would, in Plato's mature metaphysics, be counted as knowledge of the Form of knowledge.

[9] Note in this connection that at *Charm.* 168a, in another anticipation of *Republic* V, Socrates reveals his assumption that not only ἐπιστήμη but also δόξα must have its own distinct external object.

[10] In the *Charmides*, even though his closing summary (175b6–7) declares without qualification that the argument has disallowed any such option, at 169a1–b1 Socrates has in fact left open the possibility that a sufficiently great man might still be able to show that there can after all be knowledge of knowledge. But Plato did not resume the idea in subsequent dialogues, and I assume him to have eventually abandoned it in the light of *Rep.* 5's redefinition of ἐπιστήμη as requiring an unchangeable object, an abandonment which I read the close of the *Theaetetus* as tending to confirm.

his new-found *sōphrosunē* lies. Is this new *sōphrosunē* an intellectual virtue, a moral virtue, or both?

On the one hand it is characterized in moral language, reminiscent of Charmides' opening definitions of *sōphrosunē* in terms of modesty, keeping oneself to oneself, etc. Henceforth, Theaetetus is told, "you will be less burdensome to those whose company you keep" (ἧττον . . . βαρὺς τοῖς συνοῦσι), and to that extent a nicer (ἡμερώτερος) person. This is not just a matter of curbing a young man's irritating self-confidence. Those who think they know what in fact they do not are well exemplified by Meletus, Socrates' accuser mentioned just a few lines later – in the dialogue's final sentence (210d2–4), as Socrates hurries off to face his judicial hearing. They are equally familiar to Plato's readers in the person of the frightful bigot Euthyphro, whose misplaced confidence that he knows all about piety leads him to the most high-handed conduct imaginable towards his own father. Most striking of all, the expression "less burdensome to those whose company you keep" (ἧττον . . . βαρὺς τοῖς συνοῦσι) finds an echo in the later *Politicus*, where tyranny is of all regimes the "most burdensome to live with" (302e12, βαρυτάτη συνοικῆσαι). The tyrant is Plato's favoured model of the extreme depths of moral vice; so Theaetetus, by his emerging self-awareness, has moved even further away from the tyrannical end of the moral scale. We need not doubt, therefore, that Theaetetus' new-won *sōphrosunē* is a significant moral improvement, of strongly Socratic stamp.

On the other hand, that same moral improvement is being cast in pointedly intellectualist terms. Theaetetus has improved intellectually by arming himself against the belief that he knows what he in fact does not. Thus at the dialogue's close, much as in its opening pages and, in the Digression, at its mathematical midpoint, moral and intellectual virtue converge on each other. The Socratic project of intellectualizing virtue has not been eclipsed by the complex psychology of the *Republic*, but remains a vital part of Plato's agenda.[11]

[11] For helpful comments I am grateful to audiences at Prague in October 2007 and Paris in February 2008, especially Jakub Jirsa, Tim Chappell, Julius Tomin, Laszlo Bene, and Dimitri El Murr. I would also like to thank Jan Szaif and Andrea Nightingale for valuable written comments. A predecessor of the present chapter appeared under the title "The *Theaetetus* as an ethical dialogue" in the proceedings of the 2007 Prague conference: A. Havlicek, F. Karfik, and S. Spinka (eds.), *Plato's Theaetetus: Proceedings of the Sixth Symposium Platonicum Pragense* (Prague, 2008), 319–30.

CHAPTER 5

Contemplating divine mind

Allan Silverman

This essay is a bit of bronze in exchange for the gold of Tony Long's conversation, teaching, and especially friendship over the past quarter century.

For both Plato and Aristotle, the doctrine of becoming like god is one of the outcomes of the inquiry into the question that matters most to us humans, namely the question of how one ought to live one's life. This is the most practical of questions for both Plato and Aristotle, involving how we manage our affairs, order our desires and choose our actions with the aim of living the best life possible, namely, a happy life. For both, becoming like the divine as much as possible is one way of describing the nature of human happiness. Striving to be like, or better *modeling ourselves* on, the divine mind is one way of expressing what we humans do in trying to realize our happiness, whether or not we are aware of our striving to achieve this. What thus begins as the most human of inquiries threatens to end with the recommendation that we should flee what is human in order to be something else, i.e., divine. I will refer to this as the "flight interpretation." Indeed many readers of Plato have concluded that the search for happiness leads the philosopher to turn his/her back on the mundane world and eschew practical activity as much as possible. Not a few readers of Aristotle find that ultimately he recommends a similar outcome. What differences Plato and Aristotle have concerning the nature of human happiness might plausibly be viewed as disagreements over the nature and activities of the divine mind. Disagreements may also appear over the manners in which a human being, or a human mind, can be like this divine mind. In order to assess the differences and similarities, I want to look at their accounts of the (self-)understanding of those who strive to be like god – how they incorporate being like the divine in the way they plan their lives, how they should achieve assimilation with the divine, and how that affects their actions and activities for the remainder of their lives. I do not think that

Plato is properly viewed as espousing the flight interpretation of becoming like god. Aristotle might well be best seen as its advocate. A critical question is how they treat an agent's thinking about the good.

In the case of each it is hard to fathom the relation of the divine being to the good: in Plato's case the relation of the Demiurge to the Form of the Good; in Aristotle's the manner in which the focal account of being and the focal account of good converge on the same primary actuality.

In Aristotle's case we worry about the mind of the prime mover. With respect to Plato, matters are murkier. Here we have, I suggest, two leads to follow: the activity of the *Republic*'s philosopher-ruler in pursuit of knowledge of the Good and the activity of the Demiurge of the *Timaeus*.[1] In both we find a divine mind engaged in an activity of reason, indeed the best activity of reason. In Plato, the activity of the Demiurge and the best activity of the fully developed philosopher seem inextricably tied to his contemplation or understanding of the Good. In Aristotle, on the other hand, the activity of reasoning about the good seems to be distinct from the reasoning of the divine mind. That is, only in Aristotle, and only somewhat late in his career, do we find a divine mind that only contemplates, i.e., engages in *theōria* (the exercise of theoretical wisdom), as something distinct from another activity of reason, namely exercising *phronēsis* (practical wisdom). For Plato, then, the contemplative understanding that is reasoning about the good seems to be the activity that is sufficient for, if not constitutive of, human happiness. Not so for Aristotle, where reasoning about the good seems the special province of a secondary exercise of reason. It is this difference, the difference between practical and theoretical reason, that I want to explore in this essay, to see what lessons we can draw about the ways in which each philosopher thinks that a human being can be as divine as possible. In a nutshell the puzzle can be posed thus: is all reasoning about the good *eo ipso* practical? This will require, at a minimum, some remarks about the nature of these activities and about their objects. I am sure that what I will say will only scratch the surface of the problem.

With respect to Plato, the central books of the *Republic* are key, especially the characterization of the mind of the philosopher-ruler who, having escaped the Cave, is pondering the return. Plato's *Republic* begins with

---

[1] I stipulate the identity of the Demiurge and *nous* (mind), and I am prepared to treat the Demiurge and *nous* and the cosmic world soul as one phenomenon. This is controversial, not least because it depends on how one stands on the question of whether Plato believes in the creation or not. I think that the account is not literal but rather "for the sake of instruction," though obviously I cannot defend that claim here. Given my reading of the *eikōs muthos*, for my purposes, nothing turns on identifying the world-soul and the Demiurge.

Socrates' question: how ought one to live? Broadly speaking, Socrates believed philosophy or rational inquiry could answer the question. Given his inquiry into and assumptions about human nature and the human soul, Socrates believed that happiness lies in a state of the rational soul achieved through this inquiry, i.e., a state of knowledge. In my view, the argument of the first four books of the *Republic*, despite the non-Socratic theory of the tripartite soul, show that Plato affirms this identification of happiness with knowledge. Critical to his answer to Glaucon's challenge, namely, to prove that (the life of) justice is in every way better than (the life of) injustice, is the thesis that reason should rule over the other two parts of the human soul. Reason exercises its rule when each of the parts is just, i.e., doing its own job. In these circumstances the soul (and the person) possesses moderation, bravery, and especially wisdom, and the condition of such a soul is harmonious. This state of psychological harmony constitutes happiness. Reason exercises its rule because it alone can consider the good, that is what is best, for each of the parts and for the soul as a whole. In so acting, reason exercises its special virtue of wisdom. Thus in exercising its wisdom it rules each of the parts in their and its own interest.[2] It seems that by the end of Book Four what it is for reason to do its job is to exercise both wisdom and rule the soul. If Plato is to avoid violating the principle of specialization to the effect that each one part perform one job, the foregoing suggests that these need not always be separate tasks.

My claim that psychological harmony constitutes happiness is, of course, controversial. According to many, the answer to Glaucon's challenge requires only that the virtues be sufficient for or dominantly contribute to happiness, but not that they be the whole of happiness. Happiness itself has other components, small contributors though they may be, namely other final goods alluded to in the threefold division of goods at 357b–358a.[3] This account relies on what Vlastos labeled the eudaimonist axiom, the idea that all one's rational actions are done for the sake of one's own happiness.[4] In order to reconcile the fact that some of the things we do we do for reasons

---

[2] This rule of reason in virtue of its wise reasoning about the good of each of the parts and the whole soul puts more flesh on Socrates' remarks in the function argument of Book One (353d) that the job of the soul is to care for, to rule, and to deliberate and such, and that since the excellence of soul is justice, the just soul and the just man will live well. It would seem from Book Four that one could be ruling one's lower parts via reason without any theoretical awareness of Forms, since we learn about Forms only in the next books. Ruling the lower parts and theorizing thus seem to be distinct activities.

[3] The role of non-moral goods in the account of happiness harks back to discussions in the Socratic dialogues (e.g., *Euthd.* 278e3–281e5, *Men.* 88e5–d3) of conditional or dependent goods, items such as health or wealth that are good provided that their possessor is virtuous. See Bobonich 2002: 123–215.

[4] Vlastos 1999: 108.

or ends other than the virtues, say for pleasure or health, we could say that pleasure and health become minor constituents of happiness, alongside the dominant virtues. It is also characteristic of this type of account that happiness is a scalar notion. While no two virtuous individuals can differ with respect to their virtuosity, and while no unjust person can be happy, one virtuous person can be happier than another, for instance by having more pleasure: the philosopher off the rack is happier than the one on the rack. Indeed, it is taken to be a virtue (sic) of the account that it comports with this seemingly intuitive assessment.[5] For those of us who identify happiness with the virtues, none of these non-moral goods matters to happiness. Insofar as our knowledge is up to us, our happiness is up to us and does not vary with contingent circumstances. But whether happiness is scalar is separate from the issue of whether non-virtuous goods are to be included in happiness. For while no two philosophers can differ with respect to their virtuosity, many would contend that they can differ in happiness if one has more occasions to contemplate than the other. And this thought is key to those who advocate the flight interpretation of becoming like god. How do we get there?

At the end of Book Four we have yet to learn what it is that reason knows that allows it to unify the soul and how it comes by this knowledge. The third and greatest wave, that philosophers must be rulers and rulers philosophers, addresses this issue. At the end of Book Five (476e–480), Plato distinguishes Forms from the ordinary objects of the material world and their properties, and he sets two powers of reason over these objects. Knowledge is set over the former and is always true; belief is set over the latter and is true and false. The metaphors of Sun, Line, and Cave present a more fine-grained range of objects and powers of the rational soul. The Good has a special place among the objects of knowledge, not least in that only in coming to know the Good can one in the strictest sense have knowledge of the Forms, including Justice and the other virtues.

The objects represented in the analogies of the Line and Cave are comparably easy to characterize and distinguish from one another, with the profound exception of the objects of the sciences, i.e., the objects in the first segment of the intelligible portion of Line assigned to discursive thought or *dianoia*. Harder to understand are the different powers, the transitions between them, and the claim that powers have their own exclusive objects, implying that there is no belief about Forms and no

[5] Most recently, Heinaman 2002: 322, n. 27.

knowledge of the material world.[6] What transformations, reflective or otherwise, take one from belief, or *dianoia*, to knowledge? And once acquired, what does knowledge do to or for your other powers? But more importantly for my purpose, once one has achieved the knowledge envisaged in the metaphors of the central books of the *Republic*, what does one do? On the one hand, it seems that the best activity the philosopher can engage in is to (continue to) exercise *nous*, i.e., theorize or contemplate the Good and the other Forms. There is much to say about what this might mean. To the extent that Knowledge of the Good is the last to be gained, perhaps continuing contemplation is the study of other Forms with the aim of achieving knowledge of the Good. Or, it might be that one can achieve knowledge of the Good prior to knowing all the Forms. Then the philosopher, when continuing in contemplation, will be pursuing knowledge of other Forms. Since this activity makes use of only Forms and arrives at Forms, contemplation is cut off from any this-worldly activity. Yet, Plato seems to maintain here that without knowledge of the Good, one lacks knowledge of any Form (508e–509b, 511, 517b–c). This requires care, lest we end up with the conclusion that the Good must be the Form known first, since it is required in order to know anything. For those who are holists, one comes to know the Good along with and as it were simultaneously with all the Forms.[7] But in this circumstance, the philosopher knows all that there is to know. There is nothing left for him to contemplate. What then does the philosopher do next?[8]

If the matter is viewed in this holistic light, it is difficult to see what is to be gained by advocating a scalar conception of happiness with respect to contemplation. Since there is no more knowledge of more Forms to be

---

[6] A strong reading of this passage maintains that in acting upon and in this material realm, one never exercises knowledge, only *doxa*. A weak(er) reading allows that some kind of knowledge might be available in this world, not least because this seems to best justify why the philosopher is best suited to rule. On either reading, however, the philosopher enjoys much better epistemic conditions than those who lack knowledge. See especially Fine 1999a.

[7] In both the Sun analogy and the Allegory of the Cave, the Form of the Good illuminates the other Forms and thus makes them knowable. Whether they can be known without knowing the Form of the Good is the question. (Compare whether one can be virtuous without knowing the Form of the Good.) In speaking of holists, I have in mind the sponsors of what is sometimes labeled a field theory of knowledge or understanding, where Plato's highest cognitive state requires understanding the relations between the various elements or Forms in a discipline, science, or field (as opposed to an individual Form or proposition). As with all epistemological holisms, one needs a principled way to limit domains or to mark off one science from another. Lacking such a demarcation, Plato's synoptic vision seems inevitably to include every Form in its field, a conclusion a field theorist rightly shrinks from advertising. Holists of varying stripes include Burnyeat 1990, Fine 1979, and Nehamas 1984.

[8] These worries are independent of the special nature of the Good in Plato's theory. That is, the same worries about holism would arise were the One to be the master Form. See Santas 1999.

gained through additional acts of contemplation, one would have to fall back on the idea that since acts of contemplating (apparently the same Field of Forms) are in themselves especially pleasant, additional acts would increase one's happiness by contributing more pleasure. Now, while it is true that Plato finds the satisfaction of rational desires most pleasant, and arguably satisfaction of the desire for knowledge the most pleasant, no such argument is apparent in these central Books. And for good reason: Plato does not advocate climbing out of the Cave in order to secure the greatest pleasure. The flight interpretation founded on contemplation of Forms seems ill suited to the epistemology of the central books.[9]

But the special role of the Good suggests that there is more to worry about than holism. Plato's ontology relies on three distinct but related items: unchanging Forms, the objects of knowledge; physical becoming, the objects of belief and the senses; and rational souls, intermediaries not only capable of grasping the intelligibles but also capable of acting on and bringing about changes in physical becoming, ideally as a response to their understanding of Forms. When it comes to assessing or understanding the very intelligibility of the Forms, and *a fortiori* in assessing what rational minds do in understanding the Forms, modern philosophers, as well as ancient scholars influenced by Aristotle's division of practical from theoretical wisdom, tend to see the relations between Forms primarily in terms of formal relations between concepts or relations between beliefs, or the regulation of beliefs.[10] Here ethical Forms are either ignored, or, while allowed to be central in our considerations of how we are to live or act in the material world in which we live, are accounted for through alternative means, e.g., through a focal analysis or analogically.

For these thinkers, the onus of the distinction between theoretical and practical wisdom falls on those aspects of our lives that involve acting on affairs in this world, and on deliberating about what to do, and perhaps most especially about what to do to achieve what (we take to be) our ends as agents. This wisdom is practical insofar as we aim to bring about changes in others, the physical environment, and ourselves. By contrast, theoretical reason is, *ex hypothesi*, limited to changes in beliefs or other

---

[9] If one can know the Good prior to knowing all the Forms, then one could think that the time spent in contemplation would be devoted to coming to know more Forms. This would be the position most favorable to the flight interpretation. But if one is to secure the grounds for flight, I think that in addition to explaining how isolated knowledge of the Good (or any Form) is possible on Plato's account of the epistemology, one would also have to show that pursuing this kind of additional knowledge is more conducive to doing the good than other activities such as ruling. Defense of this claim is the subject of another work.

[10] An excellent starting point for the differences between practical and theoretical reason is Wallace 2003.

(representational) cognitive states, conceived to be independent of desires, or not concerned with actions or items that can change. On this account of the objects of theoretical science, we do not in any way think about or act on particulars, or particular instances of the properties studied by the sciences. Testing ideas, or collecting data and studying outcomes, seem excluded from theoretical reason's domain, eliminating on the surface at least explanation and prediction as part of theoretical science. Ethical reflection, or the science of ethics, is not conceived to be a theoretical study on this account.

There does seem to be a difference between thinking about objects that can change and thinking about at least some objects that are necessary or unchanging. I am not sure that this is best conceived as the exercise of different kinds of reason, or reason acting or functioning differently, or just reason thinking about different things. It seems as if the basic idea is that something is an act of *theōria* if one is not acting on others, other physical things or oneself, save for the reflective mental activity that is theorizing. In this regard everything other than the activity and object is a distraction. Insofar as our thinking is entirely up to us, we are self-sufficient. Insofar as the objects of *theōria* are not part of the contingent world, our theoretical thinking is impervious to changing circumstances (though of course changes in one's circumstances can, for instance, cause one to desist from theorizing). If thinking about the good requires that one involve oneself in thinking about how to bring about change (for the better), then thinking about the good is not *theōria*.

In my view, the framework of the *Republic* not only resists this demotion, it places the Good (and other ethical Forms) at the heart of the intelligibility of all Forms. This can and has been one reason to try to find an ethically neutral aspect of the Good, roughly by treating it as a Form of Forms. Here, I think, we tend to overlook the role of the soul as mediator between the so-called two worlds, and in particular shrink from embracing the idea that thinking or reasoning is a dynamic process with its own standards and goals, a process that changes with changing circumstances, even while it preserves, to the extent possible, its gains, i.e., whatever knowledge it obtains. Perhaps Aristotle finds coherent a universe of intelligence and intelligible that is static and unchanging, an act or moment of contemplation, the unchanging vision of an unchanging vista. But this does not seem to me to be Plato's picture in the *Republic*, not only because he explicitly promotes the Form of the Good, which is absent from Aristotle's realm of theoretical intelligibles, but because unlike Aristotle's promotion of mathematics and theology to the front ranks of theoretical inquiry, Plato accepts among the Forms the Forms of the Virtues as well as many that pertain to physical becoming (think of collection and division in the *Sophist* and *Statesman*).[11] Moreover, after discussing the five mathematical disciplines in which the twenty-somethings are to be trained, and the requirement that they spend their first five years of graduate school in dialectic, Plato insists that the would-be philosopher spend the next fifteen years in state-administration. This stage is much the longest in the educational cursus and seems inevitably to redirect the synoptic gaze down from the objects of dialectic and the mathematical and astronomical heavens. Plato seems to think that serving in these jobs is in some way conducive to coming to, if not part of, knowledge of the Good.[12]

Finally, Plato assigns to the rational part of the soul an essential desire for the Good,[13] which, as the highest intelligible, may be thought of as the ultimate focus of rational desire. In asking what one does with knowledge of the Good, we might be asking whether the (rational) desire is satisfied with the mere acquisition, desiring perhaps to retain what one has. Rather, I think that Plato's point is that in satisfying the thirst for knowledge we come to desire, in light of our knowledge of the Good (and the satisfaction of our desire), to make more good, though perhaps we can add that in making more good we are satisfying our desire to retain what we have striven to achieve. Insofar as we are thus moved by the Good, given whatever circumstances we find ourselves in, we create or make things good, including in particular making others good.

[11] See especially *Plt.* 258c–e, where Plato divides knowledges into two kinds, the practical, such as carpentry, and the theoretical, such as mathematics. The latter "simply furnish knowledge and do not involve or are bare (ψιλαί) of practical actions." The division in the *Sph.* (265a4–266d7) is between acquisitive and productive (ποιητική) τέχναι. Of course it is a matter of contention whether the epistemology and metaphysics of these late dialogues cohere with the metaphysics and epistemology of the middle-period works.

[12] How are we to think about the objects of the science that they engage in at this stage? Since, in the chronological order of the fantasy, these people will be working with mechanisms of the state created by older philosophers (i.e., the founders), we can speculate that they will spend their time learning first how these mechanisms were designed and why, and then solving the problems that they are designed to address, e.g., court cases, decisions about trade and other relations between the Kallipolis and its neighbors, whatever tax and revenue collection is needed to finance the activities of the military, religious and educational ministries, and overseeing the ministries. To think about the nitty-gritty details might incline one to conceive of the "objects" of this part of one's life as dwelling in the bottom half of the line, as it were, unlike, say, the objects of the sciences studied for the previous ten, which occupy at least the third level. But this I think may not be right. Consider their activities instead as settling disputes and worrying about questions of distributive justice, and finally as learning to deal with the behaviors of the non-philosophical soldiers, educators, and craftsmen. Then, perhaps, we can say that these fifteen years are spent rather in the study of rhetoric, psychology, sociology, and other social sciences.

[13] One might argue that the natural desire of the rational part is not for the Good, but rather is only for knowledge. But insofar as knowledge has Forms for objects, and insofar as the Good has its position as the unhypothetical first principle of the Forms, it would seem that the desire for knowledge leads inevitably to the Good. On reason's desire for knowledge, see Ferrari 2007.

To think that Plato's remarks about Forms and knowledge are consonant with the Aristotelian separation of theoretical reason from practical reason and the flight interpretation seems totally belied by what philosophers actually do in the *Republic*.[14] In the *Republic*, the philosopher (sometimes) goes down to rule. Here the question might be, with what attitude? I have argued elsewhere that the philosopher descends with the aim of making more good, not at the cost of his own happiness, but simply because he has the opportunity of making others better.[15] Knowledge of the Good makes his soul as well-ordered as it can be: thus knowing the Good entails being good. In this manner, Plato affirms the identity of virtue and happiness and rejects the scalar conception of happiness. Once having achieved knowledge of the Good and the other Forms, he is happy. No additional acts, and hence no additional time spent in contemplation, will augment his happiness. In this respect he is "like god," insofar as his happiness is totally up to him and not affectable by contingent or external circumstances. But secondly, it seems that in knowing the Good he desires to create or make more good: thus knowing the Good entails doing good, at least to the extent that the philosopher's reasons for action determine the goodness of his action. Thus, in descending to help others he acts on his contemplative understanding of the Good and the other Forms. (540a–b)

The *Republic*'s Kallipolis and its construction is of course an exercise in utopian thinking. But the very idea that Plato engages in philosophical study of how to bring about an ideal state reinforces the notion that, for him, contemplative understanding of the Good and other Forms does not mean that the philosopher should cut himself off from the world. To the contrary, the moral of the *Republic*, and the message of its central books on happiness, knowledge, and the Good, is that philosophical understanding drives one not only to seek outlets for using one's knowledge of the Good to bring about more good for others and oneself, but also to turn again and again to the physical cosmos to further investigate and learn from in order to expand one's understanding of the Forms. Far from isolating oneself from this world, the *Republic* teaches that philosophical understanding, whose presence secures one's own happiness, leads one not only to practical activity, but to the further study of behaviors and conditions in the polis with the aim of furthering one's efforts to make more good.

---

[14] It seems equally belied by what Plato is doing both in writing the *Republic* in the manner that he does and in general his writing and teaching. They are designed to bring about change in the reader, or at least some of the readers, whether or not the writing of dialogues is best viewed as an exercise in theoretical reasoning or as part of a process leading to *theōria*.

[15] Silverman 2007.

Now, did time permit, I would argue that the late dialogues of Plato are focused on the study of matters in the physical and social world as a part of his efforts to do philosophy, both ethics (the *Philebus*), epistemology (the *Theaetetus*), political philosophy (*Statesman* and *Laws*), metaphysics and the philosophy of language (the *Sophist*), and natural philosophy (the *Timaeus*). Since this last work has been one impetus behind the flight interpretation of the doctrine of becoming like God, let me look briefly at Plato's cosmological treatise.

Generally speaking, I take it that the *Timaeus* does not simply present a Craftsman whose making of the world is designed to offer us insight into the metaphysical structure of the cosmos. Even more important is its lesson in soul construction, where the "craftsman-like" activities of the Demiurge in fashioning the cosmos according to a pattern is the model for our own activity of fashioning our souls in the appropriate way. That is, the Demiurge is the "Form" on which we are to model our own souls. The realm of Forms itself has a structure and hence so too does the cosmos, and this structure is to be viewed by us as a system of truths, including primarily what might be best thought of as practical truths that guide (practical) wisdom in the fashioning of raw materials to serve a purpose, namely the filling out of the parts of the cosmos. Insofar as these truths and this structure are designed by Plato for the sake of instruction, we in turn can take the moral to be that we are to emulate or imitate the Demiurge insofar as we are to discover practical truths as to how we ought to live, and thus that we are to treat the "raw materials" of everyday becoming as well as our souls themselves as instrumentalities in the craft of living, i.e., as material for living well.

This decidedly practical reading of the Demiurge and the moral of the *Timaeus* is at odds with the Plotinian or flight interpretation, as presented by Sedley.[16] On this account, the aim of the philosopher is "a purely intellectual assimilation to a higher being. The moral virtues are a mere political expedient in the interests of a well-run society."[17] For Sedley, Plato wants to claim that our true self or our truest self is the rational soul, not the tripartite soul of which it is a part working in harmony: we are to identify ourselves with this rational part alone.[18] The argument of the

---

[16] Sedley 1999.

[17] Ibid. 322. This reading gains some support from remarks within the *Republic* itself, both at 518d–e and in the discussion of the demotic virtues at 500d.

[18] Compare Waterlow 1972–73 and Korsgaard 1999 on identifying with reason and identifying with the constitution ruled by reason. A crucial difference between Korsgaard and Waterlow (and others) is that Korsgaard's agent identifies not with reason but "with her constitution, and it says that

Timaeus isolates as the locus the rational soul or the circular motions which share a likeness with the motions of the world-soul with which they are kindred. The goal of each of us is to return these motions to their natural courses.

Now for everybody there is one way to care for every part, and that is to grant to each part its proper nourishments and motions. For the divine element in us, the motions which are akin to it are the thoughts and the revolutions of the whole world. Everyone should take a lead from these. We should correct the corrupted revolutions in our head concerned with becoming, by learning the harmonies and revolutions of the whole world, and so make the thinking subject resemble the object of its thought, in accordance with its ancient nature; and, by creating this resemblance, bring to fulfillment (*telos*) the best life offered by the gods to mankind for present and future time. (*Tim.* 90c–d)

Let me make three remarks on this passage. First, if we are to return our rational motions to their proper course, the clear message is that we should concern ourselves not with becoming, but with other better matters. Genesis here is not birth, but the realm of becoming. This echoes the theme laid down at the outset by Timaeus that the Demiurge's model was something that is, not something that has come to be (*Tim.* 28a–b). Emulating him in this regard by looking at something that is restores our rational motions. But this can be read in two ways. The Plotinian treats it as a blanket prohibition: neither the would-be philosopher, nor one who has resettled the circles of his soul, is at any time to concern himself with becoming. Thus, even after order has been restored, the philosopher would still dissociate from becoming, whether because of the threat of disturbing his soul, or because he is drawn to the more attractive study of what is. But it can also be seen as a recommendation to the aspiring philosopher to fix his attention on the Forms and the principles of the Demiurgic construction of the cosmos. Only by turning away from becoming to face a different direction can we become happy. But this implies nothing about our actions or interests, once we have achieved knowledge of the Good. It is open what we then do.

Second, the *Timaeus* encourages the philosopher/physicist to study astronomy and to seek to understand the mathematical physics that lies behind the cosmic cyclical motions in order to correct the circular motions in his/her soul.[19] But these heavenly orbits, admittedly the best part of

---

reason should rule" (Korsgaard 1999: 15). Compare Waterlow: "For while Plato fully acknowledges the conceptual priority of agent to actions, there is for him something prior again to the agent, namely reason itself" (Waterlow 1972–73: 36).

[19] Indeed the circular motions of the heavens seem to exert an almost attractive force on the motions of reason, causing them to move in a manner more similar to the cosmic motions, i.e., more cyclically.

the cosmos, are still part of what is created. It is doubtful that we are to stop with these cosmic motions. For instance, there is the object that is the model for the cosmos. Now the end point of this line of reasoning is to understand not just the nature of the model that always is, but also the creative and reflective activities of the Demiurge in using or working from this model. In short, the restored circular motions of reason think about the whole of the cosmos and the principles of its construction.[20]

Third, Sedley infers from his reading that "What we are urged to share with the world soul, then, does not include practical reasoning."[21] The implicit assumption is that when we are concerned with becoming in any form, we are engaged in practical reasoning. Now the very enterprise Timaeus and company are engaged in, namely physics, is concerned with becoming. We can wonder whether the *eikōs mythos* that is Timaeus' account is itself a bit of practical reasoning,[22] and hence not something that Plato would have us engage in at any point. Or we can view the relation between physics and philosophy differently, allowing one to be a part of the other once we are properly appreciative of the nature of the model and the Demiurge's activity. In this case, not only will there be a difference in our practical reasoning, since we are better informed about the nature of the cosmos and its constituents with which we interact everyday, but we will continue to study the physics of the cosmos in order to better understand the nature of the model and the Demiurgic activity.

Among the many conditions Plato lays down for understanding his physics, let me draw attention to two. First, whatever approach we take to the teleology, there is an element of necessity or contingency that is not under the control of intelligence in the physical system, i.e., in the cosmos. Along with the Forms, we have to account for this in our physics and therefore in thinking about how to live our lives. A second constraint flows from the nature of the Demiurge, namely that he is good and that he creates. Let me pause for a moment on both. That he might not create is not a possibility entertained by Plato. But in a logical sense perhaps, can one not ask whether it is possible for the Demiurge not to bring the cosmos into being? Here we might think through some scenarios having to do with the recalcitrance of the material to yield to his persuasion, or complex systems tending to have some incompatible demands or virtues, or what have you. But I don't mean this. These seem to me challenges he can overcome or recognize, should he act on his desire to create. I am worried about the question of whether the Demiurge could simply not act – is that possible for the Demiurge? Plato suggests that it is not. "Now

---

[20] Nightingale 2004.   [21] Sedley 1999: 323.   [22] Burnyeat 2005.

why did he who framed this whole universe of becoming frame it? Let us state the reason why: He was good, and one who is good can never become jealous of anything. And so, being free of jealousy, he wanted everything to become as much like himself as was possible" (*Tim.* 29e). Whatever the logical possibility, Plato's demiurge must act, that is create, because he is good, and he does so ungrudgingly, fulfilling the rational desire to bring order, beauty, and goodness to his creation.

We might then ask whether we are to think of him as antecedently or afterwards aware that the outcome of his creation is something good but not completely good, not completely under his control, i.e., that there is some random factor that makes contingency ineliminable from the world. The answer to this again seems to me to be yes. So, the constraint is that the Demiurge acts, for the sake of the good, to bring about the physical cosmos, which he understands will include randomness, the precise occurrences of which he will not be able to anticipate. Insofar as we imitate the Demiurge, we know all this too. Thus when we consider what we are to do, we are entitled to think that when we act we should act with the same expectations and aims, namely for the best, knowing that we cannot press this all the way down. However, when we come to deal with the contingent and random, as surely we will, we are now equipped to understand how it arises from the ordered and what means, physically I mean, are available to us to bring order to our cosmos.

The foregoing only scratches the surface of a number of issues pertaining to what might be thought of as the *Republic*'s "way down" the divided line and the transformations of the rational as well as the other parts of the soul effected by coming to know the good. One critical issue is whether the ruler can now be said to know things about the physical world, and whether the form such knowledge takes is the same as the knowledge of the Forms. Nevertheless, it would seem from our reflections on the *Timaeus* and Demiurgic activity that the mere fact that one's reason, once informed by knowledge of the Good and the other Forms, is directed at contingent affairs is no reason (pun intended) to think that some kind of knowledge with a distinctive structure is at work. If I am right that Plato never intends us to hive off the practical from our model divine mind, it is because he is committed to the thesis that knowing the good entails not only being good, and being imperviously happy, it also entails doing good, in whatever circumstances one finds oneself in, to the extent that doing good is possible. By such an exercise of reason, one models oneself on the divine mind.

When we turn to Aristotle, matters are much more complicated. As so often in Aristotle studies, both developmental issues and the Stagirite's dialectical or aporematic method complicate our assessment of his so-called position. From what we can tell from the *Protrepticus*, at a relatively early stage in his thinking Aristotle does not distinguish *theōria* from the exercise of *phronēsis*.[23] When we consider why Aristotle eventually splits from Plato – when he looks for a distinctive excellence of *to doxastikon*, the faculty responsible for beliefs, that qualifies as *phronēsis* as opposed to *doxa* – a typical explanation is that the objects differ, namely, changeable contingent objects versus unchanging objects. But this doesn't quite capture the thrust of Aristotle's division. Consider Richard Kraut's opening line in his *Stanford Encyclopedia of Philosophy* article on Aristotle's Ethics: "Aristotle conceives of ethical theory as a field distinct from the theoretical sciences. Its methodology must match its subject matter – good action – and must respect the fact that in this field many generalizations hold only for the most part."[24] He adds shortly thereafter that: "[H]e rejects Plato's idea that a training in the sciences and metaphysics is a necessary prerequisite for a *full* understanding of our good" (italics mine). Aristotle is not entirely consistent in his description of the theoretical sciences.[25] On the one hand, we find three different ways of being, assignable respectively to sensible substances, mathematical substances, and divine substances. If there are beings of all three kinds, the sensible and mathematical substances form a hierarchical structure focused on the way of being enjoyed by divine substances. On the other hand, we have the scientific disciplines that treat each of these ways of being: physics, general mathematics, and metaphysics. The substances of which they treat are differentiated principally in terms of being separate or not and being changeable or not. Each of these disciplines is theoretical and each in turn stands at the apex of a hierarchical structure. If one wants to further subdivide these theoretical sciences, the argument of the *Metaphysics*, as I understand it, ultimately dictates that one isolate the different ways that actuality is expressed or realized by the different kinds of beings in each general science. Thus one can perhaps hive off from the sciences theology, mathematics, and astronomy, whose beings are either immaterial, abstract, or superlunary, and thus express actuality in a purer way than any sensible substance.[26] And in this respect one can think that what holds of necessity is somehow more a mark of mathematical and divine beings than of sensible beings. That leaves us with the theoretical science of physics and its "subdisciplines" such as biology

---

[23] Jaeger's 1962, *Appendix Two*, is the classic account.   [24] Kraut 2001.
[25] E.g., *Metaph.* 7. 1. 1025^{b}3–1026^{a}33, *Top.* 6. 6. 145^{a}15–18; *Metaph.* 11. 7. 1064^{a}16–19, *EN* 6. 2. 1139^{a}26–28.
[26] *Metaph.* 6. 1. and 2.

and psychology, where in the study of sensible substance we will have to isolate matter, substantial form, and the composite of matter and form. All these sciences have a similar structure and their first principles involve definitions of the species and genera that are their subject matter. Here again we seem to have a focus, namely substantial form, i.e., soul, for it is the appropriate focus if we are to understand in which sense the being and actuality of sensible substances are related to and dependent on the being and actuality of divine substances. Now it would take a different essay to address the ways in which contingency, holding "for the most part," and necessity play out in Aristotle's analysis of matter, sensible composites, and soul. But suffice it to say that insofar as physics is theoretical science, and to the extent that a theoretical science studies what holds of necessity, or necessary beings, then there are grounds for thinking that biology and psychology are also somehow theoretical sciences and deal with what holds of necessity. In turn, I submit that if ethics is a science, and if ethics at a minimum must concern itself with biology and psychology, then it too is in some sense a theoretical science, even if a less precise one, i.e., despite the fact that its subject matter in some manner holds only for the most part or is somehow contingent. More specifically, and somewhat dogmatically, the key to understanding the peculiar way in which the substantial forms of sensible substances, i.e. souls, relate to the separate (divine) substances is to recognize that though identical with its essence and an actuality, the form of a sensible substance involves potentiality. This is because it is realized in matter and, perhaps more crucially, essentially contains an element of potentiality in that (a) not all the activities of life for which it is responsible are exercised all the time and (b) some of the activities of which the soul is capable are acquired. Divine substance in no way involves potentiality, but rather is pure actuality. To return to the opening lines of Kraut's entry: it is hard to know what the force of training in the sciences amounts to, but, on the face of it, the nature of the prime mover is a subject studied by metaphysics and the sciences. And if our good is implicated with the pure activity of the prime mover, then while some understanding of our good is perhaps possible without them, a *full* understanding would seem to require metaphysics and the sciences.

Each of these three aspects of potentiality implicates contingency in a manner relevant to ethical theory. Because our soul is realized in matter, ethics must concern itself with both material goods and ethical virtues. Because all life activities are not exercised all the time we must choose between them and decide when to exercise those activities of which we are currently capable. Because some activities are acquired, we must determine which of them to pursue and how we might acquire those we wish to pursue. Thus all these seem to involve choices and actions, leading to the canonical understanding of ethics as a practical science. But the foregoing suggests that the mesh of practical science and theoretical science is hard to determine. It is possible to see the prospects for tension in Aristotle's general teleological account of the idea of the human good at the outset of the *Nicomachean Ethics*. It is that end for the sake of which all our rational endeavors aim. As Gavin Lawrence puts it:

The human good so understood is thus also a principle, a focus, of organization: all other ends we rationally pursue are organized focally, in some way or another, e.g. constitutively or instrumentally, around this highest humanly attainable good. And as the greatest humanly attainable good, it is the formal object of practical rationality, both to define or specify, and to secure: for it would be irrational to aim at less than the greatest practicable good – a *grammatical* remark that expresses a constitutive principle of practical rationality.[27]

The *Nicomachean Ethics* is designed to aid the well-educated but not yet virtuous individual in achieving the highest attainable human good. Since it engages the youth who not only has yet to achieve full rationality, but also is still trying to understand what factors should go into securing and organizing one's life around whatever turns out to be the highest good, it is aimed at the capacity of practical reason, for that is in fact the kind of reason which is exercised by the youth seeking instruction at this juncture of his life in matters of this sort, regardless of whether he is aware of the kind of reason he is exercising. But the determination of this higher good is, I think, a different matter. This seems clearly the product of either theoretical rationality or whatever rationality is at work in the study of metaphysics or psychology (or at least not successfully concluded without bringing to bear the fruits of those inquiries). While the writer of the treatise has determined that *theōria* is that highest attainable good, the fact that Aristotle delays for almost ten books its explicit elevation signals that it will not be initially well received or fully understood by the student.

The good at which we aim has conditions, which are arrived at by some act of reason reflecting on its own nature and situation, as well as possible situations through which it might or must navigate. For Aristotle two conditions are paramount, unconditional finality and self-sufficiency. Especially because of worries over unconditionality, both these conditions are fraught with ambiguity and controversy. While it seems clear that as "final" the human good must be an end not simply for a further end, it

---

[27] Lawrence 2006: 1.

is argued that as unqualifiedly final, it must be an end that doesn't lead to any other ends beyond itself. The problem here is how to think about what the "itself" is beyond which there can't be an end. Consider again the Demiurge acting without jealousy – is the world he creates an end beyond the Demiurge himself? It is, I think, another thing, for he brings it into to being, but it is, *ex hypothesi*, another good (thing). So, in some sense being perfectly good and bringing about another albeit less perfect good might be thought not to be beyond itself. In the case of the prime mover, there seems to be an analogous situation with respect to his thinking of the substantial forms bringing them into actuality. And this is the same problematic for unconditional goodness or reason acting in full knowledge of the good: it doesn't act in order to create more good for itself, though its actions lead to a good and its purpose is to lead to that good. We may say that it is expressing its goodness, though this third or second person account is not reason's – it does not act in order to express its goodness, it acts simply to create more goodness. As final, the activity must also be an end "for its own sake." That is, it must not have the conceptual structure of a process, but be an activity that has its end in itself, and so, conceptually, can be engaged in *ad infinitum*. This, again, makes for difficulty in assessing whether our reason can be held to the same standards as divine reason.[28] While the *Metaphysics* perhaps drives us to think that any activity can, considered in its own right, be engaged in *ad infinitum*, all the work is being done by the phrase "considered in its own right," where we conceptually abstract away all the conditions for, or that surround, the activity. Indeed, we have here an argument for activity that precisely parallels the argument of *Metaph.* 7. 3 against matter as substance – there may well be only one activity that can be metaphysically engaged in *ad infinitum*. Viewing our reason in this manner would be a mistake, however, and would confuse what one could plan and deliberate for with what one might wish – though I suspect that no one would wish it for himself.

The dialectic of self-sufficiency plays out in a similar fashion. The practical good must by itself make life worthwhile. If we had only it, we would be happy. This then works itself into the thought that our practical good is what it is independent of everything else, that it finally can only be invulnerable to circumstance if it is entirely up to us as creatures with minds.

---

[28] In the *Timaeus* (35a–b), the mixture of divided and undivided being, sameness and difference, somehow is degraded by the time the Demiurge mixes the ingredients that will serve as the rational element in our souls.

This raises the question of what exactly it would mean for practical reason to determine and organize one's life around *theōria* as the final, unconditional good. Let me begin by remarking that I do not think we know what contemplation is for Aristotle. One set of problems arises from the *Nicomachean Ethics* and especially the tenth book, where we are compelled to adjudicate the relation of practical reason to theoretical reason, and in turn the relation of the life of political virtue to the life of intellectual virtue. A second set of problems arises from Aristotle's remarks in the *Physics*, *De anima*, and *Metaphysics* about the character of divine contemplation.[29] Of course the two are related, in so far as Aristotle insists that we are to liken ourselves to this divine activity:

> If intellect is divine, then, in comparison with man, the life lived according to it is divine in comparison with a human life. But we must not follow those who advise us, being men, to think of human things, and being mortal, of mortal things, but must, so far as we can, make ourselves immortal, and strain every nerve to live in accordance with the best thing in us . . . (*EN* 10. 1077^{b}30–34)

All the divine does is contemplate.[30] It does so continuously because, metaphysically and epistemologically speaking, the argument of the *Metaphysics* and *De Anima* leads to the thesis that the divine is an unchanging, immaterial intellect, a being which, lacking any matter and (hence) any possibility of potentiality, cannot act otherwise, and which "can in no way be otherwise than as it is" (*Metaph.* 12. 7 1072^{b}8). It does not, then, choose to contemplate. Moreover, the life of the prime mover is most pleasant (*hēdiston, Metaph.* 12. 7 1072^{b}24). Its extraordinary pleasantness is a function of, on the one hand, the relation of the object of thought to a rational desire, and, on the other hand, the relation of pleasure to activities or actualities. Rational intellects desire to think what they deem to be their best objects and in actually thinking the object of their desire they are pleased. The divine intellect, however, has all along achieved its aim of thinking whatever are the objects of its thought. In this respect then its desire is "always already fulfilled."[31] Finally, the objects of the thinking of the divine intellect are all the immaterial essences; it thinks all these

---

[29] *Ph.* 8. 5–10, *De An.* 3. 4–5, *Metaph.* 12. 6–10.

[30] In the next chapter (8) Aristotle reiterates the contrast between the moral excellences and theoretical excellence: that complete happiness is a contemplative activity appears from the consideration that the gods are most blessed and happy and yet that we can assign to them no acts of moral virtue – they are not generous or brave or just. "If we were to run through them all, the circumstances of action would be found trivial and unworthy of gods. Still, everyone supposes that they live and therefore that they are active. . . . Now if you take away from a living being action, and still more production, what is left but contemplation?" (1178b8–24).

[31] Frede 2002: 39.

immaterial essences at once. These essences are themselves ones (unities) and the thought of the divine intellect in thinking all the immaterial essences that are the objects of its thoughts is a unity and is indivisible (*DA* 3. 6, *Metaph.* 9. 9 1051^{b}26; 12. 9 1075^{a}5–11). The thought or thinking of the divine intellect is, then, identical with these essences. So how are we supposed to understand Aristotle's recommendation that we liken ourselves, or our reason, to this? First, note that its life is such as the best we experience for a short while: I take the "such" (οἴα) to indicate that our contemplation is not even for a short while the same as god's (*Metaph.* 12. 7 1072^{b}14–16). If we consider each of the three features discussed above – choice, desire, and the continuity and indivisibility – none of them strictly speaking can be a feature of our intellects or lives. As Aristotle notes, we cannot contemplate continuously. Nor (thus) can we think of ourselves as something that can be in no way otherwise than it is. Finally, for creatures like us, the nature of desire is bound up with lack. We desire what we may not yet have and we desire to retain what we do have.

Nonetheless, the argument of the *Nicomachean Ethics* compels us to consider the relation of our life to the divine life and the relation of our intellect to God's. A crucial question seems to be how we are to think of the "perfect or best life" that is promulgated as the highest good aimed at by all of our "prohairetic" or chosen rational actions. According to one reading, we are to evaluate what is the best life by comparing the lives of all species and rational beings, including god. On this scale, the human life, or rather the human condition, will be considered a defect that an individual can suffer. Others think that that is not the right way to think about which life is best. The question concerns lives that are, as we might say, real options for us. Living the life of another species is not a real option. The task is to figure out within the human condition what is the best possible life.[32]

But this too is problematic. It seems at times that Aristotle thinks of lives in such a way that they are composed, if you will, of activities or actions, with the result that one candidate for the best possible life would be the life that contains the greatest number of acts of contemplation. On this aggregative reading, in any choice situation where one alternative is to contemplate and the other alternative is not, i.e., is merely a morally virtuous action, one always will choose to contemplate, since contemplation is, *ex argumentis*, the best possible act. We thereby imitate the continuousness of divine contemplation by doing it whenever we can.

---

[32] Lawrence's 2006 discussion is the best work on this topic.

There is another way to consider the best life, what Lawrence calls the utopian target. It is, I think, especially relevant to our Platonic problem. Grant that the target is the greatest good obtainable or the best or perfect human life. In one sense to live that life is to have the correct values and correctly to bring them to bear so as to do what is called for, or what is best, in the situation. So doing, people will do nothing they regret. But the situations they face may be defective, even tragic ones, involving circumstances which rightly they would rather had not arisen in the first place. In another sense a person lives a perfect life only if they do the above and the situations that arise for them are not defective but are the optimal ones for a human being. The target here is the best life a human can enjoy in the optimal circumstances for a human – the best that is ever available. As practically rational agents, we have both targets or ideals. We aim to live the best life we can in the circumstances that life presents us, whatever these are; and we aim that life should present us with the best possible circumstances. This is the utopian target. And this latter constitutes the norm, or measure, of unqualified success and defectiveness in human life.[33]

Maybe we wish or hope that life should present us with the best possible circumstances. But insofar as we aim that life present us with these utopian circumstances, I think Lawrence's second aim is wrapped up in his first. To aim to do the best in the circumstances life presents will often include aiming to change the circumstances for the better. But I don't think we "aim" that life (passively) presents us even with non-tragic circumstances let alone with the best possible circumstances. Lawrence's worry seems to be that sometimes we do find ourselves in defective and tragic circumstances and we recognize that it would have been better had it not turned out so. Reflecting on this situation, Lawrence seems to suggest, we might conclude not only that there is something like a life that is free of (the possibility of) any tragic circumstances, but even that the best life ever would be a life that is composed of perfect circumstances. Perfect circumstances in what sense? Well, first, since the problem is that the human condition is such that we often find ourselves having to deal with situations where bad things happen, we try to minimize our exposure to others, including circumstances that would call upon our moral virtues and practical wisdom. Similarly, since the best activity we can engage in is contemplation, we think the perfect life would be the life containing the most opportunities for contemplation.

---

[33] This paraphrase derives from private conversation with Gavin Lawrence, Lawrence 2006, and his unpublished works.

So, the life we aim at is the life of leisure, understood to be a life of disengagement from the everyday and filled with what is apparently the most leisurely of activities, philosophy.

Once more we find ourselves in circumstances of flight or conflict with our this-worldly existence. The imperfection is not in comparison to another species' kind of life; it is an imperfection within any human life that is lived with others. For the optimal life, on this reading, in effect would be one that yields as much leisure as possible as early as possible. It seems to entail that, in any choice situation, we will contemplate, and the maximal number of such situations would constitute the optimal life for a human, a life in which we need to do as little as possible so that we may at our leisure engage in philosophy. Moreover, on this view of the optimal life or the utopian target, we still labor under the difficulty of reconciling Book 10.6–8 with the rest of the *Nicomachean Ethics*, or broadly speaking of showing how theoretical virtue can be distinct from and yet be the aim of practical reason. No practical action can count as theoretical or contemplative, no act of contemplation can have any effect on this world.

Ultimately, ethically virtuous action requires *phronēsis*, the excellence of the doxastic capacity involving a perceptual sensitivity to the circumstances surrounding one's choice about what to do that is manifested in a particular judgment. This particularist excellence provides a contrast with theoretical reason, which, at least in its divine incarnation, is seemingly universal through and through. If such is the nature of practical reason, if it yearns for change as it were, it would seem that static contemplation would be off-putting, i.e., that once achieved, practical reason would recoil and seek new outlets for action. The relation of practical reason to contemplative activity is, to be sure, a matter of controversy. If *theōria* is the ultimate end of practical reason, then in some sense practical reason sets as its end something beyond itself, something it cannot experience. Of course one can learn from others that *theōria* is the best condition and thus set one's course of life to put oneself in a position to achieve it; but it would seem that unless one actually engages in theoretical contemplation, then one at best knows that but not why *theōria* is best. This begs the question of whether one can actually be a *phronimos* without being a *theōrētikos*. We are back to Plato versus Aristotle: is training in the sciences and metaphysics a necessary prerequisite for a *full* understanding of our good?

Undoubtedly, the next round of inquiry into this question would take us deeper into Aristotle's teleology and his differences, if any, from Plato. For while one might be able to think theoretically about the objects of mathematics without engaging desire, a key difference might depend on whether one would be able to think the Good, or about god, without engaging desire, or at least the same kind of desire that is engaged when one is thinking about one's own good or a good achievable by you, i.e., something that you can bring about. In the end, I suspect that the difference between them boils down to a difference in their models for a divine mind. Aristotle's account of the divine mind seems in the last analysis driven more by his account of actuality in the *Physics* and *Metaphysics*. Plato's model derives from reflection about our own mind. Contrary, then, to common belief, Aristotle's division of practical from theoretical reason directs our gaze to a world that is alien and beyond our ken. It is Plato who reminds us that we must come back down once we discover that the divine mind is no different from our own.[34]

[34] I would like to thank the audience at the 2007 Models of Mind Conference at Berkeley for their questions and comments, especially those of my commentator, G. R. F. Ferrari. To the organizers of the conference and editors of this volume I owe a special debt.

CHAPTER 6

Aristotle and the history of skepticism
Alan Code

In affectionate appreciation of my dear friend and colleague,
Tony Long.

PUZZLES AND THE SEARCH FOR KNOWLEDGE

In the interest of furthering our understanding of Aristotle's place in the
history of skepticism, A. A. Long has urged that Aristotle left to posterity
a methodology that takes certain skeptical strategies that could be used to
present challenges to claims to knowledge and employs them instead in aid
of maintaining a search for knowledge.[1] In the course of illustrating and
defending this conclusion in his article "Aristotle and the History of Greek
Skepticism", he lucidly highlights a number of respects in which Aristotle's
methodological discussions reveal an awareness of the usefulness for his
own purposes of argumentative ploys that in some form or other play a
role in the skeptic's arsenal. Aristotle in fact does exhibit an awareness of
the need to answer on behalf of his epistemology a variety of objections
that would, if successful, undermine the possibility of knowledge as he
conceived of it. In this essay I discuss some of these strategies as well as
the general shape of his attitude towards the use of puzzles in philosophy.
My focus will not be so much on the interpretation of particular texts
as on the general epistemological stance that Aristotle takes on this issue,
and accordingly I have tried to avoid matters of scholarly controversy to
the extent that they do not impact very general methodological points.
In particular, I wish to highlight his firm rejection of the requirement
that knowledge always be backed up with proof or demonstration and to
connect it with the view that puzzles are not an obstacle or impediment to
the search for principles. Puzzles about some subject matter do not always

---

[1] Long 1981: 105.

97

have to be solved before principles are established,[2] and in cases where puzzles have led some to deny or question something Aristotle takes to be a principle he sees opportunities to give helpful diagnoses of their errors and persuade them of the truth.

Towards the beginning of his seminal article, Long schematically compares a skeptical with an Aristotelian attitude towards the role of puzzles, or *aporiai*, in philosophical inquiry. Although puzzles play a crucial role both in the account that Sextus Empiricus gives of the origin of skepticism and in Aristotle's own treatment of philosophical methodology in his *Metaphysics*, Aristotle's attitude towards them is strikingly different from that exemplified in the various forms of ancient skepticism. For Aristotle the statement and subsequent elaboration of puzzles puts one in a better position to discover the truth. One role of this kind of examination is, in Long's words, that it "exposes the problems to be considered and provides possible material for their solution."[3] When discussing the need for an examination of puzzles as a preliminary to investigation, *Metaphysics* 3.1 tells us that somebody who has not first explored the puzzles is like a traveler who sets out on a journey without knowing their destination.[4] Puzzles can help structure an inquiry, and familiarity with them makes one a better judge of the truth.[5] Far from being an impediment to knowledge, the puzzles make clear a goal or destination for philosophical inquiry. Going through puzzles puts one in a better position to know that one has found the truth about some matter.[6]

By way of sharp contrast, the examination of puzzles leads to suspension of judgment for the proto-skeptic as described by Sextus. The proto-skeptics initially proceeded to examine the puzzles in an attempt to determine what is true and what is false, and did so with the goal of ceasing to be troubled as to what they ought to give their approval to. One striking observation that Long has made about this is that as described so far this account could almost be borrowed from Aristotle.[7] However, Long further explains that the attempts to settle the discrepancies led the proto-skeptic to the original goal in a completely unexpected way. The attempt to find a

---

[2] In some cases he will urge that a rival view makes a puzzle on some central issue irresoluble, whereas given his own distinctions and positive views there is no longer a problem. Such is his attitude about the unity of definable objects (*Metaph.* 8.6.1045[a]20–25). Although he seems to arrive at the views that solve the puzzle independently of considerations about the puzzle, their ability to solve it is a point in its favor.

[3] Long 1981: 84. As we shall see, they can also provide a clarificatory function after positive results have been obtained.

[4] *Metaph.* 3.1.995[a]34–36.   [5] *Metaph.* 3.1.995[b]2–4.   [6] *Metaph.* 3.1.995[a]36–b2.

[7] However, as will be shown below in connection with a puzzle about change from the *Physics*, for Aristotle the treatment of a puzzle can come after the truth has already been ascertained.

criterion to settle the puzzling issues did not for them in fact end up with a criterion, but rather led to the conflicting opinions having equal weight, and from there led to a suspension of judgment. Without now pausing to consider the nuances of this account, it is enough for his point that the described result of the proto-skeptic's examination of puzzles is suspension of judgment. Sextus is clearly not describing somebody who has been put in a better position to decide or judge which opinions are true, and is not describing a methodology that succeeds in reaching knowledge.

DEMONSTRATIVE KNOWLEDGE AND THE NEED FOR PRINCIPLES

In connection with "the material which forms the basis of the Pyrrhonist's *tropoi* or 'modes' for suspending of judgment,"[8] Long calls attention to the fact that Aristotle shows familiarity with argumentative strategies that later turn up in the five modes of Agrippa. In particular, he finds Aristotle to be anticipating and responding to the second, fourth, and fifth of these Pyrrhonist strategies in his attempts to avoid the charges that demonstrative knowledge is vitiated by *infinite regress* or by the use of *hypothetical premises* that themselves are not known, or is possible only on the condition that *circular proof* be allowed. Additionally, Aristotle is aware of the polemical use to which the modes invoking either *diaphonia* (irresoluble conflict) or relativity, the first and third modes of Agrippa, can be put. Thus all five of these general strategies play some kind of role in Aristotle's attempts to establish epistemological theses of his own.

A form of knowledge that was of particular importance and interest to Aristotle was demonstrative knowledge. Such knowledge is restricted to necessary truths, and is arrived at by deducing conclusions from immediate truths that are themselves in need of no further explanation. For Aristotle the scientific inquiry that leads to the resolution of perplexity and puzzlement is preeminently a search for such explanatory principles, or starting points of knowledge. All theoretical understanding proceeds rigorously from indemonstrable first principles. General truths can be known and understood by tracing observable facts and features of the world all the way back to their explanatory sources, and then locating eternal and unchanging truths in their proper place in an axiomatic structure. Aristotle conceives of demonstrative knowledge as requiring syllogistic proofs that use as premises principles that are "true and primitive and immediate and more familiar than and prior to and explanatory of the conclusion."[9] The idea here is to analyze a scientific demonstration as a syllogism (or

---

[8] Long 1981: 85.   [9] *APo.* 1.2.71^{b}21–22. All translations are from Barnes (1984).

string of syllogisms) in which every premise is either an indemonstrable first principle or is itself proven.

Although conclusions will themselves be true if the argument is valid and the premises true, more than these two features are required for genuine demonstration. Among other things, a proof must proceed from principles, and Aristotle thinks that the first principles of a science must not themselves be in need of proof or explanation. Accordingly, he rejects the thesis that all things knowable must be demonstrated, and insists that scientific proof ultimately proceeds from indemonstrable starting points. In rejecting the thesis that everything knowable must be proven he commits himself to the view that some principles are known without proof, and charges those who do not understand which propositions do not require demonstration with a lack of education.[10] Not everything has or requires an explanatory account, and it is improper to look for such an account where none can be given. Indeed, he goes so far as to claim that the very people who make this kind of unreasonable demand show by their actions that they are not really convinced of their own thesis.[11] His claim that principles are known without demonstration is neither itself a principle nor something that he proves, but rather something he takes to be embodied in the attitude of all who engage in epistemological discussion.

It is at this point that we reach a claim that is crucial to Aristotle's own response to a variety of attacks on his version of a foundationalist epistemology. The resolution of puzzlement and the discernment of scientific truth requires that there are principles that are not known by deducing them from something else, but rather are immediately known in a non-deductive manner. The first principles are not known through demonstration, but rather are known in a better way than the scientific theorems that they explain. He says that they are the objects of *nous*, or "intellect," rather than demonstrative knowledge.[12] The kind of knowledge that we have of principles is superior to demonstrative knowledge. As we will see, Aristotle explicitly considers challenges to this picture mounted by those who would insist – contrary to what he himself believes – that all knowledge is demonstrative. If this opposing view were correct, then there would be no such thing as *immediate* knowledge of principles.

[10] *Metaph.* 4.4.1006^{a}5–6.
[11] *Metaph.* 4.6.1011^{a}8–13. Exactly which aspects of their behavior he has in mind is not specified.
[12] *APo.* 2.19.100^{b}5–15, esp. 12.

In the *Posterior Analytics* Aristotle considers two different kinds of opponent to the type of epistemological foundationalism that this treatise
presents and endorses.[13] As Aristotle puts it,[14] "some think that because
one must understand the primitives there is no understanding at all"; alternatively, the necessity of knowing the primary things has made some people
think that it does exist "but that there are demonstrations of everything."
Both types of opponent share in common the un-Aristotelian assumption that all knowledge is demonstrative, but they differ as to whether
knowledge is possible.

The opponents from Party One assume the following disjunction: either
there is an infinite regress of demonstrations or demonstration depends
upon undemonstrated premises. To put it more fully, either the process of
demonstrating the premises by means of new deductions continues without
an end, or at some point the regress of deductions comes to a halt, and there
is a deduction that uses a premise that is not itself demonstrated. Since this
opponent is assuming that all knowledge is demonstrative, this leads to
the conclusion that knowledge is not possible. In Long's words "either the
move from the posterior to the prior is an infinite or a finite series; if it is
infinite, the primary truths can never be reached; if it is finite, the primary
truths cannot themselves be known since they cannot be demonstrated."[15]

Let us now consider the second type of objector. An opponent from Party
Two does not deny the existence of knowledge, but nonetheless holds a
position that has an obvious affinity with a kind of skeptical strategy.
This opponent believes that there is knowledge and, like the opponents
from Party One, agrees that all knowledge is demonstrative. However, this
opponent takes it that the premises of one demonstration are conclusions
of another. This move allows one to avoid the charge of infinite regress
and yet still maintain that all knowledge is demonstrative. However, by
allowing for the possibility of circular demonstration, this position rejects
Aristotle's claim that the premises of a syllogistic demonstration are better
known than the conclusion. On this un-Aristotelian view knowledge does
exist, but there is no privileged set of first principles that are known in a
better manner, or known non-demonstratively.

Long urges that in response to this second type of opponent Aristotle
plays the skeptic's game to a *certain extent* by rejecting the possibility of
circular proof. However, Aristotle's own rejection of circular proof rests on
the idea that premises that ultimately explain why other things must be the
case cannot themselves be just as much in need of explanation as whatever

---

[13] See Long 1981: 86.   [14] *APo.* 1.3.72^{b}5–7.   [15] Long 1981: 87.

it is they purport to explain.[16] The first principles are both known and knowable in a way that does not constitutively involve their being deduced from anything else. According to Aristotle, the first principles are known in a non-demonstrative manner. Rather than acquiesce in an epistemological stance that makes room for the existence of knowledge by countenancing circular demonstration, he accepts the second horn of the dilemma stated above. The series from the posterior back to the prior terminates in a finite number of steps, and hence with premises that cannot be demonstrated. However, since it is not part of Aristotle's own position that all knowledge is demonstrable, accepting this horn of the dilemma for him does not require agreement that the premises at which the regress terminates are unknowable.

Of course this does not settle the issue, since Aristotle's claim that there is non-demonstrative knowledge in turn leads to questions as to the nature of the faculty by means of which the premises are known. As Long points out, one way in which such questions could arise is by an opponent issuing a challenge along the lines that a non-demonstrative faculty of *nous* itself requires a criterion to justify its knowing anything. Although Aristotle himself does not develop a puzzle along these lines, he does think that there are puzzles about how the first principles come to be known and concerning the faculty by means of which they are known. However, he is optimistic that clarity will be reached on these issues after a preliminary examination of relevant puzzles.[17] One upshot of this examination is that there are two kinds of undemonstrated knowledge. In addition to the first principles of a science and a faculty for knowing them, there is also perceptual knowledge and a faculty of perception. In a highly condensed passage that gives rise to many interpretative challenges he describes an account of how we arrive at knowledge of scientific first principles beginning with individual perceptions.[18] There is no requirement that any particular sense-perception

---

[16] According to *APo*. 1.2.71^{b}29–30 the first principles are better known than the conclusions that they explain.

[17] *APo*. 2.19.99^{b}17–19.

[18] *APo*. 2.19.99^{b}34–100^{a}14. In this passage Aristotle describes a progression from these initial starting points to memory, and from there to experience (here characterized as being constituted by a plurality of memories of the same kind of thing). Perception is responsible in this way for a non-scientific grasp of universals (100^{b}4–5). At least this much is attributed to the perceptual faculty, and does not yet involve knowledge that is arrived at through a process of reasoning. At some point induction comes into the picture (100^{b}3–4), and eventually we acquire an intellectual state by means of which we grasp the truth of principles. The details have given rise to much scholarly controversy, but regardless of how they are interpreted Aristotle is committing himself to the view that there is perceptual knowledge, that it is not based on reasoning or demonstration, and that in some way or other the knowledge of first principles ultimately comes about from perception (100^{a}10–11).

should be absolutely certain, and no attempt to use perceptual knowledge to explain (much less demonstrate) the truth of the first principles.

That said, whether or not Aristotle ultimately has the resources to ward off such attacks, both the manner in which he delineates the two types of opponent and his rejection of their shared assumption shows that he was familiar with the use of the types of general argumentative strategies that show up later in three of the modes of Agrippa. Aristotle both saw their relevance to philosophical argumentation about the possibility of knowledge, and had thought about what stance to take towards them at least in connection with his own positive claims about the possibility and nature of demonstrative knowledge.

PUZZLES AND FIRST PRINCIPLES OF A SCIENCE

Central to Aristotle's considered response to the three Agrippan skeptical strategies that we have considered is his insistence on the existence of indemonstrable knowledge. As is well known, in *Posterior Analytics* 1.2 there are three types of indemonstrable first principles for a demonstrative science, and these first principles of a science are divided into axioms and "posits." The axioms are common to all of the sciences, and without them scientific reasoning is impossible. A chief example of an axiom is one that he considers the most fundamental principle of all reasoning, the principle of non-contradiction. We will briefly consider this principle shortly. Since each science has its own domain of inquiry, in addition to the common axioms, scientists need to employ special principles that are appropriate to the kind of objects that science studies. These are what Aristotle calls "posits," and are divided into two types, definitions and suppositions. Definitions are statements that give the essence of a definable object, and say of something definable what it is, whereas a supposition or hypothesis says of something that it is (or is not). On the general picture that emerges from the *Posterior Analytics* definitions, or statements of essence, function as explanatory middle terms in demonstrative proofs of theorems.

Up until now our discussion of Aristotle's response to various opponents to his epistemology has been general and abstract, but for our purposes it is useful to consider them within the context of examples of his own practice. Here I will make some brief remarks about the deployment of these ideas in the pursuit of a genuine branch of knowledge – natural philosophy. One place where we can find him investigating existence claims and definitions is in Books 3 and 4 of his *Physics* where he goes to work on the concepts of motion, the infinite, place, the void, and time. For each of these topics he sets out to establish whether or not it exists (and how it does or does not) and what each is. Each, if it does exist, is so basic that it is a candidate for a principle of the science, and as such its existence and nature are not demonstrable. This is not the occasion for an extended look at the methodology at work in these discussions. Instead, I will use just one example to help illuminate a role that puzzles can play in inquiry into definitions. Although the treatment of each of these topics involves *aporiai*, each discussion also leaves us with definite, positive results.

Consider Aristotle's solution of a puzzle to which he alludes in the opening line of 3.3. Although he does not explicitly formulate this puzzle as to where a change takes place, it is clear that his treatment of it makes use of a definitional principle that has already been accepted. It is important to note that his invocation of this puzzle takes place *after* the first chapter has already given us his definition of change as the *entelecheia* of the potential as such, and that the immediately preceding chapter has already asserted that the "soundness of this definition is evident both when we consider the accounts of motion that the others have given, and also from the difficulty of defining it otherwise."[19] In the other cases in *Physics* 3 and 4 the puzzles come before his own positive account, but in this case the examination of the puzzle is not part of an attempt to determine the truth about the topic under investigation (change).[20]

He starts 3.3 with the claim that "the solution of the difficulty is plain: motion is in the movable."[21] He does not here say just what puzzle about the place of change he has in mind, but material from the immediately preceding chapter could suggest something like the following. That chapter claimed that, given his definition, the cause of motion is going to be "contact with what can move."[22] Due to this contact of agent and patient, there will be some change in the agent as well, provided that the agent is the kind of thing that can move. Given that the change requires contact of agent with patient, and that if the agent is the kind of thing that can be changed it is itself changed when acting on the patient, this could give rise to a question whether the change in question is *in* the agent.

[19] *Ph.* 3.2.201^{b}16–18.
[20] Henry Mendell, in comments on this essay prepared for the Models of Mind conference, has usefully classified the puzzle on change as "clarificatory" owing to the role that it plays in an investigation, and distinguishes such puzzles from the "probative" puzzles concerning the infinite, place, the void, and time. These play some kind of role in establishing the conceptual groundwork for a positive result. In either case, Aristotle is using puzzles as part of his own development of a principle and does not even consider the possibility that examining them would lead one to withhold assent (or give up the search for truth).
[21] *Ph.* 3.3.202^{a}13–14.   [22] *Ph.* 3.2.202^{a}8.

For instance, suppose that a housebuilder transmits the form of a house to some building material through some kind of direct or indirect contact with it. Aristotle has just argued that in such a transaction the housebuilder would be changed. Consequently, there must be a change that takes place *in* the agent. In that case one might reasonably wonder why housebuilding is not what is taking place in the housebuilder. However, Aristotle thinks that having given his own definition of change, and defended it by arguing for its superiority to rival attempts, he is now in a position to say that the solution to the puzzle (whatever it may be) as to where change takes place is clear. This is not simply an unrelated afterthought appended to the tail end of his discussion of change. The claim is not that the solution is clear to everybody, but rather that once we are in possession of his correct definition of change the solution is now evident.

Given his definition of change, it is clear that the change of housebuilding takes place in the materials, not in the housebuilder, because change is defined as the actuality of the *changeable*. In the case at hand, the change is housebuilding, and this is by definition the actuality of that which is able to change in such a way as to be a house. Whatever change the housebuilder may undergo owing to contact with the material, *that* change is not housebuilding because the housebuilder is not able to turn into a house, and hence is not a potential house. There is both an active and a passive or receptive capacity involved in this change, the former in the agent and the latter in the patient. The material has its own passive or receptive capacity, and housebuilding is the actuality of the potential house by the agency of something with an active power, or capacity, to affect just that change – i.e., housebuilding. Housebuilding itself is the joint actuality of both the active and the passive capacity, and there is just *one* change that is the exercise of both. This one change takes place in the patient.[23]

Here, then, is one example of one kind of use of puzzles in an actual science. Aristotle's use of the puzzle does not lead to suspension of judgment,

---

[23] Aristotle goes on to say that this result itself has a "logical" difficulty (202ª21–22). If acting and being acted upon are different, we may further puzzle over what these two motions are in. Is the agency in the agent and the patiency in the patient, or are both in the patient? Although I do not here attempt to analyze this further development, it is worth pointing out that Aristotle's discussion involves the clarification that agency and patiency, the one being the *entelecheia* of the agent and the other the *entelecheia* of the patient, are different with respect to the account of what it is to be. Although Aristotle does not explicitly say so, unclarity on this point would be an impediment to understanding the definition of change as the *entelecheia* of the potential as such. Even though the active capacity to bring about a change is in the agent and the corresponding passive capacity is in the patient, there is nothing to prevent these two items from having a single *entelecheia* located in the patient. Solving this additional logical puzzle clears up confusion that would prevent one from understanding the definition. The removal of this confusion is necessary (though not by itself sufficient) for knowing the definition *as* a first principle.

nor is this one left unresolved. Rather, he uses a previously established first principle – his definition of change – to show how it is to be solved. The definition of change can be used in an explanation of the proposition that change takes place in the patient, and such an explanation establishes that something is the case and shows why it must be. The definition was arrived at prior to the solution of the puzzle; he is not using the puzzle to discover or establish the correct definition of change, and he does not think that it poses a serious challenge to the truth of the principle he has already articulated.

THE PRINCIPLE OF NON-CONTRADICTION

The general considerations concerning circular proof, infinite regress, and the like are for Aristotle problems about universal scientific knowledge, not problems about the determination of individual matters of fact about individual perceptual objects. Although perception plays a crucial role in the acquisition of knowledge of principles, the kind of foundationalist epistemology that he endorses does not take the form of seeking a secure perceptual foundation in certain or indubitable truths about *individual* objects of experience.[24] Furthermore, although he does think that the sense-perceptions of the proper objects of the senses are the least prone to error, his treatment of scientific knowledge does not present an epistemology according to which that kind of sensory knowledge is extended by deduction to other pieces of sensory knowledge of further facts about individual, perceptible objects.[25] In addition to perceiving colors, sounds, tastes, and so on (the special objects of the senses), there is perception of the common sensibles (motion, magnitude, shape, and number), as well as coincidental perception of various sorts (we can see the son of Diares, for instance).[26] These are less reliable modes of perception, and no attempt is made to put them on a more certain basis by suggesting that we syllogistically deduce claims of that sort from the more certain perceptions

---

[24] Long 1981: 97 is quick to point out that Aristotle is not responding to a challenge "which made perceptual certainty and criteria of truth the primary problems of philosophy." He is in agreement with the statement in Burnyeat 1981 that "Aristotle does not take his starting point to be the problem of perceptual certainty."

[25] Although scientific knowledge as such is universal, insofar as particular cases can be subsumed under scientifically knowable universals there is a way in which universal truths could be applied to particular cases to extend knowledge about sensible particulars. This could be done even from inductive generalizations that did not count as scientific knowledge in the unqualified sense. However, our perceptual knowledge of sensible objects is not acquired in this way.

[26] *De An.* 2.6.

of the special objects of the senses. When Aristotle does discuss problems and puzzles concerning the perception of particulars, his aim is not to set perceptual knowledge on a certain and secure foundation. When looking for indemonstrable starting points he is interested in securing the starting points for scientific knowledge rather than for particular matters of fact about perceptible objects.

It is in this connection that Long has also shown the relevance to Aristotle of the different typology of skeptical strategies exhibited in the ten modes of Aenesidemus. Unlike the Agrippan modes, these classify what could be characterized as "a large body of evidence"[27] that includes all sorts of general facts about sense-perception. Not only do humans differ from animals in their perceptions, but perceptions differ from one human to another, and even in the case of a single person the perceptions of one sense differ from those of another. Additionally, our perceptions vary both when our condition differs (awake, asleep, healthy, ill, etc.), and when the external conditions vary. Much of this material pre-dates Aristotle and is as old as Xenophanes, Heraclitus, Parmenides, and Democritus. Some of it would have been familiar to Aristotle from the use that Plato makes of conflicting appearances in the refutation of Protagoras in the *Theaetetus*, and many of these considerations turn up in *Metaphysics* 4 in connection with his discussion of the principle of non-contradiction. In fact, he claims that those who deny this principle out of genuine puzzlement arrived at their position on the basis of perceptible objects.[28]

At least some of the considerations that led them to this view are similar to or almost the same as material found in the ten modes. In the context of his discussion in the *Metaphysics* of various facts about how perceptions differ and vary, Aristotle does not seem to distinguish the thesis that the same thing is both true and false from the related, but clearly different, theses that everything is true and that everything is false. Perhaps for his purposes it is not incumbent upon him to do so since he is reporting the views of others, but in any case he obviously thinks that use of material from these modes fails to support any of these formulations of the thesis.

The principle of non-contradiction is for him the firmest and most secure of all of the principles, and must be known by anybody who knows anything at all.[29] It is formulated in a number of different ways by Aristotle, but for now the following will suffice: "The same attribute cannot at the same time belong and not belong to the same subject in the same respect."[30]

[27] Long 1981: 89. [28] *Metaph.* 4.5.1009^{a}22–23.
[29] *Metaph.* 4.3.1005^{b}17–23. [30] *Metaph.* 4.3.1005^{b}19–20.

There can be no scientific demonstration of this principle precisely because there is nothing prior to and explanatory of it. For him the principle of non-contradiction is a basis for all reasoning. It is so fundamental to our ability to reason that there simply is nothing more fundamental that could be appealed to in order to show *why* it must be true. Hence this is the example *par excellence* of something that one ought to accept without demonstration.

There is, though, a sense in which it can be demonstrated. According to Book 4.4 it is possible to give an *elenctic* proof in which the premises are supplied by an interlocutor who denies the principle.[31] The basic idea is that if an opponent who denies it says something significant, then Aristotle thinks such an interlocutor must grant premises that will refute his own view. Of course the opponent might simply refuse to talk, and then there could be no discussion or argument, and even if Aristotle does succeed in refuting the opponent, the opponent might refuse to admit defeat. After all, if the opponent claims that contradictories can be true at the same time, showing him that his own admissions lead to a conclusion that contradicts his claim might even be viewed by him as further support for his thesis.[32] The style of argument he employs for those who deny the principle for the sake of argument is indirect in that it attacks their conclusion as absurd, but does not try to expose some error in their reasoning.

However, Aristotle distinguishes the kind of opponent who denies the principle for the sake of argument from those who are led to it through perplexity.[33] These latter are in a state of *aporia* and have been led to their denial of the principle by the kind of material similar to that which later turns up in the ten modes. Unlike merely contentious opponents, Aristotle thinks that such people can be *persuaded* to see the error in their thinking. Although he here offers no analysis of persuasion as an argumentative mode, he does indicate how one can go about relieving them of their perplexity. After diagnosing the acceptance of one of their misguided conclusions as resulting from the use of one of a variety of arguments from conflicting appearances he goes on to show how to solve the puzzle in question. The solutions he offers focus on drawing distinctions (e.g., potential versus actual being, or different kinds of change) which are then applied to their mistaken reasoning in order to show both the extent to which their views contain the truth and where they go wrong. Like the puzzle about

---

[31] *Metaph.* 4.4.1006ª11–13.
[32] In *Metaph.* 4.6.1011ª15–16 Aristotle points out the futility of trying to contradict in argument somebody who starts out by contradicting himself.
[33] *Metaph.* 4.5.1009ª16–22.

the location of change from the *Physics*, these puzzles are also examined after the relevant first principle has been announced, and they play no role in discovering or searching for the principle. Furthermore, Aristotle approaches the puzzles with the confident expectation that if somebody has been led to denial of the principle owing to one of these puzzles, then it will be *easy* to cure them of their ignorance.[34] They are simply wrong, and the puzzles are not serious obstacles to knowledge.

It is obvious how this contrasts with our earlier description of the proto-skeptic. The proto-skeptic inquired in order to solve *aporiai*, but eventually argument conforming to various modes led to a suspension of judgment. However, if Aristotle is right, material such as is found in the ten modes has led them into a condition in which they are not saying anything at all.[35] They are no longer really inquiring, but neither are they saying anything determinate. If so, there simply is no challenge to his own principles for him to meet.

Although arguments from conflicting appearances have led some into confusion and puzzlement, for Aristotle the puzzlement is the result of improper education, and is betrayed in the demand, unreasonable by his lights, that a proof be given of everything. Here too, as in the case of scientific first principles, Aristotle is confident that puzzles are not an impediment to the discernment of truth. And to express this point one can do no better than quote Long's own words: "he left to later philosophers a series of defences against skepticism, some of which they adopted, and a methodology which turns the skeptic's grounds for giving up the quest for knowledge into reasons for maintaining the search and hoping for a solution."[36] In response to those who sincerely believe that there are puzzles that render the truth of his principles problematic he offers not proof, but the promise of persuasion.[37]

---

[34] *Metaph.* 4.5.1009ᵃ18–19.   [35] *Metaph.* 4.4.1008ᵃ30–31.   [36] Long 1981: 105.

[37] I would like to thank Peter Klein and Henry Mendell for their comments on a previous draft, as well as the participants in the Ancient Models of Mind conference.

CHAPTER 7

Stoic selection

Objects, actions, and agents

Stephen White

Selection (ἐκλογή, *selectio*) is a key concept in Stoic ethics. It has a prominent role in attempts by Diogenes of Babylon and Antipater of Tarsus in the second century BCE to explain and defend the Stoic conception of the good life or human *telos*. It is a major target of ancient criticism from their contemporary Carneades down to Plutarch and Alexander. And it is central to recent attempts to reconstruct Stoic moral psychology, which take selection to be a distinctive kind of motivation, a species of rational "impulse" (ὁρμή) that differs both from the uniquely virtuous "dispassions" (εὐπάθειαι) of a sage, and from the inherently defective "passions" (πάθη) found in everyone else. So construed, a selection is simply an impulse to act in pursuit of an objective viewed as "indifferent": not as either good or bad (as in dispassions correctly and passions incorrectly), but as "preferred" or "dispreferred," on the basis of its "selective" value or disvalue. This intermediate form of motivation, which is common to everyone, sages and others alike, is supposed to help explain how we can make "progress" from vice toward virtue: simply by transforming our passions into selections, that is, by viewing as "indifferent" but "preferred" much of what we ordinarily consider "good." It also underpins recent accounts of practical reasoning in Stoicism: the correct way to decide what to do is simply to select the available option that promises the greatest selective value.

This account of selection is not without problems. One is a puzzle about deliberation that Rachel Barney has pressed: How can the selection of indifferents underwrite principled acts of courage, let alone the heroics of Stoic exemplars like Heracles and Socrates, or Regulus and Cato? Why should anyone ever select an option liable to cost them their life?[1] A more basic problem concerns the nature of selection itself. Contrary to prevailing views, it does not appear to be an impulse at all; and its proper objects are not actions but physical bodies and their states. That may sound like a

---

[1] Barney 2003; for a systematic response, see Brennan 2005: 182–230.

trivial point. But it rests on a basic distinction in Stoic ontology, and it has major implications for ethics. Crudely put, current views reflect a model of deliberation that is primarily object-oriented, centered on preferred bodies and bodily states. But Stoic ethics, and its underlying model of mind, is distinctly action-oriented, centered not on *what objects* to pursue, avoid, or deploy, but on *how to respond* to our situation. Moreover, a proper response depends in the first instance on *who we are*, as defined by the networks of personal, social, and cosmic relations we inherit, create, and continually adjust, and only in the second instance on the "selective value" of *what* we seek. In short, *who we are* determines a set of actions to perform – a set of *kathēkonta* or "duties"; and those duties typically have (or should have) deliberative priority over any selection of essentially indifferent objectives, which are only the "material" of our conduct and emotional life. All that is very crudely put. The burden of what follows is to fill out this sketch by articulating the conceptual structure behind the Stoic account of selection and exploring the ethical significance of that account. The first step requires reviewing some abstract doxographical texts, mainly from the outline of Stoic ethics preserved by Stobaeus; the second focuses on a single discourse of Epictetus.

WHAT DOES SELECTION SELECT?

At the heart of Stoic ethics is a contrast between goodness and value. Only virtue and things that partake of virtue (virtuous people, attitudes, and activities) are good. Everything else has at most only "value" – because it is liable to misuse, hence at most sometimes beneficial, and therefore neither necessary nor essential to "living in agreement with [human and cosmic] nature." An exhaustive ontological division marks this contrast: everything that "is" – every being, which is to say, every body or bodily state – is either good or bad or indifferent; and every indifferent is either (1) "preferred," because it has value (standard examples are health and wealth); or (2) "dispreferred," because it has disvalue (standard examples are illness and poverty); or (3) neither, because totally indifferent (a standard example is having an odd number of hairs on your head).[2] This division is the basis for a number of parallel divisions, including one that directly concerns our topic. The Stoics maintain that all and only what is good – virtue and anything virtuous – is "choiceworthy" or "worth choosing" (αἱρετόν).

---

[2] Stob. 2.57 and 79, D.L. 7.101–04. The second division oversimplifies. Some evidence suggests two further classes: things that have some value or disvalue but too little to be either preferred or dispreferred. But I ignore that distinction since it appears to be irrelevant here.

What has value is only "worth getting" (ληπτόν); and this class comprises the normal objects of selection. As Stobaeus reports:

They say that "worth choosing" and "worth getting" differ: what stimulates a sufficient impulse is "worth choosing" [editors and scholars supply a parallel formula for "worth getting"; but paucity of evidence makes any supplement overly conjectural]; and something "worth choosing" differs from something "worth getting" to the same degree that something inherently "worth choosing" differs from something inherently "worth getting," and in general something good from something that has value.[3]

This parallelism between choosing and getting on the one hand, and goodness and value on the other hand, appears to be the main basis for an inference that underlies the idea that selection is a kind of impulse. On this view, the attitudes of choice and selection are directly analogous and differ simply in the way in which we view our objective, in particular, whether we evaluate it as good or bad, or rather as preferred or dispreferred. The Stoic analysis of passions as kinds of impulse (namely, "excessive" rational impulses), hence complex beliefs, provides a template to formulate the difference schematically:

A **choice** (αἵρεσις) is a belief (either knowledge or opinion) that something available is a good that I should pursue (ὀρέγεσθαι).

A **selection** (ἐκλογή) is a belief (either knowledge or opinion) that something available is an indifferent that I should pursue.[4]

If and only if the agent is a sage, these beliefs qualify as knowledge or understanding (ἐπιστήμη); otherwise, they are merely opinions (δόξαι), either false or weakly assented, or both. That epistemic contrast marks a crucial difference between passions and dispassions. A sage's choices are invariably correct and firmly assented, hence understood or known. Anyone else's choices are either incorrect or weakly assented, hence merely opinions. In the case of prospective pro-attitudes, or wanting, a sage has "volitions" but everyone else has "desires":

---

[3] Stob. 2.75.1–6 (unsupplemented), cf. 64.13–17, 72.14–22, 82.20–83.9. Value is primarily an attribute of types, and in some situations, tokens of a preferred type (healthy meals), while still "worth getting" (ληπτά), are not "to be gotten" (ληπτέα), and conversely for dispreferreds; accordingly, our sources report token-variability in duties "according to circumstance," but no corresponding variability in value by circumstance, no circumstantial preferreds or dispreferreds.

[4] Neither formula is attested; but αἵρεσις, as a species of ὄρεξις (Stob. 2.87.20–2), is plainly an impulse, and selection would then be directly parallel (unless ὀρέγεσθαι should be replaced by λαμβάνειν). See Brennan 2005: 93–100, elaborating his account in Brennan 1998: 35–6 and building on Inwood 1985: 198–215; cf. Voelke 1973: 65–72, Inwood 1999: 698, Sorabji 2000: 53, Graver 2002: 168, Barney 2003: 321–4, Brennan 2003: 269–72, Graver 2007: 48. I omit the converse attitudes of avoidance (generically ἔκκλισις, or specifically fear and caution: φόβος and εὐλάβεια) and disselection (ἀπεκλογή) only for the sake of clarity.

A **volition** (βούλησις) is knowledge that something available is a good that I should pursue.

A **desire** (ἐπιθυμία) is an opinion that something available is a good that I should pursue.

One attraction of this schema is that it offers a *tertium quid* between vicious passions and virtuous dispassions, namely selections, which accordingly enable us to bridge the gulf we have to traverse in making progress toward virtue. Anyone can have correct attitudes of selection, whether virtuous or not; and we achieve moral progress by replacing our misguided passions with correct selections – by learning to view what we want as "preferred" (or dispreferred) rather than "good" (or bad).[5] Another attraction is that it offers a plausible model of practical reasoning and deliberation. The rational way to determine what to do, whether we are sages or not, is simply to estimate and compare the value of our available options; if we select the option with the greatest value, we act correctly, since to select an option is simply to have an impulse to act, and so (on Stoic theory) to act accordingly. So if we estimate value correctly, we act correctly, which is to say we act "in line with" or "in accordance with" virtue: we do *what* a virtuous sage would do, even if not sages ourselves, though not entirely the *way* a sage would do it, with all the same attitudes and consequent modulations in conduct.

Despite its attractions, this account of selection faces serious objections. One, noted long ago by Tony Long, is simply a shortage of evidence: the term nowhere appears in any surviving list of emotions and impulses.[6] To be sure, evidence is meager all round: "selection" is a technical term not well attested outside of discussions of Stoic ethics.[7] But the argument from silence is confirmed by what evidence we do have, where the grammar shows that selection has a different logical structure than impulses do. Simply put, the proper objects of selection are not actions, as specified by verbs (or verbal nouns), but bodies or bodily states, as specified by substantives (or substantival phrases). Consider the *telos*-formulae of Diogenes and Antipater, which I mentioned at the outset:

---

[5] Brennan 1998: 61 n. 31 felicitously calls this "the domestication of desire"; cf. Brennan 2005: 100–4. Selection is loosely analogous to "cognition" (κατάληψις): each is a form of assent that can but need not figure in understanding; cf. Brennan 2005: 111 n. 11. But the analogy should not be pressed too far: cognition is always veridical and reliably grounded, but selections (contra Brennan 2000: 150 n. 6) are often false (misevaluations) or poorly grounded (based on misperception or misconception).

[6] Long 1976: 81.

[7] Otherwise rare in philosophical texts, apart from what may be derivative uses in logic (Alexander) and medicine (Galen); for these uses, which in effect localize selection to specific disciplines, cf. Stob. 2.73.10–15.

being reasonable in the selection and disselection *of natural things* [τῶν κατὰ φύσιν];... continuously selecting *natural things* and disselecting *unnatural things* [τὰ παρὰ φύσιν]. (Stob. 2.76; cf. Clem. *Strom.* 2.129.2, D.L. 7.88. Plut. *CN* 1072F)

Diogenes' formula uses the noun "selection" with an objective genitive; Antipater's uses the participle "selecting" with object accusatives. Both constructions are well attested, and regularly found with the same or very similar characterization of the objects, in both Greek and Latin.[8] The point of grammar is in turn confirmed by abundant evidence for what the Stoics count as "natural (or unnatural) things": invariably either states of our own bodies or bodily parts, or external bodies and their states. Witness two typical lists in Stobaeus:

Things like this are natural: health, strength, soundness of sense-organs, and the like.... Preferreds concern the soul, the body, or externals. Concerning the soul are things like these: talent, progress, memory, quickness in thinking, a disposition to stick to duties, and any skills that can contribute mainly to a natural way of life. Bodily preferreds are health, sensory acuity, and the like. Externals include parents, offspring, suitable property, and popular favor. (Stob. 2.79.20–80.1, 80.22–81.6; cf. D.L. 7.106)

In Stoic materialism, the soul is itself a body, and its attributes are states of that body, namely, dynamic "tensile" states of psychic pneuma. Bodily attributes like health are likewise states of the soul–body complex that is a living animal, hence similarly dynamic material structures. External factors (literally external to an agent's body) are also reducible to materialist analysis, though extant sources offer little guidance here, where the details are more complicated. Wealth or respect, for example, can be analyzed as relations between an agent and a set of other bodies belonging to her (her wealth), or relations among a set of people whose psychic states include favorable attitudes toward one of them (their respect for her). In any case, the items in all three classes of preferreds must be strictly corporeal, either bodies or their states (including relational states). After all, preferreds are the sorts of things that "stimulate an impulse"; but to stimulate is to act as (at least a partial and proximate) efficient cause, which is something only bodies can do.[9]

What we select, then, are exclusively corporeal items: bodily states either of our own souls or bodies, or of other bodies "external" to our own.

---

[8] Chrysippus in Epict. 2.6.9 (*SVF* 3.191); Plut. *CN* 1069–72 *passim*; Alex. *Mant.* 160–6 *passim*; Cic. *Fin.* 3.20, 3.31, 4.46; Sen. *Ep.* 92.11–13 (using *electio*).

[9] Stob. 2.79, cf. D.L. 7.104. An impulse, as a "motion" (φορά) in someone's soul (a motion of their psychic pneuma), is a bodily event. But its intentional object or goal is incorporeal: not food or health *tout court*, but getting, maintaining, or using those or other corporeal items in eating, working, playing, and the like – which are instantiations of predicates; cf. Graver 2007: 38–9.

Impulses, by contrast, have twin objects: not only bodies that figure as direct objects or "targets" of an action but also incorporeal "predicates" that represent the action (or emotional reaction) itself.[10] These actions (or reactions) are typically designated by infinitives, which serve as grammatical complements for an impulse-term. "Desires" and "volitions" are impulses *to do* (or undergo) something, be it walking, talking, or simply "reaching" out in pursuit (ὀρέγεσθαι generically) of things; and conversely, "fears" and "cautions" are impulses *to avoid* active or passive events of the same ontological sort. To "select" a predicate, however, would be a category mistake. As predicates, actions (and undergoings) are incorporeal; they are what we "choose" or otherwise "desire" or "will" (or conversely avoid or fear).[11] Thus, you *choose* to sit down in a chair, regardless whether you think doing so is virtuous or indifferent but preferred. All you *select* is the chair (a corporeal object or "being"), not your sitting down (an incorporeal predicate). In short, what we choose are actions (and reactions), and what we select are bodily objects, namely, those with or for or on which we act (or react). When you choose to sit down, you must also select a seat on which to sit; and which you do first may matter, as we shall see.

Selections and impulses are fundamentally different kinds of attitudes. But difference does not entail dissociation, and what we have seen suggests that they are closely related. Recall the two-part structure of impulses, which are standardly analyzed as complex beliefs: both an evaluative belief that this or that is good or bad, preferred or dispreferred; and also a correlated prescriptive belief that one should do (or undergo) such and such regarding this or that. What the first belief evaluates is regularly a body or bodily state. An obvious hypothesis, then, is that "selection" is a technical Stoic term for the evaluative beliefs that figure in prospective attitudes of pursuit, whether vicious "desires" or virtuous "volitions"; and that "disselection" analogously refers to the evaluative beliefs that figure in prospective attitudes of avoidance, both vicious "fear" and virtuous "caution."[12] In short:

---

[10] For clarity, I omit reference to the "impressions" that mediate the process: even bodies in our immediate vicinity stimulate action only via our perceptual awareness, hence via impressions (themselves pneumatic states of soul) of their states and relations; likewise for imagined and other non-perceptual objects *mutatis mutandis*.

[11] Choosing anything corporeal would likewise be a category mistake; cf. Stob. 2.78.7–12: wisdom, as a bodily state, is something we may choose to pursue or exercise, but strictly speaking, what we choose is the predicate "being wise" and not wisdom itself.

[12] So construed, selection and disselection should also figure in the corresponding retrospective attitudes of pleasure or joy and sorrow (contra Brennan 2005: 101); cf. Stob. 2.88.12–21 on "leading" and "supervening" passions. But decisive evidence is missing.

A **selection** is a belief that something is worth pursuing.

Two points call for emphasis. First, unlike a choice or any other rational impulse, a selection has no prescriptive component. While not motivationally neutral as non-evaluative beliefs are, it is insufficient to induce any action (or reaction) on its own. At most, a selection has something like potential energy, which is readily transformed into kinetic energy when appropriately linked to prescriptive beliefs, but otherwise remains dormant.[13]

Second, if selection differs from choice in the way I propose, it would be very odd to restrict selection to considerations of value and impulse to considerations of goodness. For if a selection is simply the evaluative component of a choice (or any other form of impulse), every choice has a selection embedded in it. True, our evidence regularly associates selection with indifferents and choice with virtue. But the point of that contrast, I suggest, is not to indicate a merely subjective difference in the way someone views a situation, as indifferent but preferred or as virtuous and good. Rather, it marks a crucial objective difference, one based both on Stoic ontology and on Stoic ethics. The ontological point is simply that we select only bodies and bodily states, and we choose only actions (and reactions). The logically *proper* objects of selection are corporeal, and the logically *proper* objects of choice are incorporeal. But of course, logical propriety does not ensure ethical rectitude: not every *proper* object is *correct*. That is one reason why the evidence has proved so misleading, because it reasonably focuses on the *correct* objects for each attitude: what we *should* select are indifferents (normally preferreds), and what we *should* choose are actions in line with virtue. In any case, the decisive difference is not simply psychological. The key ethical difference is not whether we view things "under different descriptions" as preferred rather than good (or the contraries), but whether we focus on objects rather than actions.[14] Selections evaluate bodies or bodily states; choices instigate actions involving those bodies or states, either pursuing or avoiding them, whether correctly

---

[13] Cf. Graver 2007: 38–46 on "the pathetic syllogism." On my account, selections are simply what she calls "simple ascriptions of value," which have the form "objects of type T have value"; and those lead to action only when conjoined with relevant "appropriateness beliefs," which have the form "if a valued object is in view, it is appropriate to do A."

[14] Chrysippus' notorious comment that it makes no difference if we call indifferents "good" so long as we don't go astray in other ways (Plut. *SC* 1048a: *SVF* 3.137), though often cited to support this view, actually shows that redescription can leave our attitudes unchanged. What matters is not whether we view something as good or preferred (whatever subjective difference that might make or reflect) but whether we have the correct objective: not only an object truly worthy of pursuit but first and foremost an act truly right to perform.

or incorrectly, virtuously or not. In short, selection differs from choice not in disregarding goodness (or badness) in favor of value (or disvalue), but in assessing objects rather than the actions we might undertake in their pursuit (or avoidance).

The prevailing view of selection, then, goes wrong on two counts: both in mistaking it for a kind of impulse, and in restricting it to an interest in value as opposed to goodness. But both points highlight a major gap in my alternative account. If all we select are objects to pursue (or avoid), then how do we tell what to do with them or how to get them in the first place? In particular, how are we to ascertain which available actions are correct, or to form the further prescriptive beliefs that figure in any and every choice? On the prevailing view, selection is supposed to supply answers to both questions: we simply calculate which option promises the greatest value, then settle on obtaining that value. But here again problems arise. As Barney (2003) emphasizes, such a procedure appears to leave few constraints or limits on our actions; and Stoicism certainly does not endorse the unrestrained pursuit of natural value.[15] Moreover, such an approach runs counter to the emphasis found in our sources, which pay relatively little attention to selection (recall the shortage of evidence) and focus rather on *kathēkonta* or duties: on cataloguing, analyzing, and explaining what kinds of actions are correct in various situations and circumstances. Not only did the leading early Stoics devote entire works to this task; so did Cicero and Seneca, and the same emphasis is evident in Epictetus, his teacher Musonius, Hierocles, and Marcus.[16]

The prominence of duties in extant texts points to an alternative model of deliberation that harmonizes neatly with my alternative account of selection. Instead of first selecting what objects to pursue (or avoid) and then adopting an expedient or efficient course of action to obtain them, the correct approach is typically first to determine what we need to do or accomplish and only then to select objects that warrant our attention. In short, the normal procedure in Stoic contexts is roughly the reverse of that found in many recent discussions. Before we turn to Epictetus to

---

[15] Nor did any rival theory, not even later Pyrrhonism; Carneades reportedly defended the position only for dialectical purposes (Cic. *Fin.* 2.42, 5.20).

[16] Titles attested for Zeno (D.L. 7.4), Cleanthes (7.175), Sphaerus (7.178), Chrysippus (*SVF* 3.174, 688, 752), Panaetius (test. 92–103 Alesse), Hecato (frs. 10–14 Gomoll), and Posidonius (frs. 39–41 EK); cf. Cicero's *De officiis* and Seneca's *De beneficiis*, and similarly Epictetus 2.10, Musonius in Stob. 4.48.67 (cf. 4.75.15, 4.79.51), Hierocles in Stob. 1.3.53–4 (cf. 2.9.7, 3.39.34–6, 4.84.23), and Marcus, *Med.* 2.5, 5.31, 6.39.

illustrate this contrast, let me outline how this reversal of priorities bears on selection, since selection has only a minor role in his discussion.

Recall the two-part structure of any impulse: both an evaluative belief (namely, a selection) and a prescriptive belief. A key question in the analysis of Stoic deliberation is how these two beliefs are related. Current models suppose that deliberation moves from the former to the latter: we first select objects, then settle on actions. On the model I propose, the normal procedure – at least normatively, though often not in practice – runs in the opposite direction: we (should) first consider what to do, then select suitable objects for acting accordingly. The leading deliberative question, then, is not what objects to select but what actions to perform; and the answer to this question, at least as a deliberative question, rests largely on who we are, not only as specimens of a natural kind (as rational but mortal beings), but also and pervasively as related in manifold ways to many other individuals, of the same and different kinds alike.[17] In short, our duties reflect the various "roles" or *personae* (πρόσωπα) we inherit and acquire and adjust over the course of our lives. It is no accident, then, that the logical grammar of duties corresponds exactly to the prescriptive beliefs embedded in impulses: both highlight predicates, typically designated by infinitives (honoring parents, worshipping gods, and so on), and often governed by deontic operators like "should" or "must" (Greek δεῖ or χρή) or characterized by gerundives with deontic force like "to be chosen" or "to be done" (αἱρετέον, ποιητέον, *expetendum*, etc.).[18] Some definitions of passions even formulate the prescriptive factor as a duty, either explicitly as *kathēkon*, or implicitly via deontic operators.[19] For example, as children or students, we (should) recognize honoring our parents and teachers as something "reaching us" (to recall the root idea behind Zeno's adoption of the term καθῆκον, D.L. 7.108), hence something we "should" do and hence "to be chosen."[20] How exactly we go about honoring someone, what objects to employ in what situations or circumstances and so on, is then a

---

[17] I say only "as a deliberative question" because the theoretical justification for these norms runs in the other direction, often or perhaps even always: the relative value of objects provides the ultimate ground for all or most norms of conduct; see the oft-cited remark by Chrysippus in Plut. *CN* 1069a, and Cic. *Fin.* 3.22–3. But that is a question for another occasion.

[18] See Stob. 2.86.5–9 on predicates (some with χρή), and 78.7–17, 97.15–98.13, and 59.4–7.

[19] See Stob. 2.90.16 for καθήκει (cf. 86.18); Andron. *Pass.* 1 for δεῖ; Galen, *PHP* 4.2.4, 4.4.2, 5.7.29 for χρή; Cic. *Tusc.* 3.25 for *rectum* and *oportere* (cf. 3.74, 3.79, 4.14, 4.59).

[20] On Zeno's construal of καθῆκον, see Cooper 1998: 268–9, who aptly proposes "incumbent" as its translation. I retain the traditional rendering "duty" mainly for simplicity; but cf. Annas 2002 on the affinity of F. H. Bradley's notion of "my station and its duties" to the Stoic emphasis on balancing the competing demands of our "dual citizenship, in the embedded circumstances of our life [especially family and social relations] and in the community of reason" (109).

matter for selection – though always subject to any number of other duties entailed by our many other roles and relations. But there is no need to dwell on my examples when Epictetus provides more telling ones.

MODEL STOIC DECISIONS

In one of his more familiar discourses, Epictetus discusses a series of deliberative scenarios to illustrate a thesis that inverts the prevailing account of selection. To calculate our options solely in terms of indifferents, as that account would have us do, is to ignore who we are (1.2.14):

For if someone stoops just once to considering things like that [τῶν τοιούτων] and counts up the values of externals, he is very near those who have completely forgotten their own role.

The scope of this claim is uncertain. Some, struck by the dismissal of "counting up values" even "once," have taken it as a general proscription of deliberation.[21] But the mention of value is plainly a gloss on "considering things like that"; and the point of reference there (the antecedent of τῶν τοιούτων) is evidently restricted to situations like the ones described in the preceding lines, where a Roman Senator wonders whether to accede to a degrading request by Nero. To settle this question thus requires situating the passage in its context. But before we proceed, three points call for immediate emphasis. First, assuming that "counting up values" refers to a process of selection (or something very much like it), it is clear that Epictetus views it as playing the leading role in deliberation for at least some people at least sometimes. Second, it is equally clear that he considers this deeply misguided, on at least some occasions. And third, what he proposes in its stead is adhering to who we are and the distinctive roles we have (note τοῦ ἰδίου προσώπου). To clarify these claims, and to see *why* Epictetus makes them, requires a wider view. The discourse as a whole examines "how someone might preserve on every occasion what fits their role" (to cite Arrian's title), and it addresses two closely related questions: Why do we do what we do, and how can we tell what we *should* do? Epictetus answers the first question clearly at the outset, where he claims that people (always and only) do what they think is *reasonable*, no matter how unnatural it may be in fact or seem to others (1.2.1–4).

For a rational animal, only what is unreasonable [ἄλογον] is unbearable; what is reasonable [εὔλογον] is bearable. "Aren't beatings unbearable by nature?" How so?

---

21 See Lloyd 1978: 244–45; cf. Inwood 1985: 44–45.

See how Spartans are whipped once they learn that it is reasonable. "And hanging isn't unbearable?" Well, whenever anyone feels that it is reasonable, he goes off and hangs himself. In short, if we pay attention, we'll not find people *afflicted* by anything so much as the unreasonable, nor again *drawn* to anything so much as the reasonable.

The initial thesis, that people put up with anything they *consider* reasonable, is illustrated by a pair of familiar but paradoxical examples. Beatings and whippings are plainly unnatural, hence dispreferred, since they inflict severe physical pain, or even lasting damage; likewise hanging, which throttles the natural drive to self-preservation. Yet, as both cases show, some people voluntarily seek out such dispreferreds: Spartan youths at the festival of Artemis Orthia; and the suicidally distraught, from tragic heroines on.[22] Epictetus renders no verdict on either case. His point is not that either group is right to act as they do, only that people readily do things that are unnatural and dispreferred, provided they themselves consider their actions reasonable. We are often wrong, of course, and our actions unreasonable. But *believing* that an action is reasonable is sufficient for us to act.

That raises the second question: How are we to tell which acts are *truly* reasonable? Or to cast the question in Stoic terms, how can we tell what our duties are, since duties are simply those acts that (once done) have a reasonable justification.[23] Epictetus presents his answer by discussing a series of vivid examples. He begins with a general principle, that what is *truly* reasonable (not just seemingly so) differs for different people (so too "good and bad" or virtuous; and "expedient and inexpedient" or preferable). In short, different people have different duties (5). But that makes it more difficult for each of us to determine our own duties. Education can help, he allows, but the key is evidently something more personal, in particular, recognizing our own distinctive or peculiar roles (6–7).

Especially for this reason [sc. the variation in what is reasonable etc.] we need education, so as to learn how to apply the concept [πρόληψιν] of what is reasonable or unreasonable to particular objects in conformity with nature; and to decide what is reasonable or unreasonable we employ the values not only of external things but also of what accords with our own individual role [τῶν κατὰ τὸ πρόσωπον ἑαυτοῦ].[24]

The education invoked here by *paideia* may extend beyond general acculturation and the standard "encyclic" training to include advanced

---

[22] The Spartan custom was a stock example; cf. Cicero *Tusc.* 2.34, 2.46, 5.77.

[23] Stob. 2.85.14–15, D.L. 7.107, Cic. *Fin.* 3.58, *Off.* 1.8, etc.

[24] On this and the following passage, see Kamtekar 1998: 150–51, Long 2002: 238–40; on Stoic notions of ethical "roles" (πρόσωπα or *personae*), see Gill 1993 and Frede 2007.

studies, even philosophical study with a Stoic teacher. But whatever its scope, such education is insufficient. To determine what is reasonable to do, we must consider not only "the values of external things" but also our station in life and its diverse and distinctive roles; and that is something each of us must do for ourselves, though not without discussion with others, as some of the following cases show. To illustrate how this works, Epictetus sketches a series of deliberative scenarios, some of which raise life-or-death questions. The first case, perhaps because of its focus, is duly anonymous (8–11):

For one person finds it reasonable to carry someone's chamber pot, since he looks only to this, that if he does not carry it, he'll get a beating and won't get any food, but if he does carry it, he won't suffer any rough and painful handling. But someone else finds it unbearable not only to carry another's but also to put up with anyone carrying one for him. So if you ask me, "Shall I hold the pot or not?", I'll tell you that getting food has more value than not getting any, and getting flayed has more disvalue than not getting flayed. Hence, if you measure your affairs by those standards, you'll go off and carry it. "But that's not for me."[25] That is something you have to bring to the inquiry yourself, not me; for you are the one who knows yourself, how much you value yourself and what price you set on yourself; for different people set different prices on themselves.

The prospect of being a toilet slave is plainly meant to seem both disgusting and degrading, and not only servile but utterly demeaning (cf. "untouchable" dalits). On the scale of natural value, the alternative falls even lower: hunger and a debilitating beating (note "flayed"). As Epictetus observes, the choice is easy according to the calculus of natural value and preferreds: carrying someone's toilet is a small price to pay for food and safety, and severe beating a stiff price for refusing. But that is only his rhetorical gambit. A defiant interjection (by a real or imagined listener) emphasizes that many consider the opposite choice equally obvious, which shows that the calculus of selection according to natural value is inadequate. Many rely instead on a personal calculus of self-worth, a calculus based on self-knowledge, including both their self-image or self-conception, and their awareness of the network of roles and relations they have. This personal calculus, and its implications for duties, is what Epictetus highlights in the following examples, which pose loftier choices with graver consequences and invoke exemplary Romans from the days of his own youth. The first is from the 60s CE, when the elite frequently had to decide how to act under Nero (12–13).

---

[25] The elliptical "for me" (κατ' ἐμέ) may allude to duty: καθήκει μοι.

For that reason, when Florus was considering whether he should attend Nero's festival, and thus perform in it as well, Agrippinus said, "Attend." And when Florus asked, "Why aren't you attending?" he said, "Because I'm not deliberating either."[26]

The initial deliberative question looks simple: to attend Nero's festival or not. But its consequences are momentous, as the following lines make clear. To attend was to risk being "asked" to perform onstage, which entailed severe legal sanctions as well as disgrace (*infamia*) for members of the Roman nobility;[27] and to refuse was to risk execution – "beheading." The choice, in short, is between life and death (15–16).

So why do you ask me, "Is death more worth choosing, or life?" I say life. "Pain or pleasure?" I say pleasure. "But if I don't perform in the tragedy, I'll have my head cut off." Well then, go off and perform in it; but I won't perform in it.

As Epictetus has Agrippinus emphasize, the calculus of selective value yields a clear answer: choose life over death, pleasure over pain, hence obedience, attendance, and performance over resistance and execution. Then why does Agrippinus nonetheless refuse? Epictetus presents his explanation in two stages. The first, an editorial comment that interrupts the anecdote (14), is the sentence I cited first: to count up natural advantages, as the calculus of selection does, is in some situations to abdicate personal integrity at the outset. As Agrippinus puts it here, even deliberation itself can be a sign of moral failure – or at least of a devastating decline in moral aspiration. Anyone who even begins to weigh his options, as Florus has, is already on a very slippery slope; and in this case, to worry about natural preferences is to neglect the prior demands of one's role (or ethical persona) – the duties it entails on its own and regardless of natural preferences. What the relevant role is here, and why it entails risking one's life, emerges first in figurative terms (17–18).

"Why not?" Because you consider yourself one of the yellow threads in the tunic. "So what?" You should have been thinking about how to be like everyone else, just as the thread is unwilling to stand out among the rest. My wish, however, is to be a purple strand, small but gleaming and responsible for the others looking

---

[26] Editors and translators treat ὅτι as a subordinating conjunction introducing a direct statement that begins with ἐγώ. But the train of thought clearly favors including ὅτι in Agrippinus' reply: "because" answers the preceding question "why?" (Διὰ τί), as it does again in 17: Διὰ τί; Ὅτι σὺ σεαυτὸν ἡγῇ (in both cases an emphatic nominative of a personal pronoun follows in initial position). Paconius Agrippinus was exiled by Nero along with Helvidius Priscus in connection with the trial and execution of Thrasea and Soranus in 66 (Tac. *Ann.* 16.33; cf. Epict. 1.1.28–32).

[27] Edwards 1993: 123–6; sanctions included loss of citizen rights, including immunity to corporal punishment.

decorous and fine. "So why do you tell me to make myself like the many? How will I still be purple?"

The decisive factor, as Epictetus explains, is one's own priorities. Simply by looking to his own natural advantage, Florus reveals that he is unwilling (οὐδ'... θέλει) to live up to the duties of his station as a senator. Instead of worrying about being disgraced onstage, "he should have been thinking about" his own personal preference, which was not to be in any way "outstanding" but rather to blend into the social fabric, the underlying "woof" that is neither dyed nor blanched beforehand, just left in the tawny color it had on the backs of sheep. Agrippinus, however, chose to act differently because he had higher aspirations. The difference is not only in what he decides to do – to risk reprisal by not attending – but also in how he reaches that decision. His choice clearly reflects his priorities. Those priorities differ so fundamentally that his process of decision differs too. He never even weighs his natural advantages: "I don't even deliberate" (13). Even before doing so, he recognizes the duties entailed by his station, and here at least, that tells him outright what he must do. In effect, his commitment to his role "silences" his interest in safety and other natural values, at least in the present situation.[28] Since his "volition" – his *reasonable* desire – is to perform the role of a senator ("to be purple," i.e., to wear the robe that is the badge of his rank), he must not attend. Not only would performing onstage disgrace his rank; obeying Nero's orders would violate his obligation to uphold the independence of the senate.

Another example from the following decade reinforces this picture of the duties of public service – or at least of the patricians who formed the primary Roman political class (19–21):

Helvidius Priscus knew this too, and he acted accordingly. When Vespasian sent for him and told him not to attend the Senate, he replied, "It is up to you not to allow me to be a member; but so long as I am, I must attend." "Very well, but when you attend, remain silent." "Do not ask me for my vote and I'll stay silent." "But I must ask." "And I too must say what appears right." "But if you speak, I'll kill you." "So when did I tell you I am immortal? You will do your part, and I will do mine: yours is to kill, mine to die without fear; yours is to banish, mine to depart without sorrow."

The imaginary exchange between princeps and senator succinctly highlights the primacy of duties over selective value; and while there is no explicit mention of *kathēkonta*, the exchange echoes key Stoic doctrines.

---

[28] This idea of "silencing" goes back to Plato's Socrates, whom Epictetus cites repeatedly; see *Ap.* 28b, *Crito* 48c–d, and Vlastos 1991: 209–14. Cf. Dobbin 1998: 83–84.

Helvidius' first reply focuses squarely and solely on the conduct required by
his rank, the duties of his station, expressed in the deontic language often
used to articulate them: "I must attend" (δεῖ). His second reply drives Vespasian to parrot his terms ("must ask": δεῖ), which his third reply implicitly
reiterates in turn: "I too (must) speak." Only at this third stage does any
reference to virtue enter the debate, and it does so only indirectly, not as any
act it entails Helvidius must perform, but simply as a blanket label for what
he must say when the assembled senate, in accord with standard procedure,
is asked to voice its views. Then, and only then, Helvidius promises, will he
say "what appears right." (Describing his response as "what appears" suits
the Stoic focus on "impressions" and avoids reference to inherently flawed
"opinions"; it also allows that Helvidius might be mistaken, in keeping
with the "reservation" inherent in "reasonable" judgments, as well as sena-
torial norms of open debate and majoritarian rule.) The confrontation then
descends to its lowest denominator. Vespasian bluntly reveals his despotism
by threatening to execute Helvidius, who responds with a succinct Stoic
sermon. First a classic maxim on mortality: "I'm not immortal," a theme
for *praemeditatio* and widely attributed to exemplary philosophers.[29] Then
a generalization about divergent roles: "your part and mine"; both tyrants
and senators have their peculiar norms of behavior. And finally a twofold
allusion to the doctrine of dispassion: remaining fearless in the face of
death, and accepting exile without sorrow, succumbing to neither of the
"negative" emotions caused by excessive concern over ills that Stoicism
counts as indifferent.

This miniature dialogue and its concluding sermon exhibit the "reasonable" response of an exemplary Stoic, if not a sage, at least a committed "progressor" well advanced on the path to virtue. What it exhibits,
moreover, is not a deliberative process of weighing options, but a gradual
unveiling of the principles and priorities of reasonable character. Nothing
Vespasian says (or could say) does anything to sway Helvidius, whose suc-
cessive replies simply track the reasons underlying his decision that make
it secure against any threat or opposing argument. His replies, and the
course of action they report, rest in the first instance on his awareness of
what his role as senator requires. That awareness in turn is rooted in his
abiding commitment to principles of Stoic ethics: that external advantages
are of only secondary value at best, and their loss no occasion either for
acting unreasonably or for reacting with the "excessive impulses" that are
passions. But Epictetus has more to add, and by pressing the rationale or

---

[29] Anaxagoras in Cic. *Tusc.* 3.30, 3.58, Val. Max. 5.10 ext., Plut. *Co. Ira* 463D, *Tranq.* 474D, [Plut.]
Cons. Ap. 118D, Ael. *VH* 3.2, D.L. 2.13; Xenophon in D.L. 2.55, etc.

justification behind Helvidius' stance a step further, he links this case to
the previous ones. The further step is simply to ask (22–4), What good can
such stoical resistance do?

So what good did Priscus do, though a single man? What good does the purple
do for the whole cloak? What else than stand out like purple and provide a fine
example for the others? Someone else, if told by Caesar in a similar situation not
to attend the Senate, would have said, "I thank you for excusing me." A man like
that Caesar would not even bother to prevent attending; he would know that the
man will either sit still like a jug, or say what he knew Caesar wants to hear, and
pile on still more.

The unstated basis for this worry is that Helvidius was in fact executed
by Vespasian. Surely resistance did the victim no good. On the contrary,
Epictetus claims, it preserved who he was. Despite costing him his life, his
conduct preserved his character and personal integrity: he lost his life but
lived correctly so long as he lived. His willingness to forgo not only natural
advantages but life itself is integral to his correct and therefore genuinely
"reasonable" choice. And his answer to the question whether to cling to
life hinges not on any calculus of selective value but on his commitment
to personal roles and the consequent personal integrity.[30]

The argument, while not overtly judgmental, plainly favors Agrippinus,
Helvidius, and principled resistance. Patrician purple, in the ethos assumed
by Arrian and most of his readers, far surpasses plebeian beige. Yet as
Epictetus reminds them with yet another example, patrician purple is not
for everyone. His point in so doing is not to endorse or condone Florus or
the benchwarming "jugs" (24) who demeaned the Senate by acquiescing
in autocracy. It is rather to emphasize that Stoic principles are demanding
and require rising above popular preoccupations with selective value. All
the same, he also allows that lower aspirations and lesser achievements have
a place in the fabric of society and the natural world.

Another case, of an athlete dying young, involves a choice of integrity
over life much lower down the social scale. Yet on two counts it is even
more emphatic: both in the suffering entailed, and in the primacy of roles
and their attendant duties in reasonable decision (25–8).

Likewise, an athlete was in danger of dying unless he had his genitals amputated.
His brother – the fellow was a philosopher – came to him and asked, "Well,

---

[30] In this respect, Epictetus' examples appear to run counter to the model of deliberation found
in Cic. *Fin.* 3.60–1, which has stimulated acute debate; see Cooper 1989, Barney 2003, Brennan
2005: 182–230. Whether the contrast reflects internal Stoic debates, or issues peculiar to suicide, or
distortion by Cicero, or a deeper problem, is an important question, but one too large to pursue
here.

brother, what are you going to do? Do we amputate these parts and enter the gymnasium again?" But he refused and remained firm until he died. Someone asked how he had done that, as an athlete or a philosopher. "As a man," he replied, "and a man who had competed at Olympia and been proclaimed victor there, who had spent his life in places like that, not newly anointed in a gladiators' ring."[31] Someone else would have had his head cut off as well, if he could live without it. That is what it is to act by your role, and that is how strong it is for those who have made it a habit to bring it to bear in their deliberations.

The case is deceptively simple. The natural choice for many if not most – what they would *find* "reasonable" even if mistakenly so – would be castration. The (roughly contemporary) Stoic Hierocles illustrates the self-awareness that enables even sub-rational animals to recognize what is "appropriate" to their nature and hence *kathēkon* for them (their natural "duty") by citing a beaver's similar response to similar options.[32] The injured athlete's rejection of the natural choice therefore demands an explanation, which an interlocutor duly requests. But the explanation turns out to have little direct connection to either of the two roles that figure explicitly in the anecdote. The athlete rejects castration neither as an athlete nor as a philosopher (26). Neither does he choose to maintain or restore his athletic prowess, since his decision entails not recovery but death. Nor does he adopt a philosophical stance, which would assign physical fitness and strength strictly instrumental value and hence favor castration and survival over a stubborn insistence on dying that verges on suicidal. The basis for the athlete's decision is rather that he is a "man"; and Epictetus uses not the generic term "human" (ἄνθρωπος) but the fully gendered "man" (ἀνήρ). At first glance, the logic looks impeccable but absurdly circular: males must avoid emasculation at all costs. But the explanation avoids circularity by highlighting the anonymous athlete's personal history: his lengthy training and great success, even in Olympic games, where he not only competed but emerged victorious. For such a victor, longevity has no appeal – no use or advantage – without the requisite testosterone.

If Epictetus expressed a verdict on the athlete's decision, Arrian does not record it. The point of the anecdote, and its ethical basis, is rather to illustrate the power of personal commitment in decision-making.[33] To

---

[31] Who replies? Translators assign the whole reply to Epictetus. But the first sentence equally suits the athlete's own words, which someone else then explicates; alternatively, the whole reply could come from the brother, who was presumably the source for the anecdote and is labelled a philosopher (in 25, where ἐκεῖνος apparently refers to the brother).

[32] Hier. *Elem.* (*PBerol* 9780) 3.10–19; cf. Plin. *NH* 8.109, Ael. *NA* 6.34.

[33] Epictetus appends, with more than a trace of irony, an ostensibly parallel demand on his own integrity (29): "'Well then, Epictetus, shave off your beard.' If I'm a philosopher, I say I won't shave it off. 'But I'll cut off your head.' If you think that's better, then cut it off."

embrace a role wholeheartedly, whether rightly or wrongly, is to make certain standards or principles personally inviolate; and those standards or principles then effectively determine one's response to any situations that put them in play, since they "silence" any competing interests, however attractive those might otherwise be. Just as the athlete (like the toilet slave introduced initially) was *psychologically* unable to decide contrary to what he considered most reasonable, so Helvidius and Agrippinus were *morally* incapable of submitting to tyranny. The athlete presumably does not deserve the same admiration: ancient athletics was blood sport, but sport all the same. Politics, by contrast, is essentially moral, and for Stoics, closely related to theology insofar as it takes the rational administration of the common good as its aim.

Arrian rounds off the discourse with two more exchanges that are thematically related but appear to be temporally separate. In the first, Epictetus confronts the question of how we are to discern what our roles are. In short, as the discussion has hitherto addressed the deliberative question of how we may tell what to *do* by invoking our roles (as determinants of duties), so he now faces the further question of how we may discover and specify our proper *roles*. A fuller response can be pieced together from other discourses (most notably 2.10 on "how to discover duties from words").[34] All Arrian provides here is an appeal to animal parallels (30–32).

Someone asked, "Then how are we each to be aware of our role?" How, he replied, is the bull alone aware of his own capability when a lion attacks, and how does he stand as a bulwark in front of the whole herd? Or is it clear that right away, together with having that capability he also has an awareness of it? In our case too, therefore, whoever has such a capability will not be unaware of it. A bull does not become capable suddenly, nor a man steadfast; it requires training all year round to become capable, and not leaping haphazardly into wholly unsuitable efforts.

Despite his quaint example, Epictetus formulates a powerful general principle. Simply put, if you have a "capability" of the relevant sort, you recognize that you have it. But the scope of the principle is far from clear. How reliable is this self-awareness? How far does it extend? Does it also tell us when and how to deploy our capabilities? Nor is it clear how we acquire the relevant capabilities. The example suggests native ability: a bull's instinctive reaction to aggression. But the term itself, literally "preparation" (παρασκευή), points to some sort of practice or training, as in the athlete's case. And the cases discussed previously, which are presumably meant to fall under the principle as well, would extend the range of capabilities

---

[34] See Long 1983: 188–94, Kamtekar 1998: 147–52, Long 2002: 231–44.

to include commitments to moral and political principles.[35] In fact, the following lines, which conclude the discourse, assume an entirely general principle, embracing the full triad of soul, body, and externals (33–37).

> Only consider what price you set for selling your own priorities. If nothing else, human that you are, don't set a low price. Outstanding greatness suits others, perhaps, Socrates and any like him. "Then why, if we're made for that, do we not all of us or most of us become like that?" Do all horses become swift, all dogs good trackers? "Well then, since I have no talent, shall I give up cultivation [τῆς ἐπιμελείας] on that account?" Not at all. Epictetus won't be superior to Socrates; but in that case, it's enough for me if I'm not his inferior. Nor shall I be Milo; yet still I don't neglect [οὐκ ἀμελῶ] my body. Nor shall I be Croesus; yet still I don't neglect my property. Nor in general do we give up our cultivation in any other area because we don't expect to excel.

The central point in Epictetus' conclusion draws on one of his favorite refrains, that our priorities, commitments, and assessments are "up to us": within our power and control, subject only to our own choice. That power or freedom (to use a hotly contested word in its simplest sense), which he repeatedly cites as a distinctive mark of being human, depends on reason. Many misuse it and enslave themselves to misguided priorities. That is what Epictetus counts as "setting a low price" and "selling ourselves cheap." The correct course, the genuinely human course, which alone is truly reasonable, is to set a high price, to aim high and challenge ourselves. And in what may seem a surprising turn, Epictetus recommends that we also attend to bodily and economic factors. Acknowledging that "outstanding greatness" is inevitably rare, he nonetheless counsels aspiration; and presenting himself as a model, he professes to emulate Socrates in cultivating his soul ("not his inferior") but also to follow Milo in "not neglecting" (οὐκ ἀμελῶ) his body, and even Croesus in "not neglecting" his property.

It may seem that we have left roles and duties far behind. But the concluding passage serves to counter the main thrust of the discourse in two ways. First, it aims to forestall any tendency to concentrate our attention *too* narrowly, whether to cultivate philosophy without regard to our many other roles and duties, or vice versa. Everyone also has physical and material needs and interests. Second, it rejects a parallel tendency to concentrate solely or heavily on areas where we *excel*, on special capabilities at the expense of other roles and duties. Few have any chance of rivaling

---

[35] Cf. 4.8.41–3, using the same example of bulls but focused on the effects of philosophical doctrines; also 1.1.31 on "cultivating" (μελετᾶν) the principles that "prepare [παρεσκευακέναι] pursuit and avoidance to resist hindrance or reversal." In Stob. 2.87.18–19, the term appears to be a technical label for capabilities acquired by prior effort (πρᾶξις πρὸ πράξεως); cf. Hier. *Elem.* 1.52–53, with the example of bulls in 2.3–7.

Milo, but that is no reason for anyone to neglect fitness entirely. Both points allude to selection and the importance of correctly evaluating natural needs and values. Some duties, after all, concern ourselves, and self-preservation requires attention to health and external resources as well. Both points are also concessive. Cultivation of the soul (cast in positive terms: ἐπιμέλεια) is what Epictetus puts first, here as elsewhere (cf. 2.5, esp. 6–9), and he adds bodily and external matters mainly as an afterthought (cast in negative terms: οὐκ ἀμελῶ). That too is fully in line with their relative rank in selective value (Stob. 2.81.19–82.4). But if his language seems to highlight objects, it would be a mistake to infer that he assigns selection deliberative priority. The focus in the finale falls squarely on "cultivation" (underscored by verbal repetition: noun and verb each used twice); and in keeping with the central theme of the entire discourse, the term refers to action, and in particular to correct actions or duties (cf. 1.1.31 and n. 35 above).

To conclude, selection concerns the evaluation of bodily objects and their states. It plays an important part in deliberation and choice. But it is neither itself a form of impulse, nor adequate by itself to motivate action. The key to action, both in moral psychology and in ethical theory, is rather the concept of suitable and reasonable conduct labelled "duties" or *kathēkonta*. To put my central thesis baldly, too baldly no doubt, selection belongs to the Stoic theory of value (to use their preferred label for most of what is conventionally called good), and duty belongs to their theory of conduct. One major aim of Stoic ethics, I suggest, is to establish the practical priority of conduct: acting correctly matters most both in deliberation and in assessing the true quality of a life. The order may differ in the theoretical justification of conduct; but that is a story for another occasion.[36]

---

[36] A worry arose at the Berkeley conference that my account of selection verges on Aristo's heterodox absolutism, which counts everything but virtue and vice as absolutely indifferent and thereby eliminates any other factors (including any value in preferreds and dispreferreds) from sound deliberation. But first, my case for the deliberative priority of actions over objects (and specifically duties over values) leaves abundant room for distinctions of value in the theoretical justification of duties, for both general rules and particular cases; and second, selective value remains a crucial factor even in deliberation, for once we choose what to do (to honor someone, for example), we must still find and select suitably valuable objects with which to do so (such as a topic to address). In the present case, the selection was easy: my first serious encounter with Stoicism I owe to Tony Long, and his discerning scholarship, passionate teaching, and enthusiastic mentoring remain for me a model of how to approach ancient philosophy. With deep admiration and abiding gratitude I happily dedicate this chapter to him. I am also grateful to Keimpe Algra for helpful comments, to Margaret Graver for challenging questions, and to the editors for organizing a model meeting of minds.

CHAPTER 8

Beauty and its relation to goodness in Stoicism
Richard Bett

I

It is well known that the concept of *to kalon* in ancient Greek occurs in a wide variety of contexts. It applies to physical beauty, but it is also common in ethical contexts, where "honorable" or "noble" are often appropriate English translations, and where Cicero regularly Latinizes it as *honestum*. Nor does this exhaust the possible applications of the concept, to judge from the range of objects that receive the label *kalon* in Plato's dialogue devoted to the topic, the *Hippias Major*; not only gods and beautiful young women, but also horses, lyres, cooking pots, and soup ladles are described as *kala*, apparently without controversy. In the last two cases, at any rate, what seems to entitle them to the epithet *kalon*, if it is justified, is not anything to do with a pleasing physical appearance, but, roughly, their *appropriateness* for the job they are supposed to do. No doubt this multiplicity of possible applications is one reason why Socrates and Hippias fail to find a satisfactory definition of *to kalon*, and why their various attempted definitions are so extremely different from one another. Although it is a recurring contention of Socrates in Plato's dialogues that each word must have a unitary sense in all of its various occurrences, the example of the term *to kalon*, as illustrated by the *Hippias Major*, seems to put that contention into question.

Yet Plato was clearly not willing to abandon the idea that these many different applications of the term *to kalon* are importantly related to one another. For in the *Symposium* he famously has Socrates describe a process of intellectual and emotional ascent which begins with the admiration of particular beautiful bodies and ends with the contemplation of the Form of Beauty itself – encompassing several other items in between, each of which deserves the label *kalon*. Indeed, the clear suggestion of the text is that it is the *same* quality present at every stage; we have an ascent covering a number of items falling under the same concept, but to a progressively greater degree.[1] But despite this, it is clear that although the first stages of the ascent emphasize physical beauty,[2] there is also a powerful connection between *to kalon*, at least in its higher manifestations, and goodness, including ethical goodness. One might have guessed this from a comparison with the *Republic*, where the Form of the Good is at the pinnacle of a long process of intellectual ascent, just as the Form of Beauty is at the pinnacle in the *Symposium*; surely the two are closely related in Plato's mind. But the *Symposium* itself gives sufficient evidence of the same point. For the grasp of the Form of Beauty is said to give rise to virtue (true virtue, not merely a simulacrum of virtue, 212a4–5); and among the things one contemplates in the course of the ascent are laws and ways of life (*epitēdeumata*, 210c3–4), the "beauty" of which must consist at least in part in their ethical excellence. *To kalon* and goodness, then, are not ultimately separable; yet *to kalon* covers a multitude of contexts, including some that we might not immediately associate with goodness. Both these points seem to be important aspects of Plato's outlook, at least as revealed in the *Symposium*.

The Stoics can hardly be said to accord such transcendent importance to *to kalon* as does Plato. But it nonetheless plays a significant role in their ethical thinking. My concern in this essay is with the Stoics' use of the concept of *to kalon*, including the question how far they are in this respect (as in many other aspects of their ethical theory) the heirs of Plato and Socrates. That there is an important ethical dimension to *to kalon* in Stoicism is uncontroversial. But this by itself does not indicate any specifically Platonic legacy; the everyday Greek notion of the *kalos kagathos* illustrates that *some* connection between *to kalon* and ethical excellence was widely taken for granted. What is also not so clear is whether there is, in the Stoics' minds, any connection between *to kalon* in its ethical aspect and physical beauty as we ordinarily understand it. This is the issue with which I begin.

[1] This is even clearer if Frisbee Sheffield is right that the goal of this entire process is to discover the true nature of beauty, seeing the common feature present in all of its various instances – much as Socrates in other dialogues is attempting to find the nature of piety, courage, etc. See Sheffield 2006: ch. 4.1, 4.2. Sheffield also argues persuasively that there are just three stages – body, soul, form – and that "laws, practices and so on are examined in extension of an interest in beauty of soul" (126, cf. 114, n. 3), rather than constituting separate stages of their own. I take this to be fully compatible with my account in this paragraph.

[2] Although even here, according to Sheffield 2006: 118–19, the lover's interest is intellectual at least as much as sexual: he is "reflecting upon the nature of this beauty" (119). I return to this point, comparing Plato with the Stoics, in the last section.

II

It looks at first as if physical beauty and *to kalon* (as discussed in ethical contexts) are in the Stoic view quite separate from one another. On the one hand beauty, *kallos*, is referred to as an indifferent, not a good; it occurs in Diogenes Laertius' summary of Stoic ethics (7.102) in a list of things that "neither benefit nor harm," along with life, health, pleasure, strength, wealth, good reputation and good birth (and their opposites). As Diogenes goes on to explain (7.103), the good is *guaranteed* to benefit, and the bad to harm, because they have benefiting and harming respectively as their "special property" (*idion*). The only things that genuinely benefit or harm in this very stringent sense are virtue and vice respectively; and anything less than this does not count as benefiting or harming at all.[3]

Beauty is indeed a *preferred* indifferent – as are life, health, etc.; that is, it has value (*axia*) – and, according to Sextus Empiricus (*M* 11.62–63) and Stobaeus (2.84.21–22), a considerable amount of value – which makes it by nature something generally worth pursuing. Diogenes (7.106) says that anything with value is a preferred indifferent, but this is probably an oversimplification; the more complicated and, I suspect, more accurate picture reported by Stobaeus and assumed by Sextus requires that the amount of value be substantial. But no amount of value, in this sense, can make something a good; despite the objections of unsympathetic critics such as Plutarch (e.g., *Comm. not.* 1060B–C), there is a fundamental gulf between the good and the preferred indifferent. Preferred indifferents – indeed, any indifferents that have value or are "according to nature" (*kata phusin*) – are described as "to be taken" (*lēpta*, Stobaeus 2.82.20). More specifically, beauty is "to be taken" for itself, and not, like wealth, "to be taken" for the sake of other things that can be obtained by means of it. But "to be taken" (*lēpton*) is not the same as "to be chosen" (*haireton*); the latter term applies only to the good (Stobaeus 2.75.1–6).[4] It is not entirely

---

3   The talk of "special properties" might be taken to suggest that health, wealth, etc. do benefit, but only contingently and only sometimes. And this might seem to be reinforced by Diogenes' comparison with heat and cold, whose "special properties" are heating and chilling respectively; for surely there are other things that do heat and chill, but not in this necessary way. However, the Stoics never allow that anything other than virtue and vice (together with certain things necessarily connected with them, such as virtuous actions, virtuous people, etc.) are either good or beneficial, and they never allow for a category of contingent, temporary benefiting. Brennan 2005: 120 has it right: "Wealth is never, in any sort of case, a good; it is always and in every case an indifferent. For . . . if this portion of wealth on this occasion really were a good, that is, if it really benefited its possessor, then an agent would have reason to feel that the loss of that wealth on that occasion . . . really was a loss of something genuinely good; and this is not a conclusion the Stoics would support."
4   For these terms, cf. White, this volume, pp. 110–29.

clear what this distinction amounts to, beyond an act of terminological legislation. But one thing that seems to follow from the preceding points is that a *haireton* is unconditionally and in all circumstances worth striving for, whereas a *lēpton* is something that there is typically reason to pursue – and in the case of preferred indifferents, strong reason to pursue – but only typically, not invariably. In any case, the level of worth accorded to the good is of a wholly different order from that accorded to indifferents, even preferred indifferents; in a very literal sense, the two are not comparable.[5]

That *kallos* in these contexts refers specifically to physical beauty is confirmed by two of the texts to which I have appealed. It is "beauty of the body" (*kallos sōmatos*, 2.83.4) that Stobaeus speaks of as one of the things that are "to be taken" for themselves. And Diogenes (7.106) distinguishes three types of preferred indifferents, one of them being preferred indifferents of the body; it is to this type that beauty is said to belong.

Now, it is a very different matter when *to kalon* is spoken of in ethical contexts. Here we are told that the perfect good (*to teleion agathon*) is *kalon* (DL 7.100), that every good is *kalon* (D.L. 7.98–99, Stob. 2.69.11–13, 78.4), that only the *kalon* is good (e.g., Cic. *Fin.* 3.50, *Paradox. Sto.* 6–15, Plut. *Sto. rep.* 1039C), that the terms *kalon* and *agathon* are equivalent (D.L. 7.101), and that *to kalon* is "to be chosen" (*haireton*) for its own sake (Plut. *Sto. Rep.* 1040C) – not merely "to be taken." Some of these ideas are ascribed to Zeno (Cic. *Acad.* 1.35, *Leg.* 1.55) and Cleanthes (Clement, *Protrept.* 6.72.2=*SVF* I.557), the earliest leaders of the school, and some of them to Chrysippus'

---

[5] This picture of the Stoic conception, according to which there are two different types of value, has been challenged, at least for the early Stoics, by McCabe 2002, esp. section V. Drawing on Diogenes Laertius' talk of "special properties" (see n. 3), she argues for a distinction between goods in themselves and derivative goods; the latter can never become the former (just as, in another repeated Stoic analogy, the courtiers to whom the king gives preferred places at court can never *become* king – Stob. 2.85.5–11, Cic. *Fin.* 3.52), but both are genuinely goods, and this is no accident. For these "special properties" of things have causal powers and exert their influence on other things; "the good is what makes other things good . . . just as the hot is what makes other things hot." On this reading, then, the argument is "not about two sorts of value, but rather about the explanatory relations between what is good by itself and whatever derives its goodness from that" (392). Now this would indeed make the Stoics' view much closer to some passages of Plato with which it is often compared (*Meno* 87e6–88d3, and especially *Euthydemus* 281b–e). But I do not see how it is compatible with the considerable evidence from Diogenes Laertius (7.94–101), Stobaeus (2.68.24–74.20), and Cicero (*Fin.* 3.33–34, 55) concerning what kinds of things the Stoics recognized as goods. The classifications are quite elaborate. But none of them ever suggests a category of derivative goods; indeed, Diogenes (7.101) insists that there is no ranking of goods – they are all equal. And none of them suggests that items such as health or wealth are good or beneficial in any sense; instead (see again the previous note), all goods either are virtues or have a necessary relation to the virtues. (There is a distinction between final and instrumental goods – D.L. 7.96–97, Stob. 2.71.15–72.13, Cic. *Fin.* 3.55; but this is a distinction between things that *confer* benefit, such as friends, and things that simply *are* benefit.) It is no doubt true that the Stoics learned from Plato in this area; but they also departed from him on crucial points. On this see the cautions of Brennan 2005: 119–21.

book *Peri tou kalou* and Hecaton's book *Peri agathōn* (DL 7.101, Plut. *Sto. rep.* 1039c). Clearly the notion of a strong interconnection between *to kalon* and the good is deeply embedded in Stoic thinking.[6] Cicero at one point reports a disagreement between Chrysippus and Aristo, and makes it sound as if Chrysippus denied that only *to kalon* is good (in Cicero's words, *quod honestum sit id solum bonum esse*, *Fin.* 4.68), a view held by Aristo. But the broader context of the passage makes clear that the disagreement, here as in many other places, has to do with whether, in addition to the good, one should recognize a category of preferred indifferents. The extremist Aristo held that only *to kalon* is good, and that besides *to kalon* (or *to agathon*), nothing has any positive value whatsoever. The orthodox Stoics hold that some indifferents do have value; but they nonetheless maintain that the good and the indifferent are on entirely different levels, which allows them to agree with Aristo that only *to kalon* is good.

As noted earlier, the only things that meet the Stoics' very high standard for being good are the virtues, to which may be added various things that necessarily accompany the virtues, such as virtuous persons, virtuous activities, etc. In keeping with this, and again reflecting the intimate connection between the good and *to kalon*, we are also told that on the Stoic view, *to kalon kagathon* is equivalent to "virtue and what partakes of virtue" (Stob. 2.78.1–4). An etymological explanation is also reported concerning the question why virtue is *kalon*: it is of a nature to call (*kalein*) towards itself those who strive for it (Stob. 2.100.21–22). The Stoics' penchant for etymological explanations tends to strike us as childish, especially since the etymologies themselves are mostly false by the standards of modern philology. But the Stoics are in this respect the upholders of a venerable tradition in Greek thought, represented most famously in parts of Plato's *Cratylus* but stretching back to Homer, that sees words as containing real and valuable information about the character of the things to which they refer.[7] The purported etymology of *kalon*, then, is supposed to tell us something genuine about virtue; and in doing so it cements still further the connection between *to kalon* and the good.

---

[6] How exactly we should conceive the connection is perhaps not as clear as it might be. The claim that *kalon* and *agathon* mean the same thing (*isodunamein*, D.L. 7.101) seems to suggest outright identity; but the other passages just quoted need not be taken as implying anything stronger than extensional equivalence. Cicero's somewhat vague statement (quoted in the next section) that beauty of soul "follows virtue or contains the very force of virtue" (*virtutem subsequens aut virtutis vim ipsam continens*, *Tusc.* 4.31) possibly reflects a lack of precision on this point in the Stoic sources.

[7] For an excellent account of the Stoics' views in this area, see Allen 2005. On Allen's interpretation, the Stoics' ideas differ substantially from those discussed in Plato's *Cratylus*.

We appear, then, to have two quite different and unrelated notions: physical beauty, referred to by the noun *kallos* and consigned to the realm of the indifferent, and the ethically admirable quality designated by the neuter adjective with the definite article, *to kalon*, which qualifies as good, and indeed is virtually indistinguishable from the good itself. One might think that the Stoics are using the verbal difference precisely in order to draw attention to the distinction between the two. There are cases in Stoicism where a distinction is drawn between two different terms using the same root; Stobaeus, for example, reports a subtle distinction between *haireton* and *haireteon*, both of which might naturally be translated "to be chosen" (2.78.7–12). *Kallos* and *to kalon* could represent another (rather more obvious) example of the same kind of thing.

But it would be a mistake to conclude that there is no connection between the two notions – whatever we may think about the choice of terminology. For the noun *kallos* is not applied only to beauty of the body, but also to beauty of the soul. And beauty of the soul is described explicitly by analogy with beauty of the body, yet is also clearly understood to carry with it a form of ethical excellence. Here, then, is a link between *kallos* as physical beauty and the ethically admirable quality designated by *to kalon*. And this may help us to better understand *what* this ethically admirable quality is – a matter that I have so far left purposely vague.

Central to the beauty both of body and of soul is the concept of *summetria*. Beauty of body is defined as "symmetry of the limbs with respect to one another and to the whole," and beauty of soul is defined analogously as "symmetry of reason and its parts with respect to the whole of it and to one another" (Stob. 2.63.1–5). The same passage of Stobaeus also includes definitions of the health and strength of the soul, again by analogy with the health and strength of the body. Galen quotes a number of passages of Chrysippus on these subjects, and it is clear that Stobaeus' summary follows Chrysippus closely (*PHP* 5.2–3). Galen complains that Chrysippus fails to mark a clear distinction between the health of the soul and its beauty, whereas the distinction is clear in the case of the body – and hence, that the soul/body analogy is flawed. Galen compares the Stoics unfavorably with Plato in this respect; the main reason, in his view, why Plato does better is that he allows genuinely distinct parts of the soul, whereas for the Stoics the soul (or at least the *hēgemonikon*, the "leading part" of the soul) is unitary. In the same vein, he questions what the Stoics can mean by the "parts" of reason in the above definition, and does not find any acceptable answer. The answer that he quotes from Chrysippus – "They are the parts of the soul through which its reason and the disposition of its reason are constituted" (*PHP* 5.2.49 DeLacy) – does indeed appear disappointingly vague. So Galen may be right that the Stoics are not in a position to define the health and the beauty of the soul in ways that are both (a) clearly distinct from one another, and (b) precisely analogous to their definitions of health and beauty in the body.

But this should not seriously trouble us. For it is clear that according to the Stoics' conception of the soul, reason or the *hēgemonikon* has a number of different aspects or functions, and that, in the wise person's soul, these aspects or functions will complement one another and fit together in a felicitous and harmonious way. The Stoics agree with Plato at least to this extent: the soul of the wise person is maximally *well-ordered* (though they may differ as to what that good order consists in). Even if we agree that this well-ordered state might just as well be called health as beauty, it remains true that *summetria* is an appropriate term by which to characterize it, and that there is a clear analogy between this and the *summetria* that the Stoics take to constitute physical beauty. The analogy may not apply in every detail, but neither is it far-fetched or implausible.

I have already begun to speak of the wise person as the one whose soul has beauty, as so described. For if beauty of the soul consists in the soul's good order, then it is clearly the person who has wisdom or virtue (and these two, of course, are for the Stoics inseparable) whose soul is beautiful. Virtue and goodness are frequently characterized in the sources in terms that emphasize their orderliness and harmony. Virtue is described as a "disposition in agreement" (*diathesin . . . homologoumenēn*, D.L. 7.89). This recalls Zeno's definition of the *telos*, the ethical end, as "living in agreement" (*homologoumenōs zēn*, Stob. 2.75.11–12), which is glossed with the words "that is, living in accordance with a single consistent reason – on the assumption that those who live in conflict are unhappy" (75.12–76.1). "In agreement," then – when it is used by itself, and not as part of a longer phrase such as "in agreement with nature" – seems to refer to the internal consistency or harmony of one's reason.[8] Cicero, too, understands the Stoic notion of *homologia* in terms of the "order and harmony in doing things" (*rerum agendarum ordinem et . . . concordiam*, *Fin.* 3.21). And Seneca speaks in very similar terms of the unmistakable signs of virtue; they are the person's "order and elegance and consistency, and the harmony among all

---

[8] Here I depart from Brennan 2005: 138. I have argued for this interpretation in a little more detail in Bett 2006: 532–33. See also Striker 1996: 223–24, and Bett 2008.

his actions" (*ordo eius et decor et constantia et omnium inter se actionum concordia, Ep.* 120.11). Both wisdom and the virtues are also described as species of knowledge (*epistēmē,* Aetius 1, Preface 2, Stob. 2.59.4–10), and knowledge, in turn, is understood as a stable system of interrelated apprehensions (Stob. 2.73.19–74.1).

Beauty of soul, then, belongs to the wise or virtuous person, and *only* to such a person; for the vicious person's soul, of course, is characterized in the opposite way, by disorder and instability – and everyone is either virtuous or vicious. It is not surprising, then, that beauty of soul, along with health and strength of soul, is referred to, in the passage where the body/soul analogy was introduced, as a virtue – albeit as a virtue that supervenes on the four primary virtues and their subspecies, and is not itself a form of knowledge (Stob. 2.62.17–20). In a passage of the *Tusculan Disputations* that is explicitly borrowing Stoic definitions, Cicero draws the same analogy between beauty of body and beauty of soul, adding that beauty of soul "follows virtue or contains the very force of virtue" (*virtutem subsequens aut virtutis vim ipsam continens,* 4.31).

So beauty, *kallos*, is not, after all, unrelated to *to kalon* as used in ethical contexts, which we might be more inclined to translate by "honorable" or "noble." Clearly the person who has beauty of soul is also the person who exhibits *to kalon* in his or her attitudes and actions; indeed, it can hardly be doubted that these are just two ways of saying the same thing. The connection is made particularly clear in a report in Diogenes Laertius: "They call the perfect good *kalon*," he says, "because of its having in full the quantities required by nature, or perfect symmetry [*to teleōs summetron*]" (7.100). The reference to "quantities" (*arithmous*) hints at a notion of mathematical proportion, which is hard to understand in this context except metaphorically; but the explanation in terms of symmetry precisely recalls the definition of beauty of soul.[9] Diogenes goes on to say that there are four forms of *to kalon*; these correspond with the four primary virtues, but with one interesting variation. *To kalon* is said to be wise, courageous, and just. But in place of an aspect corresponding to the usual fourth virtue, *sōphrosunē*, we are told that *to kalon* is "orderly" (*kosmion*). In the *Republic* Plato had defined *sōphrosunē* as a harmony among the parts

---

[9] Compare the definition in Stobaeus of the *katorthōma* ("right action") as a *kathēkon* (appropriate action) "that possesses all the numbers" (*pantas epechon tous arithmous,* 2.93.14–15). A *kathēkon,* though it is in fact the correct action on the occasion in question, is not necessarily performed with the correct disposition. *Katorthōmata* are the special subset of *kathēkonta* that are both correct and performed correctly, in this sense; in other words, they are *kathēkonta* as performed by the wise, whose souls have the requisite symmetry or proportion.

of the soul. Given their different conception of the soul, the Stoics cannot follow this; they define *sōphrosunē* as a form of knowledge (Stob. 2.59.8–9), and it is also characterized in texts apparently appealing to Stoic ideas as "a state that preserves the decisions of *phronēsis* in choices and avoidances" (Sextus, *M* 9.174, cf. Clement, *Strom.* 2.18.79.5). But the Stoics do echo the Platonic picture to the extent of including *kosmiotēs*, orderliness, as one of the subspecies of *sōphrosunē* (Stob. 2.60.20, D.L. 7.126). And it is not surprising that when the subject is the forms of *to kalon*, itself so closely connected with the notion of good order, the subordinate virtue *kosmiotēs* should be made to stand in for *sōphrosunē* as a whole.

It might still be suggested that physical beauty and the qualities exhibited by the wise or virtuous person are entirely distinct; there may be an analogy between beauty of body and beauty of soul, but this, one might say, does not tell against the fundamental discontinuity between the two. However, this too is open to question. For nature, according to the Stoics, is unified in a very strong sense. It is unified because it is directed, down to the last detail, by a rational divine being. Not only directed, but permeated; the divine reason takes the form of an all-pervading breath (*pneuma*) that constitutes the soul of the cosmos. And one of the most visible manifestations of this divine reason – and one of the strongest reasons for believing that it exists – is the orderliness of the cosmos. Cleanthes' *Hymn to Zeus* speaks of the divinity "making crooked things straight and ordering what is without order [κοσμεῖν τἄκοσμα]," and adds "you have fitted together (συνήρμωκας) everything into one" (Stob. 1.2.12 = *SVF* I p. 122,14–16). And in *On the Nature of the Gods*, Cicero has the Stoic Balbus report from Cleanthes four reasons why people believe (correctly) in the existence of gods, of which the most important is the order and stability of the motions of the heavenly bodies (2.15). The orderliness of the world as a whole, then, is a result of the perfect rationality of the divinity; the cosmic soul, like the soul of the wise person, is orderly, and so imparts order to whatever it affects.

But now, as we saw, it is precisely a kind of orderliness, referred to as *summetria*, that constitutes *beauty*, whether physical or psychic. It is not surprising, then, that Balbus also speaks in the same passage (2.15) of the beauty of the cosmic order; indeed, the words *pulchritudo* and *ordo* are simply juxtaposed, with no connective. It is also not unreasonable – although, as far as I know, this is not explicitly reported in the sources – to think of the various examples of physical beauty in the world as being especially vivid illustrations of the all-pervading divine reason. If the cosmic divinity is revealed in the orderliness of the world, then that divinity shines with particular intensity in the *summetria* that constitutes physical beauty.

So beauty of body and beauty of soul are not merely analogous in some accidental way; they are both manifestations of rationality functioning at its best. That someone is physically beautiful does not, of course, guarantee that he or she also has beauty of soul (although even here, as we shall see later, there is more of a connection than one might have expected). But physical beauty is a supreme product of the rationality of the divine soul, which is itself presumably as beautiful as any soul can be.

Another indication of the continuity of beauty in the Stoic view of the world is a surprising argument reported by Sextus Empiricus in *Against the Ethicists*. In this part of the work Sextus has argued that nothing is by nature either good or bad. To close the chapter he considers, and rebuts, two objections, one from the Epicureans and one from the Stoics, both of which appeal to animal behavior to show that certain things are naturally to be chosen. According to Sextus, the Stoics, characterized as "those who believe that only *to kalon* is good,"[10] say that "some noble (*gennaia*) animals, such as bulls and cocks, fight to the death even though no delight or pleasure is in store for them" (99), and that this can only be explained on the assumption that *to kalon* has an inherent attractive power. In my commentary on *Against the Ethicists*,[11] I referred to this Stoic argument as "ill-advised," because – as Sextus does not hesitate to point out – the Stoics hold that only rational beings (which excludes all non-human animals) can aspire to ethical excellence. But the argument does seem to suggest that the Stoics do not wish to restrict *to kalon* and one's responses to it solely to the realm of the ethical outlook and behavior of rational beings. Just as physical beauty and beauty of soul are not wholly unrelated phenomena, so too *to kalon* as a motivating force in human behavior is not wholly distinct from what motivates some non-human animals.

IV

I have taken the argument for the continuity of *kallos* and *to kalon* as far as it can go. For clearly the *way* in which *to kalon* motivates

---

[10] The Stoics are not actually named in the passage. Bernard Besnier has suggested to me that the view here discussed might have been held by someone influenced by the Stoics but not in agreement with every point in their ethics – an Antiochean, perhaps. In this case it might not be subject to the rather obvious objection that Sextus raises (see below). But the phrase "those who believe that only *to kalon* is good" would clearly be understood to refer primarily (even if perhaps not exclusively) to the Stoics, and would even more clearly be understood to include them. I find it hard to believe that Sextus, in however mischievous a frame of mind, would use this phrase to refer to a group that specifically did *not* include the Stoics.

[11] Bett 1997: 126.

non-human animals, if it does, must be quite different from the way
in which it motivates the wise person, or even humans in general. Animals
cannot initiate any action using the *concept* of *to kalon*; their action in this
domain must rather be some kind of instinctive response, which the divine
being has designed them to undergo in certain kinds of circumstances. But
since what is crucial about the wise person is precisely the attitude with
which he or she approaches the world, such a person does indeed stand
apart from all the other instances of *kallos* or *to kalon* in the world – except,
of course, for the soul of the divine being itself. The Stoics, then, are subject to conflicting pressures. On the one hand they have good reason to
draw attention to the interconnection among the different types of beauty
in the world, from physical beauty to the beauty of the sage's disposition
and actions; on the other hand they have good reason to emphasize the
uniqueness of the sage. I shall return to this point near the end. For the
moment I want to examine in more detail the latter tendency, i.e.,
the tendency to stress the exceptional character of the sage. This is exhibited
in a particular twist that they give to the notion of beauty in some contexts,
where they claim that, regardless of physical appearances, the sage is the
only one who is beautiful.

   This, of course, is just one of numerous claims known as the "Stoic
paradoxes"; this particular paradox is one of several that are reached by
beginning with an ordinary concept, but arguing that the only person
who meets the conditions for the application of that concept, properly
understood, is the sage. That only the wise person is beautiful is not one
of the paradoxes treated in Cicero's *Paradoxa Stoicorum*; but the last two
of Cicero's paradoxes, that only the wise person is free, and that only the
wise person is rich, follow a similar pattern. In the case of beauty we do
not, as far as I know, have a complete argument surviving; but there are
several suggestive testimonies. A scholium on Horace's *Satires* reports that
the Stoics claim that the sage "is most beautiful, even if he is most ugly"
(*pulcherrimum esse, etiamsi sit sordidissimus*, SVF III 597, p. 155, 40–41).
The thought is not expressed as lucidly as one might like, but given the
points discussed earlier, it is not hard to guess the underlying idea: while
the sage's outer physical appearance may be unattractive, he is beautiful
in the only way that really matters, namely in the orderliness of his soul.
In the same vein Cicero says that the sage will correctly be called beautiful
because "the outlines [*liniamenta*] of the soul are more beautiful than those
of the body" (*Fin.* 3.75). Neither of these texts actually says that *only* the
sage is beautiful. But Cicero does elsewhere attribute this stronger claim to
the Stoics (*Acad.* 2.136), and we also have a report to this effect from Sextus

Empiricus. Along with saying that only the sage is wise and only the sage is rich, the Stoics, according to Sextus (*M* 11.170), say that "only the person worthy of love [*axierastos*] is beautiful, and only the sage is worthy of love; therefore only the sage is beautiful."

This in turn depends on a Stoic definition of love (*erōs*) as "an attempt to form a friendship because of beauty manifested [διὰ κάλλος ἐμφαινόμενον]" or ". . . because of a manifestation of beauty [διὰ κάλλους ἔμφασιν]" (Stob. 2.66.11–13, 2.91.15–16, D.L. 7.130).[12] The definition sometimes includes "of young people at their prime" (νέων ὡραίων) in connection with the word "beauty" (Stob. 2.115.1–2); and Sextus, who mentions the definition in another context, says that these words are assumed even if they are not stated (*M* 7.239). But the notion that only the sage is beautiful seems to call this into question. If one omits the words "of young people at their prime," then there is a question: in whom does true beauty reside? And according to some powerful strands in Stoic thinking, that question has only one possible answer, however unconventional – namely, the person who has achieved true ethical and epistemic excellence. Compared with the beauty of soul of such a person, so-called beauty of body is simply not worth taking seriously as such. And, by the same token, it is only the sage who is genuinely worth loving – even, perhaps, in the sexual sense normally conveyed by the word *erōs*.

Like other Stoic paradoxes, the idea that only the sage is beautiful encountered criticism and ridicule. Alexander of Aphrodisias complains that the Stoics are misusing language; they know perfectly well

---

[12] I follow the translation in Price 2002. I do not, however, accept the implications that Price draws from this reading of the Greek; see nn. 17, 18. Others have generally translated "because of the appearance of beauty"; Schofield 1991/99: 112–13 argues that this "appearance" must be a *mere* appearance; for, if virtue is the only truly beautiful thing, the young persons usually singled out by the Stoics as appropriate objects of love (contrary to the syllogism reported by Sextus) are *not* really beautiful. But *emphainomenon* does not mean "merely apparent"; what is ἐμφαινόμενον is *exhibited* or *shown forth* – there is no room for illusion. The noun *emphasis* can sometimes refer to an image or impression (or a reflection in a mirror or water, Aristotle, *Meteor.* 373b24, 377b17, *Div. Somn.* 464b12); and such impressions can, of course, sometimes be deceptive. But in these cases the ἔμφασις is called an ἔμφασις "as if" or "as" of something. Diogenes Laertius, for example, reporting on the Stoic theory of appearances (*phantasiai*), refers to those appearances that have no real objects as "ἐμφάσεις that are as if [ὡσανεί] from existing things." When ἔμφασις is used with a simple noun in the genitive, the clear implication is that the thing referred to by the noun is real. For example, Galen (*PHP* II.8.15 = *SVF* II.909) quotes Chrysippus commenting on a passage of Hesiod and saying that it "provides the manifestation" (ποιοῦντ᾽ ἔμφασιν) of a different, allegorical meaning – in other words, points (truly) towards such a meaning. The beauty of which there is an ἔμφασις is, then, genuine, not merely apparent; and so, as we shall see, is the resulting tension in the Stoic conception (as Schofield in fact seems to accept. Although I arrive at my conclusions by a somewhat different route, I take myself to be in agreement with him on most of the central points).

what the sage's characteristics are, but they choose to misrepresent these characteristics by calling them wealth, beauty, or noble birth (*In Ar. Top.* 2.134,13–16 = *SVF* III, p. 155, 20–23). Plutarch goes further; for him, the idea that only the sage is beautiful is a prime example of the Stoics' absurd departure from "common conceptions," according to the sizeable work that he devotes to that topic (*Comm. not.* 1072F–1073B). According to Plutarch's report, the Stoics claim not only that the sage is beautiful, but that the young are ugly, "since they are inferior and without reason." One might suspect Plutarch of exaggeration here, and he does not offer any verbatim quotations from Stoics. But if true beauty is beauty of the soul, and if everyone is either virtuous or vicious, then the only natural alternative to being beautiful in this genuine way is being ugly – and all non-sages, including all young people, would fall into this category.

Plutarch's evidence does, however, contradict that of Sextus in one respect. According to Plutarch, the consequence (accepted by the Stoics) of the young being ugly is that love is directed towards the ugly – and that, if and when these ugly persons *become* beautiful (that is, become sages), they *cease* being either loved or worthy of love. Plutarch's version of the Stoic position thus preserves the common idea of the young being appropriate objects of love, but breaks the usual connection between love and beauty. Sextus' version, on the other hand, preserves the latter connection, but speaks of the sages, not the young, as being "worthy of love." Now Sextus is alone on this last point. No other source refers to sages as being worthy of love; the *axierastoi* are elsewhere always young people who are not (yet) sages. For this reason Malcolm Schofield has accused Sextus of "bluffing."[13] But Sextus may be reporting an alternative Stoic line of thought that attempts to take seriously the implications of the idea that the sage, and no one else, is beautiful – as Plutarch's version arguably does not.[14]

v

While both Sextus and Plutarch are often unfair to the Stoics, it is hard not to feel some sympathy with their reactions to Stoic views on this topic.[15] But what is perhaps of more importance than our own intuitive responses is the fact that the Stoics themselves do not manage to sustain this extreme position about beauty and (if we follow Sextus) love. For one

[13] Schofield 1991/1999: 113 n.1.   [14] Here I repeat a view first proposed in Bett 1997: 188–89.
[15] Nussbaum 2002: 84–85 also expresses sympathy for Plutarch's view, though with emphasis on a slightly different aspect of it.

thing, the definition of *erōs* as "an attempt to form a friendship because of a manifestation of beauty" is clearly worded in such a way as to conform to the ordinary conception of love; this is particularly obvious if "of young people at their prime" is added, but it is surely correct (as we saw Sextus saying elsewhere, *M* 7.239) that this is the normal implication, even if it is not actually stated. Secondly, while it appears that this definition was intended to include both a good and a bad variety of *erōs* – one kind being virtuous and the other vicious[16] – it is clear that both kinds include a response to physical beauty. It is also clear that the *sage* will form erotic relationships with beautiful young people who are not (or at any rate, not yet) themselves sages; on this conception, then, even the good kind of love is substantially different from the kind imagined in the notion that only the sage is beautiful (and, on Sextus' version, worthy of love).

One of the places where the definition of *erōs* is quoted in Stobaeus (2.91.15–16) is in the middle of the discussion of the passions, all of which, of course, are forms of irrationality and are alien to the sage's mentality. *Erōs* is classified as one of the subspecies of desire (*epithumia*), which is one of the four primary passions. However, it is notable that what comes under this heading is not *erōs* tout court, but *erōtes sphodroi* (2.91.2) – that is, violent or excessive sexual passions. The distinction between this and the kind of love appropriate to the sage is explained in another passage. We have just been told that the sage does everything in accordance with all the virtues (2.65,12–13); Stobaeus then adds that it follows from this that the sage also acts "sensibly and dialectically and sympotically [i.e., in a manner appropriate to a symposium] and erotically" (16–17). Not surprisingly, this requires some explanation, and there follow some additional remarks about symposia and erotic behavior.

The passage continues, "But the erotic person is spoken of in two ways: the person of a kind that accords with virtue, who is excellent, and the person of a kind that accords with vice, who is subject to blame – a kind of sex maniac, as it were" (2.65.17–20). The latter kind of person is now dismissed, and the good sympotic and erotic attitudes are further explored. These are both counted as virtues (2.66.3–4), and therefore, given the usual Stoic account of virtues, as species of knowledge. The erotic virtue is

---

[16] DL 7.113 actually restricts the definition to the bad kind, and says that good people do not have this kind of love. (I owe this observation to Inwood 1997.) The second point is contradicted by the rest of the evidence, where the definition clearly can apply to the sage's love; but the passage does suggest that the inferior kind of love is at least included in the definition, and Stobaeus 2.91.15–16, cited in the next paragraph, confirms this. (Both passages occur in catalogues of the passions.) Schofield, too, sees the definition as ethically neutral (Schofield 1991/99: 114). Price 2002: 183 takes it to be restricted to the good kind. But this is connected with his distinctive interpretation of the definition, on which I comment below (n. 17).

defined in general terms as "knowledge of loving nobly" (ἐπιστήμην τοῦ καλῶς ἐρᾶν, 66.8); interestingly, then, *to kalon* appears in the description of the ethically admirable attitude of the lover. But *kallos* also appears in the same passage as the stimulus to love, in the definition of *erōs* that we have already seen (2.66.12–13). The passage emphasizes that *erōs*, of the good kind now under discussion, is *not* a desire (*epithumia*) and is not directed at inferior objects – as distinct from the broader phenomenon of 'loving' (τὸ ἐρᾶν), which is an indifferent and can occur in inferior people. But still, the *kallos* in the definition is clearly intended to refer to the physical beauty of young people. For the erotic virtue is also characterized, more fully, as "knowledge of the hunt for young people of fine natures [εὐφυῶν], which spurs them on to the knowledge consisting of virtue" (66.7–8). The beloved, then, is a young person with a strong *potential* for virtue, and the erotic relationship itself will encourage the development of his or her virtue. But at least at the start of the relationship, the young person does not have virtue, and the beauty he or she possesses can only be beauty of the body.[17]

---

[17] Price 2002 has denied this. He takes the beauty "manifested" to be beauty of character, which is revealed by the young person's outward appearance. D.L. 7.129, cited in the next paragraph, does indeed speak of these young people as "manifesting" (ἐμφαινόντων) a promising character (though not, it should be noted, beauty, of any kind) through their outward appearance. But a "manifestation" of something does not have to occur *by means of* something else. If I take off my shirt, for example, I manifest my torso, pure and simple; no medium is required. And ἐμφαίνω is sometimes used in this way. A particularly pertinent example occurs in Xenophon's *Cyropaideia* (1.4.3), during an account of the youthful Cyrus: "just as in the body, with those who are young but have taken on their size [i.e., have reached their full adult size], youthfulness nonetheless is manifested in them [ὅμως ἐμφαίνεται τὸ νεαρὸν αὐτοῖς], which gives away their lack of years." Here the "youthfulness" does indeed point to something else. But since what it points to is "lack of years" (ὀλιγοετίαν), the "youthfulness" itself must be a youthful *appearance* – fresh face, absence of wrinkles, minimal beard, etc. And it is this youthful appearance, and *not* what it points to, that is described as being "manifested" – that is, obvious on the surface. (For other examples of such "surface manifestations" see Ar. *Pol.* 1254a30–31, and Philo, *De somniis* 1.145 (= *SVF* 2.674), where what is "manifested" is a dark patch on the face of the moon.) Now, if the beauty that the young person "manifests" is bodily beauty, then what is manifested is again obvious on the surface; and hence, as Schofield 1991/99: 112–13 notes, ἐμφαίνω is used in different ways in the definition of love and in DL 7.129. But there is nothing particularly troublesome about this. And the fact is that there is nothing else the young person's beauty could be. If young persons are not sages, they do not have the other kind of beauty, beauty of soul. Price recognizes this difficulty, but a key point in his response to it seems to me unconvincing; see below, n. 18. A number of other proposals also seem to me to founder on this point. One might suggest that (1) the young person's beauty consists in his or her *potential* for virtue – or that (2) the sage is not really responding to actual, physical beauty, but to the potential for beauty/virtue in the soul (this latter appears in Nussbaum 2002: 79). But (1) the potential for virtue, on the Stoic view, is not beauty; only fully attained *summetria* constitutes beauty, and that must be either (fully attained) virtue – which the young person does not have – or physical beauty. And (2) it is beauty, not the potential for beauty, that the definition describes the lover as responding to; it is real and not fake (see above, n. 12), and it is present and actual, not future or potential. One might also try (3) reinterpreting beauty of the body "upward," so to speak, so that, properly understood, it is indistinguishable from beauty of soul. But in that case, again, the young person does not have it; only the sage does.

The point is repeated in a later passage in Stobaeus, where the definition of *erōs* is repeated, this time with the closing phrase "of young people at their prime," and is supplemented by the words "therefore the wise person will be erotic and will love those worthy of love, who are well-born and of fine natures" (2.115.2–4). "Worthy of love" (*axierastos*) was defined in the earlier passage as "deserving of love that is excellent" (ἄξιον σπουδαίου ἔρωτος, 2.66.2). By itself this is hardly informative. But again, it is clear that the persons "worthy of love" in this sense, whom the sage will love, are young people who show promise in their growth towards virtue, but who are not at present virtuous, by whose physical beauty the sage is attracted (though not, of course, in a violent or excessive way).

A similar point appears in Diogenes Laertius' summary of Stoicism (7.129), but with an interesting addition. According to Diogenes, the Stoics hold that the sage will love "those young people who manifest [ἐμφαινόν-των] through their form [εἴδους] a good natural tendency towards virtue [πρὸς ἀρετὴν εὐφυΐαν]." While Diogenes emphasizes that the goal of this attachment is friendship (*philia*), not sexual gratification (130), the sage's attraction to the young person's physical appearance is not denied; "form" (εἶδος) in this context, as in many others, refers to beauty of shape. But this beauty of shape is here said to be an outward sign of the person's potential for virtue. One is tempted to object that appearances can be deceiving, especially in such an emotionally charged context as that of love. But the sage, of course, is not subject to emotion in the same way as the rest of us; the sage does not have *pathē*, but only *eupatheiai*, which do not have the same violent and uncontrollable character. And the sage does not make mistakes of judgement. For those who can judge correctly, then, there is a connection between physical beauty – or at least, some instances of physical beauty – and an inner potential for developing the beauty of soul that goes along with virtue. Here is yet another respect in which, as in the contexts we were examining earlier, beauty of body and beauty of soul are related to one another. A similar connection is suggested when Diogenes adds (130) that they define *hōra* – that is, the bloom or beauty of youth – as "the flower of virtue" (ἄνθος ἀρετῆς). Indeed, this seems to go too far; for it seems to have the misleading implication that any beautiful youth is automatically already virtuous.[18]

---

[18] Schofield 1991/99: 114 makes essentially the same point. (Indeed, on one understanding of the phrase, one could say that almost everyone enjoys "the bloom of youth" at some point in their lives.) Price 2002 draws attention to the fact that the blossom (ἄνθος) on a tree precedes the arrival of the fruit, and interprets ἄνθος ἀρετῆς as again referring to the youth's *prefiguring* of virtue. In calling it the "blossom," though, the Stoics are indicating that "the beauty of virtue is *beautifully*

Diogenes also refers to specific books by Zeno, Chrysippus, and Apollodorus that expressed this view. The work of Zeno is his *Republic*; and there is reason to believe that the *Republic* portrayed *erōs* as an important mechanism for cementing a community. There is some dispute about precisely what kind of "community" this work imagined – whether it was a literal (albeit ideal) city, like its Platonic predecessor, or some more abstract form of fellowship among sages the world over, these being the only true citizens of the *polis* that is the cosmos itself.[19] But whatever kind of community it was, *erōs* was said to hold it together. Athenaeus (561C = L&S 67D) reports that Zeno "supposed Eros to be god of friendship and freedom, and also to be a producer of concord [*homonoia*], but of nothing else. And for this reason he said in the *Republic* that Eros is a god who is a contributor to the safety of the city." Despite the reference, as in Diogenes, to friendship "and nothing else" as the goal of *erōs*, later critics such as Sextus Empiricus treated the Stoics', and especially Zeno's, political theory as a prescription for indiscriminate sexual relations (e.g., *M* 11.190–92). Zeno's *Republic* (like Plato's) did indeed call for a "community of wives" (D.L. 7.33, 131), and it does appear that the erotic component in his political theory was a matter of some embarrassment to later Stoics.[20] But the community of wives applied only to sages; and that, for the reasons examined just now, makes a fundamental difference. At any rate, as we have seen from Diogenes, later

prefigured" (186, emphasis in original). This proposal seems to me to have several difficulties. First, the definition of love refers to beauty, not to a prefiguring of beauty (see again n. 17). Second, the prefiguring of beauty of which Price speaks is very hard to understand, in Stoic terms, as itself beautiful; beauty is *summetria*, not the prospect of *summetria*. A person who becomes virtuous is not in *any* way virtuous until the moment of becoming (entirely) virtuous. If beauty of soul is virtue, any beauty that prefigures it would have to be a quite different type of beauty, of which (unless it is physical beauty, which Price is denying) we hear nothing in the sources, and which the Stoics' tendency to think in all-or-nothing terms would not lead one to expect. And third, this construal of ἄνθος is far-fetched; when used in this metaphorical way, it seems uniformly to refer to the *peak* of something, not the promise of it. See LSJ, ἄνθος (A) II.2, with several relevant examples. (Price cites Plato's *Symposium*, saying that "the ἄνθος of the body [183e3] is not its physical prime or ἀκμή . . . but its visual peak" [185]. But that still leaves it as a peak of some sort; and the passage makes clear that the passing of this ἄνθος marks a decline – in the specific respect drawn attention to, of course – not a progression towards some higher goal.) Price mentions an intra-Stoic dispute about whether temperance (σωφροσύνη) is the ἄνθος of beauty or vice versa (D.L. 7.23). But σωφροσύνη is a conjecture of Wilamowitz; the manuscripts say something quite different (and very obscure).

[19] On this and other matters concerning Zeno's *Republic*, see Schofield 1991/99 and Vogt 2007.

[20] On this see Schofield 1991/99: chapter 1, especially 9–10. Chrysippus did also endorse the idea of a "community of wives" (D.L. 7.131), and he is quoted by Sextus alongside Zeno as sanctioning incest (*M* 11.192). Zeno is the one with whom the idea of *erōs* as a force for political harmony is particularly associated (see just below in the main text); but there is no reason to think that Chrysippus actively differed from him on this point. Evidence of embarrassment at, and even suppression of, Zeno's works seems to belong to a later stage; Athenodorus, mentioned in this context in D.L. 7.34, appears to have lived in the early first century BCE. On this point see Schofield 1991/99: 9.

Stoics did not hesitate to express the same view of *erōs* in general – even if they perhaps did not give it such an explicitly political dimension; the works of Chrysippus that he cites are *On Lives* (Περὶ βίων) and *On Erōs*, and that of Apollodorus is *Ethics*.

The type of erotic relationship imagined here sounds like an idealized version of the type celebrated in several of Plato's dialogues, which was itself modeled on (and is surely also an idealization of) a type that was standard in Athenian society: a relationship between an older man and an adolescent boy, in which there was a sexual component of some sort (the details are a matter of some dispute, and in any case surely varied), but also a strong pedagogical component. Apart from the greater idealization of both parties – a Stoic sage on one side and a future Stoic sage on the other – one important possible difference between the Stoic and Platonic models is that in the Stoic model it is not clear that either party necessarily had to be male. The Stoics are more consistent than Plato in allowing that women are capable of achieving virtue; it seems to follow that either the older sage or the younger potential sage (or both) might be female.[21] This is why I have translated νέων ὡραίων by "young people in their prime" rather than "young men in their prime"; the Greek leaves it open whether only young males are intended, and there seems no compelling reason to assume so.[22] But despite this significant possible innovation, the picture of *erōs*, and of the sage's appropriate response to beauty, suggested here seems to be recognizably related to normal human responses, and particularly to the erotic responses that were normal at this time and place in history – unlike the picture according to which only the sage is beautiful and worthy of love, which is clearly unrelated to any time or place in human history.

VI

As noted earlier, we have here a tension; it is a tension of a kind that is not unusual in Stoicism. On the one hand the Stoics stress the unity of nature and the providential character of the universe. But they also stress the very exceptional character of the sage and of the good, and the

---

[21] On this point, and on how far Zeno, for one, may or may not have lived up to it, see Schofield 1991/99: 43–46.

[22] On the other hand, as Nussbaum 2002: 78 puts it, "the reference to the prime or *hōra* of the beautiful person is especially familiar within the conventions of male–male love." And Michael Trapp has pointed out to me that, although in the abstract the phrase could refer to either males or females or both, it would surely be *heard*, given the cultural context, as referring to males. Again, then, the extent to which the Stoics could actually live up to their aspirations to gender equality is not so clear.

unbridgeable gulf between the good and the indifferent – the indifferent including a great many of the things that most of us care about. These competing tendencies lead to a dilemma as to whether to treat the sage, and the ethically correct attitudes that the sage embodies, as related to and continuous with other phenomena in the world, or as wholly distinct and unique. This dilemma is displayed, for example, in the Stoics' treatment of the notion of *technē*. They offer a definition of *technē* that appears to be designed to conform to everyday examples of *technai* such as medicine or shipbuilding: "a system of apprehensions organized together for some end useful in life." But they also consider correct ethical thinking to be a *technē* for life (τέχνη περὶ τὸν βίον); and they are sometimes inclined to speak as if this is the only true *technē* – because, after all, ethical excellence is the only thing that truly deserves to be called useful. There is a hint of this last idea in connection with our main topic. In *De officiis*, which is much concerned with the apparent conflict between the ethical and the useful, Cicero cites as a standard Stoic view that if anything is *honestum* (that is, *kalon*), it is useful, and that there is nothing useful that is not *honestum* (3.11). Cicero may be framing the Stoic position in this way for the purposes of his own treatise. But the point seems closely related to something that is at the center of their ethical thinking, namely that only virtue truly benefits (ὠφελεῖν, e.g. D.L. 7.103); and Cleanthes lists 'useful' (χρήσιμον) as well as 'beneficial' (ὠφέλιμον) among the characteristics of the good (Clement, *Protrept.* 6.72.2 = *SVF* I.557). Yet this, of course, as Cicero acknowledges, is worlds apart from usefulness as ordinarily understood.

In any case, the same kind of dilemma is apparent in the Stoics' ideas on beauty. They have strong reasons for thinking of the beauty apprehended by the senses, and the beauty of soul that is synonymous with ethical excellence, as related to one another, and as both genuine types of beauty. According to this line of thinking, there is nothing surprising in the sage's responding favorably to the beauty of the young, and seeing this as a symptom of their promise for developing inner beauty of soul. But they also have strong reasons for thinking of beauty of soul, or *to kalon* as it appears in ethical contexts, as being immeasurably superior to any kind of physical beauty; and it is an easy step from there to saying, as they sometimes do, that it is only the sage – meaning, of course, the sage's inner disposition – that is truly beautiful, the implication being that physical beauty is not really beauty at all. It is not clear to me that this dilemma is ever properly resolved.

I return, finally, to the question introduced at the beginning and touched on at a few other points: in their reflections on beauty, how far are the

Stoics the heirs of Plato? At least one Stoic clearly thought of his school as following Plato on this topic. Antipater wrote three books entitled "On the fact that according to Plato only *to kalon* is good." Our source, Clement (*Strom.* 5.14.97.6 = *SVF* III, p. 252, 30–34), tells us that in this work, Antipater "shows that according to him [i.e. Plato] virtue is sufficient for happiness, and proposes many other doctrines that agree with the Stoics." The general claim of agreement is uncontroversial. And while Plato may not have said precisely that virtue is sufficient for happiness, this is an easy translation into Stoic terminology of the central message of Plato's *Republic*. It is perhaps less obvious where exactly in Plato Antipater detected the idea that only *to kalon* is good, which he presumably took to be connected with the idea that virtue is sufficient for happiness. Certainly, as I noted at the outset, Plato sees a strong connection between *to kalon* and goodness. But Plato does not have such a restricted view of what qualifies as good, because unlike the Stoics, he does not have a clear and explicit distinction between the good and the indifferent. However, since the idea that only *to kalon* is good is closely connected in Stoicism with other ideas – such as that virtue is sufficient for happiness – for which there are obvious antecedents in Plato, Antipater may have felt justified in attributing this idea to Plato as well.

This report on Antipater, then, does not take us very far. But we need not rely only on the verdicts of the Stoics themselves. What is peculiar to the Stoics and Plato on the subject of beauty, I would suggest, is a juxtaposition of two points that are seemingly in tension with one another: on the one hand, their emphatic devaluing of physical beauty as compared with ethical or psychic forms of beauty, and on the other, their willingness to take physical beauty (when responded to correctly) as having an important role in ethical and intellectual improvement. As we have seen, the Stoics in their most severe mood refuse to follow the second of these two tendencies, and stress the first to the extent of holding that the sage's inner beauty is the only beauty that there is. Alcibiades' reference in Plato's *Symposium* (216d–217a) to Socrates' inner beauty (as compared with his Silenus-like exterior), along with Socrates' devaluation of physical beauty in others (e.g., *Tht.* 185e, *Meno* 76b, even if he seems superficially to be obsessed by it), goes some way in this direction; and of course denigration of the body in general is an important theme in some Platonic dialogues, notably the *Phaedo*. So the Stoics may well have looked to Plato in arriving at their "most severe" position; but in this mood, at least, they seem clearly to be going beyond him. However, as we have seen, they also have another mood in which physical beauty is really beauty, and is in some sense a stepping-stone towards ethical or psychic beauty, even if its inferiority to that form of beauty needs to be kept firmly in mind. And here Socrates' own speech in the *Symposium* looks like a significant precedent.[23] (One might think also of his second speech in the *Phaedrus*; but the response to physical beauty in the *Phaedrus* looks rather more violent than the Stoics would like.)[24]

The central connection in Stoicism between beauty and *summetria* is also something that they could easily have found in Plato; *Philebus* 64e6–7 makes the connection in so many words. Admittedly the same connection can be found in Aristotle as well (*Met.* 1078a36–b1).[25] But in Plato, unlike in Aristotle, the beauty of the universe as a whole, which is connected with its good order, is the direct result of the power of the cosmic soul, also known as Zeus; this point also appears in the *Philebus* (30b–d), but related thoughts are easy to find in the *Timaeus*. And this cluster of ideas concerning beauty, order, and the divine directedness of the cosmos look like clear forerunners of the Stoic conception.

The Stoic and Platonic pictures are not, of course, identical. We saw earlier that differences between Plato and the Stoics concerning the structure of the soul led to some differences in how they are each to conceive beauty, or symmetry, of soul. Again, the Stoics' immanent and micromanaging Zeus differs in important respects from most Platonic conceptions of divinity. And, to return to the comparison with the *Symposium*, there is nothing quite like the ascent to the Form of Beauty in the Stoics, because the Stoics reject the whole idea of Platonic Forms. The youth's outer beauty may be a sign of his or her potential for developing the higher, inner beauty of soul. But beauty of soul, in Stoicism, is not "higher" than beauty of body in the same sense in which, in Plato, the Form of Beauty is higher

---

[23] If we follow Sheffield 2006 in thinking of the initial concentration on physical beauty as itself driven by the desire to discover what beauty is (see again n. 2), then physical beauty does not have an *independent* value; it is valuable only insofar as it starts one towards the grasp of the Form. (This is not to deny that it can also be enjoyed for its own sake; but that by itself would be insignificant.) But a similar thing might be said of the Stoic picture: physical beauty is valuable only insofar as it enables the sage to recognize the young person's potential for virtue, and then to help this virtue to become actual. On both views, physical beauty is not to be dismissed as unimportant, or as not really beauty; but its role is primarily as a bridge to something else.

[24] By the same token, although physical beauty is still, as in the *Symposium*, a conduit to the Form, the experience of physical beauty in its own right is given considerably more weight in the *Phaedrus'* account (compare the previous note). To the extent that the Stoic picture resembles, in this respect, that of the *Symposium*, it is correspondingly less close to that of the *Phaedrus*. For contrasting views (appealing to other aspects than those I have just mentioned) on the closeness of the *Phaedrus* and Stoicism on beauty and love, see Nussbaum 1995 and Price 2002.

[25] The relevance of this to Aristotle's ethical theory is nicely brought out in Richardson Lear 2004: ch. 6, "Moral virtue and *to kalon*", esp. sections 1 and 2.

than beauty of body; this simply follows from their having very different ontologies. Equally, beauty of soul does not enjoy the same preeminence in Plato as it does in Stoicism. For the Stoics to achieve beauty of soul is to achieve perfection and assimilation to the divine. For Plato it is much less momentous – and not just because beauty of soul is lower on the ladder than the Form of Beauty, but because the *Symposium*'s standards for what qualifies as beauty of soul seem to be considerably more relaxed.[26]

There are other, less central respects in which Plato's explorations of beauty may have served as a model for the Stoics. As I mentioned at the beginning, the *Hippias Major* explores the possibility of understanding beauty in terms of what is useful or beneficial; it is here that the beauty of cooking pots and soup ladles enters the discussion. A related idea appears, incidentally, in Xenophon's portrait of Socrates, with which the Stoics were also familiar; in Xenophon's *Symposium* (5), Socrates playfully argues that he – that is, his face – is the most beautiful because his features are best adapted for their respective functions (the bulging eyes for looking in all directions, the lips for kissing, etc.). All of this is at a rather mundane level. But this basic idea of the beautiful as the useful or beneficial may have helped the Stoics to develop the much more elevated conception, alluded to a few paragraphs back, of *to kalon* as the only thing truly useful or beneficial.

Another attempted definition of *to kalon* in the *Hippias Major* is "the pleasant through sight and hearing" (299b–c), and there is an interesting echo of this in a book title of Chrysippus, "On the beautiful and pleasure" (Περὶ τοῦ καλοῦ καὶ τῆς ἡδονῆς, D.L. 7.202). We know very little of the contents of this work; Athenaeus quotes or refers to it a number of times, but it is hard to extract much information from these passages. In general, the Stoics' attitude towards pleasure appears to be somewhat inconsistent; or, perhaps, they refer to several different things by the same word *hēdonē*. It is named as one of the four primary *pathē* (Stob. 2.88.15), and as such it was of course viewed in a negative light. However, it is also referred to by Diogenes more positively, as the by-product of a thriving animal constitution (7.86). In keeping with this, Diogenes lists it as a preferred indifferent (7.102 – although Sextus, *M* 11.73, seems to qualify this, citing Stoics for whom it was an indifferent but *not* preferred). But if there is an intrinsic connection between pleasure and *to kalon*, as Chrysippus' title suggests, then one might expect pleasure to be ranked even higher – at

---

[26] 210b–c gives the impression that encountering someone with beauty of soul is not a particularly rare occurrence.

least, if *to kalon* here has its usual Stoic connections with ethical excellence. And this appears to be the case in a curious remark attributed to Cleanthes, that "the good and beautiful are the pleasures" (τὸ ἀγαθὸν καὶ καλόν... εἶναι τὰς ἡδονάς, Epiphanius, *Adv. haer.* III, p. 508, 25 = *SVF* I.538). No explanation is offered of this remark; but it at least seems to suggest, if we can take the text at face value, that the Stoics were prepared to connect pleasure with *to kalon* in its ethical aspect. Again, we are some distance from the *Hippias Major*, where it is sensory pleasure that is connected with *to kalon*. But the connection may nonetheless have been one that the Stoics saw as worth developing, albeit in a rather different direction.

These comments are very superficial; and an adequate treatment of Plato's thoughts about beauty is certainly beyond the scope of this essay. I merely wanted to hint at the nature of the inspiration that the Stoics may have drawn from Plato, in central and also in more peripheral respects. Such a legacy – if I am right that it exists – is in no way surprising; Stoic ethics is full of developments of Socratic or Platonic ideas. As is usual when one is attempting to determine philosophical influence, the interest lies in the details of where the later philosophy follows the earlier one, where it diverges from it, and why.[27]

---

[27] In addition to the version presented at the Berkeley conference, an earlier version of this essay was presented at the Centre d'études sur la philosophie hellénistique et romaine, University of Paris, and at the Institute of Classical Studies, University of London. I thank the participants at all these venues for their many valuable comments, especially Bernard Besnier, José Turpin, Verity Harte, M. M. McCabe, Anthony Price, Frisbee Sheffield, and Michael Trapp. I also thank Julia Annas and Katja Vogt for reading and commenting on the earlier version, and the editors, Andrea Nightingale and David Sedley, for suggesting a number of improvements that I happily adopted. The essay is much improved as a result of all this feedback. Finally, and in a much more general way, I thank Tony Long, who first stimulated my interest in Hellenistic philosophy. Without the inspiration I drew from a memorable seminar of his on Stoics and Sceptics in the spring of 1984, it is quite possible that my career would not have gone in remotely the direction it in fact has – in which case neither this essay nor many others of mine would ever have been written.

CHAPTER 9

How dialectical was Stoic dialectic?

Luca Castagnoli

For Tony Long

T1   [Chrysippus] became so renowned in dialectic that most people thought that if there were dialectic among the gods, it
would be no different from that of Chrysippus.[1] (D.L. 7.180
= Long and Sedley 1987 [henceforth L&S] 31Q)

The enthusiastic view reported by Diogenes Laertius has been far from
unanimous across the centuries, and Stoic *dialektikē* has come under the
fire of many ruthless critics, both in antiquity and in modern times. The
most recurrent charge has been that of empty and rigid "formalism" (in
modern jargon),[2] or of paying too much attention to "words" (sterile
terminological quibbles and logical puzzles) rather than to the "things
themselves",[3] with no real improvement (and indeed some regrettable
devolution) in comparison with the heights reached by its main rival,
Aristotelian logic.[4] The revival of the study of Stoic logic in the twentieth
century was prompted by a fresh understanding and appreciation – inspired
by the modern development of formal *Aussagenlogik* – of those very features
disparaged earlier, and in particular the rigorous and formalized character
of Stoic syllogistic.[5]

    One charge that neither ancient nor modern critics ever levelled against
Stoic *dialektikē* is that, despite all their terminological zeal and subtle

---

[1] An interesting question, which I cannot pursue here, is why the gods are supposed *not* to have dialectic,
    as the imperfect indicatives used in the conditional sentence (εἰ παρὰ θεοῖς ἦν ἡ διαλεκτική, οὐκ
    ἂν ἄλλη ἦν ἢ ἡ Χρυσίππειος) suggest.
[2] Cf. e.g. Prantl 1855–70, vol. I: 408.
[3] This is how the ancient critics typically phrased their indictment: cf. e.g. Alex. Aphr. *In Arist. APr.*
    84, 12–19; Gal. *Inst. Log.* 3.2 and 3.5.
[4] Cf. the related ancient charges of plagiarism and excessive taste for innovation (καινοτομία). Other
    recurrent ancient charges emphasize that Stoic dialectic is not an *ars inveniendi*, that there are
    interminable logical disputes even within the school, and that the building of Stoic dialectic is flawed
    at its very foundations (cf., e.g., Academic and Pyrrhonian attacks on the principle of bivalence for
    "assertibles" and on the notions of validity and proof).
[5] For discussion of some drawbacks of this approach cf. Castagnoli 2004 and pp. 169–79 below.

taxonomies, the Stoics adopted a misleading label for this branch of their philosophy (or philosophical "discourse" [λόγος]).[6] If we give a cursory look at most ancient and modern accounts of Stoic *dialektikē*, there seems to be a compelling case to be made for the complaint that there is very little which is "dialectical" in Stoic dialectic, and some serious work to be done to explain why *dialektikē* is not, after all, an inappropriate label.

To address this issue, let us first recall, summarily, what subdivisions and main subjects Stoic *dialektikē* encompassed (see schema on p. 155).

Broadly speaking, most of the subjects we would consider of "logical" interest were included by the Stoics in the section dealing with "things signified" (τὰ σημαινόμενα, also referred to as τὰ πράγματα), which is only one of the two main subdivisions of *dialektikē*, which in turn is only a branch of Stoic "logic" (λογική, the science of "rational discourse"). However, there is no strict correspondence even between "our" logic and the subsection of *dialektikē* on "things signified".[7]

But what semantic connotations would the term *dialektikē* have carried outside the Stoic school? For the various uses of *dialektikē* in currency in the formative years of the Stoa, I limit myself to adopting here a broad-brush map outlined by Long and Sedley (L&S, vol. I: 189):

(1) Socratic/Platonic dialectic: the method of inquiry into, and testing of, definitions, principles, and forms. (This is variously manifested as Socratic conversation (διαλέγεσθαι) and *elenchus* in the early Platonic dialogues; "hypotheses" in the *Meno* and the *Phaedo*; ascending–descending dialectic in the *Republic*; division and collection in the *Sophist*, *Statesman*, *Phaedrus*, and *Philebus*.)

(2) Aristotle's dialectic: the method by which one can argue validly and convincingly (albeit not demonstratively) about any problem whatsoever by taking up *endoxa* ("acceptable opinions") as one's premises and testing them.

(3) The "Dialectical School": the name of the school associated with Diodorus Cronus, which specialized in logical puzzles (e.g. Sorites, Liar, Master Argument) and sophisms (e.g. Veiled Man, Horned Man).

(4) Sceptical dialectic in Arcesilaus' Academy: the ability to answer every claim to knowledge or belief with an argument of equal force on the opposite side, in order to produce suspension of judgement.

---

[6] On this distinction cf. Ierodiakonou 1993: 58–61, Gourinat 2000: 26–28.

[7] Some Stoics treated the investigation of definitions as a part of logic separate from dialectic (cf. D.L. 7.41); others included it in the subsection of dialectic concerned with signifiers (cf. D.L. 7.44). For discussion of the problematic position of epistemology within the Stoic system, signalled by the dotted lines with question marks in the schema on p. 155, cf. n. 33 below.

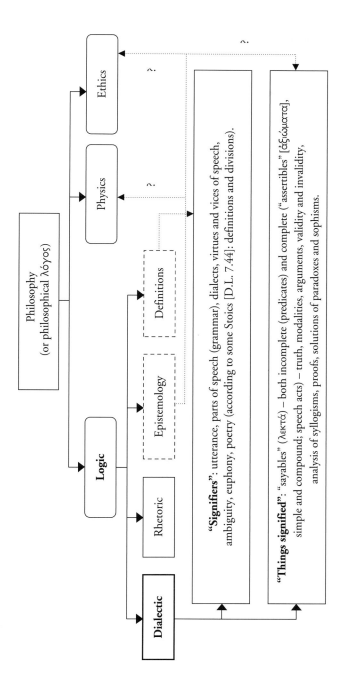

Commenting upon these four distinct, albeit overlapping, notions of "dialectic", Long and Sedley suggest that

common to all of these practices is the notion that arguments are questions put to an interlocutor and that their premises require his positive answer if they are to proceed. Hence all users of dialectic, whatever their particular aims and methods, could agree that it is argument by question and answer. (L&S, vol. I: 189)

One might object that this is slightly overstated and refer, for example, to Aristotle's aporetic scrutiny of the notable views of earlier philosophers in the *Metaphysics*, *De anima* or *Nicomachean Ethics*, or to Carneades' notorious 155 BCE Rome embassy and opposed speeches (for and against justice) on consecutive days; these are not in dialogical, question-and-answer form. Although these argumentative styles are often called "dialectical" in the scholarly literature, however, there is actually no clear evidence to suggest that they were considered examples of *dialektikē* by those who used them and by their contemporaries.[8] Long and Sedley's remark thus conveys the indisputable truth that at Zeno's time the meaning of the noun διαλεκτική remained inextricably rooted in that of the verb διαλέγεσθαι ("converse", "discuss") from which it had perhaps been coined by Plato himself some decades before.

If one surveys the few extant ancient summary accounts of Stoic dialectic,[9] or some standard modern monographs on Stoic logic,[10] or just considers the list of topics in my schema above, one might wonder what on earth Stoic *dialektikē* had to do with these roughly contemporary uses, if they were all so deep-rooted in the idea of dialogue and argument by question and answer.[11] Why was the term itself adopted by the Stoics in the first place? The mystery, however, is not so deep after all. There is at least one attested historical link between Stoic dialectic and one of those

---

[8] For this reason, the fourth sense of dialectic distinguished by Long and Sedley can be accepted only if we take it to mean that dialectic in the sceptical Academy was the (Arcesilean) practice of arguing *against* a certain position, and not the (Carneadean) one of arguing *for* the opposite side, or arguing *in utramque partem* (for this distinction cf. L&S, vol. I: 448). For the "prehistory" of dialectic cf. Gourinat, forthcoming.

[9] Cf. e.g. the seventh book of Diogenes Laertius, most likely dependent on a late Stoic handbook datable to the second/first century BCE, or various sections in Sextus Empiricus' *PH* 2 and *M* 7–8.

[10] Cf. e.g. Mates 1961, Mignucci 1965, Frede 1974, Baldassarri 1984.

[11] As Long (1978/96: 88) puts it, for example, "the detailed summary of Stoic logic in Diogenes Laertius has nothing whatsoever to say about how 'to discourse correctly on arguments in question-and-answer form'" (which, as we shall see, might have been Zeno's own definition of διαλεκτική; cf. T11 below).

contemporary uses of *dialektikē*. We know that Zeno of Citium was an admirer of the major exponents of the Dialectical school:[12]

T2 [Zeno] used to discuss carefully with Philo the Dialectician and to study along with him; hence Zeno, his junior, admired him [*sc.* Philo] no less than his teacher Diodorus. (D.L. 7.16 = Hülser 1987–88 [henceforth *FDS*]: 108)

Diodorus Cronus (whom Sextus calls διαλεκτικώτατος,[13] "the most dialectical"), Philo, and the other διαλεκτικοί were not single-mindedly obsessed with logical puzzles and petty sophisms, as some hostile ancient sources would have us think. From what we can gather from our (regrettably scanty) evidence, the "Dialecticians" laid down the foundations of propositional logic[14] and syllogistic,[15] did groundbreaking work in the theory of modality,[16] and reflected on the nature of language and meaning.[17] It is not wild speculation that Zeno's dialectic, i.e. Stoic dialectic at its birth, was not only strongly influenced by the *dialektikē* of these *dialektikoi*, but also *named* after it; in fact, it is possible that Zeno's dialectic might not have differed much from that of his teachers, since Zeno himself is not recorded as having offered any insightful contribution to the subject.[18]

The next question is, of course, why these Dialecticians themselves came to be known as *dialektikoi*: the bare list of their logical interests which I have just sketched does not make the rationale for this choice immediately transparent. Diogenes Laertius explains why Dionysius of Chalcedon (a contemporary of Diodorus Cronus) first adopted the label *dialektikoi*:

T3 [That name] had first been given to them by Dionysius of Chalcedon because they used to put their arguments in the form of question and answer (πρὸς ἐρώτησιν καὶ ἀπόκρισιν). (D.L. 2.106)

---

[12] Or *tendency*: "it may well be that the Dialectical school was bound together by a community of interests rather than of beliefs, and that it lacked the clear doctrinal stamp that characterized most contemporary sects" (Sedley 1977: 76). To speak of a *Dialectical* school, distinct from the Megaric one, is itself controversial (cf. Sedley 1977, Döring 1989, Ebert 1991, Barnes 1993). But this issue is not important for our present purposes.

[13] S.E. *M* 1.310.

[14] Cf. e.g. Clinomachus' pioneering writings on predicates and ἀξιώματα (D.L. 2.112) and the quarrel between Philo and Diodorus on the truth conditions for συνημμένα (e.g. S.E. *PH* 2.110–1).

[15] Philo wrote a treatise on τρόποι, i.e., probably, on "inference schemata" (D.L. 7.194); the "Dialecticians" may have formulated a taxonomy of invalidity (cf. S.E. *PH* 2.146–50 and Ebert 1991: ch. 6).

[16] Cf. Bobzien 1993. On Diodorus' celebrated "Master Argument" cf. Gaskin 1995.

[17] On Diodorus Cronus' varied interests and crucial influence on Hellenistic philosophy cf. the seminal Sedley 1977. On the other members of the school and of "neighbouring" schools cf. also Döring 1972, Muller 1988, and Giannantoni 1983–90.

[18] Cf. e.g. Cic. *Fin.* 4.9 = L&S 31I. On the possible Aristotelian influences on Stoic logic cf. Barnes 1999a.

The dialogical focus of the Dialecticians' argumentative practice, also confirmed by the numerous uses of terms such as ἐρωτήματα ("interrogations"), ἐρωτήσεις ("questions"), and ἐρωτάω ("ask") to refer to their arguments,[19] emerges time and again in our sources. As the evergreen anecdote goes, Diodorus Cronus himself died in despair, consumed by the shame of having been unable to solve on the spot some "dialectical arguments" which his arch-rival Stilpo had proposed to him (literally, *asked* him) at a banquet in the presence of king Ptolemy Soter (D.L. 2.111–12).

Zeno's reported attitude towards the *dialektikoi* and *dialektikē* is not straightforward, however. On the one hand, he studied with the master Dialecticians of his time (T2) and encouraged his own pupils to study dialectic:

T4 When a Dialectician showed him [*sc.* Zeno] seven dialectical forms in the Mowing Argument, he asked how much he was selling them for. Having being told a hundred drachmas, [Zeno] gave him two hundred. (D.L. 7.25 = *FDS* 107)

T5 [Zeno] used to solve sophisms, and to encourage his pupils to take up dialectic because of its power to do this. (Plut. *Stoic. Rep.* 1034E = L&S 31L)

On the other hand, Stobaeus attributes to him what appears to be a less than flattering assessment of the Dialecticians' skills:

T6 Zeno used to compare the skills of the Dialecticians to correct instruments of measure which do not measure wheat or anything else worthwhile, but chaff and dung. (Stob. *Ecl.* 2.2.12 = *FDS* 206)

Zeno's simile is reminiscent of those which the Cynicizing Stoic Aristo, the author of an *Against the Dialecticians* (D.L. 7.163), adopted to put dialectic and its practitioners on trial: dialectic is "nothing to us"; it is useless, like artistically woven spider webs; it is annoying and dangerous, like mulch in the street, which sticks to your shoes and can make you trip; it can even be potentially deadly, like hellebore, which is purgative in large grains, but makes you choke and suffocate if assumed in fine powder; indeed, the dialecticians themselves are like crab-eaters, condemned to chew the bones[20] because of the lack of flesh in their subject.[21] Should we postulate that the different tone of our testimonies (T6 vs. T2, T4 and T5) reveals a change of mind on Zeno's part, perhaps a transition from an earlier Cynicizing phase which utterly rejected dialectic to a newly found

---

[19] Cf. e.g. D.L 2.108, Epict. *Disc.* 2.19.1; on the use and significance of these terms cf. Glucker 1989 and pp. 164, 173–74 below.
[20] Cf. the Stoic similes for the tripartition of philosophy (T7–T10 and T14 below).
[21] Cf. *FDS* 208–15.

appreciation of the worth of some dialectical skills?[22] Such a developmental conjecture is unnecessary: Zeno may have valued the refined techniques of the Dialecticians, but at the same time, and for this very reason, he may have regretted that they were not used constructively (as they could and should have been)[23] but only negatively, to devise worthless sophisms and logical puzzles, or at most to solve them. Therefore, while commentators are certainly correct when they emphasize that in early Stoicism *dialektikē* was *primarily* a defensive tool against one's adversary's attacks (and, thereby, an intrinsically dialectical tool), some notion of a possible (and desirable) constructive and systematic use of *dialektikē* on "quality matters" might lurk behind Zeno's simile in T6 (cf. also Zeno's own notorious syllogisms,[24] which were not cast, however, in what would later become Stoic canonical form).[25] Here is a small sample of testimonies stressing the defensive function of Stoic dialectic and logic:

T7 The Stoics themselves, too, say that logic comes first, ethics second, and physics occupies the last place. For the mind must first be fortified (κατησφαλίσθαι) for the task of guarding (φυλακήν) its heritage impregnably, and the dialectical section makes the intellect secure (ὀχυρωτικόν). (S.E. *M* 7.22–3 = *FDS* 20)

T8 [Epictetus complains against those who devote themselves to the study of logic too single-mindedly]: "Have you ever seen anyone building a coping without putting it on a wall? What door-keeper stands where there is no door? But you are practising your skill at proving – proving what? You are practising so as not to be shaken away through sophisms – away from what? Show me first what you are guarding (τηρεῖς)." (Epict. *Disc.* 3.26.15–6)

T9 For just as the enclosing wall (τεῖχος) is a guard (φυλακτήριον) for the fruits and plants of the field, keeping out those who would like to enter to plunder, in the same way the logical part of philosophy is the most secure (ὀχυρωτάτη) protection (φρουρά) of those two, ethics and physics; for it discloses double and

---

[22] Cf. e.g. Ioppolo 1980: 72n. 36.

[23] For the idea that logic, like a scale, might be fruitless in itself but has the crucial function of measuring *everything else*, cf. Epict. *Disc.* 1.17.4–12. Cf. also Epictetus' concerns with his pupils' *misuse* of logic and erroneous views about its *intrinsic* value (on which see Long 1978/96: 104–06, 2002: 116–21 and Barnes 1997: 24–77).

[24] For discussion of Zeno's (possibly dialectical) syllogisms, cf. Schofield 1983 and Gourinat 2000: 245–55. According to D.L. 7.179, Chrysippus wanted to be taught only the doctrines of Cleanthes, and would find out the *demonstrations* by himself (*pace* Babut 2005: 86, according to whom Stoic dialectic retained throughout *exclusively* the defensive function of preserving truths already accepted independently on purely non-logical grounds).

[25] We shall encounter below an argument attributed to Zeno which is closer to Stoic canonical form (T16).

amphibolous expressions and dissolves the plausibility produced through sophisms and the seductive deception . . . [26] (Philo *De agr.* 15–6 = *FDS* 23)

The same defensive tendency emerges from some well-known similes which the Stoics used to illustrate the tripartition of their system:

T10 [The Stoics compare philosophy] to an egg: logic is the outside, ethics what comes next, and physics the innermost part; or to a fertile field: its surrounding fence (φραγμόν) corresponds to logic, its fruits to ethics, and its land or trees to physics; or to a city which is well fortified (τετειχισμένη) and governed according to reason. (D.L. 7.40 = L&S 26B)

To conclude this summary reconstruction of the initial phase of the history of Stoic *dialektikē*, consider one of the attested Stoic definitions of *dialektikē*, usually taken to be early, and most likely accepted and proposed by Zeno himself:

T11 The science (ἐπιστήμη) of correct discussion (τοῦ ὀρθῶς διαλέγεσθαι) in regard to discourses conducted by question and answer (ἐν ἐρωτήσει καὶ ἀποκρίσει). (D.L. 7.42 = L&S 31A)[27]

This is contrasted with the kind of continuous, 'macrologic' speech which is the subject matter of rhetoric.[28] The similarity between this "science" and the form of dialectic nurtured by the Dialecticians and, ultimately, the model of Socratic dialogic dialectic is evident. It is not to formalize arguments in your philosophical treatises that you need *dialektikē*; it is in oral disputation structured by questions and answers that dialectic will make you proficient.

The essentials of my outline of the original dialectical thrust of Stoic *dialektikē* are – I surmise – hardly controversial. Most scholars, however, will certainly want to claim that this is only the initial and least original and exciting phase of the Stoic inquiry into logic. According to Long and Sedley, for example, it is with Chrysippus, the most creative logician of the school (the "dialectician of the gods") that some decades later Stoic *dialektikē* expanded well beyond its original limited scope to become that

---

[26] Cf. also Cic. *Fin.* 3.21.72 =*FDS* 90: dialectic does not establish the Stoic doctrine on good and evil, but preserves (*tenere*) and defends (*tueri*) it from "captious plausibility" (*captiosa probabilitate*). For a possible example of the way in which proficiency in dialectic could help one to defend Stoic doctrine, see the Stoics' reply to Alexinus' "parallel" argument (παραβολή) to Zeno's theological syllogism at S.E. *M* 9.108-10 (on which cf. Schofield 1983).

[27] Cf. also *FDS* 55–59, 64. Some sources have εὖ διαλέγεσθαι or *bene disputandi*, and make it explicit that dialectic is *so called* from "discussing in the form of question and answer" (*FDS* 58, 64).

[28] Cf. Zeno's simile of the clenched fist and the open palm to illustrate the difference between dialectical brachylogy and rhetorical macrology but also, perhaps, the "agonistic" nature of *dialektikē* (Quint. *Inst.* 2.20.7).

systematic science concerning "signifiers and things signified" (D.L. 7.62)[29] encompassing the wide variety of topics listed in the schema on p. 155. Chrysippus and his successors proposed the discrimination of true and false impressions, *quite generally*, as the primary positive goal of this powerful dialectic, "thus fully integrating it with epistemology":[30] "dialectic, in its concern with truth, knowledge, definitions etc. assumes a significance in Stoicism which is fully comparable to the Platonic conception" (L&S, vol. I: 190). According to such a reading, this extension of the role of *dialektikē* is also confirmed by the definition of dialectic as "the science of what is true and false and neither (ψευδῶν καὶ ἀληθῶν καὶ οὐδετέρων)"[31] attributed to Posidonius in D.L. 7.62, but often taken to be originally Chrysippean.[32] I find it dubious, however, that, from Chrysippus onwards, epistemology became the central part (or even *a* part) of Stoic *dialektikē*,[33] or, even more strongly, that in mature Stoicism the dialectician, *qua* dialectician, is not merely a skilled disputer or logician, but someone who "has knowledge of reality", in a fully Platonic sense.[34] As Barnes pithily puts it, Stoic "dialectic is neither a superscience nor an omniscience":[35] it cannot discriminate,

---

[29] Cf. *FDS* 63–5.

[30] Cf. also Gourinat 2000: 107: "La vertu dialectique inclut donc en elle toutes les vertus de l'assentiment", and 72: "la dialectique apparaît essentiellement comme la science qui distingue, différencie et apprécie représentations et propositions."

[31] Cf. *FDS* 60–4.

[32] Cf. e.g. L&S, vol. I: 190, Alesse 2000: 266. Note, however, that in D.L. 7.62 this definition immediately *precedes* the specific remark that, *according to Chrysippus*, dialectic deals with signifiers and things signified; this seems to make it unlikely that Diogenes' sources attributed the Posidonian definition to Chrysippus himself.

[33] I can just recall here that epistemology (the part "concerning canons and criteria") was clearly treated by *some* Stoics as a part of λογική *distinct* from dialectic and rhetoric (cf. D.L. 7.41), and there is no indication that even those who did not do so included epistemology *under dialectic* (from Diocles' summary in Diogenes Laertius and the κατὰ μέρος exposition of Stoic logic beginning at 7.49 it is quite clear that the treatment of epistemology *preceded* that of dialectic). In fact, it is not even obvious that epistemology was constantly discussed by the Stoics as a part of logic: there are no epistemological titles in the D.L. catalogue of Chrysippus' logical works (on which cf. Hadot 1994, Barnes 1996, Gourinat 2000: 95–106), whereas there are some in the ethical section, and we know that some epistemology was dealt with by Chrysippus in his *Physics* (D.L. 7.54). In Cic. *Ac.* 1.40–2 Zeno's epistemological innovations are treated by Varro as belonging to the "third part of philosophy", which is discussed after ethics and physics, and therefore belonging to logic, but, again, not specifically to dialectic, to which, as we have seen, according to Cicero himself Zeno did not make any contribution worth mentioning (moreover, this division might reflect a late, Antiochean arrangement of the material). On the thorny issue of the position of epistemology within the Stoic system cf. Mansfeld 1986; Brunschwig 1991; Gourinat 2000: 88–107; for the most recent defence of the idea that Stoic epistemology was a central part of Stoic dialectic cf. Togni, forthcoming.

[34] Cf. Long 1978/96: 97. The most promising piece of evidence adduced, D.L. 7.83 (the Stoic dialectician examines what each thing is and how it is called), does not appear to be clinching.

[35] Barnes 1999b: 66.

for example, among the truths and falsehoods of physics, ethics, or non-philosophical sciences.[36] The following passage from Cicero's *Lucullus* is instructive as to the correct (and more modest) way in which I suggest we should interpret the definition of dialectic as the "science of what is true and false and neither":

T12 You say that dialectic was discovered as the arbiter and judge, as it were, of truth and falsehood (*veri et falsi quasi disceptatricem et iudicem*). What truths and falsehoods, and in what subjects? Is the dialectician going to judge what is true or false in geometry, or in literature, or in music? No. But he does not know such subjects. In philosophy, then? What does a question about the size of the sun have to do with him? What ability does he have to judge what the highest good is? What will he judge, then? What conjunctions and disjunctions are true; what is stated ambiguously; what follows from each thing and what conflicts with it (*quae coniunctio, quae diiunctio vera sit, quid ambigue dictum sit, quid sequatur quamque rem, quid repugnet*).[37] (Cic. *Luc.* 91)

It is by establishing the truth conditions of sentences that include connectives or clarifying ambiguities that dialectic acts as a sort of arbiter of truth and falsehood; but in doing so dialectic does not transform into a part of epistemology (e.g. it does not offer any criterion of truth for simple assertibles, or any account of different cognitive states), let alone into broader "knowledge of reality".

In fact, I suggest that it is by no means necessary to take as mutually exclusive (1) the original "dialectical definition" of *dialektikē* as the science of correct discussion by question and answer, (2) Chrysippus' remark on its scope (signifiers and things signified) and (3) the definition attributed to Posidonius. This claim can be bolstered by the following three points:

(1) To discuss (διαλέγεσθαι) well (εὖ) or correctly (ὀρθῶς) is, according to the Stoics, to say *what is true*[38] (Alex. Aphr. *In Arist. Top.* 1, 8–14 [= *FDS* 57]; An. *Proleg. in Hermog. de Stat.* 192, 3–15 [= *FDS* 49]).

(2) Various sources associate Chrysippus' and Posidonius' accounts, presumably on the grounds that "assertible" σημαινόμενα (i.e. ἀξιώματα, simple and compound) are either true or false, whereas signifiers and non-assertible σημαινόμενα are neither true nor false.[39]

(3) At D.L. 7.42, Posidonius' "semantic" definition is presented as a *consequence* of Zeno's "dialectical" definition (ὅθεν), probably on the grounds

---

[36] Since the Stoic wise man (σοφός) is the only true dialectician (cf. pp. 167–69 below), of course the dialectician, *qua wise man*, will also have knowledge of physics and ethics; but he will not have this knowledge *qua dialectician*.

[37] Cf. also Cic. *Tusc.* 5.23.68, 72; Phld. *Rhet.* 1.

[38] As opposed to winning the dialectical contest or persuading one's interlocutor.

[39] On the Stoic defence of bivalence for ἀξιώματα cf. Barnes 2007: ch. 1.

that in dialogical exchanges answers can be either true or false, whereas questions are neither true nor false.[40]

This is not to deny the uncontroversial fact that with Chrysippus logic (and especially *dialektikē*) developed into a much more refined, extensive, and systematic part of Stoic philosophy. It might have been this advancement that prompted Posidonius to introduce a new and fortunate simile for the tripartition of philosophy, more apt to illustrate the interdependent character of all its parts:

T14 Since the parts of philosophy are inseparable from one another, whereas plants are observed to be different from fruits, and walls to be separate from plants, Posidonius said he preferred to compare philosophy to a living being: physics to the blood and flesh, logic to the bones and sinews, and ethics to the soul.[41] (S.E. *M* 7.19 = L&S 26D)

Logic, and therefore its principal branch, *dialektikē*, are now depicted as what gives internal structure and cohesion to the body of philosophical discourse, as bones and sinews do to animal bodies, and not solely as an *external* shell or armour for something which, at least in principle, might exist independently of them.

The typical scholarly emphasis on the distinctive achievements of Chrysippean and post-Chrysippean *dialektikē* (e.g. in linguistic and grammar, theory of modalities, propositional logic and syllogistic, and, allegedly, epistemology) risks obscuring those genuine dialectical traits which it is reasonable to suppose that Stoic *dialektikē* retained throughout. Is mature Stoic *dialektikē* not only *better*, but also *less dialectical* than Zeno's original *dialektikē*? (In the eyes of those interpreters who applaud the formal character of Stoic logic, these two qualifications are related.) This is the impression one gets from a survey of modern accounts of Stoic dialectic: interpreters have tended to look at it through the lenses (sometimes distorting) of our "classical" propositional logic, largely confining their attention to those sections which correspond to the most formal chapters of that logic, and are thereby less dialectical (seldom, indeed, do they use the term "dialectic" itself, simply replacing it with "logic").[42] This general tendency has exceptions, and some scholars have stressed the necessity of taking into more serious account the original dialectical background of Stoic "logic" and of

---

[40] Diogenes of Babylon did not perceive any contrast when he defined διαλεκτική as *ars bene disserendi et vera ac falsa diiudicandi* (Cic. *De orat.* 2.38.157–59 =L&S 31G). For sensitive discussion of the various Stoic definitions of διαλεκτική and their mutual relationships, cf. Gourinat 2000: 69–72.

[41] Cf. also D.L. 7.40. On the Stoic tripartition of philosophy and the various similes illustrating it, cf. Hadot 1991, Ierodiakonou 1993, Gourinat 2000: 19-34, Annas 2007.

[42] As noticed by Gourinat 2000: 9.

trying to understand the significance of Stoic *dialektikē* as an integral part of Stoic philosophy (and life).[43] As Gourinat remarks when summarising the findings of his *La dialectique des Stoïciens*, "la conception complexe, à première vue multiple équivoque de la dialectique stoïcienne, correspond donc à une unité focale, qui se trouve dans l'unité de son origine . . . c'est ce centre *toujours présent* à partir duquel elle rayonne, ce *noyau central* auquel elle se ramène tout entière: la dialectique est la *science du dialogue*" (2000: 328, italics mine). Having emphasized the spectacular blossoming of Chrysippean dialectic into a wide-ranging and ambitious "science of what is true and false and neither", Long and Sedley clarify in a similar vein that

at the same time, by furnishing analysis and techniques of argument, it retains the original concern with logical puzzles and training against opponents . . . The Stoic view of argument had a dialectical background in which each premise was posed as a question to an interlocutor and required his agreement. Despite the great formality imposed by the logical handbooks, *this dialectical aspect was never lost sight of.* Arguments are standardly "asked", not just stated, and although the texts only rarely set out the premises in interrogative form the reader is nevertheless expected to take them that way. (L&S, vol. I: 190, 218, italics mine)

We can find confirmation of this remark by considering some pieces of Stoic logical jargon: verbs such as ἐρωτάω and συνερωτάω ("ask") and nouns like λῆμμα ("what is accepted")[44] and πρόσληψις ("what is accepted in addition") are clear reminders of the dialectical origin of Stoic logic. Moreover, various sophisms which excited Stoic logicians are transmitted in interrogative form or clearly presuppose it.[45] Finally, a careful reading of Epictetus reveals that rule-governed exchanges by question and answer were still widely practised by the Stoics in the second century CE, at least as a kind of intellectual gymnastic or sport (Epictetus even complained that the relevant dialectical skills were in fact pursued with excessive eagerness by Stoic pupils).[46]

---

[43] Cf. especially the seminal Long 1978/96, Long 1986: 121–45, Gourinat 2000.

[44] Cf. also the apparently dialectical background of the accounts of λῆμμα in the definitions of ἀπόδειξις at *PH* 2.136 and *M* 8.302 (conjecturally attributed, respectively, to Zeno and Cleanthes by Brunschwig 1980).

[45] Cf. e.g. the so-called "changing arguments (μεταπίπτοντες λόγοι)" (on which see Barnes 1997: 99–125), the Horned Man sophism, and the sorites; cf. also Gourinat 2000: 262–64. Papyrus Parisinus 2 is an isolated interesting example of the survival of *some* dialectical structure in a written logical text (Stoic? Dialectical? Academic?) in the third century BCE (cf. Cavini 1985: 116).

[46] The point is investigated in depth in Barnes 1997 (on Epictetus' attitude towards logic cf. also Crivelli 2007). In the second century BCE Antipater was criticized and ridiculed for his excessive reliance on *writing* to tackle the Sceptics' challenges against the Stoa (cf. Burnyeat 1997). Cf. also Gellius 16.2.

But are these dialectical strands in mature Stoic *dialektikē* dead *relics* of its early history, with no vital function to play within the developed system? For example, was it always a purely extrinsic matter (like, say, the choice between different notations in modern systems of formal logic) whether one chose to formulate one's argument in a dialectical context (and in interrogative form) or in written declarative form? In other words, was Chrysippean *dialektikē*[47] only *derivatively* dialectical, both chronologically and because the same logical expertise which it afforded in arguments quite generally did continue having some application in live exchanges taking the form of question and answer? Even the most scrupulous interpreters of Stoic dialectic within its historical context seem to answer "yes" to all these questions. According to Long, for example, Chrysippus did not "assign an important heuristic function to discussion by question and answer" (1978/96: 92); "he certainly thought the wise man should be excellent at questioning and responding in formal debates, but nothing suggests that he shared Plato's views about the cognitive value of such encounters" (97). I shall argue that these remarks might benefit from some further qualification. Barnes, while noticing that "formal syllogizing is hardly the rule in ancient philosophical writing", has suggested, more boldly, that the dialogical setting in which so many ancient arguments were framed, and so prominent especially in Plato, is *always* "extrinsic":

> Plato conceived of thoughts as an interior dialogue, not as an interior monologue (*Sophist* 264a). Members of his school, the Academy, trained their private faculties in public dialogues, for which various rules were laid down. The rules made up the art of "dialectic" . . . and this art had a permanent influence on the terminology of later Greek logic . . . Nonetheless, the dialogue form is *extrinsic* in this sense: Plato's arguments can *all* be turned into monologues without any logical or philosophical loss. The ancient commentators were aware of this, and they frequently bared Plato's arguments of their *conversational clothing* in order to reveal their logical force. (Barnes 2003: 27–28, italics mine)

Although Barnes does not refer to *Stoic* arguments here, the context makes it quite clear that his contention concerning the merely extrinsic value of the dialogical setting would apply, *a fortiori*, to Stoic syllogisms.[48]

In the second part of the present chapter I wish to challenge this idea, by examining an instructive example of how *deeply* dialectical Stoic *dialektikē* remained throughout. First, however, let us consider a few additional

---

[47] Under the heading "Chrysippean διαλεκτική" I also include the subsequent developments, with full awareness that mature Stoic dialectic cannot be simply identified with Chrysippean dialectic.

[48] Barnes' remarks are excerpted from a *general* introduction to 'Argument in Ancient Philosophy.'

clues to the lasting importance of dialectic *as dialogue* in mature Stoicism. Plutarch informs us that, according to Chrysippus, Socrates (and not, notably, Plato or Aristotle) was the keenest student of *dialektikē* among "the ancients":

T15 In the third book of his *On Dialectic* [Chrysippus] remarked that dialectic was keenly studied by Plato and Aristotle and their followers up to Polemo and Strato, but especially by Socrates . . . as though it were among the greatest and most indispensable capacities.[49] (Plut. *Stoic. Rep.* 1045E–1046A = *FDS* 217)

This is a first hint that in Chrysippus' eyes *dialektikē* had not lost its tight and *primary* connection with live conversation, unless we prefer to saddle him with the idea that Socrates had written treatises on syllogisms or lectured on signifiers.

There is one different but related sense of "dialectical", involving discussion and criticism of one's opponent's views (albeit not necessarily in live conversation), in which Chrysippus' later attitude towards argument might be described as *more dialectical* than Zeno's. The founder of the Stoa is reported to have argued that, once one has listened to one side of a dispute, hearing and assessing the reasons for the opposite side become redundant:

T16 In response to him who said "Do not pass judgement until you have heard both sides," Zeno stated the contrary thesis, using an argument of the following kind: "The second speaker must not be heard, whether the first speaker proved his case (for the inquiry has its end) or did not prove it (for that is like his not having complied when summoned, or his having complied by prattling). But either he proved his case or he did not prove it. Therefore the second speaker must not be heard." (Plut. *Stoic. Rep.* 1034E = L&S 31L)

Zeno's dilemmatic argument, clearly tailored to judicial contexts, can be easily transposed to philosophical exchanges, producing a very anti-dialectical attitude:[50] if your role is that of trying to establish a certain conclusion, and your opponent's that of refuting it, your success in supporting your positive point is already a clear-cut triumph for you and your thesis, independently of the strength (or weakness) of your opponent's

---

[49] For analysis of this passage cf. Brunschwig 1991 (in which Chrysippean dialectic is read, however, through excessively Aristotelian spectacles).

[50] Glucker (1989: 488) suggests that "the anecdote as we have it is no piece of philosophical doctrine, taken out of one of Zeno's serious books, but an amusing χρεία"; certainly this does not imply, however, that the argument itself must be a mere sophistic joke, *pace* Glucker.

reasons, which need not be assessed and countered.⁵¹ By contrast, Chrysippus says that

T17 he does not completely disapprove of testing dialectically the opposite case (τὸ πρὸς τὰ ἐναντία διαλέγεσθαι), but he recommends that this be used cautiously, as in the courtroom, not to advocate it but to solve its plausibility. (Plut. *Stoic. Rep.* 1035F = L&S 31P)⁵²

Let us come now to the Stoic tenet that the "wise man" (σοφός) must be proficient in *dialektikē*, and actually is always⁵³ a dialectician (D.L. 7.83) and the only true dialectician (Alex. Aphr. *In Arist. Top.* 1, 8–14 =*FDS* 57), because *dialektikē* is a virtue and the wise man must be all-virtuous. Our main evidence on the notion of dialectical virtue and its various species is provided by Diogenes Laertius and an anonymous Herculaneum papyrus:⁵⁴

T18 They [*sc.* the Stoics] take dialectic itself to be necessary, and a virtue which incorporates specific virtues. Non-precipitancy is knowledge of when one should and should not assent. Uncarelessness is a strong rational principle against the plausible, so as not to give in to it. Irrefutability is strength in argument, so as not to be carried away by argument into the contradictory. Non-randomness is a disposition that refers impressions to the correct rational principle... Without the study of dialectic the wise man will not be infallible (ἄπτωτον) in argument, since dialectic distinguishes the true from the false, and clarifies plausibilities and ambiguous statements; and without it it is impossible to ask and answer questions methodically (ὁδῷ ἐρωτᾶν καὶ ἀποκρίνεσθαι)... Only in this way will the wise man show himself to be penetrating, sharp-witted and, quite generally, formidable in argument. For it belongs to the same person to discuss correctly and to reason correctly (ὀρθῶς διαλέγεσθαι καὶ διαλογίζεσθαι), and to test dialectically what is under discussion (πρὸς τὰ προκείμενα διαλεχθῆναι) and to respond to what is asked (πρὸς τὸ ἐρωτώμενον ἀποκρίνασθαι); all these things belong to the man skilled in dialectic. (D.L. 7.46-48 = L&S 31B; L&S's translation modified)

T19 [Wise men] cannot be deceived (ἀνεξαπατήτους) or err (ἀναμαρτή-τους)... if dialectic is, according to us, the science of how to discuss correctly

---

⁵¹ Conversely, if your role is that of trying to refute a certain thesis, and your opponent's that of defending it, your failure to bring home your negative point is already the victory of your opponent and of the thesis he is defending, independently of the strength (or weakness) of your opponent's reasons. Plutarch goes on criticising Zeno's argument as overtly inconsistent with Zeno's own practice of writing against Plato and solving sophisms.

⁵² At 1036B–C Plutarch complains that actually Chrysippus developed the case for the opposite side with excessive zeal, and was then unable to demolish it convincingly, thus lending powerful anti-Stoic material to his adversaries (especially Carneades).

⁵³ Reading ἀεί with L&S and *FDS*.

⁵⁴ We have no reason to suspect that these texts reflect early views later abandoned by Chrysippus and subsequent Stoics. In fact, the list of dialectical virtues is often attributed to Chrysippus himself (cf. e.g. Long 1978/96: 92), albeit on the basis of very circumstantial evidence.

(ἐπιστήμη τοῦ ὀρθῶς διαλέγεσθαι) . . . [the wise man] must be expert in discussion (ἐν τῷ διαλέγεσθαι), and he who is expert in discussion must thereby be skilled both in answering and in questioning (καὶ εὐερωτητικὸν καὶ εὐαποκριτικόν) . . . [wise men] are irrefutable (ἀνεξέλεγκτοι) and self-sufficient in their apprehension of the assertibles, refuting in addition the hindering argument and prevailing upon their opponents; for they must both be unmoved by refutation and be fortified (πεφραγμένως) in their assent against the opponents. (PHerc. 1020, coll. I–III; selection of the relevant sections of the fragmentary text [cf. *FDS* 88])

Apart from "non-randomness" (ἀματαιότης), the precise meaning of which is difficult to pin down, the three other species of dialectical virtue mentioned by Diogenes Laertius ("non-precipitancy" [ἀπροπτωσία], "uncarelessness" [ἀνεικαιότης] and "irrefutability" [ἀνελεγξία] in Long and Sedley's translation)[55] are most naturally interpreted as defensive skills which the Stoic will exhibit *primarily* when engaged by some opponent *in argument by question and answer*, as confirmed by the explicit references to this context in the middle of T18 and in T19.[56] In particular, the wise dialectician will be irrefutable because he is not liable to be deceived by the tricks ("plausibilities")[57] of his dialectical foes;[58] he is "fortified" against them (recall the similes of the fenced field and the walled city in T7–T10), and thus can preserve the truth in his soul and avoid being dislodged from his status of infallibility[59] (this defensive character of the four dialectical virtues also transpires from the neologisms coined for them, all beginning with a privative α-).

The final observation in T18, that dialectical expertise is essential for the σοφός, since "it belongs to the same person to discuss correctly and to

---

[55] For discussion of the Stoic dialectical virtues cf. Long 1978/96: 92–94; Gourinat 2000: 73–79.

[56] Cf. Long 1978/96: 93: "The *main emphasis* in both texts is upon *dialectic in the limited, argumentative sense*. We seem to be closer to the science of discoursing correctly by question and answer (Zeno's probable conception of dialectic) than to the larger, epistemological activity which I have attributed to Chrysippus"; Gourinat 2000: 79: "Il paraît donc en ressortir que les vertus dialectiques du sage sont les vertus de l'assentiment qui s'exercent dans toutes les circonstances de la vie et sont donc liées à l'exercice des vertus non logiques, les vertus naturelles et éthiques, mais qu'elles *s'exercent malgré tout primordialement dans l'activité du dialogue par questions et réponses*" (italics mine). Gourinat's "dans toutes les circonstances de la vie" must be too strong: caution in assenting to perceptual impressions in non-ideal visual conditions, for example, is unlikely to be a fruit of the *dialectical* virtue of ἀπροπτωσία (*pace* Perin 2005: 395), although there might well be a corresponding "epistemological" or broadly "logical" virtue which the wise man possesses.

[57] Cf. T9 and T17.

[58] Cf. also Epict. *Disc.* 1.7.26: the wise man (φρόνιμος) is skilful in question and answer and cannot be deceived (ἀνεξαπάτητος) and tricked by sophisms (ἀσόφιστος); Marcus Aurelius 7.55.

[59] Cf. also the Stoic definition of ἐπιστήμη as "certain cognition unmovable (ἀμετάπτωτος) by argument" (*FDS* 385–90). On the Stoic notion of *elenchus* cf. Repici 1993.

reason correctly (ὀρθῶς διαλέγεσθαι καὶ διαλογίζεσθαι),"[60] offers crucial evidence of the strict relationship between dialogue and argument in Stoicism: correct reasoning, quite generally, is based on the same dialectical knowledge (of signifiers and things signified) and follows the same rules which secure correctness and success in dialogical exchanges, both in the role of questioner and in that of answerer (remember that "correct" and "correctness" must stand for "true" and "truth" respectively). While we are not told that for the Stoics reasoning and judging are a sort of silent inner dialogue one entertains with oneself, in Platonic vein,[61] some analogous model of human thinking[62] might be in the air; compare also the idea that human beings differ from animals by their λόγος ἐνδιάθετος ("inner discourse"),[63] although we have no further information on whether this λόγος was conceived to have monologic or dialogic form. The concession I have made above on behalf of the standard interpretation, that by being a master formal logician (διαλεκτικός) a Stoic σοφός will also be a master debater (διαλεκτικός), may be too weak, then, and may reverse the actual direction of explanation: it is because (and insofar as) the σοφός is a master debater that he is a master arguer and a master thinker more generally.

But the conclusion I would like to establish is, again, stronger. It is *only* on a *strictly* dialectical model that we will be able to understand correctly the logic of at least some of the arguments used by the Stoics,[64] arguments which make very little sense, or no sense at all, if we cheerfully strip them of their "conversational clothing", as Barnes suggests. I am referring to the arguments based on περιτροπή (literally, "reversal", "turnabout", typically rendered as "self-refutation"). In his first seminal

---

[60] For a different translation, which seems to me to miss partially the point of the passage, cf. L&S, vol. I: 184: "for the person whose job it is to discuss and to argue correctly is the very person whose job it is to discuss debating topics and to respond to the questions put to him." Cf. also Gourinat 2000: 80, who does not translate ὀρθῶς.

[61] Cf. e.g. *Tht.* 189d–190a, *Soph.* 263d–264b, *Phil.* 38c–e; cf. also Arist. *Metaph.* Γ 4, 1006b8–10.

[62] Perhaps as opposed to *divine* thinking? Cf. n. 1 above.

[63] Cf. e.g. Gal. *Plac. Hipp. et Plat.* 3.7.42–3: "Speaking must be from the mind, and speaking within oneself, and thinking, and going through an utterance in ourselves, and sending it out." On the notion of λόγος ἐνδιάθετος (which probably was not specifically Stoic, however) cf. Chiesa 1991. On the relation between language and thought in Stoicism cf. Long 1971.

[64] The only other scholar whom I could find making this stronger claim is Gourinat (not surprisingly, given his excellent constant emphasis on the dialectical nature of Stoic *dialektikē*): "Et bon nombre de syllogismes ou de sophismes ne peuvent pas se comprendre si l'on fait abstraction d'un contexte dialectique" (2000: 324). However, as far as I could ascertain, he does not present examples of *Stoic syllogisms* which cannot be stripped of their dialectical garb, and analyses some of the syllogisms which on my reading would be excellent examples of his general claim in a way which seems to me inadequate exactly because it overlooks their dialectical context (cf. T22 below).

study of ancient self-refutation, Burnyeat clarified that although "any refutation, of course, establishes the contrary of what it refutes", in Hellenistic
and post-Hellenistic philosophical jargon περιτρέπειν and περιτροπή
tended "to be used of the special case where the thesis to be refuted itself
serves as a premise for its own refutation, where starting out with '*p*' we
deduce 'not-*p*' and so conclude that the original premise was false" (1976:
48).[65] Starting from this general account, Burnyeat developed a much more
nuanced analysis of περιτροπή arguments, stressing how in *some* of them
the deduction of the contradictory not-*p* from *p* is not purely formal,
but can be understood and justified only if the argument is examined in
the light of its original dialectical context. Other readers, however, both
before and after Burnyeat, have tended to oversimplify the matter: a clear
illustration of this tendency is Barnes' sweeping generalisation that all
"περιτροπή . . . turns on the exotic truth that anything which implies its
own negation is itself false" (1997: 31). In other words, ancient περιτροπή
has often been read through the lenses of modern formal logic, thus ending up being identified with the tautology of the classical propositional
calculus

$$(\text{CM}) \quad (p \to \neg p) \to \neg p \qquad (\neg p \to p) \to p$$

known as *Consequentia Mirabilis* ("the marvellous consequence"):[66] any
proposition implying its own contradictory is (necessarily) false, and conversely any proposition implied by its own contradictory is (necessarily)
true.

I shall now focus on a single passage, to illustrate how the construal
of περιτροπή as a formal deduction by CM is misleading, and to argue
that we need to appreciate fully the intrinsically dialectical nature of the
περιτροπή argument in order firmly to grasp its logic. We are almost at the
end of the second book of Sextus Empiricus' *Against the Logicians*; having
presented a battery of arguments against the existence of any sound proof

---

[65] This argument pattern was "a commonplace of later Greek controversy, available to disputants of
any persuasion to confute the other side of the debate" (Burnyeat 1976: 57), and the Stoics made
great use of it.

[66] Often the name *Consequentia Mirabilis* (attested for the first time in the seventeenth century among
Polish Jesuit scholars) is primarily attributed to the formula $(\neg p \to p) \to p$, dubbed also *Lex Clavii*,
and only consequently to $(p \to \neg p) \to \neg p$, which follows from it by substitution of the variables
and the law of double negation (however, the two formulae are not equivalent in all systems:
in intuitionistic logic, for example, only $(p \to \neg p) \to \neg p$ is valid). For a comprehensive history of
Consequentia Mirabilis see Nuchelmans 1991: 124–37; Bellissima and Pagli 1996; for a cautionary
discussion of its actual existence in antiquity and in Stoicism cf. Castagnoli 2007, 2009 and 2010.

(ἀπόδειξις),[67] Sextus invites his readers to have a look at the opposite one (presumably, in defence of the existence of proof):

T20 The dogmatic philosophers think that he who maintains that proof does not exist incurs self-reversal (αὐτὸν ὑφ' αὑτοῦ περιτρέπεσθαι), and that he affirms proof by the very means by which he denies it. Hence in withstanding the Sceptics they also say: "He who says that proof does not exist says that proof does not exist either by using a bare and unproved assertion or by proving such a thing by argument. And if it is by using bare assertion, none of those who are receiving the proof will trust him, who uses bare assertion, but he will be checked by the contradictory assertion, when someone says that proof exists. But if it is by proving that proof does not exist (for they say so), then he has thereby admitted (ὡμολόγησε) that proof exists; for the argument which proves the non-existence of proof is a proof of the existence of proof." (*M* 8.463-64)

Although Sextus himself does not reveal the identity of these "dogmatic philosophers",[68] the context, style, and language of the argument and of other similar ones we find in Sextus' corpus (in defence of the existence of cause, criterion, sign, and in defence of the reliability of appearances)[69] offer strong circumstantial evidence to support those commentators who have confidently identified these dogmatists as Stoics.[70]

The context of the περιτροπή charge is overtly dialectical. If the denier of the existence of proof limits himself to bare assertion,[71] he will not be credible (no more, at least, than any opponent who merely counter-asserts that proof exists). It is in the second horn of the dilemma that the περιτροπή charge properly resides: whoever supports his denial of proof by offering proof of the non-existence of proof has thereby *admitted* (ὡμολόγησε) the existence of proof, thus contradicting his own denial. The precise logic underlying this charge is difficult to establish: while the conclusion of the περιτροπή, the Sceptic's admission of the existence of proof, is compatible with a purely *ad hominem* dialectical retort ("since you advance what *you* claim to be a proof of your view, you are thereby

---

[67] For the dogmatic definition of ἀπόδειξις cf. e.g. *PH* 2.143: "A proof, then, ought to be an argument which is conclusive and true and has a non-evident conclusion which is revealed by the power of the premises; and for this reason a proof is said to be an argument which, by way of agreed premises and in virtue of inference, reveals an unclear conclusion." On the Stoic definitions of ἀπόδειξις cf. Brunschwig 1980.

[68] *Pace* Burnyeat, who claims that "the Stoic origin of these arguments is attested at *M* 7.445, 8.298, 470" (1976: 51 n. 14), perhaps misled by Bury's (1935) liberal insertions in his translation.

[69] Cf. *PH* 3.19, *M* 9.204 (cause), *M* 7.440 (criterion), 8.279–82 (sign), 360–1 (reliability of appearances).

[70] For some defence of this claim cf. n. 86 below.

[71] As Bett (2005: 180 n. 134) notes, Sextus' "none of those who are receiving the proof" is misleading phrasing, "since the argument presents demonstration and bare assertion as alternatives."

unwittingly admitting the existence of at least one proof, thus refuting yourself"), Sextus' wording seems to refer instead to actual, and not merely purported, proof of the non-existence of proof. This would guarantee a stronger "pragmatic" self-refutation, in which the propositional content of an assertion is *falsified* by the actual way it is advanced ("by proving your claim that proof does not exist, you have thereby produced a proof of the existence of proof, thus falsifying your own claim").[72]

Pragmatic self-refutation also underlies, *prima facie*, the second horn of a slightly different dilemmatic argument formulated immediately below:

T21 And, in general, the argument against proof (ὁ κατὰ τῆς ἀποδείξεως λόγος) either is a proof or is not a proof; and if it is not a proof, it is not credible, but if it is a proof, proof exists. (*M* 8.465)

The λόγος against proof cannot be here the statement "Proof does not exist"; it must be the *argument* against the existence of proof. That the Sceptic has argued for the non-existence of proof is thus being taken for granted in T21, unlike in T20, and the issue is now whether his argument is or is not a proof: if it is not a proof, it will be unconvincing; but if it is a proof, proof does exist.[73] Actual proof of the non-existence of proof seems to be presupposed in the second horn, for a pragmatic περιτροπή which would establish the absolute existence of proof, rather than simply force the Sceptic's dialectical admission.[74] However, this raises two problems. First, it seems that such a pragmatic περιτροπή actually could never occur, since, strictly speaking, a sound proof of the non-existence of sound proofs is an impossibility, a monstrous logical chimaera, at least if a sound proof must possess all the characteristics the Stoics attributed to it, including, crucially, a true conclusion.[75] Second, there would be a disturbing asymmetry in the

---

[72] As I argue in Castagnoli 2010: 160–63, Mackie's influential account of the logic of pragmatic self-refutation (1964: 193–4) is not sufficiently clear in distinguishing the two objections.

[73] The parallel passage in *PH* (2.185) begins at once by formulating this second dilemma and clarifies that its second horn contains a περιτροπή: "The dogmatists, attempting to establish the contrary, say that the arguments propounded against proof are either demonstrative or non-demonstrative; and if they are not demonstrative, then they cannot show that proof does not exist; if they are demonstrative, then they themselves conclude the existence of proof by περιτροπή."

[74] Cf. Burnyeat 1976: 54.

[75] This might be reflected in the (otherwise difficult to explain) parenthesis "for they say so", towards the end of T20: if the Sceptic says that proof does not exist by proving that it does not exist (as the dogmatists *improperly* put it) then he admits the existence of proof. A more appropriate way to formulate the charge would have been "by *purporting* to prove that proof does not exist". There is, however, a different sense in which a proof of the non-existence of proofs could exist: an anti-dogmatic argument can apparently fulfil all the other requirements for demonstrativity set by dogmatic logic (cf. n. 67 above), but conclude that no proof exists, which amounts to a form of *reductio ad absurdum* of the whole dogmatic conception of proof *cum* self-elimination of that argument (cf. *M* 8.480–81 and Castagnoli 2000, 2010: 290–307).

dilemma, since its first horn is not enough for, and indeed cannot be aimed at, proving the existence of proof: that the sceptical arguments against proof are not probative is far from entailing, by itself, that proof does exist. (In fact, this would not even seem to be sufficient to force an *admission* of the existence of proof by the Sceptic in a dialectical exchange; things change, however, as soon as we import the kind of considerations underlying Zeno's argument in T16.)[76]

It would be hasty to assume that, despite appearances, in T21 the Stoics cannot be marshalling a pragmatic self-refutation argument on the sole basis that such an argument seems to us deeply objectionable, i.e. on the sole basis of a liberal application of the principle of charity. Yet these difficulties encourage us to explore alternatives. In the light of what we have seen so far about the dialectical character of Stoic *dialektikē*, the clear dialectical background of the immediately preceding and strictly related argument of T20, and various close parallels of περιτροπή in Sextus and elsewhere, it is not outrageous to speculate that T21's argument might be a compressed formulation of a dialectical dilemma. The Sceptic has offered an argument concluding that proof does not exist. The Stoic presses him: "Is this argument of yours a proof, or not?" Suppose the Sceptic answers "no"; by doing so, he will be losing any credibility. Alternatively, he can answer "Yes, my argument is a proof," thus immediately dooming himself to reversal, i.e. to the *admission* that, at the end of the day, (at least one) proof does exist. Either way, he is in bad shape and loses the dialectical exchange, not because of some truth which the very existence of his argument reveals (i.e. by pragmatic self-refutation), but because of what he has been forced to admit, rightly or wrongly, within the rules of that exchange.

The same exegetical approach would help to solve the difficulties posed by the subsequent dilemma propounded by "some" people (ἔνιοι δὲ καὶ οὕτω συνερωτῶσιν) at *M* 8.466:

T22 (1) If proof exists, proof exists $\qquad\qquad\qquad\qquad\qquad$ $p \rightarrow p$
$\qquad$ (2) If proof does not exist, proof exists $\qquad\qquad\qquad$ $\neg p \rightarrow p$
$\qquad$ (3) Either proof exists or it does not exist $\qquad\qquad$ $p \vee \neg p$
$\qquad$ (4) Therefore, proof exists $\qquad\qquad\qquad\qquad\qquad\quad$ p

---

[76] Those considerations appear to be operative at *M* 8.296: "And if he [*sc.* the dogmatist who claims that sign exists] cannot prove by a sign that sign exists, he is forced by reversal into admitting (περιτρέπεται εἰς τὸ ὁμολογεῖν) that sign does not exist."

This is as neat an example as any of the Stoics' much disparaged, or much acclaimed (depending on philosophical taste), "formalism."[77] The logical schema underlying this argument appears to be a *Consequentia Mirabilis* in the form $\neg p {\rightarrow} p \vdash p$, expanded with the addition of the truistic premises (1) and (3). Although the schema is formally valid, however, its key premise, (2), if taken at face value, looks far from *mirabilis* (how on earth could the existence of proof ever be a consequence of its non-existence?), and the justification offered for its truth borders on irrelevance: the conditional (2) "If proof does not exist, proof exists" is true – according to Sextus' dogmatists (i.e. Stoics) – because

T23 the very argument which proves the non-existence of proof, if it is demonstrative, confirms the existence of proof. (*M* 8.467)

This would be a decent support for (2) only on the controversial and possibly question-begging assumption that proof could be non-existent only if it were demonstrably so.[78] But if we are ready to supply such an unstated assumption to salvage T22's dilemma, why not supply instead a dialectical framework which is explicitly outlined or strongly suggested in the case of analogous arguments (including T20 above), and was, more generally, as we have seen, the default background of Stoic *dialektikē*? Notice that the dilemma is introduced as, literally, something *asked* (συνερωτῶσιν). The occurrence of the verb συνερωτῶ cannot by itself guarantee the presence of a live dialectical context for the argument, since sometimes it might be only a relic of the dialectical *origin* of ancient reflection on logic; however its use, here and elsewhere to introduce similar dilemmas,[79] is an additional clue in favour of a dialectical transposition and expansion of T22 along the following lines: "(3) Do you *say* that proof exists or that it does not exist? (1) If you *answer* that it exists, you are already on my side, *admitting* that proof exists; (2) if you *answer* that it does not exist, you'd better produce at least one argument, and a demonstrative one, if you hope to persuade me; but once you have agreed to advance a proof of your view, you have thereby *admitted* that some proof does exist; (4) in any case, therefore, you

---

[77] The same argument occurs at *PH* 2.186, where we also find a succinct description of its logic in quite formal terms: "whatever follows from contradictories is not only true, but also necessary." The same schema also occurs at *PH* 2.131 and *M* 8.281 (p = "sign exists"), and *M* 9.205 (p = "cause exists").

[78] I can only signal here in passing that some such assumption would appear more palatable within a modern intuitionistic framework.

[79] (Συν)ερωτῶ is also used in all the four other occurrences of the schema in Sextus (cf. n. 77).

are bound to *agree* with me that proof exists (unless you give up *dialektikē*, by limiting yourself to unconvincing assertions)":[80]

(1) If <you answer that> proof exists, <you yourself admit that> $p \rightarrow r$
     proof exists

(2) If <you answer that> proof does not exist, <you must advance $q <\rightarrow s \wedge s> \rightarrow r$
     a proof in support of your claim, and thereby admit that>
     proof exists

(3) Either <you answer that> proof exists or <you answer that> $p \vee q$
     proof does not exist

(4) Therefore, <in any case you must admit that> proof exists r

In the present context of a dispute over the existence of sound proofs, the assumption that in order successfully to support one's thesis one must produce a sound proof of it seems to beg the question almost as blatantly as the different assumption required by a more literal interpretation; nonetheless, it is at least an assumption we meet time and again in Sextus' reports of the dogmatists' περιτροπή arguments, including, crucially, T20, only a few lines above T22.

The syllogism of T22, which has often been read at face value as pivoting on a nifty formal deduction by *Consequentia Mirabilis*,[81] is best interpreted as an elliptical and enthymematic formulation of a more complex dialectical manoeuvre. How can we explain this formulation? I suggest that T22's dilemma, and the other parallel ones, might have been adopted to summarize, in a pedagogically memorable way, more complex and discursive pieces of dialectical reasoning, and not to reveal their underlying logical form[82] (incidentally, this might also account for the way in which Aristotle's cognate φιλοσοφητέον argument in the *Protrepticus* is reported by most of our late sources).[83] But it is only when read as a dialectical manoeuvre

---

[80] Of course the occurrence of συνερωτῶ *alone* cannot guarantee that the dilemma was expanded, dialectically, in the way just proposed. All the dialectic there was could have amounted to asking the interlocutor's preliminary assent to each premise and to the conclusion, formulated exactly as they appear: "Is it the case that if proof exists, proof exists?" "Yes." "Is it the case that if proof does not exists, proof exists?" "Yes." . . .

[81] Cf. e.g. Kneale 1957: 63, Bellissima and Pagli 1996, Gourinat 2000: 247–8.

[82] As Schofield (1983: 53) suggests for Zeno's syllogisms.

[83] In Castagnoli 2010: ch. 11 I argue that Aristotle's original argument was not in the pattern of CM, but followed the same lines as just sketched for the Stoic anti-sceptical dilemma in T22:

  (1) If <your position is that> one must philosophize, then <you yourself $p \rightarrow r$
      admit that> one must philosophize

  (2) If <your position is that> one must not philosophize, then <you must $q <\rightarrow s \wedge s> \rightarrow r$
      reflect on this choice and argue in its support, but by doing so you are
      already doing philosophy, thereby in fact admitting that> one must
      philosophize

within the framework of the direct confrontation with the sceptics, and
expanded accordingly, rather than as a formal demonstration by CM of
the "logical truth" of a certain proposition ("proof exists"), that the Stoic
dilemma makes sense from a logical point of view. Moreover, there is a
further complication in trying to take T22 at face value as an instance of
CM. As I have argued elsewhere, there are compelling reasons to believe
that the (most likely Chrysippean) conception of conditional proposition (συνημμένον) dubbed συνάρτησις ("connectedness") involved the
truth of what has come to be known in the literature as "Aristotle's
thesis":

$$\text{(AT)} \quad \neg(p \rightarrow \neg p) \qquad \neg(\neg p \rightarrow p)$$

[No proposition implies or is implied by its own negation]

If this is correct,[84] since συνάρτησις was Stoic orthodoxy for some time
(cf. e.g. D.L. 7.73) a literal non-dialectical reading of T22 and cognate
dilemmas would have been unacceptable in mainstream Stoicism, and
for serious logical reasons: for whoever endorses AT any argument in the
pattern of T22 will be materially false, because of the necessary falsehood
of its key premise (in modern jargon, any such argument would be only
"degenerately" valid). I have examined elsewhere a passage by Galen (*Plac.
Hipp. et Plat.* 2.3.18–20) that could be interpreted as evidence that, as
a matter of fact, Chrysippus himself never employed arguments in the
pattern of the anti-sceptical dilemmas.[85] It is in fact reasonable to suppose
that T22's dilemma in defence of the existence of proof, and the parallel
ones in defence of the existence of cause and sign, originated as a response
to those who disputed the existence of proof, cause and sign, and it is
likely that the major attacks on those notions started *after* Chrysippus: we
know that the Carneadean Clitomachus wrote a *Refutations of Proof* (cf.
Galen, *Libr. Propr.* 19.44, 7), that Aenesidemus opposed the aetiologists
with his eight modes against causal explanation (cf. e.g. S.E. *PH* 1.180–6)
and argued against sign (cf. Phot. *Bibl.* 212.170b12–14), and that Agrippa
devised a series of arguments against proof, sign and cause (cf. D.L. 9.90–
91). The anti-sceptical dilemmas might have been introduced by *later Stoics*,
urged by the necessity to devise new incisive ways to defend the foundations

---

(3) Either <your position is that> one must philosophize or <your position $p \lor q$
    is that> one must not philosophize
(4) Therefore, <you must admit that> one must philosophize r
[84] For in-depth discussion of this issue and the details of the complex scholarly debate surrounding it
    cf. Nasti De Vincentis 2002, Castagnoli 2004, 2009 and 2010: chs. 6 and 10.
[85] Cf. Castagnoli 2009, 2010: 183–85.

of their epistemology and physics from the more and more pressing attacks of Academics and Pyrrhonists.[86]

Sextus' passage could only be, of course, a test case, insufficient by itself to establish my point concerning the nature of περιτροπή. But the parallel passages in Sextus' corpus[87] corroborate the picture I have offered of Stoic περιτροπή as an intrinsically dialectical manoeuvre, as opposed to some logical property of propositions or style of formal demonstration:

(1) What is charged with reversal is a *person* who says something (*PH* 3.19, *M* 8.281–82, 9.204: ὁ λέγων κτλ; *M* 7.440: ὁ Σκεπτικός . . . λέγων). When the subject of περιτροπή is a λόγος (*M* 8.360–61), it is clear that an actual *statement* is being referred to, and not an abstract propositional content or unasserted thesis;

(2) The person who will incur περιτροπή always has an interlocutor, who must be persuaded and who is ready to oppose him. The *setting* is dialectical;

(3) The reversal *consists in* the fact that the person who says that *p* ends up *admitting* that not-*p* in the act of/as a consequence of saying that *p*. There is no indication that the *proposition p* is thereby falsified;

(4) All the different cases share the same general *cause* of περιτροπή: broadly speaking, the person who claims that *p* must do so in a *way* which commits him to the admission of not-*p* (this "way" varying from case to case: adding a cause, relying on apparent things as evidence, trying to prove *p*, uttering significant words);

(5) The reversal is usually *occasioned by* the dialectical framework: it is the need to avoid bare assertion that presses the person who eventually incurs reversal to present *p* in the way which will doom him. And bare assertion is to be eschewed, typically, because it fails to be persuasive (*PH* 3.19, *M* 7.440, 8.279, 360–61, 9.204) and the opponent can

---

[86] At any rate, the group of those adopting those dilemmas does not seem to coincide with, and is possibly narrower than, the number of those using the corresponding περιτροπή manoeuvres: "*Some* (ἔνιοι) also propound the following argument . . ." (*M* 8.466); "*It is also possible* to propound the argument . . ." (*M* 9.205); "*Some* (τινες) also propound the following argument . . ." (*M* 8.281). That those dilemmas were not Stoic *at all* seems instead more difficult to maintain: when reporting the justification of their validity or attacking them Sextus consistently uses Stoic technical jargon (e.g. τὸ πρῶτον, τὸ δεύτερον, τὸ ἡγούμενον, τὸ λῆγον, συνημμένον, διεζευγμένον, διαφορούμενον, λήμματα, ἐπιφορά, ἀξίωμα, just to limit ourselves to the dogmatists' justification of the validity of T22's dilemma at *M* 8.466–69) and Stoic tenets (e.g. at *PH* 2.188–92 that dilemma is criticized on the grounds that its premises are "mutually destructive" on the basis of the συνάρτησις truth conditions for the συνημμένον and the Stoic conception of διεζευγμένον). Gourinat (2000: 248) suggests that the anti-sceptical dilemmas can be plausibly attributed to Zeno of Citium, but his arguments (they are Stoic but cannot be Chrysippean and resemble Zeno's dilemmatic argument T16 and Aristotle's φιλοσοφητέον argument in the *Protrepticus*) underdetermine this conclusion.

[87] For detailed analysis of these passages cf. Castagnoli 2010: ch. 10.

always counter-assert its contradictory with equal (un)persuasiveness (*M* 8.281–82, 360–61).[88]

There are cases, then, in which the dialectical form could not just be for the Stoics an archaic, crystallized, and purely extrinsic way of formulating arguments which might have been cast equally well, and more rigorously, in declarative form, i.e., by stripping them of that "conversational clothing" which hides their underlying logical force. On the contrary, the dialectical context is something which, even when *not* made explicit by our sources,[89] as in T22, must be intended as implicitly meant (on the basis of stringent textual, contextual, and logical considerations), since it is an *essential* and *intrinsic* ingredient of the περιτροπή argument itself. And although I have suggested that dialectical περιτροπή does not (and cannot) aim at establishing the "absolute truth" of a certain proposition *in vacuo* (so, in *this* sense, we can agree that it has "no *heuristic* function"), it is more difficult to accept that it has "no independent cognitive value": after all, it is meant to protect some cornerstone of Stoic logical theory (here, the notion of sound proof) which has immense cognitive value, by defeating and silencing its attackers. Whether it succeeds even in this defensive task is, of course, an entirely different question (and, indeed, if we consider

---

[88] I can only add here, dogmatically, that Barnes' "reductionist" approach fails for ancient self-refutation arguments quite generally, with very few exceptions in late antiquity (cf. Castagnoli 2007, 2010).

[89] The nature of our sources on Stoic logic (mainly late paraphrases, summaries, and handbook excerpts) clearly favours the dropping of the dialectical context from our reports. There are cases, however, in which that context is explicit and yet stripped away too casually by the interpreters. Consider the short chapter of Epictetus' *Discourses* entitled "How is logic necessary?":

When someone in the audience said "Convince me that logic is useful", he [*sc.* Epictetus] said "Shall I prove this to you?" "Yes." "Then must I use a demonstrative argument?" And when [the questioner] agreed, [Epictetus asked]: "How then will you know if I deceive you sophistically?" When the man remained silent, he said: "Do you see how you yourself admit that this [*sc.* logic] is necessary, if without it you cannot even come to know this very thing, whether it is necessary or not?" (*Disc.* 2.25)

Substitute "one must philosophize" for "logic is necessary" (or "logic is useful") and you get an interesting variant of Aristotle's lesson of the φιλοσοφητέον argument (cf. n. 83 above): even if the burden of proof were not on you, and thus you did not need logic to argue for its uselessness, you would still need it to assess (and, if necessary, unmask the fallacies of) the arguments of others who try to persuade you that logic is useful. For this reason, you must admit that logic is useful after all. Barnes (1997: 59–60) attempts to reconstruct Epictetus' argument as a non-dialectical proof of the necessity of studying logic:

In order to know whether or not it is necessary to study logic, it is necessary to study logic;
But you ought to know whether or not it is necessary to study logic;
Therefore: you ought to study logic.

The dialectical context of the argument is lost in translation, and thus the second premise becomes difficult to accept: it is no surprise then that Barnes is forced to conclude that, although "it is a nice question . . . whether such a form is valid or not", at face value the argument "reads, no doubt, like a sophism."

carefully Sextus' comebacks which follow at *M* 8.470–81, the answer could be a loud "no").[90] But the point I wanted to establish here is a different one: even at the end of our story, when Stoic *dialektikē* might seem to have blossomed into something different and more "modern" (formal logic), we still find it where Zeno had originally placed it, guarding the luxuriant garden (or regimented citadel) of Stoic dogmatism by talking (more precisely, by διαλέγεσθαι) would-be plunderers out of breaking in and causing havoc.

ACKNOWLEDGMENT

I am delighted, and indeed honoured, to be able to dedicate this chapter to Tony Long. Tony's enthusiastic, inspiring, and gracious teaching and supervising throughout the year I spent in Berkeley as an exchange student in 1998/9 and his generous support and friendship since then have earned more gratitude than I could express here. I can only hope that at least some glint of what I have learnt from Tony's unique scholarship is reflected in this chapter. That I will have the opportunity to learn much more from him and his work in the future, I have no doubt.

Many thanks also to Andrea Nightingale and David Sedley for inviting me to participate to the 2007 Berkeley conference in honour of Tony and for their very helpful suggestions and their kind assistance in the process of revision of this chapter. I would also like to thank audiences in Cambridge and Berkeley for their constructive responses to earlier versions of this chapter, and especially Jean-Baptiste Gourinat for his detailed and thought-provoking oral and written comments and suggestions. The ideas on the nature of περιτροπή sketched in the final pages of this chapter are part of a broader research project on ancient self-refutation arguments which has benefited in the last few years from the invaluable input of many friends and colleagues. I wish to express my gratitude here in particular to Myles Burnyeat, Walter Cavini, Nick Denyer, Valentina Di Lascio and, again, Tony Long and David Sedley. The bulk of this chapter was researched and written during my Lumley Research Fellowship at Magdalene College, Cambridge (October 2004-August 2007); I am glad to be able to acknowledge here the College's support.

[90] Cf. n. 75 above.

CHAPTER 10

Socrates speaks in Seneca, De vita beata *24–28*
James Ker

Only once does Socrates say more than a few words in Seneca: in the final chapters of *De vita beata*, written in 58 CE, when Seneca was at the height of his power and wealth as Nero's adviser.[1] In response to an imagined accuser who asks how it is that someone can study philosophy *and* be so wealthy (*VB* 21.1), Seneca has Socrates speak at length, including the following (*VB* 25.4):[2]

Make me conqueror of all the world. Have that luxurious chariot of Liber carry me in triumph from the rising of the sun all the way to Thebes.... I will be thinking of myself as human precisely when I am greeted by one and all as a god. Then follow this lofty pedestal with a radical transformation. Let me be placed on someone else's float to decorate the procession of a fierce and arrogant conqueror. I will not be carried any more humbly beneath another's chariot than I would if I had stood in my own. So? I nevertheless prefer to conquer than to be captured.

When the text breaks off several chapters later, Socrates is still speaking.

What kind of Socratic voice is this? Below I consider four aspects, partly of the voice itself and partly of the content of the utterance: (1) The voice belongs to a prosopopoeia. (2) Socrates espouses the Stoic doctrine of preferred indifferents. (3) He invokes recognizably Roman examples such as the triumph. (4) Partly overlapping with these other aspects, Socrates speaks with some prescience of his own later reception. Studying these aspects together in the context of *De vita beata*, I argue, gives us a more detailed understanding of Seneca's appropriation of the philosophical tradition, including how he deploys it to shape perceptions of his own life-course.

I thank Tony Long as a most inspiring mentor to all of his students. I am grateful to the participants of the conference, to Brad Inwood for a generous response, and especially to Andrea Nightingale and David Sedley for their exacting comments; also, to the two anonymous readers.
[1] For introduction and commentary, see Viansino 1992–93 and Schiesaro 1996.
[2] I use the OCT text by Reynolds; translations are mine unless otherwise indicated.

SOCRATISMS

Our passage belongs to the broader reception of Socrates in ancient philosophy.[3] In his 1988 article, "Socrates in Hellenistic Philosophy,"[4] Tony Long demonstrated that doctrines of the early Hellenistic schools were in many cases formed through a serious, and varied, reflection on Socrates. For most of these schools, Socrates is a philosopher of ethics who has turned away from the study of nature; for many, he is already the Socrates of Xenophon rather than the Socrates of Plato; and his characteristic irony and self-confession of ignorance are mostly absent. But his doxographic profile varies on points of doctrine, and oscillates between knowledge and scepticism. Long shows, for example, how the Platonic Socrates' argument of *Euthydemus* 278e3–281e5 allowed for divergent readings by the early Stoics Zeno and Aristo and thus served as a basis for their divergent doctrines on indifferents: Zeno classifies some indifferents such as health and wealth as having some value and being preferred, whereas Aristo completely rejects value for all indifferents. A similar observation about the Stoic, indeed Senecan, engagement with the Platonic Socrates has been made more recently by Brad Inwood in a chapter of his *Reading Seneca*. When Seneca describes Socrates as having waited out his time in prison (rather than, say, starving himself sooner) partially *ut praeberet se legibus*, "in order to submit to the laws" (*Ep.* 70.9; trans. Inwood), Inwood notes the echoes of Plato's *Crito* in particular with its personified Laws of Athens, and argues that the Socratic appeal to "rationality and fairness" is being used by Seneca to clarify how he sees "our relationship to the law of nature, in particular the law of mortality."[5] Studies such as Long's and Inwood's illustrate how specific Socratic scenarios could be mined for their potential to develop or dramatize Stoic doctrine.

Along with Socratizing doctrine, there is also the question of Socratizing discourse. Long has more recently turned to the Socrates of Epictetus in his book *Epictetus: A Stoic and Socratic Guide to Life*, where he argues, *inter alia*, for Epictetus' use of an "elenctic" mode in the *Discourses* as they were written up by Arrian, a mode adapted and customized to be sure (especially given Arrian's own emulation of Xenophon), but with clear origins in Plato's dialogues. Turning to Seneca or any other philosophical writer, we may ask whether the way in which he writes, or even the way in which he represents Socrates speaking, can be identified with any characteristically "Socratic" mode(s), whether dialectic, mythic monologue, the forensic

---

[3] See further Döring 1979.   [4] Reprinted in Long 1996: 1–34.   [5] Inwood 2005: 241–43.

rhetoric of the *Apology*, or any other form of discourse. But there is also the converse question to be asked, namely, to what extent various philosophical writers retroactively attribute to Socrates a manner of speaking that is post-Socratic (or post-Platonic) in origin. Gretchen Reydams-Schils has shown how the practices of "self-assessment" widely used by the Roman Stoics, and especially "the so-called *meditatio*, the examination of conscience, in which one's firm adherence to philosophical principles is tested against reflection on concrete, practical challenges," are in turn attributed by Epictetus to Socrates himself, who is alleged to have variously used interior dialogue and writing as forms of exercise.[6] These approaches to Stoic Socratism, then, ask us to remain attentive to the voice of Socrates, whether in the preservation of an "original" mode or in the back-projection of a later one.

There is a third feature of Socratism which recent studies have also singled out: his function as an exemplum. In his *Exemplum Socratis* (1979), Klaus Döring emphasizes how Socrates is the focus of an especially mimetic approach to exemplarity, in which *imitatio Socratis* includes becoming exemplary oneself in turn – an approach that we may note is characteristic not only of Seneca but of what Matthew Roller calls the Roman "loop of exemplarity."[7] But Döring emphasizes the extent to which Socrates is reshaped by Seneca even as he imitates him. In Döring's account, Socrates' appearance in *De vita beata* is just the biggest instance of this; in fact, the *ethopoeia* has little to do with the historical Socrates and more to do with the "abstract ideal form" of the sage and with the particular scenario in which he is speaking, namely the defense of Seneca himself against charges of hypocrisy before an audience of Roman contemporaries.[8] Inwood also poses important questions regarding Seneca's use of the *sapiens* in general, and Socrates in particular, as models. Discussing a complex passage in letter 120 in which Seneca appeals to our memory of an unnamed perfectly morally consistent individual, Inwood argues that even if Socrates or Cato or some other historical individual is meant, "his primary use in our moral epistemology is not as a direct model for imitation or analysis, but as a foil in the analytical process of concept formation," and as an "idealized *persona*."[9] On the other hand, Inwood also acknowledges Seneca's striving for naturalism in his examples – whether in seeking someone from his own experience or in the use of literature to make a wise man accessible.[10] Such approaches as Döring's and Inwood's identify the different epistemological frameworks which may be at play in Socrates' function as an *exemplum*.

---

[6] Reydams Schils 2005b: 9–10.   [7] Roller 2004.   [8] Döring 1979: 28–30.
[9] Inwood 2005: 295.   [10] Inwood 2005: 296.

In the thirty-six distinct passages where Seneca mentions Socrates, scholars have already noted obvious and significant patterns, such as a recurring focus on Socrates' imprisonment and death (16 times) and his frequent pairing of Socrates with Cato and other Roman heroes (26 times), as well as implicit comparisons between Athens (under democracy or the thirty tyrants) and Rome (at the end of the republic or in the early empire).[11] A less frequent but still distinctive motif is Seneca's description of Socrates engaging in specific forms of discourse. He uses the term *disputare* to characterize Socratic dialogue in general (as against, say, the Cynic mode of *dubitare*, *Brev.* 14.1; cf. *Prov.* 3.12). But in a striking passage in *De tranquillitate animi* he relates how Socrates showed his *libertas* against the thirty tyrants in a range of different modes of rheoric:

He was in the thick of things (*in medio erat*), and exhorted those who were despairing for their country (*desperantes de re publica exhortabatur*), and censured (*exprobrabat*) the rich (who now were afraid of their own wealth) for regretting their greed so late, and carried around a great example for those willing to imitate it (*imitari volentibus magnum circumferebat exemplar*), since he was walking free despite being among thirty masters. (*Tranq.* 5.1–3)

As Reydams-Schils observes, such behaviors, not seen in the early Socratic tradition, make Socrates "a Roman Stoic *avant la lettre*."[12] In at least one instance, also, Seneca briefly has Socrates exhort Lucilius, saying: "If I have any sway with you, follow *them* [the exemplary philosophers],[13] so that you will be happy..." (*sequere... illos, si quid apud te habeo auctoritatis, ut sis beatus...*, *Ep.* 71.7). Yet equally often Seneca focuses not on Socrates' words, but on his unflappable facial expression (*vultus*) as a sign of even-keeled endurance (*Helv.* 13.4; *Ep.* 104.29). In the majority of these examples, however, Socrates is described rather than invoked; against this background, the speaking Socrates of *De vita beata* stands out.

DE VITA BEATA

In Tacitus' account for the year 58 CE we read that charges were brought against P. Suillius Rufus, a professional accuser who had flourished already under Tiberius and Claudius. Tacitus relates Suillius' trial and eventual banishment, but first describes the accusations which the professional accuser directed, apparently behind the scenes, against Seneca (*Ann.* 13.42–3.1;

---

[11] On specific features see Döring 1979; Isnardi Parenti 2000; Staley 2002.
[12] Reydams Schils 2005b: 104. [13] For this interpretation of *illos* see Inwood 2007a: 187–88.

cf. 11.5.3).[14] Although we cannot go into the Suillius episode in much detail
here, his portrayal of Seneca's career – Seneca's "most just exile" (*iustissi-
mum exilium*), "lazy studies" (*studiis inertibus*), indulgence of "the ignorance of young men" (*iuvenum imperitiae*), rhetorical polemics, adultery
in the imperial household (cf. Dio 61.10), and "precipitous rise to fortune"
(*subitae felicitati*) boosted by "usury" (*faenore*) and "legacy-hunting" (*testa-
menta . . . capi*) – has traditionally been seen as motivating the apologetics
of *De vita beata*. The work has been seen in some sense as responding to
Suillius' question: "By what wisdom, what precepts of the philosophers,
had he [Seneca] acquired 300 million sesterces in four years of friendship
with the emperor?" (*qua sapientia, quibus philosophorum praeceptis intra
quadriennium regiae amicitiae ter milies sestertium paravisset?*, *Ann.* 13.42.4).
Addressed to his brother Gallio and explaining the work's title in the terms
"what it is that produces the happy life" (*quid sit quod beatam vitam efficiat*,
VB 1.1), Seneca's text invokes the theory of preferred indifferents and associates this with none other than Socrates.

The work's first sixteen chapters are spent arguing that virtue is sufficient for living happily and fending off a quasi-Epicurean objector. From
chapter 17 onward the objector is represented as pointing out supposed
contradictions between what Seneca says and how he lives, arguing that
"You speak one way and live in another" (*"aliter . . . loqueris, aliter vivis*,"
18.1; cf. 20.1). He emphasizes themes which in many cases have resonance
with Seneca's own career, such as the exile which he had appeared to tol-
erate in *Consolatio ad Helviam*: "And yet does he, if he can, grow old in
the fatherland (*senescit in patria*)?" (21.1; cf. 17.1–2). While Seneca takes
evident pleasure in allowing the objector to heap up these and other such
accusations, in 24.4 he introduces the *sapiens* as a responder.

The *sapiens* has been foreshadowed. Seneca had earlier admitted, "I am
not wise . . . nor will I be. . . . I speak these words not for myself – since I am
in the depth of all vices – but for him who has accomplished something"
(*non sum sapiens . . . nec ero. . . . haec non pro me loquor – ego enim in alto
vitiorum omnium sum – sed pro illo cui aliquid acti est*, 17.3–4), thereby
differentiating between the person that he is in his actions and the person
whose voice he is channeling (cf. 11.1). As a failed philosopher with valiant
intentions, he puts himself in very good company: "This accusation . . . was
made of Plato, of Epicurus, of Zeno; for all of these men were saying not
how they themselves were living, but how even they themselves ought to
live (*non quemadmodum ipsi viverent, sed quemadmodum esset <et> ipsis*

---

[14] For background on Suillius see Rutledge 2001: 111–13.

vivendum)" (18.1). And he draws up further lists of those with whom his accusers are unlikely to be satisfied, including Rutilius Rufus and Cato, Demetrius the Cynic, and Diodorus the Epicurean, a recent philosophical suicide (18.3; 19). But one name standardly included in these catalogues is conspicuously absent. Seneca will be seeking his ultimate example, and advocate, not in the worthy efforts of the school philosophers but in the unquestioned moral perfection of Socrates.

Yet when Seneca finally introduces the *sapiens* as speaker, he does not initially give him a name (*VB* 24.4–5):

But he who has attained the height of human good will deal with you differently and will say: "First, you should not be allowed to pass judgment on better men (*de melioribus ferre sententiam*). It has turned out for me now – a sign of my rectitude – that I am displeasing to bad men (*malis displicere*). But if I may give you an account of how I am jealous of no mortal man, hear what I promise and at how much I value each thing (*quid promittam et quanti quaeque aestimem*). I deny that riches are a good. For if they were a good, they would make men good. But now, since that which is discovered among bad men cannot be called good, I deny them this name. But I do say that riches are to be acquired and are useful and bring great advantages to life (*et habendas esse et utiles et magna commoda vitae adferentis fateor*). Hear the reason why, then, I do not count them among good things, and what I accomplish in them different from what you do, seeing as we both agree that they are to be acquired."

This passage serves as something of a preface, in which the speaker acknowledges his accusers and introduces his topic, that is, his own axiology and his reasons for thinking that wealth is "to be acquired," though in ways contrary to the views of his opponents.

After these remarks, the speaker embarks on the first major section (25.1–8),[15] an extensive series of hypothetical scenarios and statements of preference, of which the triumph example with which we began (25.4) is representative. Only part way through these hypothetical scenarios does Seneca first identify the speaker as Socrates: *hoc tibi ille Socrates dicet* ("that Socrates will say to you the following," 25.4) – in which *ille Socrates* may mean "that famous Socrates" or may simply suggest "that 'Socrates' we have been talking about," with the name as a synonym for "wise man." But toward the end of this section he reverts to *inquit sapiens* ("the wise man says," 25.8).

In the second section (26.1–3), the speaker answers an objector who asks for further clarification of the difference between them by answering that

---

[15] The section divisions are mine, established on the basis of rhetorical markers in the text.

the wise man is the commander of his wealth, whereas "you," he says, are slaves to wealth; he compares them to *barbari* under siege who have a false sense of security because they do not understand the machinery at their enemy's disposal.

In the third section (26.4–8), the speaker is once again identified as Socrates (*VB* 26.4–5):

"There is nothing of which I have persuaded myself more," says that Socrates or someone else possessing the same feeling and the same power with regard to human things (*ille Socrates aut aliquis alius cui idem <adfectus> adversus humana atque eadem potestas est*), "than that I should avoid turning the actions of my life in the direction of your opinions . . ." This is what will be said by him who has obtained wisdom, whose mind is invulnerable to the vices and orders him to scold others not because he hates them but to offer a remedy.

The oscillation between "that Socrates" and "someone else" both deemphasizes the personality of Socrates in particular and marks his moral perfection as theoretically iterable in others. In this section the speaker compares the audience's attack on him to a barrage of superstitious and irreverent practices directed at the gods.

The fourth section (27.1–28.1), however, is introduced with the most precise and evocative reference to Socrates: "Behold Socrates (*ecce Socrates*), from that prison which he purified by entering and rendered more virtuous than any senate house, proclaims (*proclamat*) . . ." (*VB* 27.1). From this point forth, the speech takes on the ambience of the prison scene depicted in *Crito* and *Phaedo*. In this section Socrates assails the audience's madness for attacking him. When the text breaks off, he is asking an extended rhetorical question: "Surely now, even if you don't feel it, some kind of whirlwind is spinning your minds (*turbo quidam animos vestros rotat*) and twirls you as you seek and shun the same things, now raised on high, now dashed to the depths?" (28.1).

We are now in a position to consider the four aspects of this Socratic voice and the content of its utterance singled out above:

(1) Prosopopoeia

Seneca introduces another person's voice into his own rhetorical scenario.[16] This is in fact a favorite device of Seneca. In *De providentia*, for example, Seneca gives voice to Cato in his capacity as a great man matched with great misfortune, where Cato's detached third-person description of himself

---

[16] On Seneca's use of prosopopoeia, see Williams 2003: 3–4; Mazzoli 2000.

tearing his wound back open helps to establish the divine and providential perspective of Jupiter (*Prov.* 2.9–12). That perspective is given voice in the extensive final chapter of the work in which God himself appears, urging the reader, "Learn death" (*mortem condiscite,* 6.3–9) – a lesson emphasized by the closural dynamics of the work's end. The speech of Socrates in *De vita beata* is in fact quite typical, coming at what appears to be the work's ending and summoning the forms of authority that come variously from a god-like idealizing perspective and from a specific historical example, and particularly from an *exitus.*

The play of voices in Seneca's *Dialogi,* whether in prosopopoeiai or in the briefer voices of the *inquis* or *inquit* interventions, is part and parcel of these works' quasi-forensic aspect. Seneca often presents the *dialogus* as a kind of textualized legal trial: in *De providentia,* once again, he says, "I will make the case for the gods" (*causam deorum agam, Prov.* 1.1), and a similar discourse is evident in *De vita beata*: even if we don't read the work as a response to Suillius the professional accuser, the arrival of Socrates as a speaker implicitly casts Seneca's opponents as the accusers from Socrates' trial. Here, however, Socrates speaks far less agnostically than he does in Plato about his rejection of certain popular religious practices and superstitions (*VB* 26.6–8). Socrates' rectitude and his authority as an advocate for the correct way to prefer wealth are here guaranteed by the authority that Seneca summons through invoking Socrates' final suffering in prison (27.1). Seneca subtly fuses the literary-historical Socrates, the idealized Socrates, and his own present persona as a defendant.

(2) Stoic doctrine

Seneca has Socrates espouse the Stoic theory of preferred indifferents, which he had earlier espoused in his own voice (*VB* 22.4):

Who among the wise men – I mean ours, to whom the one good is virtue – denies that even these things which we call indifferent have some value in them and that some are preferable to others (*etiam haec quae indifferentia vocamus habere aliquid in se pretii et alia aliis esse potiora*)? Some of these are assigned a certain amount of honor, others are assigned much honor. To keep you from mistaking, then: riches are among the preferable ones (*inter potiora divitiae sunt*).

Seneca here presents a picture of Stoic unanimity around the Zenonian theory of indifferents, omitting the chapter in Stoic doxography represented by Aristo. It is interesting that in doing so Seneca should then go on to appeal to Socrates as the mouthpiece for this theory. As Long has observed, the Platonic Socrates had said nothing to discount Aristo's theory of valueless indifferents. What Seneca presents, though, is a Socrates who both describes and embodies the Zenonian theory. The form in which Socrates (or, to begin with, the *sapiens*) espouses the theory has a very systematic structure (*VB* 25.1–8):

(1) "Put me (*pone... me*) in the most lavish house, put me where gold and silver are in common use. I will not look up at myself (*non suspiciam me*) because of these things – even if they are with me, they are still outside of me. Shift me (*me transfer*) to the Sublician bridge and cast me among the needy. I will not on that account, however, look down on myself (*non ideo... me despiciam*) because I have settled among the number of those who stretch out their hand for alms. For what difference does it make whether someone lacks a piece of bread if he does not lack the ability to die? So (*quid ergo est*)? I prefer (*malo*) that splendid house to the bridge.

(2) Put me (*pone*) among glittering contraptions and a luxurious retinue. I will not believe myself to be in any way happier (*nihilo me feliciorem credam*) because I have a soft garment, because purple is spread under my guests. Change (*muta*) my bedding. I will not be less happily disposed (*nihilo miserius ero*) if my tired neck rests in a handful of hay, if I lie over a Circus cushion which leaks through the patches of an old cloth. So (*quid ergo est*)? I prefer (*malo*) to show off the state of my mind while wearing a noble's toga... than with my shoulder-blades bare.

(3) Let all my days go (*cedant*) according to my prayers, let one round of rejoicings be joined (*subtexantur*) to another. I will not be smug because of this (*non ob hoc mihi placebo*). Change (*muta*) these favorable times to their opposite, let my mind be assaulted from all sides by loss, grief, and various attacks, let no hour be without lament. I will not for this reason curse (*non ideo... execrabor*) a day. For I have made provision that no day of mine will count as "black." So (*quid ergo est*)? I prefer (*malo*) controlling my joy than combatting grief.

(4) That Socrates will say to you the following: "Make me (*fac me*) conqueror of all the world. Have that luxurious chariot of Liber carry (*vehat*) me in triumph from the rising of the sun all the way to Thebes.... I will be thinking (*cogitabo*) of myself as human precisely when I am greeted by one and all as a god. Then follow (*coniunge*) this lofty pedestal with a radical transformation. Let me be placed (*imponar*) on someone else's float to decorate the procession of a fierce and arrogant conqueror. I will not be carried (*non... agar*) any more humbly beneath another's chariot than I would if I had stood in my own. So (*quid ergo est*)? I nevertheless prefer (*malo*) to conquer than to be captured."

(5) I will look down upon (*despiciam*) the whole kingdom of fortune, but if it is granted I will take the better things from it (*meliora sumam*). Whatever comes my way will be made good, but I prefer that easier and more pleasant things come, things less taxing to deal with (*malo faciliora ac iucundiora veniant et minus vexatura tractantem*).

For there is no reason why you should think that any virtue is without effort, but some virtues are in need of goading on, others are in need of reining in. (6) Just as a body on an incline must be held back, but toward a hill must be pushed, so some virtues are on an incline, others are going up a slope (*quaedam virtutes in proclivi sunt, quaedam clivum subeunt*). Or is there any doubt that there is a climb, an effort, a struggle, for endurance, courage, persistence, and whatever other virtues are opposed to hard things and which overcome fortune? (7) So (*quid ergo est*)? Is it not equally obvious that there is a downhill ride for generosity, temperance, and gentleness? . . . (8) Given this distinction, I prefer to be using those virtues which must be exercised more calmly than those whose test is blood and sweat (*malo has in usu mihi esse quae exercendae tranquillius sunt quam eas quarum experimentum sanguis et sudor est*)."

First note the general progression through different categories, which move from particular to general: in 25.1, wealth represented through places; 25.2, wealth represented through clothing; 25.3, fortunes represented through times; 25.4, fortunes represented through positions in the triumph; 25.5, the "whole kingdom of fortune" (*totum fortunae regnum*); 25.5–8, the distinct sets of virtues dealing with "downhill" and "uphill" situations. Note also the structure of each unit: a hypothetical good situation to which I am indifferent, a hypothetical bad situation to which I am indifferent, and then an expression of preference with *malo*, "I prefer." Although the main point is the expression of preference, the power of this expression depends crucially on the preceding expressions of indifference; in particular, it depends on the speaker's perfectly balanced treatment of the downhill and uphill situations – an effect that is also helped by the fact that Socrates does not openly express any "*dis*preferral" of, say, poverty, and even more so by the fact that the sequence within each unit uniformly goes from positive to negative, showing how a catastrophic narrative trajectory that would ordinarily be the stuff of tragedy is neutralized through the theory of indifferents. The espousal by Socrates also goes beyond a mere description or explanation: its dramatic first-person and future-tense formulations make it an embodiment of the wise man's state of mind as he perfects the art of self-testing. And it helps that it is *Socrates* who says this, given that we know that it is predominantly the "uphill" virtues that he was eventually called upon to exercise – a fact underpinned by Seneca's later transition to the prison scene.

The discursive mode used by Socrates here closely resembles the structure of *meditatio*, and more specifically the *praemeditatio futurorum malorum*,[17]

---

[17] On *meditatio* in Seneca, see Newman 1989; Armisen-Marchetti 1986.

which Seneca models elsewhere in his writings, for example in *Epistulae morales* 24. There Lucilius is invited to undertake the same kind of quasi-theatrical "rehearsal" that we see in Socrates, using first-person hypotheticals (for example, *exul fiam*, "I will become an exile") followed by a consolatory comment (*ibi me natum putabo quo mittar*, "I will imagine that I was born in the place to which I am sent", *Ep.* 24.17). The fuller instance in *De vita beata*, however, features *praemeditatio bonorum* alongside *malorum*. It is also much more specific about the context for the *praemeditatio malorum* exercise: while Lucilius is simply implied to be in present good circumstances, Socrates emphasizes that he prepares for the worst *precisely when* things are at their best. Indeed, he later recaps his exercise in the following terms: *sapiens tunc maxime paupertatem meditatur cum in mediis divitiis constitit* ("the wise man rehearses for poverty precisely when he stands amid wealth," *VB* 26.1). This *figura etymologica* emphasizes the *meditatio* as a practice which enacts detachment *in mediis rebus*. The question remains whether this *meditatio* should be seen as the projection of a predominantly Stoic (or Hellenistic) discursive mode onto Socrates or the preservation of an essentially Socratic mode. Perhaps it is both. We do not see such systematic examples of *meditatio* before Latin literature, yet as Seneca himself reminds us elsewhere (*Marc.* 23.2), the philosopher's main task, *meditatio mortis* (μελέτη θανάτου), was first identified by Plato, who put this in the mouth of Socrates in prison as he faces his coming death with indifference (*Phaedo* 64a, 67d).[18]

(3) Roman culture

Numerous Roman details emerge in Socrates' speech – not just the triumph, but everything from the topography of the Sublician bridge (25.1)[19] and the calendrical *dies atri* (25.3) to the detail that Socrates, by entering his prison, "purified" it and "rendered it more virtuous than any senate house" ([*carcerem*] *purgavit omnique honestiorem curia reddidit*, 27.1); in other words, Socrates plays the role of an idealized Roman *censor*. Of course, Seneca consistently uses cultural models and metaphors as a way to bring his audience *in rem praesentem* (*Ep.* 59.6), but the impact of Roman models is made especially complex by Socrates' status as a Greek outsider. Below

---

[18] It is worth noting that Socrates also implicitly treats his audience's arguments themselves as indifferents, and as a test for his own *patientia* and *perseverantia*; in so doing he gives a doctrinal grounding to the Platonic Socrates' claim that Anytus and Meletus cannot harm him (cf. Pl. *Apol.* 30c), in which the Stoics showed some interest (e.g., Epict. 1.29.18).

[19] On the topography of the Roman city in Seneca, see André 2002.

I present two brief, open-ended examples in which Seneca has Socrates enlist Roman concepts to help his speech.

First, in the example of the Roman triumph quoted above (*VB* 25.4), Socrates summons up the world of Roman imperialism, with the opposed positions of the *felix triumphator* on his chariot and the conquered foreigner being carried on his platform as part of the procession. The triumph offers a snug fit for Socrates' doctrinal point. When he formulates his *meditatio* and his expression of indifference in the terms "I will be thinking of myself as human precisely when I am greeted by one and all as a god" (*me hominem esse maxime cogitabo, cum deus undique consalutabor,* 25.4), he is alluding to the custom in which the slave or other assistant who accompanies the triumphator on his chariot speaks these words into his ear: "Look behind you! Remember that you are human!" (*respice post te! hominem te memento!,* Tert. *Apol.* 33.4).[20] The philosophical use of this comparison can be paralleled in Epictetus, again with reference to indifferents and in a meditative context (Epict. 3.24.85–86):

Never give up [your power over] impressions completely, and do not allow excess to come forth as far as it wishes, but push back, prevent it, like those who stand behind triumphators and remind them that they are human (οἷον οἱ τοῖς θριαμβεύουσιν ἐφεστῶτες ὄπισθεν καὶ ὑπομιμνήσκοντες ὅτι ἄνθρωποί εἰσιν). Give yourself some such reminder, that what you love is something mortal, that what you love is nothing that belongs to you.

Note in addition, however, that in Seneca's use of the triumphator comparison the triumph mentioned is already metaphorical: the chariot is that of Liber, and the triumphal return to Thebes rather than Rome is in keeping with this allegory, since that city is the home of Dionysus' mother Semele. The image of Dionysus returning to Thebes may evoke the tragic reversals of the *Bacchae*, and it is also appropriate in light of Seneca's critiques of hedonism. In any case, Socrates acts out his disdain for wealth through appealing to a normative Roman social institution in which the *felicitas* of the triumphator is of social value only when constrained by his ritual observance of humility – a lesson also for Seneca and his *subita felicitas* (Tac. *Ann.* 13.42.4).

Second, the religious terminology used by Socrates in the third section of his speech operates within the religious universe of first-century Rome. Socrates introduces it as follows (*VB* 26.6):

---

[20] Further parallels for the triumph analogy, and for Dionysus as the original triumphator, are given by Viansino 1992–93: 2.599.

I endure your hallucinations just as Jupiter Greatest and Best endures the absurdities of the poets (*sic vestras halucinationes fero quemadmodum Iuppiter optimus maximus ineptias poetarum*). Of these, one has put wings on him, another horns, another has made him an adulterer and a night-reveler, another cruel against the gods, another unfair to men, another even the ravisher of his own kind and kin, another a parricide and an attacker of another's kingdom, and his *father's* kingdom. These have accomplished nothing except that human beings should lose their sense of shame at wrongdoing, if they believed that the gods were like this.

His statements are in keeping with, in turn, the cautious approach to defining the triumphator's state of mind mentioned earlier in the speech (the Roman triumphator was customarily dressed as Jupiter), the discussion of Athenian religion in Plato's *Euthyphro*, Seneca's own critiques of popular religion in *De superstitione* and *De situ et sacris Aegyptiorum*,[21] and, more generally, the picture of orientalizing religions during the principate that we see in authors such as Juvenal. Socrates' next step, however, suggests a space for philosophy within the religious conventions of Roman life. When Socrates commands them, "Worship [virtue] as you do the gods and its professors as temple-masters," and reinforces this with a command of ritual silence in the presence of philosophical scripture, *favete linguis* ("Watch your tongues", *VB* 26.7), he does something analogous to what Seneca does in *De brevitate vitae*, describing the great "households" of philosophy which are permanently available for us to visit in a form of *salutatio* (*Brev.* 15.2–3). In the context of Socrates' speech, however, the emphasis on ritual silence belongs to a more general strategy of disarming the voices of his audience by relentlessly satirizing them through all manner of descriptions (for example, *conviciari*, "lambast"; *vagire velut infantes*, "wail like babies," *VB* 26.4).[22]

(4) Anachronisms

Socrates speaks with a knowledge of history that transcends his own lifetime. This includes aspects we have already considered, such as his convenient attention to Seneca's present situation, his anticipation of the authority he will gain through his own death, and his speaking like a Stoic and a Roman. But in the final section of the speech, in particular, Seneca has Socrates exercise a self-conscious hindsight that reflects what has been made of Socrates himself in the literary and philosophical tradition. This comes across most clearly when he says, "I have on occasion

---

[21] On these lost works, see Vottero 1998: 19–21, 47–57.
[22] As Andrea Nightingale points out, this echoes the Socratic concern with εὐφημία already in Plato.

offered Aristophanes material for jokes, and that entire cohort of comic poets has sprayed its poisoned witticisms on me (*praebui ego aliquando Aristophani materiam iocorum, tota illa comicorum poetarum manus in me venenatos sales suos effudit*). My virtue has been illuminated through the very things with which it was attacked" (*VB* 27.2). Even if the reference to the comic Socrates were understood to refer only to satirizations during his own lifetime (though the multiplication would seem to point ahead to such representations as that by Timon in his *Silloi*), Socrates still shows a prescient awareness of himself as a figure of literature in his audience's imagination. The comparison of himself to a rock a few sentences later (*duritia silicis*, 27.2) surely implies the hypostasized post-Socratic images of the *sapiens*. Indeed, as he continues, he switches from the past-tense *praebui* to the present-tense *praebeo*, and for the rest of this section he fleshes out the image of the invulnerable sage: "I offer myself (*praebeo me*) in no way differently from a lonely outcrop in a shallow sea, which the waves do not cease to lash, from whichever side they have been stirred up, yet they do not for that reason either move me from my place or exhaust me with their endless onslaught through so many ages. Pounce, make your attack: I will overcome you by endurance (*ferendo vos vincam*)" (*VB* 27.3; 28.1). These comparisons, with their military and maritime metaphors, reflect Socrates' transformation into the *sapiens* as he is defined in Hellenistic, Roman, and Senecan commonplaces.

The transhistorical perspective is also manifested when Socrates places himself within a retrospective pageant of philosophers (*VB* 27.5):

Charge Plato with having sought money, Aristotle with having received it, Democritus with neglecting it, Epicurus with using it up. Charge me myself with Alcibiades and Phaedrus (*mihi ipsi Alcibiaden et Phaedrum obiectate*), you who will be greatly happy, as soon as you can begin to imitate [even just] our vices (*cum primum vobis imitari vitia nostra contigerit*).

Socrates brushes aside the charges of pederasty (conveniently for Seneca; cf. Dio 61.10) which were to become a negative thread in the Socratic reception. Socrates supports his moral high ground by invoking the entire tradition of philosophy to which he belongs, and for which he has become a model – as he acknowledges here by referring to *imitatio Socratis*. But what licenses Socrates to speak with an unfettered view of history? This perspective within a Senecan prosopopoeia is not unique to Socrates: in *Consolatio ad Marciam* Cremutius Cordus is allowed to amplify his annalistic historian's perspective in the afterlife, and to engage in turn with his daughter's posthumous perspective on him (cf. *Marc.* 26.5). But our best sense of a transhistorical interaction with Socrates and other philosophers comes in *De brevitate vitae*, where the philosopher gains access to a universal colloquium of sages (*Brev.* 14.2).

It may be Seneca's ability to summon Socrates and to animate him in this way that best captures the nature of his literary performance in these closing chapters of *De vita beata*. Socrates' words are themselves important in all the ways we have seen, lending advocacy to Seneca's arguments about preferred indifferents in response to a hostile audience. But Seneca's strongest answer to his detractors is to show that even as he classifies material objects as preferred but indifferent, he is simultaneously displaying a higher form of inalienable wealth, which he has appropriated through a brilliant exercise in *captatio*, an inheritance from the households of philosophy which grows only greater with each day's *salutatio* in the atria of Socrates and his like.

CONCLUSION

Let us consider, in closing, what the speech of Socrates in *De vita beata* adds to the Socratic template for Seneca's own life and career. The picture of Socrates engaged in *meditatio*, repeatedly rehearsing his indifference to "downhill" and "uphill" scenarios in succession, equips Seneca, successively a political insider and outsider, with a biographical framework that has a place for the textual performance of both downhill virtues (think *De beneficiis, De vita beata*) and, equally, uphill virtues – both earlier (*Ad Helviam*) and later (*De providentia, Epistulae morales*). This might have been only a *potential* effect, except that it is brought out so clearly by Tacitus, both in his portrayal of the interview with Nero in which Seneca actively strives to pivot from prosperity to *paupertas* (*Ann.* 14.53–56), and even more vividly in his notice regarding Seneca's refusal of a funeral: "This was as he had stipulated in his will, when he was giving thought to his last rites even while still supremely wealthy and powerful" (*ita codicillis praescripserat, cum etiam tum praedives et praepotens supremis suis consuleret, Ann.* 15.64.4). The wordplay on *praescripserat* and *praedives/praepotens* parallels (at the level of biographical narrative) the structure of anticipation that Seneca has Socrates chart out in the figure *meditatur . . . in mediis divitiis* (*VB* 26.1). Tacitus, consciously or not, registers the effect of Seneca's vivid portrayal of Socrates navigating the fortunes and misfortunes of life. Read within this biographical schema, Seneca's Socrates, invoked at the mid-point of his career, serves as a form of symbolic wealth that immunizes the author against fluctuations in his material wealth.

The speaking Socrates of *De vita beata*, however, was not the only Senecan artifact that would offer templates to later writers interested in constructing narratives of Seneca's life and career. Seneca had given voice to *multiple* characters of Athenian literature, having them speak in prosopopoeiai, in Stoic terminology, in metaphors from Roman culture, and with an uncanny hindsight on their own posthumous reception. I refer, of course, to the figures of Senecan tragedy,[23] whose voices would be echoed in the rewritings of Seneca's life and career in triumphal and tragic modes by the authors of *Hercules Oetaeus* and *Octavia*, and others.

[23] See, e.g., the recent discussion of Medea by Bartsch 2006: 230–81.

CHAPTER 11

Seneca's Platonism

The soul and its divine origin

Gretchen Reydams-Schils

To Tony, demiurge and providence

At the opening of the *Didaskalikos*, Alcinous – if in fact he is the author – provides two definitions of wisdom: first, that "it is the knowledge of divine and human matters"; second, that it entails "a loosening of the soul and turning away from the body." The first definition is also attested for the Stoics.[1] The second definition, inspired by Plato's *Phaedo*, would seem a particularly good fit in a Middle Platonist context, such as Alcinous' handbook, because it emphasizes a stark and unmitigated dualism between the intelligible and sensible realms. Precisely for that reason one would not expect such a definition to show up in a Stoic context, since Stoicism is an implicit target of criticism in Alcinous' account. Yet Seneca seems to have been quite attracted to this second view of wisdom and philosophy, and his texts are interspersed with echoes of the theme. But for all his attraction to the *Phaedo* and to other Platonic accounts, Seneca remains quite rooted in Stoic thought, even if he finds himself dreaming, on occasion, of immortality (*Ep.* 102). To get this point across, one does not need to explain away certain passages of Seneca as mere metaphors, or rhetoric in the service of practical, moral philosophy.[2] From a hermeneutical point of view such an approach is unsatisfactory because, for one thing, it does not address the question why Seneca chooses certain metaphors or rhetorical devices over others. Nor does one have to look for an explanation exclusively in earlier attempts at combining Platonic and Stoic ideas made by Panaetius, Posidonius, or Antiochus. One can focus instead on the use to which Seneca puts these allegedly Platonic themes in the context of what we know both of earlier Stoicism and of Stoicism in the imperial era.

---

[1] *SVF* 2. 35–36; 1017; Cicero *Off.* 2.5; *Tusc.* 5.7. Cf. also the discussion, below, of Seneca *Naturales Quaestiones* 1 Preface, and *Ep.* 89.5, 90.3.
[2] Cf. Gill 2006: 96–100; Inwood 2005: 31–38.

I

If we read through Seneca's *Letters* 58 and 65, which provide so much theoretical information about the Platonic–Aristotelian and Stoic modes of being (58) as well as causality (65), something odd seems to have happened with the Platonic Ideas. Here are the different types of thoughts or concepts Seneca lists:

(1) Imaginary thought-objects, i.e., the result of a *falsa cogitatio*, such as centaurs (58.15);

(2) The first Platonic mode of being, which he calls the *cogitabile* as opposed to that which can be grasped by the senses; these seem to be universals such as the designations of genera (58.16);

(3) Plato's third mode of being, *quod proprie est*, the Ideas, said to be outside the human field of vision, though not labeled as *cogitabile* here (58.18).

In *Letter* 58 Seneca is vague about the exact relation between god and the Platonic Ideas: god is the second mode of being, *per excellentiam*, that is, the highest mode of being (58.17), and is said "to dwell among the Ideas" (58.27–28). This relation is clarified in *Letter* 65: the Ideas to which god looks in order to form the universe are in his own mind (65.7: *intra se habet; mente complexus est*). Seneca alludes here to a common Middle-Platonist theme of the Ideas as the thoughts of god.[3]

What, then, is odd in Seneca's exposition? We know that the Stoics rejected the notion of the Platonic Ideas, or more precisely, their ontological status as existents in their own right. Stoics grouped the Ideas with "mere" concepts, if not with figments of our imagination.[4] In Seneca's account there is no trace of this criticism; the Ideas are distinguished both from imaginary thought-objects such as centaurs and from universals such as generic labels. This absence of criticism could be due to the fact that Seneca is reporting a friend's exposition on Plato (58.8), but the second-hand nature of the report does not prevent Stoic traits from slipping into the account, particularly in Plato's so-called sixth mode of being, which includes the Stoic incorporeals, void and time (58.22).[5]

---

[3] Alcinous 9, 163.14–15, 32–34; Dörrie and Baltes 1987–: vol. 4 (1996), Baustein 113, vol. 5 (1998), Baustein 127; Inwood 2007b: 149–67, focuses on the importance of the *Phaedo* for Seneca, rather than the *Timaeus*, and argues for the non-scholastic nature of Seneca's exposition.

[4] Called *phantasmata*: Stobaeus 1.136.21–137.6; Diogenes Laertius 7.60–61; L&S [= Long and Sedley 1987] 30. I am not concerned here with the debate as to whether imaginary objects, limits, concepts, and Ideas have the same ontological status in the Stoic theory of *genera*; on this cf. L&S 1, 27; Sedley 1985: 87–92, Brunschwig 1988: 19–127, esp. 27–42; Caston 1999: 146–213.

[5] Sedley 2005: 125–27. See also Gersh 1986: 1.180–95 and Inwood's translation and analysis of *Letters* 58 and 65 (2007b).

In *Letter* 65.7, Seneca casually states that it makes no difference whether an artisan uses a physical, external model or one that he conceives in his own mind. (In reading ancient texts, one quickly learns to be on the alert when phrases such as "it makes no difference" crop up.) In light of the Stoic tradition, however, the difference could be significant, because if the Ideas exist outside of the human mind as models, then they can have a real ontological status; *how* "real" remains to be seen. But, one may retort, Seneca here has an ordinary human artisan in mind, and to accept that such an artisan's model exists in reality does not imply an endorsement of Plato's ontology of Ideas.

Turning our attention now from external models to those which are conceived in one's mind, we can ask what happens if we posit the Platonic Ideas not as thoughts of human beings (which they derive from the interaction with their environment according to Stoic epistemology) but as the thoughts of god. Thoughts of god are not mere concepts. It is misleading and anachronistic to call these thoughts, like their human counterparts, "mind-dependent" entities. Such a label obscures the crucial difference between human and divine thoughts. Divine thoughts would not be derivative but rather would constitute the very ground of reality. In the case of the Platonic Ideas they do so as models.

Now, Seneca does not explicitly reject this theory either. Of course, he could be mentioning it as belonging to Plato, without necessarily endorsing it himself. But the notion of the "Ideas as the thoughts of god" is quite compatible with his view that there can be only one real cause – namely, god – interacting with matter, because the thoughts could be subordinated to god, as *his* thoughts. Moreover, Seneca puts the "thoughts of god" to use elsewhere.[6] Yet this still does not settle a priori the question what the "thoughts of god" would be for a Stoic. As it turns out, however, there is a possible Stoic alternative to the Platonic Ideas, namely, the *logoi spermatikoi*, as Long has pointed out.[7] These *logoi* come forth from the *logos* as divine active principle, and they are real in the sense that they embody the very structure of reality, albeit in this case not as models but as embedded in reality itself. So, for all its Platonic resonances, even a notion such as "the thoughts of god" can be put to good Stoic use, and a Stoic can exploit the structural similarity of the Platonic Ideas and *logoi spermatikoi* as thoughts

---

[6] *Ep.* 9.16–17, 79.12, *Ben.* 6.23.5, as does Epictetus *Diss.* 3.13.2–7; Reydams-Schils 2005a: 579–96; 2006: 81–94.

[7] In the context of an interpretation of Antiochus of Ascalon's views, as represented by Cicero in *Academica* 1.30 (see also *Lucullus* 30), Long 1974: 228. On the notion in Seneca, cf. Wildberger 2006: esp. 59, 206–17.

of god (namely, that both are constitutive of reality) while glossing over the crucial ontological difference between the two notions. This example sets the tone for the claim that Seneca uses Platonic themes in a Stoic manner.

The two themes examined in the remainder of this essay also occur in *Letters* 58 and 65: the detachment of the soul from the body, and its desire to turn or return to a higher reality. Seneca connects these themes as follows:

The wise man, the seeker after wisdom, is bound closely, indeed, to his body, but he is an absentee so far as his better self is concerned, and he concentrates his thoughts upon lofty things. (trans. Gummere, 65.18)[8]

A broader understanding of the dynamic of the debates between Platonists and Stoics throws light on Seneca's use of such motifs. Many Platonic-sounding notions in Seneca can be attributed, as is the case with other later Stoics such as Epictetus, to a Socratic legacy which the Stoics had already made their own in the earlier era.[9] A second strand of influence is the debate over the *Timaeus*, which helped shape earlier Stoicism. *Letters* 58 and 65, while also showing the influence of other Platonic works, can be read as a polemic about the interpretation of the *Timaeus*, as the transitions from human artisans to a divine *opifex* indicate, as well as do its echoes of the *Timaeus* (as in 58.27–28, 65.7), and even a citation (65.10), on god being good.[10]

II

Then our mind will have reason to rejoice in itself, when sent forth from this darkness in which it is dragged, it will not merely have glanced at the brightness with weak vision, but will have admitted the full light of day and will be restored to its part of heaven, when it will have regained the place that it occupied when it drew the lot of its birth. Its origin is calling it back. But it will arrive there even before it is released from this prison when it will have discarded its vices and will have leapt forth, pure and light, towards divine thoughts. (*Ep.* 79.12)[11]

---

[8] *Sapiens adsectatorque sapientiae adhaeret quidem in corpore suo, sed optima sui parte abest et cogitationes suas ad sublimia intendit.*

[9] Cf. Long 1988: 150–71, 2002; Sedley 1993: 313–31.

[10] Setaioli 1988: 126–40; Dörrie and Baltes 1987–: vol. 4 (1996), Baustein 116.1, cf. also 105.1, 106.1, 118.1.

[11] *Tunc animus noster habebit, quod gratuletur sibi, cum emissus his tenebris, in quibus volutatur, non tenui visu clara prospexerit, sed totum diem admiserit et redditus caelo suo fuerit, cum receperit locum, quem occupavit sorte nascendi. Sursum illum vocant initia sua. Erit autem illic etiam antequam hac custodia exsolvatur, cum vitia disiecerit purusque ac levis in cogitationes divinas emicuerit.* On this section, cf. Setaioli 1997.

If one did not know the author of this passage, one could easily take it for a Middle-Platonist vignette with ideas borrowed from Plato's *Phaedo*, *Phaedrus*, *Timaeus*, and *Republic*. Underlying the passage is a stark soul–body dualism. This kind of dualism is different from the dichotomy of rational and irrational soul functions, or from a distinction between different parts in the soul itself.[12]

If a marked contrast or even opposition between soul and body and a deprecation of the body constitute marks of Platonism, then Seneca is not the only one to have undergone this influence, but appears to share it with other later Stoics such as Epictetus, Marcus Aurelius, and, to a lesser extent, Musonius Rufus (VI Lutz). Epictetus and Marcus tend to reduce the body to mere "flesh," and to use the diminutive *sōmation* to express their scorn of the body.[13] Marcus even pushes his language to the brink of considering the mind incorporeal, by contrasting it with the soul-*pneuma* and the body (as in 2.2, 3.16, 4.41, 12.3).[14] What is distinctive of Seneca is his extensive borrowing of Platonic language and imagery to get the point across, but not the opposition between soul and body as such.

In spite of these resonances, what remains un-Platonic in Seneca's view of the soul? Again, features he shares with other later Stoics. First, Seneca still conceives the soul itself, as well as the *hēgemonikon*, as corporeal (*Ep.* 50.6, 106.5), and Marcus stops short of actually calling the mind incorporeal. Second, even though Seneca at times catches himself dreaming about Platonic immortality (*Ep.* 102.1–2), he adheres to the Stoic doctrine that at most posits a temporary survival of the soul after death.[15] Third, in line with original Stoicism, we are dealing with a unified psychology, not a part-based one (even though Seneca at times appears to be making concessions to Platonic psychology: see the debate mentioned above). Fourth, the "core" of a human being is fundamentally "integrated," that is, the mind or *hēgemonikon* is integrated into the soul as a whole, the soul into the body, and individual human beings into the nature and ordered universe that surrounds them. On the relation between soul and body, Seneca states, in line with orthodox Stoicism: "one's constitution (*constitutio*) consists of a ruling power in the soul which has a certain relation towards the body" (*Ep.* 121.10). Finally, as I have argued elsewhere,[16] the later Stoics have a "robust" sense of self with individual content, for which there is no

---

[12] On the latter issue, there is also debate among scholars concerning the extent of Plato's influence on Seneca, but in this context we'll put that debate aside; cf., for instance, Fillion-Lahille 1984; see also Inwood 2005: ch. 2, 23–64.

[13] Cf. Bonhöffer 1890: 33–40.   [14] Cf. Asmis 1989: 2228–52.

[15] Hoven 1971.   [16] Cf. Reydams-Schils 2005b: ch. 1, pp. 15–52.

counterpart in the Platonic view of human rationality because of its focus on the relation between reason and the Ideas.

The Platonic language and imagery in Seneca is meant to emphasize the importance of the turn inwards (*reverti* in Seneca, *De vita beata* 8.4; ἐπιστροφή in Epictetus, *Diss.* 3.16.15) and the focus on one's true self that runs like a red thread through so many later Stoic texts. In other words, Seneca uses the opposition between soul and body to underscore a genuinely Stoic reorientation in values. Even for the early Stoics, the corporeality of the soul does not prevent it from being distinguished from the body as such, and from being considered superior to the body.[17]

The Stoic reorientation of values is anchored in the doctrine of "appropriation," *oikeiōsis*, to which Seneca devotes an entire letter (*Ep.* 121). That doctrine stipulates that animals and human beings are born with a self-awareness and self-love that orient them towards doing whatever it takes to preserve themselves (L&S 57). "Appropriation" evolves in the process of maturation, as the constitution of an animal or human being changes. In human beings, as opposed to animals, this development contains the major transition into becoming rational (at age fourteen, when human beings are considered adult). In fact, there should be two transitions in a human life: first, the advent of reason, and second, the perfection of reason, of which most human beings, however, fall short.

The point that matters in this context, though, is that the advent of reason ought to change the scale of values for human beings. Whereas, at the earlier stage, self-preservation in terms of bodily health and overall physical well-being was all that mattered, henceforth virtue as the perfection of reason is the only good. The reason why most human beings fall short of this goal is that they cannot let go of the priorities of the pre-rational stage of their lives, and thus mistakenly go on ranking matters pertaining to the body and to externals among the goods. The opposition between soul and body, as Seneca and other later Stoics use it, conveys the importance of focusing on one's reason instead of the body and externals. The body can indeed drag one down and hold one back if one continues to believe that bodily self-preservation and indulgence of bodily needs are of the utmost importance and constitute goods.

In other words, Seneca and others use Plato as a kind of propaedeutic device to underscore an essentially Stoic scale of values. This is one such point for which a wider understanding of the dynamic of assimilation between Platonists and Stoics can be useful, as I indicated above. The

---

[17] Cf. Long 1982: 34–57.

Neo-Platonist Simplicius gives us a rare but very valuable glimpse in his commentary on Epictetus' *Encheiridion* of how a Platonist could do the reverse with Stoic material. By this, I mean that, like the Golden Verses attributed to Pythagoras, Epictetus' *Encheiridion* could be used in a Neo-Platonist context as a propaedeutic device preceding the regular courses of philosophy consisting first of works by Aristotle and then of Platonic dialogues.[18] Epictetus' enunciations allegedly help to detach the soul from its misguided attachments to the body and externals, and hence make pupils receptive to the further stages of Platonic teachings. In Simplicius' commentary, the *Encheiridion* is read together with Plato's *Alcibiades I* and its famous claim of the soul's superiority over the body, which the soul uses as an instrument (129e). This initial training helps to promote the so-called ethical virtues, which for the Neo-Platonists make up the lowest level in a hierarchy of virtues.[19]

Just as Simplicius' use of Epictetus remains firmly within Platonist parameters, so, I would argue, Seneca's use of Platonic discourse in his rendering of the opposition between soul and body serves a genuinely Stoic agenda. Ultimately, this dynamic should not really come as a surprise, given the pivotal importance of rationality in both the Platonic–Peripatetic and the Stoic traditions.[20]

III

[The mind] will be restored to its part of heaven, when it will have regained the place that it occupied when it drew the lot of its birth. Its origin is calling it back. But it will arrive there even before it is released from this prison when it will have discarded its vices and will have leapt forth, pure and light, towards divine thoughts. (*Ep.* 79.12)

What are the higher things, or *sublimia*, to which the mind is called once it is released from the bonds of the body? This passage can be read together with the Prefaces of the *Naturales quaestiones* (especially those of Books One and Three, which resemble the letters addressed to Lucilius), as well as the ending of Seneca's *Consolatio ad Marciam*, which in turn is an echo of Cicero's "Dream of Scipio" at the end of his *Republic*.[21] The theme of *sublimia* runs through the entire range of Seneca's writings, early as well as late. All these passages call the soul or mind to a higher realm, and are

---

[18] Cf. I. Hadot 1996: 51–60.   [19] For a good overview cf. O'Meara 2003: 40–49.
[20] Clement of Alexandria, for instance, makes an explicit connection between the Stoic turn away from the body and the Platonic one at *Strom.* 4.6.28.1–2.
[21] For this theme in Cicero, cf. also his *Tusc.* 1.18.42–20.47, and *De Legibus* 1.22.59–23.62.

therefore pivotal in an argument such as Donini's that while Seneca may have remained a Stoic with respect to ethics, in physics he was attracted to the Platonic hierarchical view of reality.[22]

Yet upon closer examination of the passage from *Letter* 79 by itself, this cannot be right. What exactly is the divine origin to which the letter refers? It talks of the mind "be[ing] restored to its part of heaven, when it will have regained the place that it occupied when it drew the lot of its birth." This too is an echo of Plato's *Timaeus*, in which the souls of humans are first assigned to heavenly bodies before being allotted a life (*Tim.* 41d8-e1; see also *Phaedrus* 246b6–247a7), heavenly bodies to which they will return once the cycle of lives is over. But this stationing refers to a higher level *within the universe*, and not to some transcendent noetic realm consisting of the Platonic Ideas.[23]

One of the peculiar features of the *Timaeus*, which made it so suitable for Stoic adaptation by both Chrysippus (Diogenes Laertius 7.88) and Posidonius (F186, 187 Kidd), is that at the end of Plato's account the cognitive functions of human souls are ordered by aligning these with the revolutions of the World Soul, embedded as it is in the motions of the heavenly bodies, that is, in the order of the universe itself (*Tim.* 90a–d). In the larger context of the *Timaeus*, Plato's readers would have known that this order of the World Soul displayed in the heavens is in turn a reflection of the higher order of Being which the Demiurge uses as his model in the shaping of the universe. But the dimension of Being is not reemphasized in the influential passage towards the end of the *Timaeus*. Like Platonism, Stoicism has its own version of the connection between human and divine reason, and Seneca does not need to cross over into the Platonic camp to make such a connection.

So, what is un-Platonic in Seneca's notion of a return to a higher realm? As stated already, humans have a connection with a divine principle that, as *pneuma*, is fundamentally embedded in the universe, and the higher realm to which we are supposed to return consists of the heavens, which are part of the universe. In our bodies we can only be a part of the whole, and this part is subject to the laws of nature that govern life and death. But our reason can "transcend" the limits of the body and adopt the perspective of the universe as a whole, by aligning itself with divine reason. This alignment can happen here and now, through a life of virtue, or it can happen after death, when souls return to their divine origin. More on this below.

[22] Cf. Donini 1979. This view has recently been endorsed again by Gauly 2004: 164–90. Donini's thesis has been criticized most thoroughly by Setaioli 1988: 505–10. Cf. also Wildberger 2006.
[23] Cf. Setaioli 2006: 354.

As with the previous theme of the opposition between soul and body, we can examine which Stoic views Seneca could use to turn our attention to higher matters. The Stoics have their own hierarchy of reality, their own version of a scale of nature. The divine principle manifests itself differently at different levels of nature: inanimate things have mere cohesion; plants have a nature (in a limited, specific sense); animals have soul; and humans have a rational soul (LS: 47). There is also a privileged connection between human and divine reason, because human reason is literally a fragment of divine reason, and this privileged connection sets human beings apart from and above the other existents.

More important for our purposes here is a notion that could be considered a corollary to the scale of nature, and to the idea that the divine principle does not manifest itself in the same manner everywhere in the universe. At the edge of the universe, that is, or in the sun, the divine principle has maintained itself in its purest form during the phase of its full cosmic deployment. The idea is attested for Chrysippus and Cleanthes.[24] It is also found in the Stoic Cornutus, a contemporary of Seneca, and one of the very few sources on Stoic physics in the imperial era:

1.2: The substance of the world is of a fiery nature, as is clear from the sun and from the other stars. From this fiery nature the aether, which is the outermost part of the world, also received its name.

2.4: [Zeus] is said to live in the heaven because that is the most dominant part (τὸ κυριώτατον μέρος) of the soul of the world. In fact, our souls, too, are fire. (trans. Hays)[25]

This kind of Stoic hierarchy is sufficient to allow for Seneca's distinction between souls that remain entangled in the wrong preoccupations and those that manage to return to their divine origin, whether in life or after death. The Stoic and Egyptian priest Chaeremon alludes to this theme (F5 Van der Horst), and Seneca's expositions about our return to the heavens and to our divine origin are very similar to passages in Manilius' *Astronomica*.[26] Given how little information we have about Stoic physics in the Roman imperial era, this convergence of approaches is striking.

---

[24] Chrysippus: Diogenes Laertius 7.139; *SVF* 2.642; Cleanthes: Diogenes Laertius 7.139; Cicero *De Natura Deorum* 2.24, 40–41, 83; Plutarch *De Facie* 928A–C.

[25] 1.2 Hays: ἡ δὲ οὐσία αὐτοῦ πυρώδης ἐστίν, ὡς δῆλον ἐκ τοῦ ἡλίου καὶ ἐκ τῶν ἄλλων ἄστρων. ὅθεν καὶ αἰθὴρ ἐκλήθη τὸ ἐξωτάτω μέρος τοῦ κόσμου ἀπὸ τοῦ αἴθεσθαι. 2.4: οἰκεῖν δὲ ἐν τῷ οὐρανῷ λέγεται, ἐπεὶ ἐκεῖ ἐστι τὸ κυριώτατον μέρος τῆς τοῦ κόσμου ψυχῆς· καὶ γὰρ αἱ ἡμέτεραι ψυχαὶ πῦρ εἰσιν.

[26] Cf., for instance, 4.866–end; this theme also made it into the rhetorical tradition as a *topos*, cf. Menander of Laodicea *Rhet.* 3.414.19–23 Spengel.

In the light of the hypothesis that the Stoic scale of nature allows for a hierarchy within the universe as a counterpart to Platonist hierarchies, let us examine more closely some passages that may appear to run counter to this claim. In his consolation to his mother Helvia, for instance, Seneca writes:

Believe me, this was the intention of the great creator of the universe, whoever he may be, whether an all-powerful god, or incorporeal reason contriving vast works, or divine spirit pervading all things from the smallest to the greatest with uniform energy, or fate and an unalterable sequence of causes clinging one to the other – this, I say, was his intention, that only the most worthless of our possessions should fall under the control of another. (trans. Basore, *Ad Helviam* 8.3)[27]

Seneca here considers the option that the maker of the universe may be "an incorporeal reason." But the Latin construction, *quisquis formator universi fuit*, reveals the gist of the argument. Whether one ends up endorsing a Stoic notion of the maker of the universe or a Platonic one, the outcome is the same: nobody can take away from us what really matters, namely, "universal Nature and our own virtue" (*natura communis et propria virtus*).

Marcus Aurelius uses an even bolder version of this strategy, with a stronger disjunction between a world governed by Providence and one consisting merely of randomly moving atoms. It strengthens the motivation to adopt a calm acceptance if that attitude would make sense even in an atomist universe: "Either there is one intelligent source, from which all things happen as to a single body – and the part ought not to grumble at what is done in the interests of the whole – or there are atoms, and nothing but a medley and a dispersion. Why then be harassed?" (9.39).[28]

Even when Seneca does allow us to peek beyond the edge of the universe, we are not looking for the Platonic Ideas (*Ot.* 5.6). Here are the questions which the notion of a "beyond" raises for him:

Our thought bursts through the ramparts of the sky, and is not content to know that which is revealed. "I search out that," it says, "which lies beyond the world – whether the vastness of space is unending, or whether this also is enclosed within its own boundaries; what is the appearance of whatever exists outside, whether it is formless and disordered, occupying the same amount of room in every direction,

---

[27] *Id actum est, mihi crede, ab illo, quisquis formator universi fuit, sive ille deus est potens omnium, sive incorporalis ratio ingentium operum artifex, sive divinus spiritus per omnia maxima ac minima aequali intentione diffusus, sive fatum et immutabilis causarum inter se cohaerentium series – id, inquam, actum est, ut in alienum arbitrium nisi vilissima quaeque non caderent.*

[28] ἤτοι ἀπὸ μιᾶς πηγῆς νοερᾶς πάντα ὡς ἑνὶ σώματι ἐπισυμβαίνει καὶ οὐ δεῖ τὸ μέρος τοῖς ὑπὲρ τοῦ ὅλου γινομένοις μέμφεσθαι· ἢ ἄτομοι καὶ οὐδὲν ἄλλο ἢ κυκεὼν καὶ σκεδασμός· τί οὖν ταράσσῃ; cf. also 3.2, 8.17, 9.40, 10.6, 7, 12.14, 24, cf. Annas 2004: 103–19.

or whether that also has been arranged into some show of elegance; whether it clings close to this world, or has withdrawn far from it and revolves there in the void; whether it is atoms by means of which everything that has been born and will be born is built up or whether the matter of things is continuous and throughout is capable of change; whether the elements are hostile to each other, or whether they are not at war, but while they differ are in harmony.[29]

In this set of questions, there is no room for a noetic realm in the Platonic sense; there are no "heads" poking beyond the rim of the heavens to catch a glimpse of intelligible reality, as in the myth of the *Phaedrus* (247c1–2: e3–4), no Ideas transcending the conditions of space and time altogether.

IV

Seneca ends his consolation to Marcia with the image of her son having gone on to better things (24.5–end). The liberation of her son's soul from his body is rendered in graphic terms: the body chains the soul, shrouds it in darkness; the soul is crushed, strangled, and contaminated by the body. In its desire to return to its origin, the soul puts up a mighty fight against the body, which drags the soul down. And before going on to the highest heavens, the soul needs an intermediary stage of purification.

Seneca has already anticipated the motif of the soul's liberation earlier in the consolation, with an explicit reference to Plato (23.1–2): the souls of people who die young are more easily released from the body, and the souls of great men yearn to be released as soon as possible, "accustomed as they are to range aloft throughout the universe, and from on high to look down in scorn upon the affairs of men." The tomb, Seneca tells Marcia, merely holds her son's body, his true self has departed.

After his death, Marcia's son finds himself in the company of divine souls, and especially in the company of great Romans, such as the Scipios and the Catos, and his own kin, Marcia's father, though "there all are akin with all." In this unknown city, the highest heaven – an allusion to the Stoic theme of the cosmopolis – his grandfather instructs him in the motions of the heavenly bodies and the secrets of nature, and shows him a new perspective on the affairs of the earth. The highest insight souls can attain consists of

---

[29] *Cogitatio nostra caeli munimenta perrumpit nec contenta est id, quod ostenditur, scire. "Illud," inquit, "scrutor, quod ultra mundum iacet, utrumne profunda vastitas sit an et hoc ipsum terminis suis cludatur; qualis sit habitus exclusis, informia et confusa sint, in omnem partem tantundem loci obtinentia, an et illa in aliquem cultum discripta sint; huic cohaereant mundo, an longe ab hoc secesserint et hic vacuo voluentur; individua sint, per quae struitur omne quod natum futurumque est, an continua eorum materia sit et per totum mutabilis; utrum contraria inter se elementa sint, an non pugnent sed per diversa conspirent.*

an understanding of the heavenly bodies and of nature as a whole. But immortality is of limited duration in this universe: periodic conflagrations lead to complete destruction before the divine active principle restarts the process of ordering the universe (26.7; 21.2).

The theme of the "universal city" occurs earlier in the consolation, and in fact constitutes one of its carefully designed literary motifs and structural devices. Seneca first compares life with a journey to a city like Syracuse, in which many wonders await the traveler, but also hardships (17.2–6). He then opens up this perspective to the human condition in general and the universe as a city "shared by gods and men – a city that embraces the universe, that is bound by fixed and eternal laws, that holds the celestial bodies as they whirl through their unwearied rounds," a city which we enter at birth. The "you" of the imaginary address here refers to both Marcia and Seneca's general audience. What is it that we get to see? First of all the stars, sun, moon, and planets – the heavenly bodies; then meteorological phenomena such as clouds and lightning; and finally the earth, with its geography and waters, as well as the products of human culture, all of this with its beauty and perils.

Two important considerations follow from this description of the universe. The "view from above" is not reserved only for life after death: through a correct use of reason human beings, including Marcia, can assume this perspective in the here and now, as Plato's *Timaeus* also stipulates. Passages discussed already above, from the *Letters* (79.12) and from the *De otio* (5), confirm this point. Nature has destined us for the contemplation of the universe, and of the heavenly bodies in particular. We can move from things that are revealed and discover the "hidden" things, such as the origin of the heavenly bodies, of the universe itself, and of human souls. "Man is part of the divine spirit," and "some sparks, as it were, of the stars fell down to earth and lingered here in a place that is not their own" (*Ot.* 5.1–5).

Moreover, the passage in the consolation to Marcia about the universal city reads like a blueprint for the *Naturales quaestiones*, and it can perhaps contribute towards a better understanding of a puzzle pertaining to the later work: even though the Prefaces direct the reader's gaze towards the highest heaven, the bulk of the work is devoted to minutiae of lesser phenomena, including meteorological ones such as snow, hail, lightning, wind, and the physics of the earth, with earthquakes and the waters. But as the consolation to Marcia indicates, the "view from above" does not limit itself to an inquiry into the heavenly bodies; it is also meant to transform our understanding of the lower levels of physical reality, as governed by the ordering of the divine active principle. In the heavens a perfection is apparent that then turns out to underlie the entire universe, including phenomena that are difficult to account for and provoke fear, such as lightning and earthquakes (cf. *Naturales quaestiones* 1 Preface 14).

The Prefaces of the *Naturales quaestiones*, especially those we now label Book One and Three (though the actual sequence of the books may originally have been different), confirm what we read elsewhere in Seneca, as in his *Letters* and the *Consolatio ad Marciam*. The Preface to Book Three summarizes the value of physics, and its connection with ethics, as follows (18):

it will be beneficial to investigate the nature of things. First, we will escape the tawdry; second, we will withdraw our mind itself (which we need to have in its highest and best condition) from the body; third, our mental sharpness, if exercised on hidden matters, will be no worse in dealing with apparent matters; nothing, however, is more readily apparent than the salutary lessons we learn in our struggle against our vice and madness, things which we condemn but do not abandon. (trans. Inwood)[30]

The right modes of inquiry into physics and ethics, or the care of the self and the study of nature, mutually reinforce each other.

The Preface of Book One focuses on theology as the highest branch of physics. The questions it asks about god, or the divine active principle, remain firmly within Stoic parameters. One such question is whether god equals only a part of the universe or the universe as a whole (*pars mundi sit an mundus*). Seneca's answer is that, while god is the mind of the universe, he is "*all* that we see and all that we do not see" (13). Here, perhaps, we are after all stumbling upon a noetic dimension of reality, one which we cannot grasp with the senses but need to pursue with thought. Seneca famously anticipates the so-called ontological proof for the existence of god, with his claim that god's magnitude is that "than which nothing greater can be *thought*" (*qua nihil maius cogitari potest*).

Throughout the *Naturales quaestiones*, Seneca contrasts the objects of sense-perception, especially sight, with the objects of thought.[31] This language echoes his claims about universals and Platonic Ideas in *Letters* 58 and 65. Yet one passage in particular points in a very different, and *bona fide* Stoic, direction. Seneca lists the physical element air among the "things

---

[30] Inwood 2005: 167; *proderit nobis inspicere rerum naturam. Primo discedemus a sordidis. Deinde animum ipsum, quo sano magnoque opus est, seducemus a corpore. Deinde in occultis exercitata subtilitas non erit in aperta deterior; nihil est autem apertius his salutaribus quae contra nequitiam nostram furoremque discuntur, quae damnamus nec ponimus.*

[31] As in 1 Preface 1, 3; 2.2.3; 6.3.2; 6.7.5; 7.30.1.

that escape the senses, but are apprehended by thought" (2.2.3), and air is obviously not the ontological equivalent of a Platonic Idea. Another clue consists of his mapping the distinction between thought and sense-perception onto the distinction between the "hidden" aspects of nature and that which lies in the open, as also attested in the summary passage from the Preface of Book Three and the passage from the *De otio* quoted above. Seneca is concerned with distinguishing the surface appearance of reality from its *depth* structure, the *pneumatic* tension that orders all of reality (or, as I have suggested above, the *logoi spermatikoi*). This inner structure of things is not immediately apparent to isolated sense-perceptions, though all thought has its starting point in sensation. If this reading holds, Seneca's move would be yet another clever appropriation of a Platonic-sounding phrase, that which can be "grasped by thought." Manilius too, in his *Astronomica*, uses a similar distinction between that which we can observe and god's hidden purpose, which we can grasp through inquiry (as in 1.247–54; 4.866–end).

The opposition between soul and body, however, and the distinction between the sensible and that which can be grasped by thought are not the only aspects of Seneca's writings that conjure up dualism. A certain tone in the *Naturales quaestiones* about the relation between the divine principle and the world also seems to point in that direction. What are we to make, for instance, of the following claim about earthquakes in Book Six?

> It will help also to keep in mind that gods cause none of these things, nor is heaven or earth overturned by the wrath of divinities. These phenomena have causes of their own; they do not rage on command but are disturbed by certain defects, just as our bodies are. At the time they seem to inflict damage they actually receive damage. All these phenomena are terrible to us since we do not know the truth, and all the more terrible since the rarity of their occurrence increases our fear. (6.3; cf. also *Prov.* 1.3)[32]

Because this passage suggests a separation between god and nature that would not be in keeping with standard Stoicism, and with its notion of a divine providence that has ordered everything well, Seneca appears to drive a wedge between divine causality and natural causes.[33] Natural phenomena, like our bodies, appear to be beset by natural defects. Seneca tries to offset the fear of earthquakes through a proper understanding of nature – but

---

[32] *Illud quoque proderit praesumere animo nihil horum deos facere nec ira numinum aut caelum converti aut terram; suas ista causas habent nec ex imperio saeviunt sed quibusdam vitiis, ut corpora nostra turbantur, et tunc, cum facere videntur, iniuriam accipiunt. Nobis autem ignorantibus verum omnia terribiliora sunt, utique quorum metum raritas auget.*

[33] A point brought out particularly well by Rosenmeyer 2000: 111–16.

is he taking the Epicurean rather than the Stoic route here? For now, let us keep in mind that he argues specifically against the supposition that earthquakes are a punishment inflicted by *the gods* – using the plural rather than the singular active divine principle. He is mounting a case against superstition (see also the extant fragments of his *De superstitione*).

It is worth recalling in this context, first, that though the Stoics endorse the thesis of a good world, it is not necessarily a comfortable one, in the ordinary, non-philosophical sense, especially in the sublunar realms of the universe. The Stoic active divine principle is both a rational agent and a natural order, consisting of clear patterns that are governed by the physical laws of *pneuma* as fire and air. Paradoxically, rational order is the order expressed by these natural patterns, and thus the very instability and mutability of the lower realms are expressions of this same order as well. Air found in the atmosphere, Seneca points out in his discussion of lightning, is by nature especially volatile and unstable in its lowest region (2.1), and it is the primary cause of earthquakes in Book Six. Musonius Rufus (F42 Lutz, also listed among the fragments of Epictetus, F8 Oldfather), Epictetus (*Diss.* 3.24.10), and Marcus Aurelius[34] all vividly underscore this point, which is also an echo of a Heraclitean legacy going back to the Early Stoa[35] that nature *is* change, allowing even for the conflagration of the entire universe.

Yet the realization that mutability constitutes the order of the lower regions of the universe is not in itself enough to get us out of the bind of the *prima facie* opposition between divine and natural causality in the passage quoted above from Book Six of the *Naturales quaestiones*. However, Book Two, on lightning and thunder, helps further elucidate Seneca's exposition on earthquakes:

lightning bolts are not sent by Jupiter but all things are so arranged that even those things which are not done by him none the less do not happen without a plan, and the plan is his. For although Jupiter does not do these things now, it is Jupiter who brought it about that they happen. He is not present at every event for every person but he gives the signal, the force, the cause to all. (2.46, trans. Corcoran)[36]

As an earlier passage in Book Two confirms, contrary to the Etruscan view of divination, Seneca and the Stoics do not believe that the highest god intervenes directly in the course of single events, be it lightning or other

---

[34] As in 2.12, 17, 4.14, 43, 5.23, 33, 6.15, 7.18, 23, 25.   [35] Cf. Long 1975–76: 132–53.

[36] *Fulmina non mitti a Iove, sed sic omnia esse disposita ut etiam quae ab illo non fiunt tamen sine ratione non fiant, quae illius est. Nam etiamsi Iupiter illa nunc non facit, Iupiter fecit ut fierent. Singulis non adest ad omne, sed signum et vim et causam omnibus dedit.*

portents. "None the less," Seneca explains, "such things are carried out by divine agency, even if the wings of the birds are not actually guided by god, nor the viscera of cattle shaped under the very axe. The roll of fate is unfolded on a different principle" (2.32, trans. Corcoran).[37]

In other words – and this is crucial – even though natural phenomena like lightning and earthquakes have their own causes, this causality is anchored in and goes back to the divine active principle as *the* cause that orders all of reality. For individual occurrences to have their own causes is not to stand in opposition to divine causality. In fate, which the Stoics describe as the unbroken series of causes (L&S 62), all causes are linked according to the structure that originates from this one cause. At the very start of a new physical cycle of the universe's ordering (διακόσμησις), all of reality is already prefigured, as it had been in previous cycles.

Such a position does not make the Stoic god analogous to later notions of the divine as a "clock-maker" who sets the clock in motion, but then withdraws. The active divine principle, in its different aspects and manifestations, underlies all of physical reality and is embedded within the universe. Hence Seneca is not contradicting himself in the *Naturales quaestiones* when he ascribes all these names to one and the same divine principle (2.45): he is "the controller and guardian of the universe, the mind and spirit of the world, the lord and artificer of this creation," fate, providence, nature, universe (cf. also *Ben.* 4.7.1). He is the Universe because "he himself is all that you see, infused throughout all his parts, sustaining both himself and his own."

Just as there is no separation between divine and natural causality in Seneca's *Naturales quaestiones*, there is no dualism of god and matter either, contrary to the claims of Pohlenz and Donini.[38] By describing the active divine principle as the one cause, and matter as entirely amenable to this cause's structuring, *Letter 65* (65.2, 23–24) is in keeping with Early Stoicism. Yet there are passages in which Seneca refers to the recalcitrance of matter, a view that aligns itself rather with a Platonist strand in the tradition of interpretations of the *Timaeus*.[39] Or, as he renders the Platonist view himself in *Letter 58*:

Let us look up to the ideal outlines of all things, which flit about on high, *and the god who moves among them* and plans how he may defend from death that which he could not make imperishable because its matter forbade, and so by reason

---

[37] *Ista nihilominus divina ope geruntur, si non a deo pennae avium reguntur nec pecudum viscera sub ipsa securi formantur. Alia ratione fatorum series explicatur.*
[38] Pohlenz 1948: I, 320–24, Donini 1979: 158–59.   [39] Setaioli 2006: 343–46.

may overcome the defects of the body. For all things abide, not because they are everlasting, but because they are protected by the care of him who governs all things; but that which was imperishable would need no guardian. The [divine] maker keeps them safe, overcoming the weakness of matter by his own might. (trans. Gummere, modified, *Ep.* 58.27–28)[40]

This is indeed a strongly dualist interpretation of the *Timaeus*: matter counteracts the divine, and the Demiurge needs to conquer the fragility of matter. But there is, in principle, a subtle but crucial difference between this Platonist view and Stoicism. The Platonic universe is the best practically possible world, and as such it is not necessarily good but results from a choice among a set of possibilities whose members may or may not be good, or good to a greater or lesser extent. By contrast, the Stoic universe is not merely the best practicably possible world, it is also maximally good. The passage from the Preface of Book One in which Seneca *raises the question* whether god is hampered by matter or is able to accomplish whatever he wants (Book One, Preface 16) is not a problem, precisely because he manages, as in the passage from the *De otio* quoted above, to include views from other schools and views other than his own. But another passage from *De providentia* is more difficult to account for: god cannot preserve human beings from certain misfortunes (6.6) because, like craftsmen, he "cannot change matter" (5.9). "Certain qualities cannot be separated from certain others; they cling together, are indivisible" (5.9). In the passage discussed above from Book Six of the *Naturales quaestiones*, Seneca mentions defects in natural phenomena and in the human bodily constitution.

For the answer to this conundrum we need to go back to a position that is attested for Chrysippus, in a passage that contains an explicit echo and response to the *Timaeus*, and which, I submit, deserves more attention in current debates.[41] The fragment in question deals with the fragility of the human head:

Similarly, when *nature* fashioned the body of humans, a rather refined reason and the purpose itself of the task demanded that the head be fashioned with the thinnest and tiniest bones. But this higher purpose had as another *consequence* a certain outside disadvantage, namely that the head became ill-protected and fragile

---

[40] *Miremur in sublimi volitantes rerum omnium formas deumque inter illa versantem et hoc providentem quemadmodum quae immortalia facere non potuit, quia materia prohibebat, defendat a morte ac ratione vitium corporis vincat. Manent enim cuncta, non quia aeterna sunt, sed quia defenduntur cura regentis: inmortalia tutore non egerent. Haec conservat artifex fragilitatem materiae vi sua vincens.*

[41] Cf. Reydams-Schils 1999: 75–76. See also Wildberger 2006: 277, n. 1335. For a different interpretation of this passage, cf. Sedley 2007: 235.

to [even] minor blows and injuries. (*SVF* 2.1170 = Aulus Gellius *Noctes Atticae*, 7.1.7)[42]

Whereas the Demiurge in the *Timaeus* faces a dilemma, because of a trade-off between longevity and mental acuity (75b–c), Chrysippus' Nature has made up its mind that the head needs to be constructed in a certain way that *entails* a degree of fragility. Aulus Gellius indicates that such features result from the structures of nature, they occur κατὰ παρακολούθησιν. The divine ordering is physical, and in nature, as Seneca admits too, certain phenomena go together with others, as an expression of that very order, not as counteracting it. A second line of reasoning which the Stoics pursue to explain the condition of human beings is that misfortunes are only apparent evils; the sole human good and happiness consists of virtue and the correct use of reason.

Epictetus, in fact, develops a line of reasoning very similar to that of Seneca's *De providentia*. Zeus is depicted as addressing Epictetus directly (1.1.10–13): it was not possible to make a human being's body and external possessions free from harm – otherwise god would have made it so – but the most important faculty, which is in fact a part of divine reason, namely, our rational ability to make correct use of our impressions, has been made such that it cannot be thwarted. Similarly, Seneca makes god respond that he has "armed human minds to withstand it all" (*Prov.* 6.6; see also *Ad Helviam* 8.3, quoted above). Given that god is the order expressed in nature, it can be said that "although the great creator and ruler of the universe himself wrote the decrees of fate, nevertheless he follows them" (*Prov.* 5.8). And this point of view is fundamentally different from a Platonist perspective that would pit god against matter, or the divine ordering against nature.

How nuanced and modest Seneca's claims about matter and its potential recalcitrance to divine ordering activity are becomes all the more apparent if we draw in the Stoic Hierocles (2nd. c. CE). Stobaeus[43] attributes to Hierocles the standard view that the gods cannot be held responsible for evil. But among the explanations of evil, Hierocles as rendered by Stobaeus, unlike other Stoics, lists matter and the distinction between a heavenly realm that is pure (τῆς εἰλικρινεστάτης οὐσίας) and orderly, and a "muddy" earthly one.[44] The argument breaks off at this point, however,

---

[42] *Sicut, cum corpora hominum natura fingeret, ratio subtilior et utilitas ipsa operis postulavit, ut tenuissimis minutisque ossiculis caput compingeret. Sed hanc utilitatem rei maiorem alia quaedam incommoditas extrinsecus consecuta est, ut fieret caput tenuiter munitum et ictibus offensionibusque parvis fragile.*

[43] *Ecl.* 2, 9, 7, 181.8ff. Wachsmuth, under the heading of how one should comport oneself towards the gods.

[44] μετά γε μὴν τὴν κακίαν δευτέρα τῶν τοιούτων πρόφασις ἡ ὕλη. τὰ μὲν γὰρ μετέωρα καὶ ὑπὲρ ἡμᾶς, ὡς ἂν ἐκ τῆς εἰλικρινεστάτης οὐσίας γεγονότα, δι' ὁμαλοῦ πορεύεται, πάντων ἐν αὐτοῖς

and its dualism has perhaps been wrongly attributed to Hierocles, by either Stobaeus himself or his source. But the passage can still serve as a good contrast case to Seneca's view, serving to underscore the latter's predominantly Stoic tenor. Even though other Stoics, including Seneca, agree that the divine principle is preserved in its purest form either at the edge of the universe or in the sun, they do not endorse the view that a lower level is the cause of evil and deficiency merely because of its lower ranking; rather, the whole of reality is the outcome of a good, divine ordering activity.

v

Seneca manages to put to good Stoic use such notions as the thoughts of god, the opposition between soul and body, or the return to a higher realm. If this assessment holds true, then the outcome of his appropriation of Platonic material is not fundamentally different from that of his use of passages taken from Epicurus. Yet, in hermeneutical terms, the manner in which he uses these two authors is still different. With the quotations from Epicurus, he is borrowing from the enemy camp; in the case of Plato, he is exploring genuine affinities, yet giving them a Stoic turn of thought. There can be no doubt that the Platonic coloring in Seneca is significant. When we compare Seneca with Epictetus, we notice that Plato is more important for Seneca than Socrates, whereas the reverse is true in Epictetus' case, as revealed in the citations and echoes.[45] This importance of Plato is attested neither in Musonius Rufus' extant work (though many of his remaining accounts seem to be a response to Plato's *Republic*), nor in that of Marcus Aurelius. Seneca himself often enough attests his independence of spirit (as, for example, in *Ep.* 33, 64, 79.6–7); but this implies that he was also capable of putting Platonic material to his own use.

   After all, a Stoic also has a right to these questions, as well as the right to look for answers within his own school:

Do you forbid me to contemplate the universe? Do you compel me to withdraw from the whole and restrict me to a part? May I not ask what are the beginnings of all things, who molded the universe, who took the confused and conglomerate mass of sluggish matter, and separated it into its parts? May I not inquire who is the master-builder of this universe, how the mighty bulk was brought under the control of law and order, who gathered together the scattered atoms, who separated

---

κατὰ τοὺς τῆς φύσεως λόγους περαινομένων· τὰ δ' ἐπίγεια καθάπερ ὑποστάθμην καὶ ἰλὺν ἔχοντα τῶν ὅλων τὴν οὐσίαν***

[45] Cf. Tieleman 2007: 133–48.

the disordered elements and assigned an outward form to elements that lay in one vast shapelessness? Or whence came all the expanse of light? And whether it is fire, or something even brighter than fire? Am I not to ask these questions? Must I be ignorant of the heights whence I have descended? Whether I am to see the world but once, or to be born many times? What is my destination afterwards? What abode awaits my soul on its release from the laws of slavery among men? Do you forbid me to have a share in heaven? In other words, do you bid me live with my head bowed down? (trans. Gummere, *Ep.* 65.19–21)[46]

[46] *Interdicis mihi inspectione rerum naturae, a toto abductum redigis in partem? Ego non quaeram, quae sint initia universorum? Quis rerum formator? Quis omnia in uno mersa et materia inerti convoluta discreverit? Non quaeram, quis sit istius artifex mundi? Qua ratione tanta magnitudo in legem et ordinem venerit? Quis sparsa collegerit, confusa distinxerit, in una deformitate iacentibus faciem diviserit? Unde lux tanta fundatur? Ignis sit, an aliquid igne lucidius? Ego ista non quaeram? Ego nesciam, unde descenderim? Semel haec mihi videnda sint, an saepe nascendum? Quo hinc iturus sim? Quae sedes exspectet animam solutam legibus servitutis humanae? Vetas me caelo interesse, id est iubes me vivere capite demisso?*

CHAPTER 12

The status of the individual in Plotinus

Kenneth Wolfe

In honor of A. A. Long, optimus magister

"Know thyself," one of the two famous inscriptions at the Temple of
Apollo at Delphi, seems to ask what the place of human beings is in the
cosmos. One interpretation of the oracle would relate it to that other saying,
"Nothing too much," and would go, "Know that you, being human, are
mortal. Know your limits. Do not strive after divine wisdom or immortality.
Do not tempt the gods." Another possible interpretation is: "Know that
you, being human, have a divine element – reason – within you. Strive to
perfect that element and become as divine as is possible for a human being."
The former interpretation may be the more traditionally religious response
and is perhaps one of the lessons of *Oedipus Rex*. The philosophers, whether
Plato, Aristotle, or the Stoics, favor the latter interpretation. Plotinus is
without doubt in this group, but what is quite striking about him is that
he takes "know thyself" to refer not only to knowing ourselves as human
beings in general but even as human individuals, and that he believes that
ultimately we are divine. So when I seek to know myself I am to ask not
only what it is to be human but also what it is for me to be the particular
human being that I am. Moreover, I am to seek not merely to be the perfect
human being, but to be the perfect me, and in fact, the divine me.[1]

For Plotinus, there is a strict correspondence between ontology and
psychology: for every level of being, there is a level of thinking or consciousness that corresponds to it. There is the basic division between
the intelligible world of "being" and the physical world of "becoming."
Within the intelligible world, moreover, there are three levels of being, the
three "hypostases" – the One, the Intellect, and the Soul. On the side of

---

[1] That Plotinus believed in Forms of individuals has now become the consensus view. For more
discussion of this issue, see Armstrong (1977), Blumenthal (1966, 1971), Kalligas (1997), Mamo
(1969), and Rist (1963, 1970). For more on the 'self' in Plotinus see O'Daly (1973), Rappe (1996),
and Remes (2007).

psychology, the lowest grade of thinking is sense-perception and the discursive reasoning that is based upon it. Above this is discursive thinking about the forms. Higher yet is the intellectual intuition of the forms. At the highest level the self transcends thinking altogether and is united with the One. Even here there is some kind of awareness, but one that transcends the distinction between subject and object (VI.9.11.4–16). Plotinus holds that every level of consciousness below the highest is individuated.

In the first place, we encounter and recognize distinct individuals on the basis of their bodies, and Plotinus agrees that the human self is in the first and lowest sense a compound of body and soul (I.1.5.8). The first sense of "Socrates" is the physical individual whose bust we can see in the Louvre. This is what most of us mean when we talk about certain individuals, since most of us, unlike Plotinus, do regard the body as an essential component of a human being.

On the other hand, we can think of the body as something that we have rather than as a part of who we really are. In this case, we are identifying ourselves with our "inner" psychic life, with our complex of thoughts and emotions. Thus I can think of myself as having a different body or even not having a body at all, but I cannot conceive of myself as continuing to exist while lacking a mind or being devoid of my basic memories and personality. Thus by "Socrates," we may be referring not to the body–soul compound but rather to a certain personality or soul.

Plotinus holds that individual souls are not only immortal but also transmigrate from one body to another (I.1.12.4, II.9.6.13, IV.3.9.5–6). What kind of body they enter into is determined by the kind of life lived by the individual in the previous incarnation.

Plotinus even believes that a soul that was once incarnate in a human being can later become incarnate in a lower animal. So if Alcibiades leads a life of lechery, his soul might enter into the body of a rabbit. Although souls thus carry with them the accumulated "karma" of their previous lives, they lose their memories. In what sense, then, are individual souls the "same" individual souls?

They can only be the same in the sense of belonging to a single causal, historical chain. This is analogous to the continuing identity of a hydrogen atom. While all hydrogen atoms are just like each other (ignoring isotopes), we can still ascribe a continuing identity to a given individual hydrogen atom if we can trace its entire history. Likewise, souls become distinct from each other only in terms of having unique histories. Souls, although being individual, all have the same essence.

What, then, has happened to the individuality of Socrates, given that his soul is not essentially different from any other soul? One possible answer is that an individual human being is a unique, accidental combination of matter and form (soul), both of which are particular existents without particular essences. The stuff of which Socrates is made is particular stuff, but it is just like the stuff of which any other human being is made. His soul, while particular, is also just like any other soul, or at least any other human soul. Plotinus rejects this possibility. It amounts to saying that all our individual differences are accidental. But to what are those accidents due? One possible answer is that matter is the principle of individuation.

Plotinus, however, is convinced that some of the differences between individuals are essential. Thus form itself becomes an individuating principle. Hence Plotinus posits the existence of forms of individuals, to which he devotes the entire, small essay, *Ennead* V.7. He argues for forms of individuals for two reasons. First, he quite explicitly believes in the existence of prime matter (III.6.9.18–19). Since matter as such has no characteristics at all, it can impart none. Whatever characteristics exist at all in the sensible world must in the ultimate analysis be due to formal principles, namely to the materialized structuring principles (*enuloi logoi*). While the proximate matter of Socrates may explain some of his characteristics, even that matter has form, and the differences of the proximate matter must ultimately be due to the differences of form. Thus, that the physical Socrates, a compound of matter and form, is a snub-nosed, pale human being is due to some conjunction of the materialized form of human being with the materialized form of the snub and the materialized form of pallor. The only question is whether or not this conjunction exists in the intelligible world as well as in the physical world. This amounts to asking whether or not the differential characteristics of human beings here in the sensible world are also differentiae of the form of human being in the intelligible world.

In V.9.12, Plotinus seems to maintain that this is so, at least to a certain extent. For example, being pale might essentially distinguish Socrates and Sally from other human beings such as Alcibiades, but even so, Socrates' pallor might differ somewhat from Sally's. Plotinus is willing to grant a certain amount of influence to such things as the matter and the environment, so that they could, for example, account for why Socrates has this kind of pallor and Sally that kind.

In this doctrine, Plotinus seems to have anticipated certain results of modern genetics. While all human beings have nearly the same genetic code, they do differ genetically in certain respects. For example, certain genes may make Socrates and Sally pale and Alcibiades swarthy, but even if we suppose that the very same genes produce Socrates' pallor and Sally's, Sally's pallor may still differ from Socrates' because, say, she ate more vegetables when she was growing up.

There is no reason to suppose that Plotinus wanted to include only corporeal differences such as pallor among those that essentially distinguish human beings. Such differences may include psychic differences as well. For example, Socrates and Alcibiades may essentially differ from each other in that Socrates is a lover of wisdom and of young men, whereas Alcibiades loves honor and women. These differences might, as we say, be "genetic," or be so to some extent. No doubt it may be very difficult for us in many cases to determine just what the role of genetics or nature is, and what the role of matter and environment is, but Plotinus is clearly grappling with the "nature/nurture" question, and believes that human beings differ from each by nature. He believes that Socrates *qua* Socrates has a different nature from Alcibiades *qua* Alcibiades. While both are human beings and in this respect have the same nature (human nature), Socrates is a Socratic human being, and Alcibiades is an "Alcibiadic" human being: Socrates instantiates the absolute Socrates or "Socraticity," and Alcibiades instantiates the absolute Alcibiades or "Alcibiadicity."

Since "Socraticity" or the intelligible form of Socrates exists in the intelligible world, it must, like all other forms, be definable and knowable by the Intellect. While the form of Alcibiades and the form of Socrates may differ by "countless" differences, these differences are in principle finite and knowable, even if they are not countable or knowable by us. While the individual forms are like other forms in being definable and knowable, they differ in being neither genera nor species, but individuals: they can no longer be divided into subordinate species or individuals. They just are unique, intelligible individuals, and knowing the essence of a particular sensible human being consists in knowing his or her intelligible form: knowing the essence of the physical Socrates consists in knowing the unique kind of human being that he is. Socrates is, we can rightly say, "one of a kind." What, though, if Socrates has an identical twin named Alexander? Identical twins are identical in form. Whatever differences there may be between them are due solely to the conditions of corporeal existence (matter, space, time, environment, etc.), so it would seem that both Socrates and Alexander must participate in the same intelligible form, which could be called either "Socraticity" or "Alexandricity." But in that case "Socraticity" would be the form not of one sensible individual, but rather of more than one sensible individual. So "Socraticity" becomes a universal like every other form; i.e., something that can be predicated of many things: both Socrates and Alexander can have "Socraticity." This does not mean, of course, that Socrates is Alexander, but simply that Socrates and Alexander are indistinguishable in form. They differ, and are thus distinguishable, only accidentally.

Plotinus, however, seriously doubts whether there actually are identical twins. He seems to believe that there always are formal differences between two human beings who appear indistinguishable, but our powers of perception are too weak to allow us to perceive these differences (V.7.3.12–13). This hypothesis may work for human beings, but what about something like a litter of kittens or different fires? Even in a litter, there may be formal distinctions which we cannot grasp. Insofar as there are formal distinctions, these distinctions have their source in the intelligible world (V.7.3.5–6). In the case of fire, however, Plotinus takes one instance of fire to be just like another (VI.5.8.21–42). Since any two fires are exactly alike in form, there is no basis upon which to divide the intelligible form of fire. Fire is a lowest kind. So we see that Plotinus is not committed to positing individual forms for everything that exists in the physical world. And he need not take such a radical step. To be in favor of "forms of individuals" all he needs to do is to posit individual forms for some things that exist in the physical world. He seems ready to posit individual forms wherever there seem to be objective differences that indicate a natural distinction. He seems particularly interested in doing so for human beings. Why so?

We now come to his second reason for introducing forms of individuals. While the first argument relied upon formal distinctions in being, that is, upon objective distinctions, this argument relies upon subjective distinctions. Since each human being can return to the intelligible world through a philosophical ascent, there must be something in the intelligible world that we are when we are there (V.7.1.1–3). For one thing, Plotinus maintains that a part of our soul has not descended: it remains always in the intelligible world. Plotinus nowhere to my knowledge addresses the possibility that more than one descended soul can be attached at the same time to the same undescended part of soul. Though he does maintain that all souls have the same essence, yet they are also still distinct in terms of their experiences and memories.

He seems to believe that for every descended soul, there is an undescended soul which the descended soul can rise to through the cultivation of the virtues and philosophy. Since each of us has his or her own soul and psychic life, there must be at least as many undescended souls at any given time as there are descended human souls. So there must be at least souls, if not forms, of individuals in the intelligible world, if we are to have a way back to the intelligible world.

Why, however, need there be an undescended soul for each of us? Why is it not possible that there is a universal human super-consciousness that all of us are capable of tapping into but few of us actually do? Our thinking prior to achieving this super-consciousness would certainly be individuated, as is clear from our ordinary experience. The rise to it must also be individuated, since not everybody actually achieves it. But neither of these facts implies that the consciousness we have once we are there is individuated.

In connection with this line of reasoning, we should recall that Plotinus maintains that when we attain unification with the One, all individuality is obliterated (VI.9.9.20–22, VI.9.11.4–16). If this is true at the level of the One, why could it not also be true at the level of the Intellect or the Soul hypostasis? Why could our "return" to the Soul not be an identification with the undescended human super-consciousness and our return to the Intellect not be an identification with the form of human being?

Plotinus is rather unclear about where in the intelligible world the soul of the individual resides. The most straightforward answer would be that it is part of the hypostasis Soul. But the upper reaches of the Soul hypostasis sometimes seem to blur with the Intellect. In the late treatise V.3, however, where Plotinus is concerned to mark the distinction between Intellect and Soul rather clearly, he says that soul is always engaged in discursive reason and is always ours and in fact what we are primarily, but Intellect knows all things at once and is not always ours, though we can come to be in accord with it and sometimes to have it (V.3.3.28). If all souls are engaged in discursive reason, then not only descended souls, but also the hypostasis Soul and whatever souls belong to it, always engage in discursive, not intuitive, reason. So it seems most plausible to take the undescended part of our souls to be that part which is always engaged in discursive reasoning, even if we (*qua* descended consciousness) are not always aware of it. What would distinguish then the undescended soul from the descended soul is that the former is engaged only in discursive reason, and is engaged in discursive reason about the forms, whereas the latter, owing to its conjunction with the body, is engaged not only in discursive reason about much lower and baser things, but even in sense-perception.

But even if we grant that there are individual souls in the intelligible world, we still do not have forms of individuals. Plotinus, however, takes this further step from individual souls to individual forms on the same grounds whereby he took the step from individual descended souls to individual undescended souls: we are able to ascend. In this case, we can ascend from discursive reasoning to intuitive knowing. We can in some way climb above the Soul and come to exist consciously on the level of Intellect: we can somehow come to be Intellect or at least an intellect. Just as formerly Plotinus did not address the possibility that several descended souls might be attached simultaneously to the same undescended soul, so too here he does not address the possibility that several undescended souls could be attached simultaneously to the same intellect. He believes that for every intelligent being there is an intellect that the intelligent being can ascend to. This is the individual's intellect. But he also holds that the Intellect is identical with the forms and that every form is an intellect, and every intellect a form (V.9.8.1–4). Thus the individual's intellect is also an individual form. Socrates' intellect is Socrates' form; it is Socraticity. And its intellection, like Intellect's intellection, must be a self-knowing. In this case, since Socrates' intellect is the intelligible Socrates, i.e., Socrates' essence, its self-knowing just is Socrates' knowing himself, that is, knowing his own essence, or what it is to be Socrates. This intellection would be expressed by something like "I, Socrates, am a human being who is pale and snub-nosed, who loves wisdom and young men, etc.," where Socrates would be aware of all his defining characteristics, whatever these may be.

This thesis that there are forms of individuals may seem to conflict with Plotinus' doctrine of the transmigration of souls. For if the soul that was at one time Socrates becomes the soul of Pythagoras, then it might seem that there is no eternal soul of Socrates nor an eternal soul of Pythagoras in the hypostasis Soul, and so that which had mediated the inference from the sensible individual to the intelligible form of the individual (the undescended soul of Socrates) disappears. Plotinus answers this objection by stating that every soul contains all the *logoi*, that is, all the rational principles, but only produces a certain set of them in any given matter (V.7.1.6–10). He thus claims that every soul is capable of participating in more than one, perhaps in every, intelligible form.

In this way, what was in one incarnation the soul of Pythagoras in virtue of participating in the intelligible form of Pythagoras becomes in a later incarnation the soul of Socrates in virtue of participating in the intelligible form of Socrates. This ingenious solution allows there still to be an undescended soul for every descended soul at any given time. The very same soul cannot be incarnate in Pythagoras and Socrates at the same time, but it can be incarnate in Socrates at one time and in Pythagoras at another time. This soul always has both a descended part and an undescended part at any given time. In this way, the number of undescended souls may be less than the number of intelligible forms. There may be at any given time certain intelligible forms which are not actively participated in by souls and made thereby incarnate in sensible particulars. Though every soul contains all the *logoi* of the forms in Intellect, each soul actualizes only some of those rational principles, and it need not be the case that at any given time every rational principle is activated by some soul. For example, Socrates is no longer alive today, but the form of "Socraticity" is eternal. Though the *logos* of Socrates is implicitly contained in every soul, no soul is currently actualizing that rational principle.

Given his belief that the universe has no beginning in time, might Plotinus be compelled to grant that the forms of individuals are infinite in number and that thus the intelligible forms are infinite in number? For if time is infinite, and individuals are always being born and passing away, then the number of sensible individuals will also be infinite. Plotinus certainly wants to avoid letting the intelligible forms be infinite in number, for if they were infinite in number, then it would be difficult to understand how they all could be knowable in principle, even by a divine intellect. If the forms are unknowable, then Intellect would be unintelligent. So, to avoid the distressing consequences of positing an infinite number of forms of individuals, Plotinus adopts the doctrine of a periodic conflagration and infinite return of the sensible universe (V.7.1.24–25, V.7.3.17). While the number of physical individuals in all of time is necessarily infinite, the number of those who ever exist within any given finite time is finite. So no matter how long any given period of the universe lasts, the number of individuals who come to be and pass away in that period is finite. If only these same individuals, or individuals identical with them in form, come to be in all later cycles of the universe, just as only they have existed in previous cycles of the universe, then the total number of their archetypes will be finite. Therefore, the number of intelligible forms of individuals will be finite.

It is not clear whether Plotinus believes that exactly the same individuals and events will recur or only the same kinds of individuals and events. Will Socrates drink the hemlock again? If exactly the same things recur, how is one to say that cycle B is "later" than cycle A? If the time in cycle B is not the same as the time in cycle A, can we not then distinguish Socrates B from Socrates A precisely by reference to which cycle each exists in? If this is so, then the supposed "form of the individual" becomes a universal like any other form, i.e., capable of being participated in by more than one sensible individual. And if "Socraticity" can serve for Socrates A and Socrates B in two different cycles of the universe, why can't it serve for two or more Socrateses in a single cycle of the universe?

Plotinus' doctrine of forms of individuals is a very good focal point for gaining insight into the nature of Plotinus' way of thinking, for in this doctrine he creatively grafts the Aristotelian doctrine of intellect and the Stoic and Pythagorean doctrine of the periodic return of the physical world onto his Platonic ontological foundation. Neither the ontological approach nor the psychological approach provides a completely satisfying argument for the existence of forms of individuals. Amidst all this philosophical gymnastics, however, breathes the mystical spirit that is so characteristic of Plotinus. If for no other reason, Plotinus believes in forms of individuals because he believes that he himself has as an individual communed with the divine Intellect. As he says,

It has happened often. Roused into myself from my body – outside everything else and inside myself – my gaze has met a beauty wondrous and great. At such moments I have been certain that mine was the better part, mine the best of lives lived to the fullest, mine identity with the divine. Fixed there firmly, poised above everything in the intellectual that is less than the highest, utter actuality was mine. (IV.8.1.1–7, tr. O'Brien)

A. A. Long: publications 1963–2009

1. BOOKS AUTHORED OR CO-AUTHORED

(1968) *Language and Thought in Sophocles. A Study of Abstract Nouns and Poetic Technique.* London.

(1974/86) *Hellenistic Philosophy. Stoics, Epicureans, Sceptics.* London/New York; 2nd edn. Berkeley and Los Angeles.

(1977) *La filosofía helenística.* Madrid.

(1987a) *The Hellenistic Philosophers*, vol. 1: *The Principal Sources in Translation with Philosophical Commentary*, with D. N. Sedley. Cambridge.

(1987b) *The Hellenistic Philosophers*, vol. 2: *Greek and Latin Texts with Notes and Bibliography*, with D. N. Sedley. Cambridge.

(1987c) *ΕΛΛΗΝΙΣΤΙΚΗ ΦΙΛΟΣΟΦΙΑ.* Athens.

(1989/1991) *La filosofia ellenistica.* Bologna; 2nd edn. Bologna.

(1992) *Hierocles: Elementa Moralia*, with G. Bastianini, in *Corpus dei papiri filosofici greci e latini*, vol. 1. Florence: 268–441.

(1996) *Stoic Studies.* Cambridge. Repr. Berkeley and Los Angeles 2001.

(1998) *Hellenisztikus Filozófia.* Budapest.

(2000) *Die hellenistischen Philosophen. Texte und Kommentare.* Stuttgart and Weimar.

(2001a) *Hellenistic Philosophy. Stoic Philosophy, Epicurean Philosophy, Sceptical Philosophy*, in Korean. Seoul.

(2001b) *Les philosophes hellénistiques*, vol. 1; *Pyrrhon; L'Epicurisme*, vol. 2; *Les stoiciens; Les Académiciens; La renaissance du pyrrhonisme.* Paris.

(2002) *Epictetus. A Stoic and Socratic Guide to Life.* Oxford. Repr. 2004.

(2003a) *Hellenistic Philosophy. Stoics, Epicureans, Sceptics*, with new preface, in Japanese. Kyoto.

(2003b) *Hellénistickå Filosofie*, with new preface. Prague.

(2006) *From Epicurus to Epictetus. Studies in Hellenistic and Roman Philosophy.* Oxford.

2. BOOKS EDITED OR CO-EDITED

(1971) *Problems in Stoicism.* London. Repr. 1996.

(1985) *Theophrastus of Eresus. On His Life and Work.* Rutgers University Studies in Classical Humanities vol. 2, with P. M. Huby and W. W. Fortenbaugh. New Brunswick and Oxford.

(1988) *The Question of Eclecticism. Studies in Later Greek Philosophy*, with J. Dillon. Berkeley, Los Angeles and London. Repr. 1996.

(1993) *Images and Ideologies: Self-Definition in the Hellenistic World*, with A. W. Bulloch, E. S. Gruen, and A. Stewart. Berkeley and Los Angeles.

(1999) *The Cambridge Companion to Early Greek Philosophy.* Cambridge.

(2001) *Handbuch frühe griechische Philosophie.* Stuttgart and Weimar.

(2005) *ΟΙ ΠΡΟΣΩΚΡΑΤΙΚΟΙ ΦΙΛΟΣΟΦΟΙ.* Athens.

(2008) *Primordios da Filosofia Grega.* Sao Paulo.

3. ARTICLES IN COLLECTIONS AND CONFERENCE PROCEEDINGS

(1971a) "Language and thought in Stoicism," in Long, ed., *Problems in Stoicism.* London: 75–113.

(1971b) "Freedom and determinism in the Stoic theory of human action," in Long, ed., *Problems in Stoicism.* London: 173–99.

(1973a) Articles on Sophocles and Plutarch, in J. Buchanan-Brown, ed., *Cassell's Encyclopaedia of World Literature*, vol. 3, 2nd ed. London: 337–8, 542–43.

(1973b) "Psychological ideas in Antiquity," in P. Wiener, ed., *Dictionary of the History of Ideas*, vol. 4. New York: 1–9.

(1973c) "Ethics of Stoicism," in P. Wiener, ed., *Dictionary of the History of Ideas*, vol. 4. New York: 319–22.

(1974) "Empedocles' cosmic cycle in the 'Sixties," in A. P. D. Mourelatos, ed., *The PreSocratics.* New York. Repr. in (1993) 2nd. ed. Princeton: 397–425.

(1975) "The principles of Parmenides' cosmogony," in R. E. Allen and D. J. Furley, eds., *Studies in Presocratic Philosophy*, vol. 2. London: 82–101. Revised reprint of article in *Phronesis* 8 (1963): 90–107.

(1977) "The early Stoic concept of moral choice," in F. Bossier et al., eds., *Symbolae* vol. **1**. *Images of Man in Ancient and Medieval Thought.* Leuven: 79–92.

(1978a) "Dialectic and the Stoic sage," in J. M. Rist, ed., *The Stoics.* Berkeley, Los Angeles and London: 101–24.

(1978b) "The Stoic doctrine of truth and the true," in J. Brunschwig, ed., *Les Stoiciens et leur logique.* Paris: 297–315. Repr. and revised in (2006) J. Brunschwig, ed., *Les Stoiciens et leur logique* 2nd ed. Paris: 61–78.

(1981) "Aristotle and the history of Greek skepticism," in D. J. O'Meara, ed., *Studies in Aristotle.* Washington D.C.: 79–106. Repr. in (1995) T. Irwin, ed., *Classical Philosophy. Collected Papers*, vol. 7. New York: 407–34.

(1982a) "Astrology: arguments pro and contra," in J. Barnes et al., eds., *Science and Speculation. Studies in Hellenistic Theory and Practice.* Cambridge and Paris: 165–92.

(1982b) "Epictetus and Marcus Aurelius," in T. J. Luce, ed., *Ancient Writers*, vol. 2. New York: 985–1002. Excerpts repr. in (1995) C. Gill, ed., *Epictetus. The Discourses*. London: 338–40.

(1983) "Arius Didymus and the exposition of Stoic ethics," in W. W. Fortenbaugh, ed., *On Stoic and Peripatetic Ethics. The Work of Arius Didymus*. Rutgers University Studies in Classical Humanities, vol. 1. New Brunswick and London, 1983: 41–66.

(1984) "Methods of argument in Gorgias' Palamedes," in K. J. Voudouris, ed., *The Sophistic Movement*. Papers of the Greek Philosophical Society. Athens: 233–41.

(1985a) "Early Greek Philosophy," in P. E. Easterling and B. M. W. Knox, eds., *The Cambridge History of Greek Literature*. Cambridge: 245–57, 751–58. Repr. in (1989) *The Cambridge History of Classical Literature*, vol. 1, Part 3, *Philosophy, History and Oratory*. Cambridge: 1–13.

(1985b) "Aristotle," in P. E. Easterling and B. M. W. Knox, eds., *The Cambridge History of Greek Literature*. Cambridge: 527–40, 805–810. Repr. in (1989) *The Cambridge History of Classical Literature*, vol. 1, Part 3, *Philosophy, History and Oratory*. Cambridge: 115–56.

(1985c) "Post-Aristotelian philosophy," in P.E. Easterling and B. M. W. Knox, eds., *The Cambridge History of Greek Literature*. Cambridge: 622–41, 835–56. Repr. in (1989) *The Cambridge History of Classical Literature*, vol. 1, Part 3, *Philosophy, History and Oratory*. Cambridge: 1–13, 149–56, 178–205.

(1985d) "Thinking about the cosmos: Greek philosophy from Thales to Aristotle," in R. Browning, ed., *The Greek World*. London: 101–14.

(1986a) "Epicureans and Stoics," in A. H. Armstrong, ed., *Classical Mediterranean Spirituality*. New York: 135–53.

(1986b) "Pleasure and social utility: the virtues of being Epicurean," in H. Flashar and O. Gigon, eds., *Aspects de la philosophie hellénistique*, Entretiens sur l'antiquité classique, vol. 32. Vandoeuvres-Geneva: 283–324. Repr. in (1993) E. N. Genovese, ed., *The Burnett Lectures*. San Diego: 102–28.

(1986c) "Ptolemy On the Kriterion: an epistemology for the practising scientist," in A. A. Long and J. Dillon, eds., *The Question of Eclecticism. Studies in Later Greek Philosophy*, Berkeley and Los Angeles/London: 176–207. Repr. in (1989) P. Huby and G. Neale, eds., *The Criterion of Truth*. Liverpool: 151–78.

(1986d) "Pro and contra fratricide: Aeschylus, *Septem* 653–719," in J. Betts and J. T. Hooker, eds., *Studies in Honour of T. B. L. Webster*, vol. 1. Bristol: 179–89.

(1989) Contributions to "On the Kriterion and Hegemonikon" in P. Huby and G. Neale, eds. *The Criterion of Truth*. Liverpool: 179–230.

(1990) "Scepticism about gods in Hellenistic philosophy," in M. Griffith and D. J. Mastronarde, eds., *Cabinet of the Muses*. Atlanta: 279–91.

(1991) "Representation and the self in Stoicism," in S. Everson, ed., *Companions to Ancient Thought. Psychology*. Cambridge: 102–20. Excerpt repr. in (1995) C. Gill, ed., *Epictetus. The Discourses*. London: 342–44.

(1992a) Articles on Cynics, Cyrenaics, Hellenistic ethics and Roman ethics, in L. C. Becker and C. B. Becker, eds., *The Encyclopaedia of Ethics*, vol. 1. New York: 234–38; 467–80; revised edition, vol. 1. New York (2001) 368–72; vol 2. New York (2001) 696–709.

(1992b) "Hellenistic Ethics," in L. C. Becker and C. B. Becker, eds., *A History of Western Ethics*. New York: 21–32

(1992c) "Roman ethics," in L. C. Becker and C. B. Becker, eds., *A History of Western Ethics*. New York: 33–44.

(1992a) "Dopo la nuova edizione degli Elementi di Etica di Ierocle Stoico," with G. Bastianini, in *Studi su codici e papiri filosofici*. Florence: 221–49.

(1992b) "Stoic readings of Homer," in R. Lamberton and J. J. Keaney, eds., *Homer's Ancient Readers*. Princeton: 41–66. Repr. in (2006) A. Laird, ed., *Oxford Readings in Classical Studies: Ancient Literary Criticism*. Oxford: 211–37.

(1993) "Hellenistic ethics and philosophical power," in P. Green, ed., *Hellenistic History and Culture*. Berkeley and Los Angeles: 138–56, 162–67.

(1993a) "Hierocles on oikeiosis and self-perception," in K. J. Voudouris, ed., *Hellenistic Philosophy* vol. I, International Center for Philosophy and Culture. Athens: 93–104.

(1993b) "Introduction" to Part V of *Images and Ideologies: Self-Definition in the Hellenistic World*, ed. A. A. Long with A. W. Bulloch, E. S. Gruen, A. Stewart. Berkeley and Los Angeles: 299–302.

(1995a) "Cicero's Plato and Aristotle," in J. Powell, ed., *Cicero the Philosopher*. Oxford: 37–61.

(1995b) "Cicero's politics in *De officiis*," in A. Laks and M. Schofield, eds., *Justice and Generosity. Studies in Hellenistic Social and Political Philosophy*. Cambridge: 213–40.

(1996a) "Notes on Hierocles Stoicus apud Stobaeum," in M.S. Funghi, ed., *Le vie della ricerca. Studi in onore di Francesco Adorno*. Florence: 299–309.

(1996b) "Skepsis; Skeptizismus," in K. Gründer, ed., *Historisches Wörterbuch der Philosophie* Band 9. Basel: 938–50.

(1996c) "The Socratic tradition: Crates, Diogenes and Hellenistic ethics," in R. B. Branham and M.-O. Goulet-Cazé, eds., *The Cynics*. Berkeley and Los Angeles: 28–46.

(1996d) "Stoic psychology and the elucidation of language," in G. Manetti, ed., *Knowledge through Signs*. Brussels: 109–31.

(1996e) "Theophrastus' *De sensibus* on Plato," in K. A. Algra et al., eds., *Polyhistor. Studies in the History and Historiography of Ancient Philosophy*. Leiden: 345–62.

(1996f) "Théories du Langage," in J. Brunschwig and G. Lloyd, eds., *Le Savoir grec*. Paris: 552–68. Translated into English in (2000) "Language," in *Greek Thought*. Cambridge, MA: 338–54.

(1997a) "Allegory in Philo and etymology in Stoicism: A plea for drawing distinctions," in D. Runia, ed., *The Studia Philonica Annual* **9**: 198–210.

(1997b) Articles on Hierocles and Ptolemy in D. Zeyl, ed., *Encyclopaedia of Classical Philosophy*. Westport: 269–70, 459–63.

(1997c) "Epicurus and Epicureanism" in D. G. Marowski, ed., *Classical and Medieval Literature Criticism*, vol. 21. Detroit: 163–92.

(1997d) "Lucretius on nature and the Epicurean self," in K. A. Algra et al., eds., *Lucretius and his Intellectual Background*. Amsterdam: 125–39.

(1997e) "Stoic Philosophers on persons, property and community," in R. Sorabji, ed., *Aristotle and After. BICS* suppl. 68. London: 13–32.

(1998a) Plato's Apologies and Socrates in the Theaetetus," in J. Gentzler. ed., *Method in Ancient Philosophy*. Oxford: 113–36.

(1998b) "Theophrastus and the Stoa," in J. van Ophuijsen and M. van Raalte, eds., *Theophrastus. Reappraising the Sources*. New Brunswick: 355–83.

(1999a) Articles on Zeno, Epicurus, Pyrrho, Cicero, Epictetus, Marcus Aurelius, Sextus Empiricus, in R. Arrington, ed., *A Companion to the Philosophers*. Oxford: 148–49, 192–93, 237–43, 455–6, 511–13.

(1999b) "Hellenistic philosophy," in R. Popkin, ed., *The Columbia History of Western Philosophy*. New York: 74–90.

(1999c) "The lives and writings of the early Greek philosophers," in A. A Long, ed. *The Cambridge Companion to Early Greek Philosophy*. Cambridge: xvii–xxix.

(1999d) "The scope of early Greek philosophy," in A. A. Long, ed., *The Cambridge Companion to Early Greek Philosophy*. Cambridge: 1–21.

(1999e) "The Socratic legacy," in K. Algra et al., eds., *The Cambridge History of Hellenistic Philosophy*. Cambridge: 617–41.

(1999f) "Stoic psychology," in K. Algra et al., eds., *The Cambridge History of Hellenistic Philosophy*. Cambridge: 560–84.

(2000) Articles on Heraclitus, Cratylus, Psyche and Nous, in E. Craig, ed., *The Routledge Encyclopaedia of Philosophy*. London: 1998.

(2002a) "Stoic reactions to Plato's *Cratylus*," in M. Canto-Sperber and P. Pellegrin, eds., *Le Style de la Pensée. Recueil de textes en hommage à Jacques Brunschwig*. Paris: 395–413.

(2002b) "Zeno's epistemology and Plato's Theaetetus," in T. Scaltsas and A. S. Mason, eds., *The Philosophy of Zeno*. Larnaka: 113–32.

(2003a) "Roman philosophy," in D. Sedley, ed., *The Cambridge Companion to Greek and Roman Philosophy*. Cambridge: 184–210.

(2003b) "Stoicism in the philosophical tradition: Spinoza, Lipsius, Butler," in J. Miller and B. Inwood, eds., *Hellenistic and Early Modern Philosophy*. Cambridge: 7–29. Co-printed in B. Inwood, ed., *The Cambridge Companion to Stoicism*. Cambridge: 365–92.

(2004a) "The Socratic imprint on Epictetus' philosophy," in S. K. Strange and J. Zupko, eds., *Stoicism. Traditions and Transformations*. Cambridge: 10–31. Trans. into French in G. Romeyer-Dherbey and J.-B. Gourinat, eds., *Les stoiciens*. Paris 2005: 403–26.

(2004b) Summary of "The Socratic imprint on Epictetus' philosophy," in V. Karasmanis, ed., *Socrates. 2400 Years since his Death*. Athens and Delphi: 449–50.

(2005a) "Law and nature in Greek thought," in M. Gagarin and D. Cohen, eds., *The Cambridge Companion to Ancient Greek Law*. Cambridge: 412–30.

(2005b) "Platonic souls as persons," in R. Salles, ed., *Metaphysics, Soul, and Ethics in Ancient Thought. Themes from the Work of Richard Sorabji*. Oxford: 173–91.

(2005c) "Stoic linguistics, Plato's *Cratylus*, and Augustine's *De dialectica*," in D. Frede and B. Inwood, eds., *Language and Learning. Philosophy of Language in the Hellenistic Age*. Cambridge: 36–55.

(2006a) "How does Socrates' divine sign communicate with him?," in S. Ahbel-Rappe and R. Kamtekar, eds., *A Companion to Socrates*. Oxford: 63–74.

(2006b) "Plato and Hellenistic philosophy," in H. Benson, ed., *A Companion to Plato*. Oxford: 418–33.

(2007a) "Stoic communitarianism and normative citizenship," in D. Keyt and F. D. Miller, eds., *Freedom, Reason, and the Polis: Essays in Ancient Greek Political Philosophy*. Cambridge: 241–61. Co-printed in *Social Philosophy & Policy* **24**, **2**: 241–61.

(2007b) "Williams on Greek literature and philosophy," in A. Thomas, ed., *Bernard Williams*. Cambridge: 155–80.

(2008) "Philo on Stoic physics," in F. Alesse, ed., *Philo of Alexandria and Post-Aristotelian Philosophy*. Leiden and Boston: 121–40.

(2009a) "L'Ethique: continuité et innovations," in J. Barnes and J.-B. Gourinat, eds., *Lire les stoiciens*. Paris: 171–91.

(2009b) "Heraclitus on measure and the explicit emergence of rationality," in D. Frede and B. Reis, eds., *Body and Soul in Ancient Philosophy*. Berlin, 87–110.

(2009c) "Seneca on the self: why now?," in S. Bartsch and D. Wray, eds., *Seneca and the Self*. Cambridge: 20–36.

4. ARTICLES IN CLASSICAL AND PHILOSOPHICAL JOURNALS

(1963a) "The Principles of Parmenides' Cosmogony," *Phronesis* **8**: 90–107.

(1963b) "Sophocles, *Trachiniae* 539–40," *Classical Review*, NS **13.2**: 128–29.

(1964a) "Abstract Terminology in Sophocles: some uses of -sis nouns," *AUMLA* (Journal of the Australasian Modern Languages Association) **21**: 53–64.

(1964b) "Sophocles, *Ajax* 68–70, a reply to Professor Fraenkel," *Museum Helveticum* **21**: 228–31.

(1964c) "Sophocles, *Electra* 1251–2," *Classical Review*, NS **14.2**: 130–32.

(1966) "Thinking and sense-perception in Empedocles: mysticism or materialism?" *Classical Quarterly* **16**: 256–76.

(1967a) "Carneades and the Stoic telos," *Phronesis* **15**: 59–90. Repr. in (1995) T. Irwin, ed., *Classical Philosophy. Collected Papers*, vol. 8. New York: 377–408.

(1967b) "Poisonous growths in *Trachiniae*," *Greek, Roman and Byzantine Studies* **8**: 275–78.

(1968a) "Aristotle, *De anima* 424b31–425a5," *Hermes* **96**: 372–74.

(1968b) "Aristotle's legacy to Stoic ethics', *Bulletin of the London University Institute of Classical Studies* **15**: 72–85. Reprinted in (1995) T. Irwin, ed., *Classical Philosophy. Collected Papers*, vol. 5. New York: 378–91.

(1968c) "The Stoic concept of evil," *Philosophical Quarterly* **18**: 329–43.

(1970a) "Morals and Values in Homer," *Journal of Hellenic Studies* **90**: 121–39. Repr. in (1999) I. J. F. de Jong, ed., *Homer Critical Assessments*, vol. 2. London and New York: 305–31.

(1970b) "Stoic determinism and Alexander of Aphrodisias *De fato* (i–xiv)," *Archiv für Geschichte der Philosophie* **52**: 246–66.

(1970–71) "The logical basis of Stoic ethics," *Proceedings of the Aristotelian Society* **71**: 85–104.

(1971) "*Aisthesis, prolepsis* and linguistic theory in Epicurus," *Bulletin of the University of London Institute of Classical Studies* **18**: 114–33.

(1975) "Alexander of Aphrodisias, *De fato* 190.26 ff.," *Classical Quarterly*, NS **25**: 158–59.

(1975/6) "Heraclitus and Stoicism," Φιλοσοφία **5/6**: 134–56. Repr. in T. Irwin, ed., *Classical Philosophy. Collected Papers*, vol. 1. New York (1995): 179–99.

(1977) "Chance and natural law in Epicureanism," *Phronesis* **22**: 63–88.

(1978a) "Sextus Empiricus on the criterion of truth," *Bulletin of the University of London Institute of Classical Studies* **25**: 35–49.

(1978b) "Sophocles, *OT* 879–81," *Liverpool Classical Monthly* **3**: 49–53.

(1978c) "Timon of Phlius: Pyrrhonist and satirist," *Proceedings of the Cambridge Philological Society* **204**: 68–90.

(1980a) "Soul and body in Stoicism," in Colloquy 36 of *Center for Hermeneutical Studies*. Berkeley: 1–17.

(1980b) "Stoa and Sceptical Academy: origins and growth of a tradition," *Liverpool Classical Monthly* **5**: 161–74, summarised in *Proceedings of the Classical Association* **76** (1979) 27–8.

(1982) "Soul and body in Stoicism," revised version, *Phronesis* **27**: 34–57. Repr. in T. Irwin, ed., *Classical Philosophy. Collected Papers*, vol. 8. New York (1995) 154–77.

(1983) "Greek ethics after Macintyre and the Stoic community of reason," *Ancient Philosophy* **3**: 184–99; also published in *Byzantina Australiensia* **5** (1984) 37–56.

(1985a) "Consciously Stoic," *Omnibus* **9**: 21–23.

(1985b) "The Stoics on world-conflagration and everlasting recurrence," *Southern Journal of Philosophy* suppl vol. 23: 13–38.

(1986) "Diogenes Laertius, life of Arcesilaus," *Elenchos* **7**: 429–50.

(1988a) Reply to Jonathan Barnes, "Epicurean signs," *Oxford Studies in Ancient Philosophy*, suppl. vol., 135–44.

(1988b) "Socrates in Hellenistic philosophy," *Classical Quarterly* **38**: 150–71.

(1989) "Stoic eudaimonism," *Proceedings of the Boston Area Colloquium in Ancient Philosophy* **4**: 77–101.

(1991) "The harmonics of Stoic virtue," *Oxford Studies in Ancient Philosophy* suppl. vol. 97–116.

(1992) "Finding oneself in Greek philosophy," *Tijdschrift voor Filosofie* **54**: 257–79. Repr. in (2006) M. van Ackeren and J. Müller, eds., *Antike Philosophie Verstehen. Understanding Ancient Philosophy*. Darmstadt: 54–71.

(1996) "Parmenides on thinking being," *Proceedings of the Boston Area Colloquium in Ancient Philosophy* **12**: 125–51. Repr. in (2005) G. Rechenauer, ed., *Frühgriechisches Denken*. Göttingen: 227–51.

(2000) "Epictetus as Socratic mentor," *Proceedings of the Cambridge Philological Society* **46**: 79–98.

(2001) "Ancient philosophy's hardest question: What to make of oneself?" *Representations* **74**: 19–36.

(2003a) "Epictetus on understanding and managing emotions," *Quaestiones Infinitae* **48**: 1–38.

(2003b) "Hellenistic ethics as the art of life," *Lampas* **36**: 27–41.

(2004) "Eudaimonism, divinity and rationality in Greek ethics," in *Proceedings of the Boston Area Colloquium in Ancient Philosophy* **19**: 123–43.

(2008) "The concept of the cosmopolitan in Greek & Roman thought," *Daedalus*, Summer 2008: 50–58.

5. BOOK REVIEWS

(1965) J. Grüber, *Über einige abstrakte Begriffe des frühen Griechischen*, in *Journal of Hellenic Studies* **85**: 198–99.

(1966a) J. Mansfeld, *Die Offenbarung des Parmenides und die menschliche Welt*, in *Philosophical Quarterly* **16**: 269–70.

(1966b) L. Tarán, *Parmenides*, in *Journal of Hellenic Studies* **86**: 223–24.

(1967) F. M. Cleve, *The Giants of Pre-sophistic Philosophy*, in *Philosophical Quarterly* **17**: 267–68.

(1968) L. Edelstein, *The Meaning of Stoicism*, in *Journal of Hellenic Studies* **88**: 196–98.

(1969) J. M. Rist, *Plotinus. The Road to Reality*, in *Philosophical Quarterly* **19**: 80–81.

(1970a) D. O'Brien, *Empedocles' Cosmic Cycle*, in *Journal of Hellenic Studies* **90**: 238–39.

(1970b) M. O' Brien, ed., *Twentieth Century Interpretations of Sophocles' Oedipus Tyrannus*, in *Phoenix* **23**: 392–94.

(1971a) G. Jäger, *'Nus' in Platons Dialogen*, in *Classical Review*, NS **21.2**: 184–86.

(1971b) E. Schmalzriedt, *Platon der Schriftsteller und die Wahrheit*, in *Classical Review*, NS **21.3**: 364–67.

(1971c) C. L. Stough, *Greek Skepticism*, in *Philosophy* **46**: 77–78.

(1972a) *Association Guillaume Budé. Actes du viii congrès*, in *Classical Review*, NS **22.1**: 93–99.

(1972b) D. Babut, *Plutarque et le stoicisme*, in *Classical Review*, NS **22.1**: 27–29.

(1972c) D. J. Furley and R. E. Allen, eds., *Studies in Presocratic Philosophy. I. The Beginnings of Philosophy*, in *Journal of Hellenic Studies* **92**: 217–18.

(1972d) M. Untersteiner, *Posidonio nel Placita del Diogene Laerzio*, in *Classical Review* NS **22.3**: 408–09.

(1972e) C. J. de Vogel, *Philosophia* I, in *Philosophical Quarterly* **22**: 361–62.

(1973a) J. Bollack, *Empédocle*, in *Archiv für Geschichte der Philosophie* **55**: 76–79.

(1973b) J. B. Gould, *The Philosophy of Chrysippus*, in *Classical Review*, NS **23.2**: 214–16.

(1974a) J. Bollack, M. Bollack, and H. Wismann, *La lettre d' Epicure*, *Classical Review*, NS **24.1**: 46–48.

(1974b) R. Hoven, *Stoicisme et stoiciens face au problème de l'au-delà*, in *Classical Review*, NS **24.1**: 232–33.

(1975a) J. den Boeft, *Calcidius on Fate, his Doctrine and Sources*, in *Classical Review*, NS **25.1**: 52–54

(1975b) K. Döring, *Die Megariker*, in *Classical Review*, NS **25.2**: 232–34.

(1975c) J. M. Rist, *Epicurus. An Introduction*, in *Mind* **334**: 291–92.

(1975d) M. C. Stokes, *One and Many in Presocratic Philosophy*, in *Mind* **334**: 289–91.

(1976a) L. Edelstein and I. G. Kidd, *Posidonius* I, in *Classical Review*, NS **26.1**: 72–76.

(1976b) M. Griffin, *Seneca: A Philosopher in Politics*, in *Times Higher Education Supplement*, 20 February: 50.

(1976c) D. Konstan, *Some Aspects of Epicurean Psychology* and D. Lemke, *Die Theologie Epikurs*, in *Classical Review*, NS **26.2**: 215–17.

(1976d) A. Manuwald, *Die Prolepsislehre Epikurs*, in *Classical Review* NS **26.1**: 134–35.

(1976e) G. Reale, *Melisso*, in *Gnomon* **48**: 645–50.

(1977a) C. S. Floratos, *Strabon über Literatur und Posidonios*, in *Classical Review*, NS **27.1**: 125–26.

(1977b) D. Pesce, *Saggio su Epicuro*, in *Classical Review* NS **27.2**: 291–92.

(1977c) C. Rowe, *An Introduction to Greek Ethics*, in *Times Higher Education Supplement*, 22 April 1977: 21.

(1978a) U. Burkhard, *Die angebliche Heraklit-Nachfolge des Skeptikers Aenesidem*, in *Classical Review*, NS **28.1**: 171–72

(1978b) C. S. Floratos, *Η ΑΙΣΘΗΤΙΚΗ ΤѠΝ ΣΤѠΙΚѠΝ*, in *Classical Review*, NS **28.1**: 171.

(1978c) A. Graeser, *Zenon von Kition*, in *Classical Review*, NS **28.2**: 361.

(1979) J. C. Fraisse, *Philia*, *Classical Review*, NS **29.1**: 80–82.

(1980a) H. Cherniss, *Plutarch's Moralia XIII*, *Classical Review* NS **30.1**: 14–16.

(1980b) G. E. R. Lloyd, *Magic Reason and Experience*, in *JACT Bulletin* **53**: 28–29.

(1980c) L. Paquet, *Les Cyniques grecs*, in *Classical Review*, NS **30.1**: 53–54.

(1980d) M. Schofield et al., eds., *Doubt and Dogmatism: Studies in Hellenistic Epistemology*, in *Times Literary Supplement* 27 June: 739.

(1980e) R. P. Winnington-Ingram, *Sophocles. An Interpretation* and R. W. B. Burton, *The Sophoclean Chorus*, in *Times Higher Education Supplement*, 8 July: 12.

(1981a) M. Billerbeck, *Epiktet. Vom Kynismus*, in *Journal of Hellenic Studies* **101**: 163.

(1981b) K. Döring, *Exemplum Socratis*, in *Classical Review* NS **31.2**: 298–99.

(1981c) H. Usener, *Glossarium Epicureum*, in *Journal of Hellenic Studies* **101**: 158.

(1982a) M. Billerbeck, *Der Kyniker Demetrius*, in *Journal of Hellenic Studies* **102**: 260.

(1982b) H. Gottschalk, *Heraclides of Pontus*, in *Classical Review*, NS **32.1**: 200–02.

(1982c) G. Reale, *Storia della filosofia antica*, in *Classical Review*, NS **32.1**: 38–41.

(1983) M. Grant, *From Alexander to Cleopatra*, in *Times Literary Supplement*, 1 April: 338.

(1984) F. Decleva Caizzi, *Pirrone, Testimonianze*, in *Classical Review*, NS **34.2**: 219–21.

(1987) M. Colish, *The Stoic Tradition from Antiquity to the Middle Ages*, in *American Historical Review*, **92**: 1187–18.

(1988a) J. Annas and J. Barnes, *The Modes of Scepticism*, in *Journal of the History of Philosophy* **26**: 474–76.

(1988b) E. Asmis, *Epicurus' Scientific Method*, in *Philosophical Review* **97**: 249–51.

(1988c) M. Nussbaum, *The Fragility of Goodness*, in *Classical Philology*, **84**: 361–70.

(1992a) T. Jahn, *Zum Wortfeld 'Seele-Geist' in der Sprache Homers*, in *Classical Review*, NS **42.1**: 3–5.

(1992b) C. Segal, *Lucretius on Death and Anxiety*, in *Ancient Philosophy* **12**: 493–98.

(1997) C. Atherton, *The Stoics on Ambiguity*, in *Ancient Philosophy* **17**: 484–88.

(1999) J. Mansfeld and D. Runia, *Aetiana*, in *Journal of the History of Philosophy* **37**: 523–24.

(2000a) "Platonic ethics: A critical notice of Julia Annas, *Platonic Ethics Old and New*," *Oxford Studies in Ancient Philosophy* **19**: 339–58.

(2000b) V. Tsouna, *The Epistemology of the Cyrenaic School*, in *Classical Review* **59.2**: 151–52.

(2001) F. Budelmann, *The Language of Sophocles*, in *Classical World* **94.3**: 278–79.

(2003a) C. Brittain, *Philo of Larissa*, in *Classical Review* **62**.2: 314–16.

(2003b) H. Tarrant, *Plato's First Interpreters*, in *Journal of the History of Philosophy* **41**: 121–22.

(2004a) H.-G. Gadamer, *The Beginning of Knowledge*, in *Philosophical Quarterly* **54**: 614–15.

(2004b) J. Warren, *Facing Death. Epicurus and his Critics*, in *Times Literary Supplement* October 8, **2004**: 11.

(2005a) J. Dillon, *The Heirs of Plato*, in *Classical Review*, NS **55.1**: 60–61.

(2005b) A. Kenny, *A New History of Western Philosophy. Vol. 1 Ancient Philosophy*, in *Times Literary Supplement*, 15 April: 4–5.

(2006a) D. McMahon, *The Pursuit of Happiness*, R. Schoch, *The Secrets of Happiness*, and D. Gilbert, *Stumbling on Happiness*, in *Times Literary Supplement*, 1 September: 9.

(2006b) J. Sellars, *The Art of Living. The Stoics on the Nature and Function of Philosophy*, in *Classical Review* NS **56.1:** 81–82.

(2007) R. Sorabji, *Self*, in *Times Literary Supplement*, 22 June: 27.

(2008) Book Notes on the Presocratics, *Phronesis* **53**: 290–302.

(2009) B. Inwood, *Reading Seneca*, in *Philosophical Review* 118.3: 378–81.

6. OCCASIONAL PIECES

(1984) Response to Thomas M. Conley, *Philon Rhetor*, Colloquy 47 of *Center for Hermeneutical Studies*. Berkeley: 35–38.

(1991/92) "The Identity Group," *Jahrbuch of the Wissenschaftskolleg zu Berlin*. Berlin: 144–51.

(1994) "Gregory Vlastos," in W. W. Briggs, ed., *Biographical Dictionary of North American Classicists*. Westport, Conn.: 664–67.

(1996) "Amos Funkenstein on the Disenchantments of Knowledge," in *Amos Funkenstein, Doreen B. Townsend Center Occasional Papers* 6. Berkeley: 9–18.

(2001) "Locating Diogenes of Apollonia," *Ancient Philosophy* **21.2**: 476.

(2003) "Memoir of Arthur Hilary Armstrong," *Proceedings of the British Academy* **120**: 3–17.

(2006) "Evolution vs Intelligent Design," *Townsend Newsletter*. Berkeley, Nov./Dec.: 3–5.

(2008) Foreword to second edition of B. Williams, *Shame and Necessity*. Berkeley and Los Angeles: xiii–xxi.

7. FORTHCOMING ARTICLES

"Aristotle on eudaimonia, nous, and divinity," in J. Miller, ed., *A Critical Guide to Aristotle's Ethics*. Cambridge.

"Cosmic craftsmanship in Plato and Stoicism," in R. Mohr, ed., *Plato's Timaeus*. Las Vegas.

"Later ancient ethics," in J. Skorupski, ed., *Routledge Companion to Ethics*. London.

"Montaigne: the eclectic pragmatist," *Republic of Letters* 1. Stanford.

"Philosophers as poets and poets as philosophers: Parmenides, Plato, Lucretius, Wordsworth," in P. Marzillo, ed., *Para/Textuelle Verhandlungen zwischen Dichtung und Philosophie in der frühen Neuzeit*. Berlin.

"Slavery as philosophical metaphor in Plato and Xenophon'," in V. Karasmanis, ed., *Presocratics and Plato. A Festschrift in Honor of Charles Kahn*. Las Vegas.

"Socrates in later Greek philosophy," in D. Morrison, ed., *The Cambridge Companion to Socrates*. Cambridge.

8. CO-EDITED SERIES VOLUMES

(1991–2007) Clarendon Later Ancient Philosophers, co-edited with Jonathan Barnes. Oxford. vol. 1, J. Hankinson, *Galen on the Natural Faculties* (1991);

vol. 2, J. Dillon, *Alcinous: The Handbook of Platonism* (1993); vol. 3, R. Bett, *Sextus Empiricus: Against the Ethicists* (1996); vol. 4, D. Blank, *Sextus Empiricus: Against the Grammarians* (1998); vol. 5, R. Dobbin, *Epictetus: Discourses Book I* (1998); vol. 6, J. Barnes, *Porphyry: Introduction* (2003); vol. 7, B. Inwood, *Seneca: Selected Philosophical Letters* (2007).

Bibliography

Ackeren, M. van (2003) *Das Wissen vom Guten: Bedeutung und Kontinuität des Tugendwissens in den Dialogen Platons*. Amsterdam and Philadelphia.

Ahbel-Rappe, S. and Kamtekar, R. (eds.) (2006) *A Companion to Socrates*. Oxford.

Alesse, F. (2000) *La Stoa e la tradizione socratica*. Naples.

Allen, J. (2005) "The Stoics on the origin of language and the foundations of etymology," in *Language and Learning: Philosophy of Language in the Hellenistic Age*, ed. D. Frede and B. Inwood. Cambridge: 14–35.

André, J.-M. (2002) "Sénèque et la topographie de Rome," in *Neronia VI. Rome à l'époque néronienne*, ed. J.-M. Croisille and Y. Perrin. Brussels: 170–77.

Annas, J. (1985) "Self-knowledge in early Plato," in *Platonic Investigations. Studies in Philosophy and the History of Philosophy* vol. 13, ed. D. J. O'Meara. Washington, D.C.: 111–38.

    (2002) "What are Plato's 'middle' dialogues in the middle of?" in Annas and Rowe: 2002: 1–23.

    (2002) "My station and its duties," *Proceedings of the Aristotelian Society* **102**: 109–23.

    (2004) "Marcus Aurelius: ethics and its background," *Rhizai* **I.2**: 103–19.

    (2007) "Ethics in Stoic philosophy," *Phronesis* **52**: 58–87.

Annas, J. and Rowe, C. (eds.) (2002) *New Perspectives on Plato, Modern and Ancient*. Cambridge, MA.

Armisen-Marchetti, M. (1986) "Imagination et méditation chez Sénèque: l'exemple de la praemeditatio," *Revue des Études Latines* **64**: 185–95.

Armstrong, A. H. (1977) "Form, individual and person in Plotinus," *Dionysius* **1**: 49–68.

Asmis, E. (1989) "The Stoicism of Marcus Aurelius," *Aufstieg und Niedergang der römischen Welt II* **36**.3: 2228–52.

Babut, D. (2005) "Sur les polémiques des anciens stoïciens," *Philosophie antique* **5**: 65–91.

Baldassarri, M. (1984) *Introduzione alla logica stoica*. Como.

Barnes, J. (1993) "A big, big D?," *Classical Review* **43**: 304–06.

    (1996) "The catalogue of Chrysippus' logical works," in *Polyhistor: Studies in the History and Historiography of Ancient Philosophy*, ed. K. A. Algra,

P. W. van der Horst and D. T. Runia. Leiden, New York and Cologne: 169–84.

(1997) *Logic and the Imperial Stoa*. Leiden, New York and Cologne.

(1999a) "Aristotle and Stoic logic," in *Topics in Stoic Philosophy*, ed. K. Ierodiakonou. Oxford: 23–53.

(1999b) "Logic. Introduction," in *The Cambridge History of Hellenistic Philosophy*, ed. K. Algra, J. Barnes, J. Mansfeld, and M. Schofield. Cambridge: 65–76.

(2003) "Argument in ancient philosophy," in *The Cambridge Companion to Greek and Roman Philosophy*, ed. D. Sedley. Cambridge: 20–41.

(2007) *Truth, etc.* Oxford.

Barnes, J. (ed.) (1984) *The Complete Works of Aristotle: The Revised Oxford Translation*. Princeton.

Barney, R. (2003) "A puzzle in Stoic ethics," *Oxford Studies in Ancient Philosophy* **24**: 303–40.

Bartsch, S. (2006) *The Mirror of the Self: Sexuality, Self-knowledge, and the Gaze in the Early Roman Empire*. Chicago.

Belfiore, E. (2006) "Dancing with the gods: The myth of the chariot in Plato's *Phaedrus*," *American Journal of Philology* **127**: 185–217.

Bellissima, F. and Pagli, P. (1996) *Consequentia Mirabilis. Una regola logica tra matematica e filosofia*. Florence.

Bett, R. (1997) *Sextus Empiricus, Against the Ethicists, Translated with an Introduction and Commentary*. Oxford.

(2005) *Sextus Empiricus. Against the Logicians*. Cambridge.

(2006) "Stoic ethics," in *A Companion to Ancient Philosophy*, ed. M. L. Gill and P. Pellegrin. Oxford and Marsden, MA: 530–48.

(2008) Review of Brennan 2005, *Philosophy and Phenomenological Research* **76**, no. 2: 504–06.

Blondell, R. (2002) *The Play of Character in Plato's Dialogues*. Cambridge.

Blumenthal, H. J. (1966) "Did Plotinus believe in Ideas of individuals?," *Phronesis* **11**: 61–80.

(1971) *Plotinus' Psychology: His Doctrine of the Embodied Soul*. The Hague.

Bobonich, C. (2002) *Plato's Utopia Recast*. Oxford.

Bobzien, S. (1993) "Chrysippus' modal logic and its relation to Philo and Diodorus," in *Dialektiker und Stoiker: Zur Logik der Stoa und ihrer Vorläufer*, ed. K. Döring and T. Ebert. Stuttgart: 63–84.

Bonhöffer, A. (1890) *Epictet und die Stoa*. Stuttgart.

Brennan, T. (1998) "The Old Stoic theory of emotions," in *The Emotions in Hellenistic Philosophy*, ed. J. Sihvola and T. Engberg-Pedersen. Dordrecht: 21–70.

(2000) "Reservation in Stoic ethics," *Archiv für Geschichte der Philosophie* **82**: 149–77.

(2003) "Moral psychology," in *Cambridge Companion to the Stoics*, ed. B. Inwood. Cambridge: 257–94.

(2005) *The Stoic Life: Emotions, Duties, and Fate*. Oxford.

Brunschwig, J. (1980) "Proof defined," in *Doubt and Dogmatism: Studies in Hellenistic Epistemology*, ed. M. Schofield, M. Burnyeat and J. Barnes. Oxford: 125–60.

(1988) "La théorie stoïcienne du genre suprême," in *Matter and Metaphysics, Fourth Symposium Hellenisticum*, ed. J. Barnes and M. Mignucci. Naples: 19–127.

(1991) "On a book-title by Chrysippus: 'On the fact that the ancients admitted dialectic along with demonstrations,'" *Oxford Studies in Ancient Philosophy* suppl. vol.: 81–95.

Burnyeat, M. (1976) "Protagoras and self-refutation in later Greek philosophy," *Philosophical Review* **85**: 44–69.

(1981) "Aristotle on understanding knowledge," in *Aristotle on Science: The "Posterior Analytics,"* ed. Enrico Berti. Padua: 97–140.

(1990) *The Theaetetus of Plato*. Indianapolis and Cambridge.

(1997) "Antipater and self-refutation: elusive arguments in Cicero's *Academica*," in *Assent and Argument: Studies in Cicero's Academic Books, Proceedings of the 7th Symposium Hellenisticum (Utrecht, August 21–25, 1995)*, ed. B. Inwood and J. Mansfeld. Leiden: 277–310.

(2005) "*Eikōs muthos*," *Rhizai* **II.2**: 143–65; reprinted in *Plato's Myths*, ed. C. Partenie. Cambridge, 2009: 167–86.

Bury, R. G. (1935) *Sextus Empiricus, vol II: Against the Logicians*. London and Cambridge, MA.

Camp, J. van and Canart, P. (1956) *Le Sens du mot theios chez Platon*. Louvain.

Carter, R. E. (1967) "Plato and inspiration," *Journal of the History of Philosophy* **5**: 111–21.

Castagnoli, L. (2000) "Self-bracketing Pyrrhonism," *Oxford Studies in Ancient Philosophy* **18**: 263–328.

(2004) "Il condizionale crisippeo e le sue interpretazioni moderne," *Elenchos* **25**: 353–95.

(2007) "'Everything is true', 'everything is false': self-refutation arguments from Democritus to Augustine," *Antiquorum Philosophia* **1**: 11–74.

(2009) "Συνάρτησις crisippea e tesi di Aristotele," in *La logica nel pensiero antico (Atti del I Colloquio, Roma 28–29 Novembre 2000)*, ed. M. Alessandrelli and M. Nasti De Vincentis. Naples: 105–63.

(2010) *Ancient Self-Refutation: The Logic and History of the Self-Refutation Argument from Democritus to Augustine*. Cambridge.

Caston, V. (1999) "Something and nothing: the Stoics on concepts and universals," *Oxford Studies in Ancient Philosophy* **17**: 146–213.

Cavini, W. (1985) "La negazione di frase nella logica greca," in *Studi su papiri greci di logica e medicina*, ed. W. Cavini, M. C. Donnini Macciò, M. S. Funghi and D. Manetti. Florence: 47–126.

Chiesa, C. (1991) "Le problème du langage intérieur chez les stoïciens," *Revue internationale de philosophie* **45**: 301–21.

Coolidge, F. (1993) "The relation of philosophy to *sophrosune*: Zalmoxian medicine in Plato's *Charmides*," *Ancient Philosophy* **13**: 23–36.

Cooper, J. M. (1989) "Greek philosophers on euthanasia and suicide," in *Suicide and Euthanasia*, ed. B. Brody. Dordrecht: 9–38; reprinted in Cooper 1999: 515–41.

(1998) "Eudaimonism, the appeal to nature, and 'moral duty' in Stoicism," in *Aristotle, Kant, and the Stoics: Rethinking Happiness and Duty*, ed. S. Engstrom and J. Whiting. Cambridge: 261–84; reprinted in Cooper 1999: 427–48.

(1999) *Reason and Emotion*. Princeton.

Crivelli, P. (2007) "Epictetus and logic," in *The Philosophy of Epictetus*, ed. D. Scaltsas and A. S. Mason. Oxford: 20–31.

De Vries, G. J. (1969) *A Commentary on the Phaedrus of Plato*. Amsterdam.

Diès, A. (1927) "La transposition platonicienne," in *Autour de Platon. Essais de Critique et d' Histoire, vol. 2*. Paris: 267–308.

Dobbin, R. (1998) *Epictetus: Discourses, Book 1*. Oxford.

Donini, P. L. (1979) "L'eclettismo impossibile. Seneca e il platonismo medio," in *Modelli filosofici e letterari. Lucrezio, Orazio, Seneca*, ed. P. L. Donini and G. F. Gianotti. Bologna: 149–300.

Döring, K. (1972) *Die Megariker*. Amsterdam.

(1979) *Exemplum Socratis. Studien zur Sokratesnachwirkung in der kynisch-stoischen Popularphilosophie der frühen Kaiserzeit und im frühen Christentum*. Wiesbaden.

(1989) "Gab es eine Dialektische Schule?," *Phronesis* **34**: 293–310.

Dörrie, H. and Baltes, M. (1987–) *Der Platonismus in der Antike. Grundlagen, System, Entwicklung*. Stuttgart.

Dyson, M. (1974) "Some problems concerning knowledge in Plato's *Charmides*," *Phronesis* **19**: 102–11.

Ebert, T. (1991) *Dialektiker und frühe Stoiker bei Sextus Empiricus*. Göttingen.

Edwards, C. (1993) *The Politics of Immorality in Ancient Rome*. Cambridge.

Ferrari, G. R. F. (1987) *Listening to the Cicadas. A Study of Plato's Phaedrus*. Cambridge.

(2007) "The three-part soul," in *The Cambridge Companion to Plato's Republic*, ed. G. R. F. Ferrari. Cambridge: 165–201.

Fillion-Lahille, J. (1984) *Le De Ira de Sénèque et la philosophie stoïcienne des passions*. Paris.

Fine, G. (1979) "Knowledge and *logos* in the *Theaetetus*," *Philosophical Review* **88**: 366–97.

(1999a) "Knowledge and belief in *Republic* 5–7," in Fine 1999b vol 1: 215–46.

(ed.) (1999b) *Plato*, 2 vols. Oxford.

(2008) "Does Socrates claim to know that he knows nothing?," *Oxford Studies in Ancient Philosophy* **35**: 49–88.

Flashar, H. (1958) *Der Dialog Ion als Zeugnis platonischer Philosophie*. Berlin.

Fortenbaugh, W. (1966) "Plato *Phaedrus* 235c3," *Classical Philology* **61**: 108–09.

Frede, M. (1974) *Die stoische Logik*. Göttingen.

(2002) "Introduction," in *Aristotle's Metaphysics Lambda*, ed. M. Frede and D. Charles. Oxford: 1–52.

(2007) "A notion of a person in Epictetus," in *The Philosophy of Epictetus*, ed. T. Scaltsas and A. S. Mason. Oxford: 153–68.

Gaskin, R. (1995) *The Sea Battle and the Master Argument: Aristotle and Diodorus Cronus on the Metaphysics of the Future*. Berlin and New York.

Gauly, B. M. (2004) *Senecas Naturales Quaestiones. Naturphilosophie für die römische Kaiserzeit*. Zetemata 122. Munich.

Gersh, S. (1986) *Middle Platonism and Neoplatonism, the Latin Tradition*, 2 vols. Notre Dame, Indiana.

Giannantoni, G. (ed.) (1983–90) *Socratis et socraticorum reliquiae*, 4 vols. Naples.

Gill, C. (1993) "Panaetius on the virtue of being yourself," in *Images and Ideologies: Self-Definition in the Hellenistic World*, ed. A. Bulloch et al. Berkeley: 330–53.

(2006) *The Structured Self in Hellenistic and Roman Thought*. Oxford.

Glucker, J. (1989) "Πρὸς τὸν εἰπόντα. Sources and credibility of *De Stoicorum Repugnantiis* 8," *Illinois Classical Studies* **13**: 473–89.

Gourinat, J.-B. (2000) *La Dialectique des stoïciens*. Paris.

(forthcoming) "Zénon d'Élée et l'invention de la dialectique."

Graf, F. (2009) "Apollo, possession, and prophecy," in *Apolline Politics and Poetics*, ed. L. Athanassaki, R. Martin, and J. F. Miller. Athens: 587–605.

Graver, M. (2002) *Cicero on the Emotions: Tusculan Disputations 3 and 4*. Chicago.

(2007) *Stoicism and Emotion*. Chicago.

Griswold, C. L. (1986) *Self-Knowledge in Plato's Phaedrus*. New Haven.

Hackforth, R. (1952) *Plato's Phaedrus*. Cambridge.

Hadot, I. (1996) *Simplicius, Commentaire sur le "Manuel" d'Épictète. Introduction et édition critique du texte grec*. Philosophia Antiqua 66. Leiden.

Hadot, P. (1991) "Philosophie, discours philosophique et divisions de la philosophie chez les stoïciens," *Revue internationale de philosophie* **45**: 205–19.

(1994) "Liste commentée de oeuvres de Chrysippe (D. L. VII 189–202)," in *Dictionnaire des philosophes antiques*, vol. II, ed. R. Goulet. Paris: 336–56.

Heinaman, R. (2002) "Plato's division of goods in the *Republic*," *Phronesis* XLVII/4: 309–35.

Horky, P. S. (2007) *Plato's Magnesia and Philosophical Polities in Magna Graecia*. Ph.D. Dissertation University of Southern California. Los Angeles.

Hoven, R. (1971) *Stoïcisme et stoïciens face au problème de l'au-delà*. Paris.

Huffman, C. A. (2005) *Archytas of Tarentum: Pythagorean, Philosopher, and Mathematician King*. Cambridge.

Hülser, K. (1987–88) *Die Fragmente zur Dialektik der Stoiker*, 4 vols. Stuttgart.

Ierodiakonou, K. (1993) "The Stoic division of philosophy," *Phronesis* **38**: 57–74.

Inwood, B. (1985) *Ethics and Action in Stoicism*. Oxford.

(1997) "'Why do fools fall in love?'," in *Aristotle and After*, ed. R. Sorabji, *Bulletin of the Institute of Classical Studies* Supplement 68: 55–69.

(1999) "Stoic ethics (i–vii)," in *The Cambridge History of Hellenistic Philosophy*, ed. K. Algra et al. Cambridge: 675–705.

(2005) *Reading Seneca. Stoic Philosophy at Rome*. Oxford.

(2007a) *Seneca. Selected Philosophical Letters*. Oxford.

(2007b) "Seneca, Plato, and Platonism: the case of *Letter* 65," in *Platonic Stoicism–Stoic Platonism. The Dialogue between Platonism and Stoicism in Antiquity*, ed. M. Bonazzi and C. Helmig. Leuven: 149–67.

Ioppolo, A. M. (1980) *Aristone di Chio e lo stoicismo antico*. Naples.

Irwin, T. (1977) *Plato's Moral Theory: The Early and Middle Dialogues*. Oxford.
    (1995) *Plato's Ethics*. New York.

Isnardi Parenti, M. (2000) "Socrate e Catone in Seneca: Il filosofo e il politico," in *Seneca e il suo tempo*, ed. P. Parroni. Rome: 215–25.

Jaeger, W. (1962) *Aristotle: Fundamentals of the History of his Development*, trans. R. Robinson, 2nd edn. Oxford.

Janaway, C. (1995) *Images of Excellence. Plato's Critique of the Arts*. Oxford.

Kalligas, P. (1997) "Forms of individuals in Plotinus: a re-examination," *Phronesis* **42**: 206–27.

Kamtekar, R. (1998) "*Aidôs* in Epictetus," *Classical Philology* **93**: 136–60.

Kneale, W. (1957) "Aristotle and the *Consequentia Mirabilis*," *Journal of Hellenic Studies* **77**: 62–66.

Korsgaard, C. (1999) "Self-constitution in the ethics of Plato and Kant," *The Journal of Ethics* **3**: 1–29.

Kraut, R. (1983) "Comments on Gregory Vlastos, 'The Socratic elenchus,'" *Oxford Studies in Ancient Philosophy* **1**: 59–70.
    (1989) *Aristotle on the Human Good*. Cambridge.
    (2001) "Aristotle's ethics," *Stanford Encyclopedia of Philosophy*.
    (ed.) (2006) *The Blackwell Guide to Aristotle's Nicomachean Ethics*. Oxford.

Lawrence, G. (2006) "Human good and human function," in Kraut 2006: 37–75.

Lear, J. (2006) "Allegory and myth in Plato's *Republic*," in *The Blackwell Guide to Plato's Republic*, ed. G. Santas. Oxford: 25–43.

Leinieks, V. (1996) *The City of Dionysos: A Study of Euripides' Bakchai*. Stuttgart.

Linforth, I. (1946) "Telestic madness in Plato, Phaedrus 244d–e," *University of California Publications in Classical Philology* **13**: 163–72.

Lloyd, A. C. (1978) "Emotion and decision in Stoic psychology," in *The Stoics*, ed. J. M. Rist. Berkeley: 233–46.

Long, A. A. (1971) "Language and thought in Stoicism," in *Problems in Stoicism*, ed. A. A. Long. London: 75–113.
    (1974) *Hellenistic Philosophy: Stoics, Epicureans, Sceptics*. London.
    (1975–76) "Heraclitus and Stoicism," Φιλοσοφία **5–6**: 132–56.
    (1976) "The Early Stoic concept of moral choice," in *Images of Man in Ancient and Medieval Thought*, ed. F. Bossier et al. Leuven: 77–92.
    (1978/96) "Dialectic and the Stoic sage," in *The Stoics*, ed. J. M. Rist. Berkeley, Los Angeles and London: 101–24 (reprinted in Long 1996: 85–106). Page citations refer to the reprint.
    (1981) "Aristotle and the history of Greek skepticism," in *Studies in Aristotle*, ed. D. J. O'Meara. Washington D.C.: 79–106.
    (1982) "Soul and body in Stoicism," *Phronesis* **27**: 34–57.
    (1983) "Greek ethics after MacIntyre and the Stoic community of reason," *Ancient Philosophy* **3**: 184–97, reprinted in Long 1996: 156–78.

(1986) *Hellenistic Philosophy: Stoics, Epicureans, Sceptics*, 2nd edn. London.

(1988) "Socrates in Hellenistic philosophy," *Classical Quarterly* **38**: 150–71.

(1992) "Finding oneself in Greek philosophy," *UIT Tijdschrift voor Filosofie* **2**: 255–79.

(1996) *Stoic Studies*. Cambridge.

(2001) "Ancient philosophy's hardest question: what to make of oneself?" *Representations* **74**: 19–36.

(2002) *Epictetus. A Stoic and Socratic Guide to Life*. Oxford

Long, A. A., and Sedley, D. N. (1987) *The Hellenistic Philosophers*, 2 vols. Cambridge.

McCabe, M. M. (2002) "Indifference readings: Plato and the Stoa on Socratic ethics," in *Classics in Progress: Essays on Ancient Greece and Rome*, ed. T. P. Wiseman. Oxford: 363–98.

Mackie, J. L. (1964) "Self-refutation – a formal analysis," *Philosophical Quarterly* **14**: 193–203.

McKim, R. (1985) "Socratic self-knowledge and 'knowledge of knowledge' in Plato's *Charmides*," *Ancient Philosophy* **13**: 23–36.

Mamo, P. S. (1969) "Forms of individuals in the *Enneads*," *Phronesis* **14**: 77–96.

Mansfeld, J. (1986) "Diogenes Laertius on Stoic philosophy," *Elenchos* **7**: 295–382.

Mates, B. (1961) *Stoic Logic*, 2nd edn. Berkeley and Los Angeles.

Matthews, G. B. (1999) *Socratic Perplexity and the Nature of Philosophy*. Oxford.

Maurizio, L. (1995) "Anthropology and spirit possession: a reconsideration of the Pythia's role at Delphi," *Journal of Hellenic Studies* **115**: 69–86.

Mazzoli, G. (2000) "Le 'voci' dei dialoghi di Seneca," in *Seneca e il suo tempo*, ed. P. Parroni. Rome: 249–60.

Mignucci, M. (1965) *Il significato della logica stoica*. Bologna.

Morgan, K. (2000) *Myth and Philosophy from the Presocratics to Plato*. Cambridge.

Muller, R. (1988) *Introduction à la pensée des Mégariques*. Paris and Brussels.

Murray, P. (1981) "Poetic inspiration in early Greece," *Journal of Hellenic Studies* **101**: 87–100.

(1992) "Inspiration and mimesis in Plato," in *The Language of the Cave*, ed. A. Barker and M. Warner. *Apeiron* **25**, no. 4: 27–46.

(2002) "Plato's Muses: The goddesses that endure," in *Cultivating the Muse: Struggles for Power and Inspiration in Classical Literature*, ed. E. Spentzou and D. Fowler. Oxford: 29–46.

Nagel, T. (1986) *The View from Nowhere*. Oxford.

Nails, D. (2000) "Mouthpiece, schmouthpiece," in *Who Speaks for Plato?*, ed. G. Press. Lanham: 15–26.

(2002) *The People of Plato*. Indianapolis.

(2006) "The trial and death of Socrates," in Ahbel-Rappe and Kamtekar 2006: 5–20.

Nasti De Vincentis, M. (2002) *Logiche della connessività*. Bern, Stuttgart and Vienna.

Nehamas, A. (1984) "Episteme and logos in Plato's later thought," *Archiv für Geschichte der Philosophie* **66**: 11–36.

(1999a) *The Art of Living: Socratic Reflections from Plato to Foucault.* Berkeley.

(1999b) *Virtues of Authenticity. Essays on Plato and Socrates.* Princeton.

(1999c) "Plato on imitation and poetry in *Republic* X," in Nehamas 1999b: 251–78. Originally published in *Plato on Beauty, Wisdom, and the Arts*, ed. J. M. E. Moravcsik and Philip Temko. Totowa, NJ. 1982: 79–124.

Nehamas, A. and Woodruff, P. (1995) *Plato, Phaedrus.* Indianapolis.

Newman, R. (1989) "*Cotidie meditari*: theory and practice of the *meditatio* in imperial Stoicism," *Aufstieg und Niedergang der römischen Welt* **ii.36.3**: 1473–1517.

Nicholson, G. (1999) *Plato's Phaedrus: The Philosophy of Love.* West Lafayette, Ind.

Nightingale, A. (1995) *Genres in Dialogue. Plato and the Construct of Philosophy.* Cambridge.

(2002) "Distant views: realistic and fantastic mimesis in Plato," in Annas and Rowe 2002: 227–47.

(2004) *Spectacles of Truth in Classical Greek Philosophy: Theoria in its Cultural Context.* Cambridge.

North, H. (1966) *Sophrosyne: Self-Knowledge and Self-Restraint in Greek Literature.* Ithaca.

Nuchelmans, G. (1991) *Dilemmatic Arguments: Towards a History of Their Logic and Rhetoric.* Amsterdam and Oxford.

Nussbaum, M. (1995) "Eros and the wise: the Stoic response to a cultural dilemma," *Oxford Studies in Ancient Philosophy* **13**: 231–67.

(2002) "Erôs and ethical norms: philosophers respond to a cultural dilemma," in *The Sleep of Reason: Erotic Experience and Sexual Ethics in Ancient Greece and Rome*, ed. M. Nussbaum and J. Sihvola. Chicago: 55–94.

O'Brien, E. (1964) *The Essential Plotinus.* Indianapolis.

O'Daly, G. (1973) *Plotinus' Philosophy of the Self.* Shannon, Ireland.

O'Meara, D. (2003) *Platonopolis. Platonic Political Philosophy in Late Antiquity.* Oxford.

Pendrick, G. (2002) *Antiphon the Sophist: The Fragments.* Cambridge.

Penner, T. and Rowe, C. (2005) *Plato's Lysis.* Cambridge.

Perin, C. (2005) "Stoic epistemology and the limits of externalism," *Ancient Philosophy* **25**: 383–401.

Pohlenz, M. (1948) *Die Stoa. Geschichte einer geistigen Bewegung*, 2 vols. Göttingen.

Prantl, C. (1855–70) *Geschichte der Logik im Abendlande*, 4 vols. Leipzig.

Price, A. W. (1989) *Love and Friendship in Plato and Aristotle.* Oxford.

(2002) "Plato, Zeno, and the object of love," in *The Sleep of Reason: Erotic Experience and Sexual Ethics in Ancient Greece and Rome*, ed. M. Nussbaum and J. Sihvola. Chicago: 170–99.

Rademaker, A. (2005) *Sophrosyne and the Rhetoric of Self-Restraint: Polysemy and Persuasive Use of an Ancient Greek Value Term.* Leiden.

Rappe, S. (1996) "Self-knowledge and subjectivity in the *Enneads*," in *The Cambridge Companion to Plotinus*, ed. L. Gerson. Cambridge: 250–74.

Reeve, C. D. C. (1989) *Socrates in the Apology.* Indianapolis.

Remes, P. (2007) *Plotinus on Self. The Philosophy of the "We."* Cambridge.

Repici, L (1993) "The Stoics and the elenchos," in *Dialektiker und Stoiker: Zur Logik der Stoa und ihrer Vorläufer*, ed. K. Döring and T. Ebert. Stuttgart: 253–69.

Reshotko, N. (2006) *Socratic Virtue: Making the Best of the Neither-Good-nor-Bad.* Cambridge.

Reydams-Schils, G. (1999) *Demiurge and Providence: Stoic and Platonist Readings of Plato's Timaeus.* Monothéismes et Philosophie. Turnhout, Belgium.

(2005a) "Le Sage face à Zeus: logique, éthique et physique dans le stoïcisme impérial, *Revue de Métaphysique et de Morale*, NS **4**: 579–96.

(2005b) *The Roman Stoics. Self, Responsibility, and Affection.* Chicago.

(2006) "The Roman Stoics on divine thinking and human knowledge," in *Eriugena, Berkeley, and the Idealist Tradition*, ed. S. Gersh and D. Moran. Notre Dame, Indiana: 81–94.

Richardson Lear, G. (2004) *Happy Lives and the Highest Good: An Essay on Aristotle's Nicomachean Ethics.* Princeton.

Rist, J. M. (1963) "Forms of individuals in Plotinus," *Classical Quarterly* **23**: 223–31.

(1970) "Ideas of individuals in Plotinus: a reply to Dr. Blumenthal," *Revue Internationale de Philosophie* **24**: 298–303.

Roller, M. (2004) "Exemplarity in Roman culture: The cases of Horatius Cocles and Cloelia," *Classical Philology* **99**: 1–56.

Roochnik, D. (1996) *Of Art and Wisdom: Plato's Understanding of Techne.* University Park, PA.

Rosenmeyer, T. (2000) "Seneca and nature," *Arethusa* **33**: 99–120.

Rowe, C. J. (1986) *Plato: Phaedrus.* Warminster.

Rudebusch, G. (1999) *Socrates, Pleasure, and Value.* Oxford and New York.

Rutledge, S. H. (2001) *Imperial Inquisitions: Prosecutors and Informants from Tiberius to Domitian.* London.

Santas, G. (1973) "Socrates at work on virtue and knowledge in Plato's *Charmides*," in *Exegesis and Argument: Studies in Greek Philosophy Presented to Gregory Vlastos*, ed. E. N. Lee, A. P. D. Mourelatos, and R. M. Rorty. New York: 105–32.

(1999) "The form of the good in Plato's *Republic*" in Fine 1999b, vol. 1: 247–74.

Schiesaro, A. (1996) "Felicità, libertà e potere nel *De vita beata*," in *Seneca, Sulla felicità*, ed. D. Agonigi. Milan: 5–26.

Schofield, M. (1983) "The syllogisms of Zeno of Citium," *Phronesis* **28**: 31–58.

(1991/99) *The Stoic Idea of the City*, reprinted with a new foreword by M. Nussbaum and an epilogue by the author. Chicago. Original publication Cambridge 1991.

Scully, S. (2003) *Plato's Phaedrus.* Newburyport, MA.

Sedley, D. (1977) "Diodorus Cronus and Hellenistic philosophy," *Proceedings of the Cambridge Philological Society* **23**: 74–120.

(1985) "The Stoic theory of universals," *The Southern Journal of Philosophy* **23**, suppl.: 87–92.

(1993) "Chrysippus on psychophysical causality," in *Passions and Perceptions. Studies in Hellenistic Philosophy of Mind: Proceedings of the Fifth Symposium Hellenisticum*, ed. J. Brunschwig and M. Nussbaum. Cambridge: 313–31.

(1999) "The ideal of godlikeness," in Fine 1999b, vol. 2: 309–28.

(2003) *Plato's Cratylus*. Cambridge.

(2004) *The Midwife of Platonism: Text and Subtext in Plato's Theaetetus*. Oxford.

(2005) "Stoic metaphysics at Rome," in *Metaphysics, Soul, and Ethics in Ancient Thought*, ed. R. Salles. Oxford: 117–42.

(2007) *Creationism and its Critics in Antiquity*. Berkeley.

Setaioli, A. (1988) *Seneca e i greci. Citazione e traduzione nelle opere filosofiche*. Bologna.

(1997) "Seneca e l'oltretomba," *Paideia* **52**: 321–67. Republished in (2000) *Facundus Seneca. Aspetti della lingua e dell'ideologia senecana*. Bologna: 247–323.

(2006) "Seneca and the divine: Stoic tradition and personal development," *International Journal of the Classical Tradition* **13.3**: 333–68.

Sheffield, F. (2006) *Plato's Symposium: The Ethics of Desire*. Oxford.

Silverman, A. (2007) "Ascent and descent: the philosopher's regret," *Social Policy and Philosophy* **24**: 40–69.

Sorabji, R. (2000) *Emotion and Peace of Mind*. Oxford.

(2006) *Self: Ancient and Modern Insights about Individuality, Life and Death*. Chicago.

Staley, G. (2002) "Seneca and Socrates," in *Noctes Atticae: 34 Articles on Graeco-Roman Antiquity and Its Nachleben*, ed. B. Amden. Copenhagen: 281–85.

Striker, G. (1996) "Following nature: A study in Stoic ethics," in G. Striker, *Essays on Hellenistic Epistemology and Ethics*. Cambridge: 221–80.

Taylor, C. (1989) *Sources of the Self*. Cambridge, MA.

Tieleman, T. (2007) "Onomastic reference in Seneca. The case of Plato and the Platonists," in *Platonic Stoicism–Stoic Platonism. The Dialogue between Platonism and Stoicism in Antiquity*, ed. M. Bonazzi and C. Helmig. Leuven: 133–48.

Tigerstedt, E. N. (1970) "Furor poeticus: poetic inspiration in Greek literature before Democritus and Plato," *Journal of the History of Ideas* **31**: 163–78.

Togni, P. (forthcoming) *Conoscenza e virtù nella dialettica stoica*. Naples.

Tuckey, T. G. (1951) *Plato's Charmides*. Cambridge.

Verdenius, W. J. (1962) "Der Begriff der Mania in Platons *Phaidros*," *Archiv für Geschichte der Philosophie* **44**: 132–50.

Viansino, G. (1992–93) *Lucio Anneo Seneca. I dialoghi*, 2nd edn., 2 vols. Milan.

Vlastos, G. (1991) *Socrates, Ironist and Moral Philosopher*. Cambridge.

(1994) *Socratic Studies*, ed. M. Burnyeat. Cambridge.

(1999) "Happiness and virtue in Socrates' moral theory," in Fine 1999b, vol. 2: 105–36.

Voelke, A.-J. (1973) *L'Idée de volonté dans le stoïcisme*. Paris.

Vogt, K. (2007) *Law and Reason in Early Stoic Political Philosophy*. Oxford.

Vottero, D. (1998) *Lucio Anneo Seneca. I frammenti*. Bologna.

Wallace, R. J. (2003) "Practical reason," *Stanford Encyclopedia of Philosophy.*

Waterlow, S. (1972–73) "The good of others in Plato's *Republic,*" *Proceedings of the Aristotelian Society* **72**: 19–36.

Weiss, R. (2006) *The Socratic Paradox and its Enemies.* Chicago.

Wilamowitz-Moellendorff, U. von (1959) *Platon. Sein Leben und seine Werke,* 2 vols., 5th edn., ed. B. Snell. Berlin.

Wildberger, J. (2006) *Seneca und die Stoa: Der Platz des Menschen in der Welt,* 2 vols. Untersuchungen zur antiken Literatur und Geschichte 84.1–2. Berlin and New York.

Williams, G. D. (2003) *Seneca, De Otio, De Brevitate Vitae.* Cambridge.

Wolfsdorf, D. (2004) "Socrates' avowals of knowledge," *Phronesis* **49**: 75–142.

Woodruff, P. (1992) "Plato's early theory of knowledge," in *Essays on the Philosophy of Socrates,* ed. H. Benson. New York: 86–106.

Woolf, R. (2000) "Callicles and Socrates," *Oxford Studies in Ancient Philosophy* **18**: 1–40.

Index